# THE FLEET THE GODS FORGOT

# THE FLEET THE GODS FORGOT

## THE U.S. ASIATIC FLEET IN WORLD WAR II

### CAPT. W. G. WINSLOW, U.S. NAVY (RET.)

NAVAL INSTITUTE PRESS
Annapolis, Maryland

Third printing hardcover, 1989
First Bluejacket Books printing, 1994

Library of Congress Cataloging in Publication Data
Winslow, Walter G., 1912–
    The fleet the gods forgot.
    Bibliography: p.
    Includes index.
    1. World War, 1939–1945—Naval operations,
American.    2. United States. Navy, Asiatic Fleet—
History.    3. World War, 1939–1945—Pacific Ocean.
I. Title.
D767.W5          940.54'5973          81-85442
ISBN 1-55750-928-X                    AACR2

Printed in the United States of America on acid-free paper ∞

To my shipmates on board
the heavy cruiser USS *Houston*
and to the officers and men
of the U.S. Asiatic Fleet
in World War II

He hath borne himself beyond the promise of his age, doing, in the figure of a lamb, the feates of a lion.

Shakespeare

# CONTENTS

Foreword     xi

Acknowledgments     xiii

**I**   **Operations**     1

1   Profile of a Fleet     3

2   Cruisers     13

3   Submarines     24

4   Destroyers     37

5   Aircraft     47

6   Gunboats     52

7   Minecraft     60

8   Torpedo Boats     63

**II**   **Battle Reports**     83

9   The Doomed Destroyer—USS *Peary* (DD-226)     85

10   The Old Lady—USS *Canopus* (AS-9)     96

11   The *S-38* in Lingayen Gulf     112

12   Disaster at Jolo     120

13   The Little Giant-Killer—USS *Heron* (AVP-2)     141

14   A First for the Navy     146

15   The Battle of Balikpapan     151

16   The Miraculous Survival of Commander Goggins     158

17   Delayed Report of a "Routine Patrol"     172

18   Through Hell and High Water     184

19   The Heavy Cruiser USS *Houston* (CA-30)     195

20   The Cruel Fate of the Destroyer USS *Pope* (DD-225)          219
21   Abandon Ship                                                 229
22   Loss of the USS *Perch* (SS-176)                             242
23   The Expendable Ship USS *Isabel* (PY-10)                     250
24   A Refusal to Surrender                                       281
     Epilogue                                                     298
     U.S. Asiatic Fleet, December 1941                            299
     Notes                                                        305
     Bibliography                                                 313
     Index                                                        319

# FOREWORD

From almost the time of the founding of the Republic, the U.S. Asiatic Fleet, along with its French, Dutch, Austrian, British, Italian, Russian, German, and Portuguese opposite numbers, served a unique role in the Orient. After the arrival of the white man in that part of the world, the little fleets of what were in Chinese eyes barbarian interlopers acted as seagoing fire departments, rushing to one or another of the political conflagrations that arose with regularity in an area where a millennial empire was disintegrating in the face of newer imperialisms with which the ancient ways could not cope.

These "fleets" were small and ill suited to traditional warfare. But they were admirably suited to protect their respective nationals, whether they were individuals in some backwater or groups of several thousand in concessions of foreign settlements immune to Chinese law, and until 1904, to Japanese law in similar concessions in Japan. From Shanghai into China's heartland, 1,300 miles up the Yangtze, these ubiquitous foreign men-of-war rode uninvited. That many of them were ancient relics was of small importance; the Chinese judged their power by the number of stacks they had. More to the point, they carried guns, and some of them armor as well, all superior to anything the Chinese could bring to bear against them.

It was an anomaly that a U.S. Asiatic Fleet of a mere 8,000 officers and men and a handful of ships, most of them obsolete, should have been commanded since 1916 by one of only four full admirals in the U.S. Navy. But prestige and rank were the names of the game. The commander in chief of that fleet wielded more real power and influence on U.S. affairs in China than did the American minister (later ambassador) at the Chinese capital.

It can be said that the Asiatic Fleet that faced the Japanese in World War II was not in any sense a fleet; it was simply an agglomeration of ships. We shall read in the following pages of the calamities that befell this small group of preponderantly elderly ships with obsolete or defective equipment; condensers leaking as a result of near-misses; boiler brickwork sagging from continuous steaming at full power; short of everything from food to fuel; no ammunition or torpedo resupply; no secure bases; blind because of an almost total lack of reconnaissance; bare of any air cover whatsoever; wrongly employed through the bungling, if not incompetence, of a too-little-and-too-late Allied combined command.

These battle-worn, used-up ships staggered to sea time and again against hopeless odds toward clearly imminent disaster. The squandering of them and the loss of thousands of veteran sailors makes the blood boil. But their small triumphs warm the heart and their individual heroism has become a part of our heritage. We are grateful to Captain Winslow for keeping these heroic performances alive in our memories.

Kemp Tolley
Rear Admiral, U.S. Navy (Ret.)

# ACKNOWLEDGMENTS

To affirm this book's historical integrity, officers who served in the Asiatic Fleet during World War II kindly reviewed those parts of it wherein they are especially knowledgeable and made constructive comments. Of the utmost importance is the fact that two of these officers, Rear Admiral Henry E. Eccles, U.S. Navy (Retired), and Rear Admiral Kemp Tolley, U.S. Navy (Retired), both meticulous naval historians and authors, devoted many long hours to a careful screening of my entire manuscript. I am also deeply indebted to the following retired officers of the U.S. Navy: Admiral Thomas H. Moorer, Admiral Harold P. Smith, Rear Admiral Welford C. Blinn, Rear Admiral John D. Bulkeley, Rear Admiral Wreford G. Chapple, Rear Admiral Robert B. Fulton II, Rear Admiral William J. Galbraith, Rear Admiral Henry W. Goodall, Rear Admiral William L. Kabler, Rear Admiral Arthur L. Maher, Rear Admiral Robert P. McConnell, Rear Admiral John H. Morrill, Rear Admiral Morris Smellow, Rear Admiral Frederick B. Warder, Captain Robert R. Barrett, Jr., Captain Thomas B. Payne, Captain Kenneth G. Schacht, Captain Jacob J. Vandergrift, Jr.

I am also indebted to Dr. Dean C. Allard, head of the Operational Archives Branch of the U.S. Naval Historical Center, for his able assistance in helping me to find the many significant documents upon which this book is based.

The naval attachés of both the British and Australian embassies in Washington, D.C., were most cooperative, and obtained for me official operational reports concerning HMS *Exeter* and HMAS *Perth*. I appreciate very much their cordial cooperation.

# THE FLEET THE GODS FORGOT

# I
# OPERATIONS

# 1

# PROFILE OF A FLEET

Admiral Thomas C. Hart assumed command of the United States Asiatic Fleet on 25 July 1939*, when relations with Japan were already strained by Japan's continuing aggression in China and its sinking, a year and a half earlier, of an American gunboat, the *Panay*, on the Yangtze River. Relations did not improve with the passing of time and, along with its growing military might, Japan's arrogance and insulting attitude toward most foreigners in China, particularly Americans, increased.

By late September 1940, the Japanese Army had moved into northern French Indochina to prevent war supplies from being routed through Hanoi to the forces of Chiang Kai-shek, and Japan had signed the Tripartite Pact with Germany and Italy. Among other things, the pact recognized Japan's right to establish a new order in Asia, and pledged that the Axis partners would "assist one another with all political, economic, and military means if one of the others should be attacked by the United States."

President Franklin D. Roosevelt responded by putting an embargo on the sale of scrap iron and steel to nations outside the British Commonwealth and the Western Hemisphere. Also, on 16 October 1940, he rushed through Congress a selective service and training act, under which sixteen million Americans registered for military duty.

To Admiral Hart, the handwriting was on the wall. He ordered the withdrawal of all major fleet units from China and, on 21 October

*To arrive at Pearl Harbor dates, subtract one day from all dates cited in this book.

1940, permanently established his headquarters in Manila. From that time on, no ships of the Asiatic Fleet, other than the gunboats in China and an occasional navy transport, operated north of Philippine waters. In addition, when replacements for the marine detachments at Tientsin and Peking arrived in the Philippines, they were not sent forward. Later, this practice was applied to the Fourth Marines stationed at Shanghai, so that as the size of all marine detachments in China decreased, the number of marines in the Philippines increased.

During the latter part of 1940, relations with Japan seemed to be heading toward the point of no return. Bombastic politicians and others in America were mounting a barrage of threatening speeches, most of them unofficial, which were headlined in newspapers throughout the world. Hart viewed such pronouncements with alarm and wrote, "nothing is ever gained by threatening the Japanese, their psychology being such that threats are likely to wholly prevent their exercise of correct judgement."* His main concern, however, was that inflammatory speeches would tend to put the Japanese on guard against preparations then being considered to shore up the pathetically weak military forces in the Philippines.

The admiral's assessment of the situation in early November 1940, concurred in by the Navy Department, was that Japan intended further aggression which, in all probability, would be directed southward. This resulted in more than 2,000 naval dependents being evacuated from the Asiatic Station by the end of December 1940. Army dependents followed a few months later.

Hart's spirits were bolstered in mid-November 1940, when he received a letter from Admiral James O. Richardson, commander in chief of the U.S. Fleet, stating that he was preparing, for possible dispatch to the East Indies, a detachment of four heavy cruisers, an aircraft carrier, nine destroyers, and four fast minelayers to operate under the command of the Asiatic Fleet.

By January 1941, all units of the Asiatic Fleet were engaged in extensive training to make them operationally ready for any eventuality. These exercises, conducted mainly in the southern Philippines, continued until the end of October. It was a rigorous period for all concerned because the ships were at sea most of the time and far removed from Manila. When they did return for other than needed overhaul, they stayed in port only long enough to replenish supplies and give their crews the relaxation of a few nights on the town.

It must be mentioned that the twenty-eight PBY seaplanes of Patrol Wing 10 and their four seagoing tenders were not exempt from the

*Hart, "Narrative of Events," p. 8.

admiral's training directive. Based at Sangley Point, across the bay to the south of Manila, the wing, unlike the rest of the fleet, never had anything to do with China. Its activities were confined to the Philippine Islands. Starting in the summer of 1939, when it was established, the wing, operating from tenders, conducted "neutrality patrols," whose principal mission was to report on the movements of Japanese ships. It also explored anchorages that might serve as seadromes in the event of war. In 1941, drums of aviation gasoline and other essential supplies were cached at several of these sites.

Admiral Hart learned, in May 1941, that the reinforcements he had been told he might get—an aircraft carrier, plus cruisers, destroyers, and minelayers—would not be forthcoming. He did, however, receive twenty-three new fleet-type submarines, which, added to the six old S-boats he already had, gave his fleet a potentially powerful striking force. That same month, it became apparent that slowdowns in British and Dutch deliveries of oil to Japan were preventing the latter from obtaining the 1,800,000 tons per annum it needed to keep its war machine and economy from foundering. The flow of other essential raw materials from the south and southwest, controlled by the British and Dutch, was also becoming more and more restricted. Japan's situation was, in fact, becoming desperate and, like a cornered rat, it would have to move quickly if it was to survive.

The Japanese made their first major move south on 24 July 1941. With no more than token resistance from the Vichy French, their army took control of all French Indochina, while their navy moved into the ports of Saigon, Tourane (now Da Nang), and Camranh Bay. To this, President Roosevelt reacted by ordering all Japanese assets in the United States frozen, and, joined by the British and Dutch, placed an embargo on oil to Japan.

The Navy Department on 20 November 1941 directed Hart that, in the event of war, he was to deploy his surface forces southward, Singapore being envisaged as the logical base for operations until heavy units of the Pacific Fleet arrived to support them. It was expected that within a few months the British would reinforce Singapore with an aircraft carrier, seven battleships, four heavy cruisers, and thirteen light cruisers. Two major warships, Britain's most powerful battleship, the *Prince of Wales*, and the battle cruiser *Repulse*, were already en route to Singapore. Scheduled to arrive with them on 2 December was the new British aircraft carrier *Indomitable*, but she had run aground and was undergoing repairs. At the time, however, the British had only three destroyers in the Far East.

In early November, the Navy Department ordered Hart to withdraw the Fourth Marines from China, a move he had previously recommended. By 1 December 1941, about 750 of these marines had arrived in Manila. Combined with marines already there, they made a crack fighting unit of about 1,600 officers and men who eventually fought, died, or were captured in the defense of Bataan and Corregidor. It was too late to evacuate the marines and navy personnel left in China, and the passenger liner *President Harrison*, in attempting to do so, was captured by the Japanese.

In mid-November, intelligence reports that considerable numbers of Japanese Army transports were moving along the coasts of Indochina and China augured either reinforcement of the occupation forces in Southern Indochina or an advance into Thailand. There was, however, no significant intelligence on Japanese naval activity. At the same time, the State Department's prolonged negotiations with Japanese Ambassador Kichisaburo Nomura and Special Envoy Saburo Kurusu in Washington, aimed at easing tensions in the Far East, appeared to be bogging down. In view of this, and convinced that Japan was planning more aggression to the south, Admiral Hart began to deploy his surface and air units to the southern Philippines and East Borneo. On 29 November 1941 he received the following ominous dispatch from the chief of naval operations:

> This dispatch is to be considered a war warning. Negotiations with Japan looking towards stabilization of conditions in the Pacific have ceased and an aggressive move by Japan is expected within the next few days. The number and equipment of Japanese troops and the organization of naval task forces indicates an amphibious expedition against either the Philippines Thai or Kra Peninsula or possibly Borneo. Execute an appropriate defense deployment preparatory to carrying out the tasks assigned in WP-46. Inform district and army authorities. A similar warning is being sent by War Department. SPENAVO [Special Naval Observer, London] inform British.

Rear Admiral William A. Glassford, Jr., commander, Yangtze Patrol, who had been ordered to withdraw his ships and staff from China, arrived in Manila on 5 December. Two of the seven gunboats in his command, the aged *Wake* (PR-3) and *Tutuila* (PR-4),* had to be left behind, but the others steamed safely to Manila. The day Glassford arrived, in the gunboat *Luzon* (PR-7), the Yangtze Patrol was dissolved, and he was designated commander, Task Force 5, with the heavy cruiser *Houston* (CA-30) as his flagship.

That same day, Admiral Sir Tom Phillips, the new commander in chief of the British Far East Fleet, arrived in Manila for a secret two-day conference with Admiral Hart and Lieutenant General Douglas

---

*Hull numbers are given with the first mention of each ship or boat. Please see "U.S. Asiatic Fleet, December 1941," at the end of the text, for a complete list.

MacArthur, who on 28 July 1941 had been recalled to active duty and placed in command of the newly formed U.S. Army Forces, Far East. The discussions centered around the Royal Navy's urgent need for two divisions of American destroyers. Only four destroyers accompanied the *Prince of Wales* and *Repulse* to Singapore, and two of the three others in Phillips's command were assigned to the defense of Hong Kong. Hart, having but three divisions of destroyers in his fleet, could not fill this need. Nevertheless, the following day, when British reconnaissance aircraft reported that a large Japanese amphibious expedition was heading westward in the Bay of Siam, Hart immediately ordered one of his destroyer divisions to steam for Singapore.

During the conference, no plans were made for Allied ships to operate jointly in the event of war. Admiral Phillips was more concerned with using British ships to protect the sea supply routes, as well as convoys bringing supplies and reinforcements from the west to Singapore. Although British, Dutch, and American naval representatives in the Far East had been informally discussing joint operations for nearly two years, nothing definite had resulted. This was unfortunate because, when such cooperation became essential a month after the war began, a combined command had to be hastily thrown together, and was forced to operate on a day-to-day basis with no common signals or codes and little coordination between fleet units; much less between land, sea, and air forces.

By 6 December 1941, war with Japan was practically assured. The only question was where it would strike. Ships of the Asiatic Fleet, unlike those in the States, had close to full complements of well-trained crews. When war did erupt, they would be ready. It was a different story, however, with the land-based forces in the Philippines.

General MacArthur's command was to consist, by April 1942, of a trained army of 200,000 men, most of them Filipinos, equipped with American tanks and heavy artillery and backed by an air arm of 256 modern bombers and 195 fighters. By the first week of December 1941, four months after its inception, this massive but belated effort to organize, build training facilities, and train recruits was progressing well. Nevertheless, MacArthur had only about 130,000 men, 100,000 of whom were recently inducted and poorly equipped Filipino trainees. Some heavy weapons, such as tanks and artillery pieces, had arrived, but not nearly enough of them. The air arm's strength had reached only 35 B-17 bombers and 107 fighter planes. That more war supplies were en route was beside the point; the army under MacArthur was in no way prepared for war.

The shock wave of the Pearl Harbor attack hit the Philippines during the early hours of 8 December 1941. The gutting of Battleship Row meant the Asiatic Fleet, which had no aircraft carriers and was not structured to take on Japanese air and sea armadas in a knock-down, drag-out war, would have to go it alone. For air support it was dependent upon the army, but that too was denied when Japanese air strikes in the Philippines knocked out two-thirds of the fighters and more than half the bombers of MacArthur's Far East Air Force.

Two days later, unopposed Japanese bombers destroyed the Cavite Navy Yard, thus eliminating the Asiatic Fleet's only overhaul and resupply facility of any significance in the Far East. Facilities at the large British naval base at Singapore, however, were available, and there was comfort in the knowledge that Britain's most powerful battleship, the *Prince of Wales*, and her battle cruiser the *Repulse* were stationed there. But once again disaster struck the Allied cause. On the same day the Cavite Navy Yard was devastated, the *Prince of Wales* and *Repulse*, rushing headlong without air support to break up a Japanese landing on Malaya, were intercepted by hordes of enemy bombers and sunk. Now Singapore itself was threatened and, if it fell, the only remaining facilities for servicing the fleet would be those of the small Dutch naval base at Surabaja, Java.

To understand the Asiatic Fleet's situation, it is helpful to compare its composition with that of the force against which it was pitted. The ships in Admiral Hart's command, discussed at length in later chapters, consisted of 1 heavy and 2 light cruisers; 13 destroyers, and their tender; 23 large fleet-type and 6 small S-type submarines, and 3 tenders; 28 PBY seaplanes, 10 single-engine utility seaplanes, and 4 tenders; 2 tankers; 6 motor torpedo boats; 6 minesweepers; 1 submarine rescue vessel; 1 fleet tug; and an assortment of coastal gunboats, river gunboats, yachts, and yard craft. The Japanese had available in Southeast Asia 10 battleships, 10 aircraft carriers, 18 heavy cruisers, 18 light cruisers, 113 destroyers, 63 submarines, and hundreds of land-based bombers and fighter planes.

These staggering odds against the Asiatic Fleet were little changed by the presence of Allied warships in Southeast Asia. The Dutch could provide only two light cruisers, a destroyer leader and seven destroyers, twelve submarines, and a few PBY seaplanes. Land-based air support for ships was nonexistent, because most Dutch fighter planes had been sent to help defend Singapore, and the few American P-40s that reached Java were soon destroyed. The British at Singapore, having lost two major warships, were hard pressed to protect their sealanes from the west, and what few cruisers and destroyers they could spare from other areas were used for that single purpose.

As a result of Admiral Hart's foresight, every major ship in the Asiatic Fleet, with the exception of the submarine *Sealion* (SS-195), which was undergoing repairs when the Cavite Navy Yard was bombed and was sunk, and the submarine tender *Canopus* (AS-9), which was held in Manila to service submarines, escaped to the Netherlands East Indies.

To meet the Japanese threat as best he could, Admiral Hart, on 2 December 1941, had divided his fleet into two task forces. Task Force 1, under his command, was headquartered in Manila, from where he planned to fight his submarines and the PBYs of Patrol Wing 10. Task Force 5, to be commanded by Admiral Glassford, was comprised of the fleet's two cruisers, all of the destroyers, and all other surface ships, save the submarine and seaplane tenders, which were needed to back up operations in the Philippines. It was planned that if war came, the ships of Task Force 5 would immediately withdraw southward and base at either Singapore or ports in the Netherlands East Indies, in spite of the fact that no arrangements for them to do so had been made with the British or the Dutch.

The advent of war and the suddenness with which Japan seized control of the skies over the Philippines forced immediate changes in the composition of both commands. For example, the light cruiser *Boise* (CL-47), having recently escorted an army convoy from the United States to Manila, was still in Philippine waters and was ordered to join Task Force 5. With enemy bombers certain to destroy them,

Admiral Thomas C. Hart, commander in chief, U.S. Asiatic Fleet, from 25 July 1939 to 4 February 1942. National Archives, 80-G-302284

Hart ordered three large auxiliaries—the aircraft tender *Langley* (AV-3) and the tankers *Trinity* (AO-13) and *Pecos* (AO-6)—being refueled and resupplied, to clear out of Manila Bay the first day of war and head south to join up with ships of Glassford's command.

Following the bombing of the Cavite Navy Yard, two of the fleet's three submarine tenders—*Holland* (AS-3) and *Otus* (AS-20)—were also ordered to the Netherlands East Indies, leaving only the *Canopus* (AS-9) to service submarines in Manila Bay. In addition, Patrol Wing 10, which in less than a week had lost more than one-third of its PBYs to enemy action, was also ordered to bases in the Indies. Thus, by mid-December, all major units of the Asiatic Fleet, less the submarines and one tender, were operating under the direction of commander, Task Force 5.

Hart's plans to fight his submarines from Manila Bay were seriously jeopardized when he had to make do with only one tender. However, all thought of operating submarines from Manila went by the board when Japanese troops landed on Luzon and, by 23 December 1941, were marching on the capital city. With his American and Filipino forces falling back to the Bataan Peninsula for a last-ditch fight and bombs falling on Manila, MacArthur had no recourse but to declare it, as of midnight 24 December, an "open city." All American military and naval activities in Manila thereupon ceased, and Hart and his staff hastily moved to the island fortress of Corregidor.

All hope of safely basing units of the Asiatic Fleet in Manila Bay, or any other place in the Philippines, having been wiped out, Hart decided to establish new headquarters at Surabaja, Java. Accordingly, on the forenoon of 25 December, he turned over command of the few naval activities remaining in the Phillipines to Rear Admiral Francis W. Rockwell, commandant of the Sixteenth Naval District, whose command post was in a tunnel on Corregidor. That night Hart and members of his staff boarded the submarine *Shark* (SS-174) which, at 0200 on 26 December 1941, got under way for the Netherlands East Indies. Thus ended a legendary naval activity in the Orient for, since Admiral Hart's departure, the flag of commander in chief, U.S. Asiatic Fleet, has not been flown on the old China Station.

Soon after Hart's arrival in Java on 15 January 1942, American, British, Dutch, and Australian forces in the Far East were formed into a unified command known as ABDACOM. Its main headquarters were near Bandung, in the mountains of central Java. In overall command was British Field Marshal Sir Archibald Percival Wavell (ABDACOM); British Air Chief Marshal Sir Richard E. C. Peirse was in command of the air forces (ABDAIR); Dutch Lieutenant General Hein ter Poorten was in command of army forces (ABDARM); and in command of the sea forces was Admiral Hart (ABDAFLOAT). Hart had little, if any, control over British or Dutch ships, which were concerned with their own areas of operations. The British operated from Singapore west to Ceylon, the Dutch in the waters around Sumatra and the Java Sea, and the Americans were responsible for all the area east of Java, with boundaries stretching from northern Borneo and the Sulu Archipelago eastward past Halmahera to the western tip of New Guinea, and south to northern Australia. Admiral Hart, however, retained control of the Asiatic Fleet, whose surface ships operated under Admiral Glassford as commander, Task Force 5, and whose submarines were under Captain John Wilkes.

On 27 January the Navy Department unceremoniously deactivated the Asiatic Fleet and placed all its ships under the newly formed Southwest Pacific Command. Glassford, temporarily promoted to vice admiral, was designated commander, Southwest Pacific, a move that created considerable confusion: by direction from Washington, Hart remained the nominal commander in chief of the "deactivated" Asiatic Fleet, which was composed of the identical forces assigned to Glassford. This confused situation persisted until 14 February 1942, when Admiral Hart, ordered back to the States, was relieved as the ABDA naval commander by Vice Admiral Conrad E. L. Helfrich of the Royal Netherlands Navy. At that point, Admiral Glassford, as commander, Western Pacific, became the undisputed commander of all American naval forces in the Far East.

Singapore fell on 15 February 1942. Ten days later, Field Marshal Wavell, relieved of his ABDA command, departed for India, and the Dutch assumed full responsibility for the defense of Java. Admiral Helfrich became commander in chief of Allied naval forces in the Southwest Pacific. Although he was in a position to direct the movement of American, British, and Australian ships, protocol dictated that he do so only after consultation with the senior staff officers of each navy. Insofar as American submarines were concerned, however, he could not direct, only suggest.

The disastrous Battle of the Java Sea on 27 February 1942 broke the back of the ABDA fleet. On 1 March, with no warships or aircraft left to defend Java and with Japanese troops, supported by fighters and bombers, streaming ashore, Helfrich had no alternative but to dissolve the Allied command. Accordingly, he advised his senior staff officers to get out of Java, then wasted no time in making good his own escape.

Admiral Glassford, accompanied by Rear Admiral Arthur F. E. Palliser, RN, who was chief of staff to Helfrich, beat a hasty retreat to Tjilatjap, on the south coast of Java, and, under cover of darkness, departed the night of 1 March for Perth, Australia, in one of the three remaining PBY seaplanes of Patrol Wing 10. Soon after arriving in Perth, Glassford was ordered to turn over his Southwest Pacific command to Vice Admiral Arthur S. Carpender, USN, and, in so doing, he reverted to the rank of rear admiral.

The fall of Java ended the first phase of the war at sea with Japan. The little Asiatic Fleet, pressed into fighting a war it could not win, had sustained appalling losses; many of its officers and men were either dead or prisoners of the Japanese, and its few battered remnants were steaming for the safety of southwestern Australia. Two months later, when Corregidor fell, all of the fleet units left to fight in the Philippines were also sacrificed.

In the chapters that follow, the operations of the Asiatic Fleet in World War II are grouped by ship types, rather than recounted chronologically. The reason for this approach is that the Asiatic Fleet was not an integrated organization, as are the fleets of today. It was a collection of ships, submarines, and aircraft, all performing their separate missions. In fact, the only way one part of the fleet could find out what another part was doing was by illegally decoding their messages.

No attempt has been made to discuss in depth the political maneuvering and petty jealousies that resulted in the removal of the very capable Admiral Hart as commander of ABDA's naval forces or the inept decisions of those charged with directing ABDA's operations. These shortcomings are not within the purview of this work. They do, however, become self-evident as the stories of Asiatic Fleet losses unfold.

# 2

# CRUISERS

Only two cruisers were assigned to the U.S. Asiatic Fleet: the heavy cruiser *Houston* and the light cruiser *Marblehead* (CL-12). When the war started, however, the light cruiser *Boise*, having just escorted an army convoy to Manila, was ordered to join the Asiatic Fleet.

The *Houston*, flagship for Admiral Hart, commander in chief of the Asiatic Fleet, with her long, low silhouette and clipper bow, was one of the most beautiful fighting ships in the navy. Just over 600 feet in length, she was rated as a 10,000-ton "treaty" cruiser, but her full-load displacement was actually between 12,000 and 14,000 tons. Her designed speed was 32.5 knots. She mounted nine 8-inch guns in three triple turrets and eight 5-inch guns for use against aircraft or surface targets. For protection against low-flying planes, she had four quadruple mounts of 1.1-inch pom-pom guns and eight .50-caliber machine guns. She also carried four single-engine seaplanes for scouting and, in time of battle, for observing the fall of shells.

A cursory assessment of the *Houston*, with her superbly trained crew, would have led to the conclusion that she was a formidable weapon of naval warfare. This she could have been, but her fighting effectiveness was diminished by her lack of radar and the fact that she was sadly in need of overhaul and modernization. Her worst problem, however, lay silent and unknown in her magazines. Not until enemy bombers were overhead and antiaircraft guns were fired in anger for the first time was it discovered that a very high percentage (Commander Arthur L. Maher the gunnery officer estimated at least 70 per cent) of her 5-inch shells failed to explode.

The heavy cruiser USS *Houston* (CA-30), flagship of the U.S. Asiatic Fleet, sunk near Sunda Strait, Java, during the early hours of 1 March 1942 by Japanese naval forces. National Archives, 80—G—424743

The *Marblehead*, commissioned in 1924, was, for all practical purposes, obsolete. She was 555 feet overall, displaced 7,050 tons, and had a designed speed of 34 knots. She was armed with ten 6-inch guns, seven 3-inch antiaircraft guns, and six 21-inch torpedo tubes. Two seaplanes for scouting and observation nested on catapults amidships. Although the *Marblehead* boasted a veteran crew, the most courageous efforts of these highly trained men were nullified by the shortcomings of their aged ship.

The *Boise* was a welcome addition to the Asiatic Fleet. Commissioned in 1938, she was a modern fighting ship, displacing more than 10,000 tons and having a designed speed of 33.6 knots. Her fifteen 6-inch guns mounted in five triple turrets and secondary battery of eight 5-inch guns were potent, up-to-date weapons. She carried two scout-observation seaplanes, and was the only ship in the Asiatic Fleet with radar. With all her potential, however, while she was a unit of the Asiatic Fleet, the *Boise* never came to grips with the enemy.

The morning bombs fell on Pearl Harbor, the major surface units of the Asiatic Fleet were dispersed well to the south of Manila Bay. The *Houston* was at Iloilo, on the island of Panay, and was joined late that afternoon by Rear Admiral William A. Glassford, Jr., the newly appointed commander of Task Force 5. The *Boise* was off the island of Cebu, and the *Marblehead* was at Tarakan, Borneo, along with five destroyers.

During the first eight weeks of the war, the cruisers were employed in the tedious but all-important task of convoying ships. To begin with, they escorted fleet support ships from the Philippines to the safer ports in the Netherlands East Indies. That done, they convoyed merchantmen, loaded with troops or war supplies, from the waters of northern Australia to ports in the Netherlands East Indies. During that time, they were not engaged in combat, but the *Houston* and *Boise* came close to it on 10 December 1941, while they and the destroyers *Paul Jones* (DD-230) and *Barker* (DD-213) were escorting the seaplane tender *Langley* and the fleet oilers *Trinity* and *Pecos* south in the Sulu Sea.

Just before sundown, lookouts reported smoke to the west. General quarters was sounded and, with all guns manned, the two cruisers and two destroyers increased speed and headed for the smoke. In a matter of minutes, three ships hove into view. At 28,000 yards, they were identified as a Japanese cruiser and two destroyers. Clearly silhouetted against a huge, blood-red, setting sun, the enemy ships were sitting ducks. The main batteries of the *Houston* and *Boise* zeroed in on the cruiser. Anticipating the momentary booms of gunfire, the crews of both ships were tense with the excitement of impending combat. Long minutes passed. Nothing happened. For some reason, Admiral Glassford, the force commander, did not give the order to open fire, and the outgunned enemy ships, along with the sun, vanished over the horizon.

The twenty-second of January 1942 was a bleak day for the Asiatic Fleet's cruisers. The *Boise*, en route to rendezvous with the *Marblehead* and some units of Destroyer Squadron 29 for a night attack on enemy ships off Balikpapan, Borneo, ripped a hole in her hull on an uncharted rock, and was forced to return to the States for repairs. That same day, a turbine malfunction reduced the speed of the *Marblehead* to 15 knots and prevented her from participating in our first offensive action of the war. The destroyers, however, went on alone and scored a thrilling victory in the Battle of Balikpapan, which is recounted in part II of this book.

The men of the *Houston*, tired of convoy duty and disgusted with the Japanese victory claims they heard, were anxious to get a whack at the enemy. Their chance came on 4 February 1942. That morning, the Dutch light cruiser *De Ruyter*, destroyer leader *Tromp*, and three destroyers, along with the *Houston*, *Marblehead*, and four American destroyers, were steaming north in the Flores Sea to attack Japanese ships in the vicinity of Makasar Strait. Suddenly, fifty-four land-based Mitsubishi-96 bombers pounced upon the striking force, concentrating their bombs on the *Houston* and *Marblehead*. With no air support, the only defense the ships had were their antiaircraft guns, and this is when it was learned that most of the *Houston*'s 5-inch antiaircraft shells were duds. The encounter was a totally frustrating experience.

For more than three hours the bombers kept up their attacks. Although three were shot down and several were probably damaged, when the planes departed, they left in their wake death and destruction. Number 3 turret on the *Houston*'s stern was destroyed by a 500-pound bomb, which also killed forty-eight of her crew and wounded fifty. The only other ship to suffer damage was the *Marblehead*. Several bomb hits and near misses killed thirteen of her crew, and wounded more than thirty. With her rudder jammed hard to port by a bomb hit and serious below-decks flooding causing her to be dangerously down by the bow, she could be steered only by use of her engines. She managed to make port but, as a combatant unit of the Asiatic Fleet, the *Marblehead* was finished.

Both ships retired to Tjilatjap,* where the dead were buried and the seriously wounded transferred to a Dutch hospital. Following emergency repairs, the *Marblehead* was ordered back to the States, but

---

*Tjilatjap is a deep-water port on Java's south coast.

The light cruiser USS *Marblehead* (CL-12). Naval Institute Collection

the *Houston*, her after 8-inch turret damaged beyond repair, was kept in the combat zone for lack of a replacement.

On 15 February, the *Houston* was again the target of Japanese bombs. Supported by the American destroyer *Peary* (DD-226) and the Australian corvettes *Swan* and *Worrengo*, she was convoying the U.S. Army transports *Meigs*, *Mauna Loa*, *Tulagi*, and *Port Mar* from Darwin, in northern Australia, to Kupang on the island of Timor. These transports were loaded with American and Australian troops, the American contingent consisting of the 147th and 148th Field Artillery. When only 150 miles north of Darwin, in an area considered safe from enemy aircraft, the convoy was surprised by a Japanese, four-engine flying boat. It immediately requested fighter protection from Darwin but, before help came, the big seaplane made two ineffectual bombing runs on the *Houston*.

Following a second attack, a lone P-40 fighter arrived, and the enemy plane promptly turned tail with the fighter in hot pursuit. Both planes were soon lost to sight, but a brilliant flash of fire on the horizon, coupled with dense black smoke, bore evidence that at least one of them had been shot down. The P-40 did not return to base, nor, according to what a Japanese officer later told survivors from the *Houston*, did the flying boat.

The next day, thirty-six twin-engine, land-based bombers attacked the convoy. This time, with 500 rounds of good 5-inch antiaircraft shells left behind by the *Boise* stowed in her magazines, the *Houston* was better equipped to fight. The attacks lasted for more than an hour and were concentrated on the *Houston*, but her effective antiaircraft fire, coupled with the skillful shiphandling of Captain Albert H. Rooks, her commanding officer, enabled her to thwart the bombers.

The last bombing attack of the day, made by a five-plane section that had previously lost one of its number to the *Houston*'s guns, was directed at the unarmed troopships. Spotting this maneuver, Captain Rooks raced the *Houston* close to the helpless convoy, and the protective curtain of bursting shells put up by her guns, the only ones capable of reaching the high-flying planes, was so effective that bombs fell close to only one ship, the *Mauna Loa*. Although the transport sustained only superficial damage, one man aboard her was killed, and another wounded by shrapnel. When the bombers had gone, the *Houston* steamed down the line of transports and, as she passed each one, hundreds of grateful soldiers roundly cheered her. Later that afternoon, when it was learned that the Japanese had landed in force on Timor, the ABDA high command ordered the convoy back to Darwin.

During the action, the *Houston*'s crew was too hard pressed to assess the results of their antiaircraft fire, but observers on other ships credited her with shooting down seven bombers and damaging several others. Upon returning to Darwin, the quartermaster of the transport *Meigs* visited the *Houston* and reported that, at times, her furious rate of fire produced a continuous sheet of flame along her 5-inch-gun decks. He said that during the action his captain stood on the bridge and shouted, "Look at those bastards go!"

When the *Houston* returned to Darwin on 18 February, her ship's company learned with misgiving that Admiral Hart had been relieved as commander of ABDA's naval forces by Vice Admiral Helfrich, a man fiercely determined to defend Java to the last ship in his command. Whereas Hart had told Rooks that he would never again send the crippled *Houston* into the dangerous waters north of the Malay barrier, Helfrich's first directive to the *Houston* ordered her to return immediately to Surabaja. Although he could have remained overnight at Darwin, Captain Rooks decided to get under way on the afternoon of the eighteenth. This was a fortunate decision because, soon after sunrise the next morning, Darwin was the object of a massive, surprise air attack. Nearly every ship in the harbor was sunk and, had the *Houston* been there, she might well have met her doom.

On 26 February two Japanese armadas were descending on Java. The most immediate threat was the force coming from the northeast: the other, coming from the northwest, appeared to be positioned to reach Java two or three days after the first had landed. There was little, if any, logic to support the assumption that the vastly outnumbered ships of the ABDA Command could stop either one of these assault groups, much less fend off the enemy bombers that roamed the skies of the Netherlands East Indies unopposed. Faced with such impossible odds, it would have been prudent to move all Allied warships south of the Malay barrier before the Japanese trapped them in the Java Sea by closing the few escape routes to the Indian Ocean. Helfrich, however, would not entertain such a thought. Instead, on 27 February 1942, he pitted his little fleet against a superior enemy force in the forlorn hope that, by some miracle of miracles, it would be able to sink enough transports to thwart the landing on eastern Java.

As the ABDA fleet headed for battle, Rear Admiral Karel Doorman of the Royal Netherlands Navy, who was in tactical command, chose to ignore proven naval tactics and deployed his force in an unorthodox fashion. The British destroyers *Jupiter*, *Electra*, and *Encounter* formed a scouting line 5 miles ahead of the main body. The cruisers steamed in column with Admiral Doorman's flagship, the *De Ruyter*, in the lead. Following, at 900-yard intervals, were the British heavy cruiser *Exeter*, the heavy cruiser *Houston*, the Australian light cruiser *Perth*, and, last in line, the Dutch light cruiser *Java*. On the port beam of the main column were the Dutch destroyers *Kortenaer* and *Witte de With*. The American destroyers *John D. Edwards* (DD-216), *Alden* (DD-211), *Paul Jones*, and *John D. Ford* (DD-228) were in column astern of the cruisers. This formation was used, no doubt, because of the motley nature of Doorman's force. He was severely handicapped by lack of a tactical communications system and by the great disparity in speed and gun power among ships that were nominally of the same type.

Doctrine dictated positioning his force in groups by types, thus permitting each to seek suitable ranges for the caliber of their guns and, at the same time, support each other. This order of battle would have placed the *Houston* and *Exeter*, with their larger guns, behind the Allied light cruisers and beyond range of the Japanese light cruisers. The American destroyers were stationed in a useless position to the rear instead of in the van, where their torpedoes could have been used to advantage. The same applied to the Dutch destroyers deployed to port of the main column.

Although detailed accounts of the battles of the Java Sea and the Sunda Strait may be found in chapter 19 entitled "The Heavy Cruiser USS *Houston* (CA-30)," certain additional points of historical importance must be mentioned.

First of all, what actually happened during the thoroughly confusing Battle of the Java Sea will never be known. Allied reports differ as to the composition of the Japanese fleet, but it is agreed that there were at least two heavy cruisers, each mounting ten guns, and two destroyer flotillas—six ships in one, and seven in the other—each led by a light cruiser. The Japanese maintain that was the extent of their forces. However, some Allied reports contend that two additional heavy cruisers, several destroyers, and one or two submarines were also in on the action. Qualified Allied observers insist that at least two Japanese heavy cruisers were damaged, and several report having seen one of them sink. The Japanese do not admit to any of their cruisers being damaged. The Allies claim to have sunk three, possibly four, enemy destroyers, while the Japanese say that only one destroyer, the *Asagumo*, was even damaged. What is known is that Admiral Helfrich's hoped-for miracle did not materialize, and the disaster suffered by the ABDA fleet signaled the fall not only of Java, but of the entire Netherlands East Indies.

During the Battle of the Java Sea, the light cruisers *De Ruyter* and *Java* and the destroyer *Kortenaer* were sunk. The destroyers *Electra* and *Jupiter* were also sunk, and the heavy cruiser *Exeter* was seriously damaged. The *Houston* and the light cruiser *Perth* retired to Tandjungpriok, Java, to refuel before attempting to escape into the Indian Ocean via Sunda Strait. The surviving destroyers and the *Exeter* returned to Surabaja to await orders. Later, the *Exeter*, escorted by the destroyers HMS *Encounter* and USS *Pope* (DD-225), tried to escape from the Java Sea into the Indian Ocean via Sunda Strait. All three ships were intercepted on 1 March 1942 by Japanese forces and sunk.

The action report of Commander Henry E. Eccles, commanding the destroyer *John D. Edwards* during the Battle of the Java Sea, contains some interesting observations:

> The manner in which U.S.S. *Houston*, H.M.S. *Exeter*, and H.M.A.S. *Perth* were handled and fought was a credit to the best traditions of the Naval Services of the United States and Great Britain. They maintained a high, accurate rate of fire against the enemy at long range which alone made this encounter a battle. The *Houston* hitting an enemy cruiser heavily at a critical time. . . . The British destroyers were handled with decision, excellent judgment and courage. It was obvious that they were commanded by cool, competent and aggressive officers.
>
> The manner in which the *Houston*, which entered the engagement with turret three completely disabled by the air attack of February 4, was fought, the aggressive way in which she at all times carried the battle to the enemy, with steady accurate fire, will long remain an inspiration to all who saw her.
>
> The Dutch fought with unfaltering courage and dogged determination. Admiral Doorman in *De Ruyter* returned to the attack time after time in a literal obedience to the signal from ABDAFLOAT (Vice Admiral Helfrich) on 26 February, "You must continue attacks until enemy is destroyed." . . . *Java*, though badly outranged and with her speed reduced by old boilers, endeavored to maintain her position throughout, firing steadily whenever her guns would range. The battle itself was a tragic commentary on the futility of attempting to oppose a powerful, determined, well equipped and organized enemy by the makeshift improvisations that were used. It was evident that the Dutch had little tactical experience. Their knowledge of communications was rudimentary and they went on the assumption that a hastily organized, uncoordinated force of ships from three navies could be assembled and taken into a major action after a one hour conference. It is impossible for anyone who did not go to sea in the Striking Force to comprehend the utter lack, in the Dutch, of any knowledge of tactical organization, and the employment of a force as a unit. They were individual ship men and went to their deaths with grim foreknowledge. The Allied Force was little more than a column of strange task groups which entered the battle with a vague general directive, and no specific mission.*

As soon as the *Houston* and *Perth* arrived at Tandjungpriok, a few miles east of Batavia, on the afternoon of 28 February, Captain Hector M. L. Waller, of the *Perth*, and Captain Rooks went to the British Naval

*Eccles, "Java Sea Battle," p. 5.

Liaison Office in Batavia for instructions. They talked by telephone to Supreme Allied Naval Headquarters at Bandung and were informed that a Dutch naval reconnaissance plane had reported as late as 1500 that day that no Japanese warships were within ten hours' steaming time of Sunda Strait. Their orders, therefore, were to proceed via that strait to Tjilatjap, where Admiral Helfrich planned to gather his few remaining ships and continue the fight.

Here it must be noted that, on 26 February, a huge Japanese invasion fleet, consisting of sixty transports, one aircraft carrier, four heavy cruisers, two light cruisers, and twenty-five destroyers had been sighted only 250 miles from western Java. Since that time, contact with this force had been lost and naval efforts to find it again had failed, but the fact that such an armada even existed was not mentioned to the two captains.

The confusion and lack of coordinated effort existing at Supreme Allied Headquarters was such that the army high command, well aware of the Japanese invasion fleet, had advised Major General Schilling, of the Royal Netherlands Indies Army, that a landing in western Java was imminent. However, although General Schilling's headquarters was in the same building in Batavia as the British Naval Liaison Office, he was not informed that the *Houston* and *Perth* were in port.

At 2315 on 28 February 1942, as they approached Sunda Strait, the captains of the *Houston* and *Perth* were astounded suddenly to find themselves in the midst of the largest amphibious landing operation yet attempted by the Japanese in the southwest Pacific. A vicious, uneven battle ensued and, for almost an hour, the two cruisers more than held their own. Surrounded at close range by transports and warships, they exacted a heavy toll, but time was running out for both of them. At 0020, the *Perth* went down, taking with her more than half her crew, including one of Australia's greatest naval heroes, Captain Hector MacDonald Laws Waller, DSO, RAN.

Following the loss of the *Perth*, the *Houston* continued to fight until, at about 0035 on 1 March, out of ammunition, gutted by torpedoes and shells, and with uncontrolled fires raging throughout her length, she sank beneath the Java Sea. Dead were two-thirds of her crew, including most of her senior officers and her valiant commanding officer, Captain Albert H. Rooks, who was posthumously awarded the Medal of Honor.

The *Houston* and *Perth* sold themselves dearly. The waters of Bantam Bay, where most of the fighting occurred, were strewn with survivors and the wreckage of sunken ships. Among the survivors in the water was Lieutenant General Hitoshi Imamura, commanding the Japanese landing forces in West Java.

The exact number of ships accounted for that night by the two Allied cruisers will never be known, but each got her share. They were no doubt helped in the confusion of battle and the dark of night by the Japanese who, on several occasions, mistakenly fired upon and launched torpedoes at their own ships.

Officially, the Japanese admit the following casualties:

| | | | |
|---|---|---|---|
| *Sakura Maru* | Passenger-cargo | 7,170 tons | Sunk |
| *Tokushima Maru* | Passenger-cargo | 5,975 tons | Sunk |
| *Horai Maru* | Passenger-cargo | 9,192 tons | Sunk |
| W-2 (AM type) | Minesweeper | ——— | Sunk |
| *Tsurumi* | Tanker | ——— | Damaged |
| *Shikinami* | Destroyer | ——— | Damaged |
| *Shirakumo* | Destroyer | ——— | Damaged |
| *Harukaze* | Destroyer | ——— | Damaged |
| *Asagumo* | Destroyer | ——— | Damaged |
| *Kinu* | Light cruiser | ——— | Damaged |

On the other side of the ledger, a careful study of the reports of Allied survivors strongly supports the belief that at least two Japanese destroyers, an 18,000-ton aircraft transport armed with a minimum of six heavy guns, and three motor torpedo boats were also sunk.

After the war, the Allies uncovered a report made by a Japanese torpedo school which stated that during the Battle of Sunda Strait eighty-seven torpedoes were expended on the *Houston* and *Perth*. No more than ten of these found their intended mark. Therefore, there must have been at least seventy-seven rogue torpedoes racing through waters jammed with Japanese ships. There can be little doubt but that some of them inflicted damage on their own forces.

Amidst the claims and counterclaims that can never be proved or disproved is a story written by Ted Sheil, an Australian journalist, and published in the *Houston Post* of 26 February 1967. Sheil wrote that a senior survivor of the *Perth* told him he was tortured because a Japanese officer, while admitting that fifteen Japanese ships had been sunk, refused to believe that only two Allied cruisers took part in the action.

# 3

# SUBMARINES

The main offensive strength of the Asiatic Fleet lay in its submarines. Under the command of Captain John Wilkes, this force of twenty-nine boats, manned by veteran crews, was trained to perfection. It had been operating under combat conditions for several weeks before the war began and, when it did, the submarine fleet was not caught unprepared. But its officers and men were destined to suffer cruel frustrations because, unknown to anyone, they sallied forth to war with torpedoes that ran deeper than programmed, and whose exploders, more often than not, failed to function.

Most formidable of the submarines were the twenty-three modern, fleet-type boats. As long as a football field, they could make 20 knots on the surface and more than 10 knots when submerged. They had a cruising radius of 12,000 miles, and could dive well below 250 feet. Their main armament consisted of eight 21-inch torpedo tubes and one 3-inch deck gun.

The six S-boats that comprised the rest of the force were smaller and older; they were built during the decade following World War I. Designed primarily for defensive purposes, not for the long-range patrols suddenly thrust upon them by the exigencies of this war, they had cramped living areas and stowage space was at a premium. They were good for 14 knots on the surface and about 10 submerged. Unlike the fleet-type submarines, S-boats had no air-conditioning and, during prolonged dives in tropical waters, their crews were unmercifully punished by foul air and sweltering heat. Although nicknamed "pig-boats," these old submarines, which had only four 21-inch torpedo tubes and a 4-inch deck gun, proved to be tough, respected weapons of underseas warfare. One of them even achieved the distinction of becoming the first American submarine to sink an enemy destroyer. This occurred off the port city of Makasar, in the southern Celebes, on the night of 8 February 1942, when the *S-37*, commanded by Lieutenant James C. Dempsey, torpedoed the 1,900-ton Japanese destroyer *Natsushio*.

To support the Asiatic Fleet's submarines were the tenders *Holland*, *Otus*, and *Canopus*, and the submarine rescue vessel *Pigeon* (ASR-6). The tenders, equipped with forges and machine shops and manned by master craftsmen, could repair or make practically anything relating to a submarine. They carried spare parts, torpedoes, fuel, food, clothing, and other supplies. Their "can do" crews worked long, hard hours to keep their fellow submariners in the fight and, had their ingenious efforts been anything less than heroic, the submarine operations of the Asiatic Fleet during the early months of the war would have slowed to a crawl.

Admiral Hart did not have enough surface ships to challenge the vast naval power of Japan. Therefore, it was planned that, in the event of war, what surface vessels he did have would immediately withdraw to the Malay barrier and await reinforcements from the Pacific Fleet. His twenty-nine submarines, on the other hand, had the potential to make any seaborne assault on the Philippines a costly venture. They, therefore, were to remain based in Manila to help defend the Philippines.

The day Japanese planes struck Pearl Harbor, five fleet-type submarines and four S-boats were en route to designated stations with war shots loaded. Two fleet submarines were undergoing repair in the Cavite Navy Yard, and the remaining eighteen boats, nested alongside their tenders in Manila Bay, were being readied for action. News of the Japanese attack spurred an already hot-paced effort to get submarines on station and, within hours, Asiatic Fleet submarines began putting to sea.

General MacArthur's Far East Air Force having been almost totally destroyed during the first two days of the war, the Philippines lay helpless before the warplanes of Japan. On the third day, 10 December 1941, the Cavite Navy Yard, across the bay from Manila, was devastated by unopposed enemy bombers. The two fleet submarines then in the yard were the *Sealion* (SS-195) and *Seadragon* (SS-194). The *Sealion* was sunk by bombs, but the *Seadragon*, lying alongside her, miraculously escaped serious damage. The loss of the U.S. Navy's only major overhaul and repair facility west of Honolulu forced the Asiatic Fleet's submarines to depend wholly on their tenders.

It was now obvious that without fighter protection in being or in prospect, no ship in Philippine waters was safe from air attack. Accordingly, Hart ordered the tenders *Holland* and *Otus* to steam for the Netherlands East Indies on the evening of the tenth, so as to place these indispensable vessels beyond the reach of enemy bombers. Only the *Canopus* and the *Pigeon* were kept in Manila to provide minimal service to submarines returning from war patrols.

In spite of the adverse operating conditions so suddenly thrust upon him, Hart was determined to fight his submarines and long-range reconnaissance seaplanes from Manila for as long as possible. Spread as thin as they were, however, the submarines were unable to intercept any of the massive Japanese invasion forces that had begun to converge on the Philippines before the war began. As time went on, they were further disadvantaged by the lack of reconnaissance aircraft to help search for enemy convoys: Patrol Wing 10, having lost eleven of its twenty-four PBY seaplanes during the first four days of war, withdrew to the Netherlands East Indies on 13 December. Compounding their plight was the continual presence of Japanese warplanes, which further inhibited their search by forcing them to remain submerged during daylight hours.

In the first two weeks of the war, when Hart's submarines did catch up with enemy shipping, their commanders attacked with great skill and daring. Time after time, they fired point-blank at choice targets only to have their torpedoes explode prematurely or not at all. There were times, too, when submariners watched aghast as their torpedoes bounced harmlessly off the sides of intended victims. Invariably, their efforts were rewarded by punishing depth-charging at the hands of enemy destroyers. Little wonder that by 24 December, Japanese troops had landed in five areas on Luzon and one in Mindanao with no more difficulty than if they had been holding dress rehearsals in friendly territory.

On the morning of 24 December 1941, with the Japanese marching on Manila from three directions and air raids becoming more frequent, MacArthur decided to save Manila from complete destruction by declaring it an "open city," effective at midnight. Hart, not having been notified that such a move was impending, was flabbergasted to learn that he had less than fourteen hours in which to close down his headquarters and get all naval personnel out of Manila.

This turn of events was indicative of the less-than-cordial relations between the army and navy commanders in the Far East. MacArthur, openly disdainful of Hart and his little Asiatic Fleet, operated mostly on his own and apparently had no interest in cooperating with his naval counterpart. As Hart later wrote:

On 23 December, the CinCAF [Commander in Chief, Asiatic Fleet] saw a copy of a USAFFE [U.S. Army Forces, Far East] dispatch which predicted an early retirement of all Army forces to the Bataan Peninsula and Corregidor. On the following morning he received definite information that such movement was in progress, that the Government and the GHQ of USAFFE would move to Corregidor that day and that Manila was to be proclaimed an open city, containing no combat elements. This eventuality had been foreseen but its coming so soon was a surprise—as was the fact that no mention of such a step had previously been made, formally or otherwise, since the war began. We immediately proceeded to uproot *Canopus* and the other Submarine installations from the Manila Harbor front and to shift all such activities to Mariveles and Corregidor.*

This precipitate move was a severe blow to the submarine command. It disorganized the operational plan, and forced the abandonment of practically all spare parts for S-boats and of many hard-to-come-by Mark-14 torpedoes for the fleet-type boats that were cached in and around Manila. Loss of those torpedoes resulted in a shortage that hampered submarine operations for the next year and a half. Also lost in the mad scramble to evacuate the city was the headquarters communication equipment.

"It was decided in full conference," Admiral Hart wrote, "that the Submarines would continue to operate from Manila Bay and keep it up as long as possible. It was hard to decide whether CinCAF should also shift his Command Post to Corregidor or accept the probability that even the Submarines would have to shift base to the southward in the near future, and make one jump of it to the N.E.I. [Netherlands East Indies]. The latter alternative was chosen."**

On Christmas Day 1941, the commander in chief, Asiatic Fleet, turned over command of all naval activities remaining in the Philippines to Rear Admiral Francis W. Rockwell, whose headquarters had been moved from the wreckage of the Cavite Navy Yard to a tunnel on Corregidor. To minimize the time he would be "out of action," Hart planned to take off for Surabaja after sundown in one of Patrol Wing 10's PBYs. That morning, however, Japanese pilots discovered the hidden seaplane and destroyed it. Fortunately, the P-type submarine *Shark* (SS-174) was available and, at about 2100, Hart and his party boarded her for a voyage that lasted seven days instead of his desired twenty-four hours.

Before he left Manila, Hart made several important changes in the staff structure of Submarines, Asiatic Command. These centered

*Hart, "Narrative of Events," p. 45.
**Ibid.

around Commander John Wilkes who, as commander of Submarine Division 14, had arrived on station in the fall of 1939 with six *Perch*-type submarines to take command of Submarine Squadron 5. Already attached to the Asiatic Fleet were six S-boats, the *Canopus*, and the *Pigeon*. These were incorporated into Wilkes's command. Squadron 5 gained strength one year later when the *Shark* and four other fleet-type boats of the *Seadragon* class arrived.

This buildup to eleven fleet-type submarines created problems in maintenance, supply, berthing, and advanced-base support that the *Canopus*, primarily an S-boat tender, could not solve. In a belated attempt to rectify the situation, the Navy Department finally responded to Hart's urgent request by purchasing the merchant vessel *Fred Morris* for conversion to a tender. Although the merchantman was commissioned the USS *Otus* on 19 March 1941, her conversion in the Cavite Navy Yard was far from complete when the war began. The Asiatic Fleet's submarine force was further bolstered by the arrival in November 1941 of Submarine Squadron 2. Commanded by Captain Walter E. Doyle, it boasted twelve fleet-type boats and the tender *Holland*.

In the interest of a more efficient chain of command, Squadrons 2 and 5 were deactivated on 1 December 1941 and combined to form Submarine Squadron 20 under the command of Captain Doyle. At this juncture, Wilkes, having completed his tour of duty with the Asiatic Fleet, was ordered back to the United States. Admiral Hart, however, held him in Manila, his justification being the simple statement that he did it "for eventualities."*

Apparently the "eventualities" Hart anticipated materialized, for on 9 December 1941—two days after the disaster at Pearl Harbor—he reinstated Wilkes, newly promoted to captain, as commander, Submarines, Asiatic Fleet, and transferred Doyle to Surabaja with orders to prepare an alternative command post for submarines. Hart's report explains that he made this abrupt change of command "on account of his [Wilkes's] experience and familiarity with the conditions obtaining—and his excellent ability, including health."** As the situation developed, it would have made little difference who was designated commander, Submarines, Asiatic Fleet, because the degree of operational control to be exercised by the holder of that billet was never clearly defined. Hart, first as commander in chief of the Asiatic Fleet and later as commander of ABDA's naval forces, issued such specific

*Ibid., p. 31.
**Ibid., p. 38.

operational directives that the submarine commander was permitted little, if any, interpretation or flexibility in their execution.

To prevent the higher echelon of the submarine command from being knocked out by enemy action, it was divided into an operational staff under Captain Wilkes and an administrative staff under Captain James Fife. Both were organized to function, if necessary, as independent operational-administrative units.

About the twentieth of December, it was determined that Surabaja, whose harbor was jammed with Allied ships, could not be effectively used to service submarines, and the tender *Holland* was sent to Darwin, where it was planned to set up a service base.

At midnight, the day after Christmas, Fife and his staff boarded the submarine *Seawolf* (SS-197) and departed Corregidor for Darwin, to set up headquarters on board the *Holland*.

Corregidor experienced its first air raid on 29 December 1941, when an estimated 340 aircraft bombed the "rock" for more than three hours and did considerable damage. Although the 3-inch antiaircraft guns of the defenders brought down a few enemy planes, it suddenly became obvious that, because of their small caliber and limited range, they could not effectively defend the island fortress and its environs against air raids.

Also attacked that day was the *Canopus*, which was lying, camouflaged, near the shore in Mariveles Bay, a few miles north of Corregidor. Even though there were 3-inch antiaircraft guns in the nearby hills, they proved no more effective than their counterparts on Corregidor. As a result, the tender was grievously damaged from a bomb hit and several near-misses.

The raid, portending grimmer days to come, underscored the futility and danger of attempting to conduct submarine operations from Manila Bay, and the swift decision to terminate them came as no surprise. Orders were transmitted that night to Asiatic Fleet submarines to head for the Malay barrier upon completion of their war patrols. The last submarine to leave the Manila area was the *Swordfish* (SS-193). She departed for Surabaja on 31 December with Wilkes and his operational staff on board. Time having run out for surface ships to escape, the *Canopus*, affectionately known to submariners as "the Old Lady," and the *Pigeon* were left behind, and were scuttled when Bataan and Corregidor fell. Their courageous crews were either killed or captured.

Toward the end of December, the U.S. War Department and Navy Department decided that Darwin had the potential to be a base of considerable magnitude and, being about 1,200 nautical miles east of

Surabaja, it provided greater security from enemy attack. Accordingly, the commander of Task Force 5, Rear Admiral Glassford, ordered all the Asiatic Fleet's auxiliaries not otherwise deployed, such as the seaplane tenders *William B. Preston* (AVD-7) and *Childs* (AVD-1), to move to Darwin.

In truth, Darwin was dismally situated for a naval base. It had a small naval station, HMAS *Melville*,* but the nearest marine overhaul and repair facility of any consequence was in southern Australia, about 1,800 miles away. Although Darwin's harbor is deep, it is cursed with a 24-foot tide, and its entrance is vulnerable to mining. No railroads came within several hundred miles of the place, and the roads were primitive, at best. Supplies in quantity could be brought in only by ship. Fighter protection was nonexistent because most of Australia's air force was fighting in Africa, Great Britain, and Singapore, and what few American combatant aircraft could be scraped together were attempting to reach beleaguered Java by staging through Darwin—not basing there.

Most of Darwin's population of 600 had fled to safer parts of the continent, leaving behind deserted streets and boarded-up stores. The sun, which bore down on the place with 110-degree intensity, could be blotted out by a sudden drenching rain. Worst of all, insofar as American sailors were concerned, lack of shipping space caused an acute shortage of beer and spirits, and entertainment, other than an occasional softball game, was out of the question.

Wilkes arrived in Surabaja on 7 January 1942 and immediately installed his staff in Hart's fleet headquarters—a large house on the city's outskirts. At about the same time, Fife and his administrative staff arrived in Darwin. In normal times, Surabaja, with its sheltered harbor, ample docking space, floating dry dock, and well-equipped machine shops, would have made an excellent submarine base. But these were far from normal times. Surabaja Harbor was overburdened with Allied naval vessels and merchant ships of many flags. Dock space was at a premium. Overhaul and repair facilities were taxed far beyond their capacity. With the tenders *Holland* and *Otus* stationed at Darwin, spare parts for American submarines were unattainable. Dutch technicians and Indonesian mechanics, unfamiliar with American machinery and hampered by a language barrier, were of little help, and submarine crews returning from grueling war patrols had to forgo much-needed rest in order to ready their boats for the next assignment. And, incredible as it may seem, the Dutch did not work in the navy yard on weekends.

---

*The Australians, like the British, name shore stations as they do ships.

It was planned to base one-third of the submarines in Darwin and rotate them with the boats operating from Surabaja, but the stark inadequacies of the Australian port doomed this hastily conceived idea from its inception. Hart's report covering the latter part of January 1942 states: "It developed to be a mistake to have sent practically all large auxiliaries all the way to Darwin, because that removed them so far from the center of gravity of operations of our ships which they existed to serve."* Accordingly, on 29 January, he directed all fleet auxiliaries to move from Darwin to Tjilatjap, upon completion of whatever work was currently under way.

When the *Holland* and *Otus* arrived on 10 February, both Tjilatjap Harbor and the long, narrow channel winding up to it from the Indian Ocean were packed with ships of all descriptions. Among the Asiatic Fleet ships present were the *Black Hawk* and *Marblehead*; the latter had been seriously damaged by bombs in the Battle of the Flores Sea six days earlier. Tjilatjap did have a small floating dry dock, but otherwise, as a fleet overhaul and repair facility, it was a farce, and the belated arrival of tenders did little to help solve the maintenance problems that were plaguing the Asiatic Fleet's war-battered ships—particularly the submarines. Besides, with ABDA's small air force all but destroyed and Japanese warplanes marauding at will over Java, it was disquieting to realize that one stick of bombs, well-placed on a ship in the narrow channel, could result in the rest of them being trapped in the harbor.

Soon after arriving in Tjilatjap, because no other ship was available, the *Otus* was given a most unorthodox assignment—to escort the crippled *Marblehead* nearly 4,000 miles to Trincomalee, Ceylon. Sparsely armed and unable to play a defensive role, the *Otus* was to rescue survivors in the event the cruiser's temporary patches gave way and she foundered. With daily bombing raids eroding port facilities at Surabaja and the area deemed unsafe for submarines, only the *Holland* remained to service Asiatic Fleet submarines.

On 18 February, Japanese forces landed unopposed on the island of Bali, giving them access to airfields within easy reach of Surabaja and Tjilatjap. The next day, 188 Japanese carrier-based dive-bombers and fighters accompanied by 54 land-based bombers demolished most of Darwin and its meager military installations. Practically every ship in the harbor was either sunk or damaged. Fearful of similar treatment for Tjilatjap, Glassford ordered the indispensable tenders *Holland*, with Fife and his administrative staff embarked, and *Black Hawk* to steam for ports in southern Australia. Accompanying them were the destroyers *Barker* and *Bulmer*, both damaged by near-hits off the coast

*Hart, "Narrative of Events," p. 65.

of Sumatra on 15 February. Escorting these ships were the submarines *Stingray* (SS-186) and *Sturgeon* (SS-187).

By 26 February, it was known that at least two enemy invasion fleets were descending on Java. Bombing raids had intensified, and the Allies, with only twenty-eight assorted combatant-type aircraft left, were powerless to stave them off. As the capital island teetered on disaster's brink, the ABDA command was dissolved and the Dutch, with the few Allied forces available to them, assumed full responsibility for the defense of Java. Now, the commander of the submarine force, John Wilkes, his boats no longer operating from bases in the Netherlands East Indies, had become supererogatory. Glassford, who had been named commander, Southwest Pacific, and given temporary promotion to vice admiral, ordered him to get out of Java while he could. The next day, Wilkes and his staff departed Tjilatjap on board the submarines *Spearfish*, *Sargo*, and *Seadragon* bound for their new headquarters in Australia.

Admiral Hart maintained strict control over the use of his fleet's submarines from the day war began until 14 February 1942, when he relinquished his ABDA command and returned to the United States. His decision to deploy his submarines primarily in the defense of points where enemy landings were anticipated did not jibe with the thinking of many submariners. They regarded waiting in low-density target areas to intercept landings that might or might not occur as a waste of time and effort, and thought it would be more productive to fight their underseas war in high-density target areas, such as off major bases and ports, and to interdict the enemy's lines of communication. To some extent this was done, but only, as Hart's report states, "insofar as numbers [of submarines] available would permit."*

Hart's plan could have been effective. It depended, however, on accurate advance information, and at no time during those early months of the war did he have adequate aerial reconnaissance. From what little information he did receive, and some of that was faulty, he was obliged to divine where and when the enemy might strike next. As a result, no Japanese landing was prevented or even seriously hampered by U.S. submarines, because, sad to say, they generally arrived on the scene after the landing had taken place.

From the beginning of the war until the fall of Java, Asiatic Fleet submarines were forced to keep to the sea for unduly long periods. It was not unusual for fleet-type submarines to be out upwards of fifty days, while the non-air-conditioned S-boats had to endure the heat of

*Ibid., p. 65.

tropic seas for thirty or forty days at a time. According to Hart: "Many of the patrols were much longer than was intended because in so many cases on the way back to base Submarines had to be rerouted to increase opposition to the enemy's advance." He went on to observe: "It was being found, however, that, in spite of the very great hardships and strain over long periods, the personnel was standing it surprisingly well. Many were in rather bad shape upon return, but appeared to recover in a very short period of rest."*

Beginning in January 1942, a few of the fleet-type submarines were diverted from war patrols to transport urgently needed supplies, mainly 3-inch antiaircraft shells and machine-gun ammunition, to Corregidor. This was necessary because surface vessels could not penetrate the Japanese blockade. On the return trip, these submarines evacuated important people who were not essential to the defense of the "rock," such as military pilots, skilled technicians, and civilian officials. They also brought out spare parts for submarines, radio equipment, and torpedoes. For example, on 20 February Lieutenant Commander Chester C. Smith in the *Swordfish* loaded thirteen torpedoes and evacuated Philippine President Manuel Quezon and his family, Vice President Sergio Osmeña, and five high-ranking staff members to San Jose, Panay Island, Philippines. The *Swordfish* immediately returned to Corregidor and evacuated the American high commissioner to the Philippines, Francis B. Sayre, his party of eleven, and five navy enlisted men. The passengers were taken to Fremantle, Australia.

The first three months of World War II will haunt the Asiatic Fleet's submariners as long as they live. From the attack on Pearl Harbor until the fall of Java, which brought about the dissolution of the Asiatic Fleet, they fired at least 223 torpedoes at some 97 enemy vessels and got only 11 confirmed kills.** It is small wonder that humiliated submarine commanders began to doubt their own or their crews' competence. The crews, in turn, knowing the fault did not lie with them, questioned the ability of their skippers. Thus, the strain generated by long, hazardous patrols, capped by repeated inexplicable failures, caused a few disillusioned and thoroughly heartsick submarine commanders to ask to be relieved.

It didn't take long for the highly competent submariners to suspect they were fighting a war with defective torpedoes, and they reported

*Ibid., p. 68.
**The figures for the number of torpedoes fired and the number of targets are extrapolated from a list of submarine war patrols contained in *Silent Victory* by Clay Blair, Jr. They are perhaps on the conservative side, but are close enough to illustrate the shocking dimensions of this tragedy.

The USS *Stingray* (SS-186), USS *Sturgeon* (SS-187), and USS *Salmon* (SS-182), pictured here with the USS *Seal* (SS-183), were part of the long-range, fleet-type submarines attached to Submarine Squadron 20. Naval History, NH 77086

their concern. Those in higher command, however, were not easily convinced, and it took nearly two years for the navy to recognize the problems and correct them. By then it was too late to salvage the careers of some promising naval officers, and many a Japanese ship that should have been rotting on the ocean floor was still plying the seas.

On the other side of the ledger, the following losses were sustained by the Asiatic Fleet's submarine force.

On 10 December 1941, the *Sealion*, commanded by Lieutenant Commander Richard G. Voge, was sunk during the bombing of the Cavite Navy Yard. Four men in her engine room were killed.

On 20 January 1942, the *S-36*, commanded by Lieutenant John R. McKnight, Jr., while traversing Makasar Strait at night in the face of strong, unpredictable currents, ran hard aground on hidden Taka Bakang Reef. Unable to work free, she was scuttled, but her crew was saved.

On 11 February 1942, the *Shark*, commanded by Lieutenant Commander Louis Shane, Jr., was depth-charged and sunk off Menado, northern Celebes, with the loss of all hands. She was the first American submarine to be sunk by surface forces in the Pacific.

On 3 March 1942, the *Perch* (SS-176), commanded by Lieutenant Commander David A. Hurt, after several days of being viciously depth-charged, was unable to submerge and, in the face of enemy gunfire, was scuttled. All hands were captured. During three and a half years as prisoners of war, nine men died, but fifty-three, including Hurt, lived through the ordeal.

On 6 April 1942, the tender *Canopus*, commanded by Commander Earl L. Sackett, left in the Manila area to service submarines, was scuttled when Bataan fell. Sackett and several others were evacuated by submarine to Australia, but the rest of the ship's company fought in the defense of Corregidor, and were either killed or captured by the Japanese.

On 4 May 1942, the *Pigeon* was sunk off Corregidor with no loss of life. During the bombing of the Cavite Navy Yard on 10 December 1941, when commanded by Lieutenant Richard E. Hawes, she rescued the minesweeper *Bittern* (AM-36) and the submarine *Seadragon* by towing both crippled ships clear of the blazing dock area. For this heroic performance, Hawes was awarded the Navy Cross, and the *Pigeon* became the first U.S. Navy ship to be awarded the Presidential Unit Citation. Lieutenant Hawes turned over command of the *Pigeon* to Lieutenant Commander Frank A. Davis on 5 January 1942 and was evacuated to Australia. Under Davis, the *Pigeon* received a second Presidential Unit Citation for outstanding performance of duty in the face of unrelenting enemy bombing attacks and artillery fire. Her crew, like many other navy men, manned Corregidor's beach defenses and fought to the bitter end. As prisoners of the Japanese, some of them managed to survive, but Davis was not one of them.

# 4

# DESTROYERS

The U.S. Asiatic Fleet had only thirteen destroyers with which to defend convoys, screen cruisers, hunt Japanese submarines, sink Japanese transports, and fight superior Japanese forces. This gargantuan task was the responsibility of Destroyer Squadron 29, commanded by Captain Herbert V. Wiley whose broad command pennant flew from the *Paul Jones*. The twelve other ships under his command were divided equally among Destroyer Divisions 57, 58, and 59.

As Admiral Hart commented, his destroyers, having been built in 1917 and 1918, were "old enough to vote." Among the last of a once-large inventory, they had seen their contemporaries scrapped, decommissioned, or turned over to the British under the lend-lease program. Their flush decks and four high stacks made them distinctive, and they were often referred to as "four pipers." They averaged 1,200 tons, were 314 feet long, and had a top speed of 32 knots. Their armament consisted of twelve torpedo tubes in four triple mounts, four 4-inch deck guns, one 3-inch antiaircraft gun designed in 1916, and a few assorted machine guns. They carried submarine-detection gear and depth charges, but had no radar and their torpedoes, which were of old design, were cursed with low speed and a small bursting charge. The destroyers of Squadron 29 were, in fact, not only inadequately armed for the warfare of the day but sadly in need of overhaul.

In the tropic sun, destroyers' decks became scorching hot, and their innards, lacking air-conditioning, heated up to oven-like intensity. Even in moderate seas they pitched and rolled like rodeo mustangs, which made it difficult, often impossible, to prepare meals that could be retained only if the consumer had a cast-iron stomach. Old these plucky little "cans" were, but they were manned by rock-hard veterans of the China Station who, under relentless, nerve-racking pressure, fought them with fierce determination and courageous abandon against fearful odds until, after three harrowing months, the Asiatic Fleet was no more.

The winds of war were blowing near gale force when, on 24 November 1941, the destroyers of Squadron 29, like other Asiatic Fleet ships, were ordered strategically deployed. The tender *Black Hawk* (AD-9) and the destroyers *Whipple* (DD-217), *Alden, John D. Edwards* (DD-216), and *Edsall* (DD-219) were sent to Balikpapan in eastern Borneo; the cruiser *Marblehead* and the destroyers *Paul Jones, Stewart* (DD-224), *Barker, Bulmer* (DD-222), and *Parrott* (DD-218) to Tarakan in northeastern Borneo. Detachment commanders were instructed to go to these oil-rich ports for fuel but to "have difficulty" in obtaining capacity loads—with a view to occupying the ports for a protracted period, if necessary.

Undergoing repairs in the Cavite Navy Yard were the destroyers *Peary* and *Pillsbury* (DD-227), which had been damaged in a near-disastrous collision. The two remaining four pipers of Squadron 29, the *Pope* and the *John D. Ford*, were on patrol in the area of Manila.

On 5 December 1941, Admiral Sir Tom Phillips, the new commander in chief of the British Far East Fleet, arrived in Manila from Singapore by seaplane for a two-day conference with Admiral Hart and General Douglas MacArthur. His presence was a carefully guarded secret. It was then that Hart first learned that the United States had assured the British of armed support in the event Japan moved aggressively against Thailand, the Malay Peninsula, the Netherlands East Indies, or Sarawak. That the Navy Department had neglected to notify the commander in chief of the Asiatic Fleet of this sensitive agreement was embarrassing, to say the least, especially because, when Phillips divulged it, he requested the immediate loan of two destroyer divisions.

Hart, however, declined to send his destroyers to Singapore unless and until there was provocation on the part of the Japanese. He noted that the only two capital ships the British had in the Far East were accompanied by four destroyers, and that the Royal Navy had two more destroyers in Hong Kong. Furthermore, his cruisers would not be fully effective if they were deprived of destroyers. Nevertheless, Hart assured Phillips that, when the time came, the promised loan of American destroyers would be made. They were, he pointed out, already deployed and readily available.

On 6 December word came from Singapore that a Japanese amphibious expedition had been sighted in the Gulf of Siam heading west in what appeared to be a strike against Thailand. That afternoon, Phillips departed Manila by plane, and, before he left, Hart informed him that Destroyer Division 57, consisting of the *Whipple, Alden, Edsall,* and *John D. Edwards,* had been ordered to sail from Balikpapan for Singapore. The *Black Hawk* was ordered to Surabaja, Java. These destroyers did not reach Singapore in time to accompany the battleship *Prince of Wales* and the battle cruiser *Repulse* in their ill-fated attempt to prevent Japanese landings in Malaya. Following the loss of both British ships and the highly regarded Admiral Phillips, the four American destroyers were ordered back to ports in the Netherlands East Indies.

The destruction of the Cavite Navy Yard on 10 December was a crippling blow to the Asiatic Fleet. It lost its only major overhaul and repair facility in the Far East, as well as its only source of spare parts. This loss immediately threw the burden of keeping the destroyers of Squadron 29 operative on the *Black Hawk.* She, like the submarine tenders, carried only limited supplies of spares, but her machine shops were manned by veteran craftsmen, and they improvised and "jury-rigged" furiously for three months to keep the ancient "cans" in the fight.

The *Peary* and *Pillsbury,* which were still in the Cavite Navy Yard at the time of the raid, narrowly escaped destruction. The *Pillsbury,* with steam up, was able to get out into Manila Bay, where she took enough evasive action to avoid being hit by the attackers. The *Peary,* on the other hand, was lying "cold iron" at the dock when bombs burst all around her. With her commanding officer struck down by shrapnel, several of her crew killed or wounded, and flames from blazing buildings threatening to finish her off, she lay helpless. The *Peary* undoubtedly would have been lost had it not been for Lieutenant Commander Charles A. Ferriter, commanding the minesweeper *Whippoorwill* (AM-35), who came to the rescue. With great daring and skill, he maneuvered his ship into position to pull the *Peary* to safety.

Hasty temporary repairs made the *Peary* seaworthy and, on the night of 26 December 1941, she escaped from Manila Bay, the last surface ship of the Asiatic Fleet to do so. En route to her destination, which was Darwin, Australia, she was attacked by both Japanese and Australian aircraft. The casualties and damage she suffered were not inflicted by the Japanese but by the Australians, who took her for a Japanese ship reported to be in the area.

The record does not come close to portraying the courage of Destroyer Squadron 29 during those first three months of World War II, when the crews and their ships were pushed without respite to the

outer limits of their physical endurance. The only relief the squadron
had from the tedium of continuous convoy duty was the *Edsall*'s sinking of the Japanese submarine *I-124* and the unconfirmed "probables"
it chalked up.

On 23 January 1942, in a daring night attack, against superior
Japanese invasion forces near the oil-rich port of Balikpapan, the
destroyers *John D. Ford, Parrott, Paul Jones,* and *Pope* won the first
surface action fought by U.S. ships in the Pacific War. With torpedoes
and deck guns they sank four cargo-transports and one patrol craft,
for a total of 23,496 tons. Several other enemy ships were badly
damaged. This attack against a force supported by cruisers and destroyers was accomplished without a single fatality, but four men were
wounded when a shell, the only one to strike home, ripped into the
torpedo workshop on board the *John D. Ford.*

On 4 February 1942, the *Stewart, John D. Edwards, Barker,* and *Bulmer*
were part of an American-Dutch task force under the command of
Rear Admiral Doorman that was ordered to attack a concentration of
Japanese ships in the vicinity of the Makasar Strait. This force was
turned back in the Flores Sea when enemy bombers attacked and
seriously damaged the cruisers *Houston* and *Marblehead.* The destroyers sustained no damage.

On the fifteenth, Doorman was ordered to take a strike force composed of American, British, and Dutch ships and intercept a large
Japanese force bearing down on Palembang, Sumatra. Before the
Allied ships, which included the *Stewart, Barker, Bulmer, John D. Edwards, Pillsbury,* and *Parrott,* reached their goal, they came under attack
by enemy bombers. Lacking fighter protection, they were bombed for
more than six hours, and their mission was aborted. Although no ships
were sunk, near-misses did extensive damage to several of them, including the *Barker* and the *Bulmer,* which were forced to retire to
Exmouth Gulf, Australia.

On the morning of 19 February 1942, the Japanese hit Darwin with
a surprise air attack, often referred to as "Australia's Pearl Harbor."
Shore installations were blasted to rubble, and almost every ship in the
harbor was sunk. Among those sent to a watery grave was the hapless
destroyer *Peary.* The raid on Darwin and the sinking of the *Peary* are
detailed in part II of this book.

That same night, about 1,100 miles to the west, the *John D. Ford,
Pope, Parrott, John D. Edwards,* and *Pillsbury* participated with Dutch
ships in the Battle of Bandung Strait. Operational control of this
mission also was given to Admiral Doorman. Its objective was to break
up a Japanese landing on the island of Bali, less than 100 miles east of
Surabaja. Based upon intelligence that failed to perceive that the

Japanese were already ashore and all but four of their destroyers and one transport had withdrawn from the area, this hastily conceived, poorly orchestrated operation should never have taken place.*

In the engagement, which pitted the Dutch cruisers De Ruyter and Java, the Dutch destroyer leader Tromp, the Dutch destroyer Piet Hein, the six American destroyers, and a few Dutch motor torpedo boats against a small Japanese force, the Allies fared badly. True, the Japanese destroyers Oshio, Asashio, and Michishio were damaged by gunfire, but the Piet Hein was sunk—Dutch sources strongly suggest this was done by an American destroyer—the Tromp badly damaged, and the Stewart so grievously shot-up that she required dry-docking in Surabaja. Nevertheless, the Allies loudly proclaimed "victory."

On 27 February, the John D. Edwards, Alden, John D. Ford, and Paul Jones participated in the Battle of the Java Sea during the hours of daylight. Two days before the battle, Doorman informed the American destroyer captains that, because their 4-inch guns could be of little value against Japanese cruisers, he wanted them to remain on the disengaged flank, ready to make torpedo attacks against enemy transports. Consequently, throughout the battle, the four pipers maneuvered furiously on the disengaged side to keep out of range of Japanese shells inaccurately fired over the Allied cruisers and to dodge stray torpedoes.

After two hours of heated combat, during which the transports were not even sighted, Doorman, wanting to regroup his ships for a night attack, ordered the American destroyers to cover his retirement. Thereupon, Commander Thomas H. Binford, flying his command pennant from the John D. Edwards, ordered a torpedo attack on the pursuing Japanese cruisers. Steaming through a storm of shells, unable to fire their own out-ranged guns and realizing that it would be suicide to close the range, the four American destroyers launched their torpedoes at 10,000 yards. Although none of them found their mark, the torpedoes forced the Japanese cruisers to turn tail and terminate the engagement. With all their torpedoes expended and their fuel running low, the destroyers retired to Surabaja.

The next morning, when Admiral Helfrich learned the extent of the disastrous Allied defeat in the Java Sea and it became painfully clear that Java was doomed, he ordered all Allied ships to run for ports in Western Australia.

*Admiral Thomas C. Hart was relieved as commander in chief of the Asiatic Fleet and commander of ABDA's naval forces on 14 February 1942, and departed for the United States the following day. Responsibility for planning this fiasco rests with his successor in the ABDA billet, Vice Admiral Helfrich.

The USS *Paul Jones* (DD-230), flagship of Destroyer Squadron 29. Naval Institute Collection

That night, under cover of darkness, the four war-weary destroyers, slowed by leaking condensers and fouled bottoms, and lacking their primary weapons—torpedoes, steamed via Madura Strait, a shortcut denied to ships of deeper draft, into Bali Strait. Their sudden appearance so surprised some Japanese destroyers patrolling off Bali that, after a brief but inconclusive gunfight, the four pipers scrambled safely past them into the Indian Ocean. They were extremely fortunate to escape to Southern Australia, because the eight other Allied warships that were on the north side of Java on 28 February all fell prey to the Japanese.

From the beginning of the war until the end of February, the thirteen fighting ships of Destroyer Squadron 29, along with their tender *Black Hawk*, led charmed lives. Although several of them suffered battle damage, only the *Peary* was sunk. The first of March 1942, however, was doomsday for four more of them.

That day, the *Edsall*, with thirty-three U.S. Army Air Forces pilots who had survived the sinking of the seaplane tender *Langley* on board, was attempting to reach Tjilatjap when she vanished in the Indian Ocean. Her fate was not known until 1952, when there came to light a Japanese film that showed the heavy cruiser *Ashihara*, at point-blank range, blasting the out-gunned four piper into oblivion. That no survivors lived to tell the tale indicates that more than 150 officers and enlisted men were wantonly massacred.

The defeat of the Allies in the Battle of the Java Sea left no major naval units in Asian waters to confront the Japanese, whose invasion forces were pouring ashore on Java. This situation, coupled with the increasing tempo of air raids, against which there were no defenses, led to all Allied ships being ordered to evacuate Tjilatjap on 1 March and steam for ports in Australia. Most ships proceeded independently, because Japanese land- and carrier-based aircraft, warships, and submarines were combing the Indian Ocean lusting for Allied blood. In dispersal lay the lone hope that some ships would get through.

Along with numerous merchant ships fleeing for their lives was a handful of lightly armed naval vessels: the destroyers *Pillsbury* and *Parrott*; the old gunboats from the China Station, the *Tulsa* (PG-22) and *Asheville* (PG-21), the minesweepers *Whippoorwill* and *Lark* (AM-21), the yacht *Isabel* (PY-10), and the Australian gunboat *Yarra*. Of all of these, the *Pillsbury* and *Parrott* seemed to have the best chance of reaching safety. The *Pillsbury*, *Asheville*, and *Yarra* vanished without a trace. Somewhere southeast of Java, in the Indian Ocean, the valiant men manning these little ships fought against impossible odds and passed unsung into the unknown.

Many of the merchant ships were torpedoed soon after they cleared the minefields protecting Tjilatjap Harbor. Others steamed on only to fall prey to enemy warships or bombers later. Their vain distress calls, which filled the air, were heartrending because there were no ships capable of responding to them.

All hell was breaking loose on Java's south coast, and the situation on the island's north coast was no different. On 1 March, the only major Allied warship still afloat there was the *Exeter*, which was damaged in the Java Sea battle and had retired to Surabaja for repairs. Escorted by the destroyers *Encounter* and *Pope*, the British cruiser had been ordered to exit the Java Sea via Sunda Strait where, unknown to the ABDA command, a powerful Japanese task force was preparing for an amphibious assault on northwestern Java. Only hours before, the cruisers *Houston* and *Perth* had unexpectedly encountered this armada and, after a furious battle, had been sunk. There is little doubt that, had the *Exeter* and her two escorts approached Sunda Strait, they would have met the same fate, but they never came close.

Early that morning, two Japanese heavy cruisers, *Nachi* and *Haguro*, spotted the Allied ships and went in pursuit. A short time later they were joined by two more heavy cruisers, the *Ashigara* and *Myoko*. The damaged *Exeter* could make no more than 26 knots and, although the destroyers tried desperately to screen her with smoke, she could not escape. Riddled by shells, she was finished off by a torpedo. Soon thereafter, the *Encounter* was sunk by shellfire.

The *Pope* was able to hide for a while in a rain squall, but enemy aircraft hunted her down and attacked. Although she did not take a direct bomb hit, near-misses ruptured her plates below the waterline and wrecked her boiler brickwork. When she began shipping water fast and her speed was so reduced that she could not take evasive action, her commanding officer, Lieutenant Commander Welford C. Blinn, ordered his crew to set demolition charges to scuttle her and abandon ship. Only one man lost his life, and that was the result of an accident when the demolition charges were being set. The 151 survivors drifted in the water, clinging to rafts and a motor launch, without food or water, for three days before they were picked up by a Japanese destroyer and made prisoners of war.

The fourth destroyer of Squadron 29 to be stricken from the list that day was the *Stewart*. Damaged during the night action in Bandung Strait on 19 February, she was in a floating dry dock at Surabaja, and there was no way she could put to sea. When placing her in dry dock, on 21 February, native workmen failed to center her on the keel blocks, with the result that, when the dock was pumped dry, she rolled to port and lay at a 37-degree angle. This mishap put her port propeller and shaft out of action, and no replacement parts were available. Two months of yard work would have been required to get the *Stewart* ready for sea, and even then she would have had only one shaft.

With the war going from bad to worse and Surabaja being bombed more heavily with every passing day, it was obvious that the *Stewart* would not escape from Java. Accordingly, all her people, other than a skeleton crew of four, were reassigned to the *Parrott, John D. Edwards,* and *Pillsbury.*

On 25 February 1942, Lieutenant Francis E. Clark, formerly the *Stewart*'s torpedo officer, returned to Surabaja with orders to strip the ship of everything of value and lay demolition charges for her ultimate destruction. Because the ABDA high command was still assuring the population that Java could not be captured, this work was done with the utmost secrecy.

Although the demolition charges were laid and ready several days before, orders to destroy the *Stewart* were not received from navy headquarters in Bandung until 1100 on 1 March. These were probably the last orders issued from Bandung because, by this time, everyone on the naval staff was racing to reach Tjilatjap before the Japanese slammed the gate, thereby barring evacuation to Australia.

When Lieutenant Clark and his four-man crew arrived at the navy yard, they discovered that the dry dock, having been hit in a bombing raid that morning, was slowly sinking, and the *Stewart*'s engine room had been gutted by a bomb. Fortunately, the leads from the bridge to the demolition charges were still intact. Clark and his men fired them and, believing the ship was wrecked beyond repair, beat a hasty retreat for Tjilatjap.

Many months later, American pilots were perplexed by the sight of what appeared to be a Yankee warship steaming with the enemy. Although the ship in question carried a tripod foremast with a raked forward stack, which were characteristic of Japanese warships, her plumb bow, flush deck, and two after stacks were definitely characteristics of American warships. The silhouette book contained nothing on the Japanese side that even closely resembled this ship, yet, every time she was sighted, she was cruising well within enemy territory.

When American occupation forces were inspecting a hodgepodge of seagoing war prizes in the Kure-Hiroshima area on 15 October 1945, they solved the puzzle. The mystery ship was the *Stewart*, which the Japanese had resurrected and named Patrol Vessel 102. On 28 October, a U.S. Navy prize crew boarded her, and the following day the venerable ship was honored when Vice Admiral Jesse B. Oldendorf, commander, Southwestern Japan Force, placed her once again in commission as a U.S. man-of-war. Because she had been stricken from the Navy Register in March 1942 and her name had been assigned to a destroyer escort, the four piper was returned to the United States without a name.

# 5

# AIRCRAFT

No unit of the Asiatic Fleet took a worse beating, during the first three months of World War II, than its air arm, Patrol Wing 10. When the war began, PatWing 10, as it was generally called, had twenty-eight twin-engine, PBY seaplanes equally divided between Patrol Squadrons VP-101 and VP-102. The wing's Utility Squadron consisted of ten single-engine aircraft; four J2F amphibians, five OS2U seaplanes, and one SOC seaplane. Its pilots and aircrewmen were among the finest in the navy. Captain Frank D. Wagner, commanding the wing, called them, "the finest in the world."

To support seaplane operations in remote anchorages, the wing boasted four seaplane tenders: the *Langley*, the largest, was the jaded hulk of a once-proud ship—the navy's first aircraft carrier; the *Childs* and *William B. Preston* were converted World War I "flush deck" destroyers; and the *Heron* (AVP-2) was a World War I "Bird"-class minesweeper. All were especially configured for the job and carried large quantities of aviation gasoline. Although lightly armed and poorly equipped to defend themselves against marauders from sea or air, all four tenders operated alone and far removed from any back-up support. They met the challenge and acquitted themselves with distinction.

When the war began, the PBY-type seaplanes flown by PatWing 10 were often referred to as "big boats," but, before long, they began to be derided as "flying coffins." They were slow, cumbersome aircraft primarily designed for long-range reconnaissance. Not having self-sealing gas tanks and armed with only two .50-caliber machine guns, one in either waist hatch, a .30-caliber machine gun in the tail, and another in the bow, their defensive capabilities against enemy fighter planes were poor. Because their oxygen equipment was rudimentary, and often inoperable, to fly at altitudes above 12,000 feet was to court the lethal effects of anoxia. Besides, with a full bomb load, the PBYs could not top 16,000 feet and, at that altitude, fly faster than 85 knots. Thus, when pressing home bombing attacks, they were always within reach of antiaircraft guns and easy prey for enemy fighters.

When Admiral Thomas C. Hart received the "war warning" dispatch from the chief of naval operations on 29 November 1941, he directed Patrol Wing 10 to begin extensive reconnaissance patrols. Three PBYs, along with the *William B. Preston*, were sent to the Gulf of Davao to search the eastern approaches to the Celebes Sea, whose waters wash the northeastern shores of Borneo and the southern approaches to the Philippines. Four single-engine seaplanes and the *Heron* were stationed on the southern tip of Palawan Island to scout for Japanese ships threatening to enter the Celebes Sea from the west. Dutch aircraft, patrolling along the northern reaches of the Netherlands East Indies, covered territory contiguous to that assigned to PatWing 10. PBYs based at Cavite and Olongapo searched the areas west to the coast of Indochina, northwest to Hainan, and north to Formosa. Thus, for all practical purposes it can be said that the planes of Patrol Wing 10, with guns loaded and ready, were cooperating with the British, Dutch, and Australians a week before Pearl Harbor was attacked.

The planes sighted nothing of great interest until 2 December, when they discovered twenty Japanese merchant ships, including transports, in Camranh Bay, French Indochina. By the third, that force had grown to fifty ships, including cruisers and destroyers. On 4 December, under cover of foul weather, this ominous armada vanished. Forty-eight hours later, however, it was spotted by British aircraft moving westward in the Gulf of Siam. It should be noted here that, coincident with the attack on Pearl Harbor, these Japanese ships were to disgorge thousands of troops on beachheads 400 miles north of Singapore to begin the invasion of Malaya.

On 5, 6, and 7 December, PBYs of PatWing 10 encountered Japanese aircraft patrolling in the vicinity of Luzon's coastline. Although machine guns were trained, no shots were fired, as, like "stiff-legged dogs," the adversaries kept wary eyes on each other.

Even while Japanese emissaries in Washington were talking peace, this movement of ships and aircraft strongly suggested that a landing in force somewhere on the Malay Peninsula, and perhaps in the Philippines, was imminent. As this word spread, there was hardly a man in the Asiatic Fleet, from Admiral Hart down to the lowest rating, who had the slightest doubt that war with Japan was about to become a grim reality, and did not cinch up his belt ready for the fight.

At 0315 on 8 December 1941 (7 December 1941 in Honolulu), when Wagner received notification of the Pearl Harbor attack, he immediately ordered two 500-pound bombs loaded on each operational PBY and sent them to four dispersal areas within 60 miles of Manila.

At the time, three PBYs were operating with the *William B. Preston* stationed far to the south at Malalag Bay in the Gulf of Davao. At 0705, when one plane was on patrol and the other two, armed with bombs, were on the water awaiting instructions, disaster struck. Without warning, Japanese carrier-based dive-bombers attacked. Bombs intended to eliminate the *William B. Preston* fell dangerously close, but caused little damage. The two PBYs, however, were not so fortunate. Both were strafed and sunk. Ensign Robert G. Tills, the pilot of one of them, was killed as he tried to get his plane airborne. He was the first American to lose his life in Asia—a distinction the young naval reserve pilot could hardly have desired.

The first day of the war was disastrous for General MacArthur's Far East Air Force: Japanese planes destroyed more than half its bombers and two-thirds of its fighters, most of them on the ground. This force was small to begin with, but when it was reduced to thirty-seven fighters and seventeen bombers, mastery of the air was at once relinquished to the enemy. The losses meant that the ungainly PBYs of Patrol Wing 10, primarily designed for long-range reconnaissance, had to assume the suicidal role of bombers.

Without fighter escort, the courageous PBY pilots and aircrewmen went to war. They tried to bomb battleships and cruisers, but in so doing, were badly mauled by antiaircraft fire and enemy fighters. By 13 December, five days after the war began, eleven of the wing's twenty-eight PBYs had been lost, and the remainder were sent to safer bases in the Netherlands East Indies. About 172 officers and men, who, for lack of space, were left behind, fought on Bataan and Corregidor.

During the desperate weeks that followed, PatWing 10's PBYs operated out of Surabaja and, backed up by the tenders *William B. Preston, Childs, Heron,* and *Langley,* out of remote coves throughout the chain of islands that comprises the Malay barrier to Ambon and south to Darwin. It was rough duty. PBY crews often slept on board their anchored planes, in native shacks, and, on occasion, in the hot, cramped quarters of the tenders. Food was in short supply and had to be rationed. Clean clothes and warm-water baths were luxuries. There were long, dangerous patrols to be flown by day and night, and rest in between was rudely interrupted by air raids. This, coupled with heartrending news of squadron mates shot down or missing in action, was enough to break the spirit of lesser men, but the airmen of PatWing 10 never wavered. Although the odds were stacked against them, they carried out their missions with grim determination and great skill. Sheer guts, however, were not enough.

By 1 January 1942, only eight of the wing's original twenty-eight PBYs were left. These were augmented by eleven PBYs of Patrol Squadron 22, which had been hurriedly flown out from Honolulu, and five provided by the Dutch, who did not have crews to man them. On the sixth, the wing underwent a change of command: Captain Wagner was ordered to Admiral Hart's staff as commander, Aircraft, Asiatic Fleet, and was replaced by Commander John V. Peterson.

Lacking sea and air power, the Allies could not stay the giant octopus of Japanese aggression whose tentacles reached ever closer to the Netherlands East Indies. With the enemy dominating the skies, not even the remotest base was safe. Even Darwin, thought to be out of Japanese bomber range, was devastated on 19 February by land-based bombers and carrier planes. At the time, four PBYs of VP-22 were based in Darwin and operating from the *William B. Preston*. One was shot down while on patrol, the other three destroyed on the water. The *Preston* took a direct hit, which killed seventeen men and wounded eleven. She was severely damaged, but managed to reach southern Australia for repairs.

Eight days later, the same day the ABDA fleet was crushed in the Battle of the Java Sea, the *Langley*, attempting to reach Tjilatjap with a deckload of fighter planes, was bombed and sunk 130 miles south of her destination. During the early morning hours of 1 March, Japanese troops swarmed ashore on Java's north coast and, meeting only sporadic resistance, moved rapidly inland. Left without warships or combatant aircraft, its army of native troops disintegrating in the face of battle, and enemy warplanes continually on the attack, the ABDA command was dissolved. With that, Glassford, Wagner, and their staffs, along with Rear Admiral Arthur F. E. Palliser, RN, Vice Admiral Helfrich's chief of staff, wasted no time in clearing out of Bandung for Tjilatjap. At the same time, Commander Peterson and his small staff left the wing's headquarters in Surabaja and headed for the same evacuation port.

That night Glassford, Palliser, Peterson, and some key enlisted men boarded a PBY and, in spite of warnings by Dutch pilots that to take off from the restricted confines of Tjilatjap Harbor in the dark was suicidal, departed near midnight, and arrived safely the next morning at Exmouth Gulf, Australia.

Just before dawn on 2 March, three of PatWing's 10's PBYs, braving Japanese carrier-based fighters in the Indian Ocean and the ever-present fighters and bombers over Java, flew in from Exmouth Gulf to evacuate Captain Wagner, his staff, and other naval personnel. Before takeoff, one of the planes, whose engine could not be started, was turned over to the Dutch to repair and use or destroy. Its crew and passengers were packed into the two other planes, which arrived safely in Australia.

Only five of the forty-four PBYs assigned to Patrol Wing 10 remained on 3 March 1942, and the Utility Squadron had lost all but one of its aircraft. The wing was temporarily out of business. Its pilots and crewmen were assigned elsewhere, but the tenders *Heron, William B. Preston,* and *Childs* stayed in Australia to service replacement squadrons.

This is not intended to be a definitive history of Patrol Wing 10. It is rather a brief summary whose purpose is to lay the groundwork for the accounts contained in part II of this book. It will suffice, therefore, to point out that besides being ordered to fly 15 bombing missions without fighter protection and more than 200 long-range patrols of one or more aircraft, the pilots of Patrol Wing 10 successfully completed 10 dangerous rescue missions. These missions, generally considered routine, encompassed landing in Japanese-controlled areas of the Netherlands East Indies to pick up Dutchmen left behind to destroy oil and other important installations, and downed army and navy airmen stranded on treacherous reef-ringed atolls or adrift on the open sea.

Patrol Wing 10 was blessed with an abundance of heroic men who will remain unknown because, in those early days of World War II, courageous feats were considered the norm. Formal patrol reports were not required, and actions were mentioned only briefly in the wing's "war" diary. The following is a typical entry for a routine patrol:

January 30, 1942. Two planes, #41 Ensign Deede and #42 Ensign Jackobson, departed on patrol of Makasar and Kendari area. Plane #42 reported being attacked by land plane fighters, and took evasive action into clouds. This plane escaped (44 holes).

The only detailed reports are those written by men who survived being shot down.

# 6

# GUNBOATS

In the spring of 1941, there were two coastal gunboats and five river gunboats assigned to the Asiatic Fleet to operate in various parts of China. These unique ships were symbols of days long past, when their mere presence was enough to command respect for the American flag and to protect American interests. But times had changed, and Japan, having captured most of China's important cities, was then the arrogant, dominating power. With Japanese shore batteries and shipboard guns literally pointing down their throats, the gunboats stayed in China only because the Japanese, not yet ready to move against the United States, disdainfully tolerated them.

Some months before World War II, Admiral Hart, sniffing the freshening winds of war, ordered the two seagoing gunboats, the *Asheville*, built in 1918, and the *Tulsa*, built in 1922, back to Manila. These boats, which had acted for years as station ships in such ports as Swatow, Amoy, Tientsin, and Tsingtao, were 241 feet long and carried a crew of 185 officers and enlisted men. In contrast with the flat-bottomed river gunboats, they had proper hulls and keels. Their main armament consisted of three 4-inch .50-caliber guns, three 3-pounders, and three 1-pounders. The main drawback of these single-screw ships was that they could make no more than 12 knots, which precluded their operating with the faster combatant units of the fleet.

The five river gunboats were assigned to Rear Admiral William A. Glassford, commander of the Yangtze Patrol, who was headquartered in Hankow, China. These lightly armed, flat-bottomed, keelless vessels were built in the late 1920s for service on the shallow rivers of China

52

and were not meant to ply the open seas. Nevertheless, in late November 1941, Hart, convinced that war with Japan was imminent, ordered Glassford, his staff, and all but the two smallest river gunboats—the *Wake* and the *Tutuila*—back to Manila.

Because of her position 1,300 miles up the Yangtze River at Chungking, China's provisional capital, the *Tutuila* was turned over to the Chinese Nationalist forces of Chiang Kai-shek, and her ship's company was ordered back to the United States for reassignment. That company, which had been reduced to two officers and twenty-two enlisted men, had an arduous journey home: they departed Chungking via CNAT (the Sino-American airline) to Calcutta, traveled across India by train to Bombay, and from there went by ship around the Cape of Good Hope to Trinidad, whence the final leg of the journey was made by aircraft—an odyssey of more than 11,500 miles.

The only escape route open to the crew of the *Wake*, which was stationed 600 miles up the Yangtze River at the Japanese-held city of Hankow, was by way of Shanghai, where they could join up with the larger gunboats *Luzon* and *Oahu* (PR-6). Ignoring bellicose Japanese demands that he stay, the *Wake*'s skipper Lieutenant Commander Andrew E. Harris, got his ship under way during the early afternoon of 24 November 1941. To make the departure date of the other gunboats, the *Wake* had to be pushed as fast as her ancient boilers would permit, and Harris was not about to let the Japanese stop him.

The fifth river gunboat, the *Mindanao* (PR-8), which was stationed in Hong Kong, was to steam to Manila unescorted.

On the afternoon of 28 November, the *Wake* arrived in Shanghai, where the *Luzon* and *Oahu*, their main-deck doors and windows covered with watertight steel shutters, and fireroom blower intakes protected by cofferdams, were making ready to put to sea at midnight. Considered not seaworthy enough to make the trip to Manila, the *Wake*, manned by several of her crew augmented by local naval reservists for a total of fourteen, was left at Shanghai. Her new commanding officer was a naval reservist, Lieutenant Commander Columbus D. Smith. The rest of the *Wake*'s company found berths in the other gunboats. Eight of the fourteen men left with the *Wake* were radiomen who were to maintain the consulate's communications and operate Smith's short-wave radio equipment ashore. Unfortunately, the day war began, the *Wake* fell easy prey to the Japanese, and her crew, along with other navy men in Shanghai, became prisoners of war.

Shortly after midnight on 29 November, the *Luzon*, with Glassford on board, got under way, followed by the *Oahu*. At dawn they were safely past the Yangtze fairway buoys, heading south in the China Sea at about 10.5 knots. To express his concern about the river-oriented ships' ability to make the trip, Glassford sent the following dispatch to Hart: "Shall make effort to run straight Manila inside Pescadores arriving if all goes well about 4 or 5 December. Should war conditions render necessary shall follow coast await opportunity final leg Manila-ward. If unable make Manila propose make for Hong Kong in hostile emergency."

As luck would have it, a typhoon was making up in the Formosa Strait. Hart, gravely concerned for the safety of the river gunboats in a treacherous ocean, sent the minesweeper *Finch* (AM-9) and the sub-marine rescue vessel *Pigeon* to tow them if necessary, or to take off their crews. It was not long, however, before these tough, little seagoing ships were themselves in trouble. In heavy seas, the *Pigeon's* rudder was damaged, making her unable to steer, and one of her two anchors was carried away. The *Finch*, having lost both her anchors, was towing the *Pigeon* toward the lee of Formosa, where repairs could be attempted.

In the meantime, the flat-bottomed river gunboats were having a terrible time of it. Pounded by mountainous seas, lashed by howling winds, and drenched by blinding rain squalls, they labored along. At one point, the *Oahu's* inclinometer recorded an astounding, near-fatal roll of 56 degrees to starboard. The terrifying experiences of those on board the gunboats during that wild voyage defy description, but Admiral Glassford gives an inkling of their ordeal:

> The 2nd and 3rd of December will never be forgotten in all their grim details. Not only were we harassed by sweeps of Japanese aircraft over-head and by insolent men-of-war ordering us to do all manner of things that we could and would not do, but as we approached the Straits of Formosa and later got well into it, we experienced a heavy, choppy sea which was almost the undoing of the personnel if not the little craft themselves. We were tossed about as by a juggler, now up like a shot to a crest from which we would fall like a stone. The ships were rolling 28 to 30 degrees on a side, with a three-second period. They were taking green seas over the forecastle and even more dangerous, surging seas over the stern.
>
> Speed had been reduced to little more than steerage way, but even so the engines raced violently, the ships shaking and trembling.
>
> What disturbed us most was whether or not the human beings on board would be worthy of these incredibly stout little ships. For nearly 48 hours there was experienced the hardest beatings of our lives at sea. There was no sleep, no hot food, and one could scarcely even sit down without being tossed about by the relentless rapidity of the lunging jerks. The very worst of all the trip was after clearing Formosa, with a quarter-ing sea. I recall just before dawn on the 4th of December, while clinging to the weather rail of the bridge deck, that our situation could not

possibly be worse and wondering just how much longer we could stand it. Not the ships, which had proven their worth, but ourselves.*

Dawn of 5 December brought a cloudless sky, a placid sea, and blessed relief to the exhausted men on board the storm-racked ships. Like a horse heading for the barn, the *Luzon* moved out for Manila at 16 knots, outdistancing the slower *Oahu*. The *Pigeon* and *Finch*, following many miles astern, were slowly but surely beating their way to Manila. That same day, Glassford, the last commander of the Yangtze Patrol, hauled down his flag and announced, "ComYangPat dissolved." To "China hands" who had experienced the mysteries of the Orient and basked in its luxury since the patrol was formally established twenty-two years earlier, and eighty-seven years after the first American warship groped her cautious way up the murky waters of the Yangtze River, it signaled a sad end to "one hell of a fine duty station."

Following the bombing of the Cavite Navy Yard on 10 December 1941, the coastal gunboats *Tulsa* and *Asheville*, in company with the minesweepers *Lark* and *Whippoorwill*, sailed south from Manila for the Netherlands East Indies. Until the day Java fell, these gunboats operated as harbor-entrance patrol vessels, mainly at Surabaja and Tjilatjap. When the Japanese landed on Java, they departed independently from Tjilatjap bound for sanctuary in Australia. The *Tulsa* made it but, on 3 March 1942, the *Asheville*, like other Allied ships fleeing for their lives, fell victim to Admiral Chuichi Nagumo's big carrier task force, and was sunk somewhere off the southeast coast of Java. Only one of her company, Fred Lewis Brown, is known to have been picked up, and he died in a Japanese prisoner-of-war camp at Makasar in the spring of 1945.

The last of the river gunboats to reach Manila was the *Mindanao*, from Hong Kong. She, too, experienced difficult times at sea, having been forced to tack 180 miles up the China coast to Swatow before being able to head down to Manila. When she arrived on 10 December, the crews of the three river gunboats, at home in the confined waters of Manila Bay, were ready to join the fight for the Philippines.

The *Mindanao* was a shade more than 210 feet in length and had a ship's company of 65 officers and men. Upon arrival in Manila, her two ancient saluting guns were replaced by two .50-caliber machine guns, which augmented her two 3-inch guns and her twelve .30-caliber Lewis and twelve .30-caliber Browning machine guns. Her sister ship *Luzon* was similarly armed, but had no Brownings. The *Oahu* was about 191

*Glassford, "Narrative of Events," pp. 30–33.

The coastal gunboat USS *Asheville* (PG–21), sunk 3 March 1942 in the Indian Ocean south of Java by Japanese warships. Only one survivor, Fred Lewis Brown, was rescued; he died in a Japanese prisoner-of-war camp at Makasar, Celebes, in the spring of 1945. National Archives, 80–G–461042

feet in length with a ship's company of 52 officers and men. She was armed with two 3-inch guns and twelve .30-caliber Lewis machine guns.

At first, the *Mindanao* was assigned as station ship for Corregidor's minefield channels. The *Luzon* and *Oahu* occasionally patrolled off the minefield entrance, but spent most of their time in Manila Bay, preventing enemy troops from infiltrating behind the lines at night. Because of the acute fuel shortage, however, these patrols had to be discontinued on 27 December.

Japanese planes heavily bombed Corregidor and the nearby anchorages on 29 December. The *Mindanao* was straddled and slightly damaged. The bombs aimed at the two other gunboats missed their targets, but they landed close enough to throw salt water over the boats' decks. This close call made Captain Kenneth M. Hoeffel, commander of the Inshore Patrol, aware of the vulnerability of the anchored gunboats, especially since the antiaircraft guns on Corregidor were, in the main, ineffective, and the vessels themselves had nothing with which to fight off high-level bombers. Accordingly, he moved his headquarters from the *Mindanao* to the navy tunnel on Corregidor and ordered the gunboats' crews ashore during daylight hours to help strengthen Corredigor's beach defenses. At night, however, they were permitted to return to their ships, where they could at least enjoy the luxury of sleeping in bunks.

During the month of January, a few night patrols were made, but by 15 February, there was too little fuel oil to permit any routine patrols. What oil was left was split between the *Mindanao* and the *Luzon* for use only in an emergency. Such an emergency arose on the night of 6 April. According to intelligence reports, the Japanese had assembled some small boats and were preparing to infiltrate behind the lines on Bataan. The *Mindanao* and *Luzon* were ordered to forestall this maneuver. For nearly seven hours they searched Manila Bay east of Bataan, but found nothing. At about 0200, however, silhouetted against a moonlit sky, they sighted eleven small craft heading for Bataan. The gunboats opened fire, but clouds suddenly blotted out the moon and enshrouded the enemy in darkness. The *Mindanao* immediately fired star shells to illuminate the targets, and both vessels again opened fire. Japanese shore batteries, alerted by the gun blasts, quickly zeroed in on the gunboats and heavy shells began falling uncomfortably close. The troop-laden Japanese boats beat a hasty retreat, but not before four of their jury-rigged invasion fleet had been sunk and several others badly shot-up. The *Mindanao* and *Luzon* then withdrew, ending what might be called the Battle of Manila Bay—gunboat style.

The bloody fighting on Bataan ended on 9 April 1942, and the bomb-battered defenders of Corregidor, all too aware that the worst was yet to come, prepared for the fight of their lives. While the abandoned river gunboats swung silently around their hooks in Corregidor's south harbor, like tethered lambs waiting for the howling wolves to descend upon them, their crews were getting ready to play a new role in the grim game of war. No longer sailors armed with 3-inch guns, they had become artillerymen assigned to guns the likes of which most of them had never seen before.

The crew of the *Mindanao* was ordered to Fort Hughes, on Caballo Island, and put in charge of Battery Craighill's four, huge 12-inch mortars of 1912 vintage. Hastily indoctrinated by several veteran artillerymen, the sailors fired twenty-six rounds at Japanese positions on Bataan and were adjudged qualified. Crewmen of the other ships were given the same perfunctory check-out. Those of the *Luzon* were assigned to Battery Gillespie, which consisted of two, mammoth 14-inch disappearing guns, and those of the *Oahu* took over a battery of 155-mm. howitzers.

River gunboat *Luzon* (PR-7) of the Yangtze Patrol. Naval Institute Collection

The inevitable end was fast approaching. On 2 May, the *Mindanao*, seriously damaged by bombs, was permitted to sink in order to ensure that the Japanese would never enjoy her services. The *Luzon*, salvaged by the Japanese, served the enemy until American aircraft sank her irretrievably in 1945. The *Oahu*, pounded by heavy artillery shells, could take no more punishment and, on 6 May, the last day Old Glory flew over the "rock," she went to her watery grave off the bloody beaches of Corregidor.

The hardened veterans of the Yangtze Patrol acquitted themelves as one would expect—with honor and courage beyond the call of duty. Eagerly, they accepted the role of artillerymen and manned their guns until they were either knocked out or could no longer bear on the enemy. Three of Battery Craighill's four 12-inch mortars were silenced by Japanese artillery, but the fourth continued to fire on the invaders until silenced by the order to surrender.

Although the Inshore Patrol was structured mainly around the three river gunboats, two other vessels, the tug *Napa* (AT-32) and the 83-foot, two-masted schooner *Lanikai*, were also assigned to it. The *Napa* was scuttled when Bataan fell, but the *Lanikai*, commanded by Lieutenant Kemp Tolley, departed Manila Bay on 26 December bound for Surabaja. The seas through which she traveled were dominated by enemy warships, yet, the little schooner and her intrepid crew arrived safely and, with the fall of Java, once again eluded the Japanese to gain sanctuary in Australia.

Another ship, the *Isabel*, sometimes classified as a gunboat and sometimes as a yacht, should be mentioned here. Although not designated a unit of the Inshore Patrol or of any other operating segment of the Asiatic Fleet, she, some years before, had served as flagship for the commander of the Yangtze Patrol. When she ceased to play that role, she remained under the operational control of the commander in chief, Asiatic Fleet, and was based in Manila.

Because she was old, in poor condition, and ill-equipped for combat, the *Isabel* was considered expendable. For that reason, on 3 December 1941, she was sent on what could have been a suicidal mission which had been personally ordered by President Franklin D. Roosevelt. With her four aged 4-inch deck guns hidden so that she would look like an innocent merchantman, the *Isabel* was directed to spy on a heavy concentration of Japanese transports and warships gathered in Camranh Bay, Indochina, even though the concentration was already being monitored by aircraft of Patrol Wing 10. The *Isabel* came within sight of the coast of Indochina, but was recalled just in time to be off Manila Bay when war with Japan broke out.

Sent to the Netherlands East Indies soon thereafter, the *Isabel* was assigned strange and dangerous missions. In that she generally operated alone and under various commands, including Dutch, her noteworthy accomplishments, among them the sinking of a Japanese submarine and the rescue of survivors from a torpedoed merchantman, went unnoticed. In fact, there were times when, in the confusion engendered by the unstoppable Japanese onslaught, her very existence was overlooked by the U.S. Navy.

Clearing the minefields at 2200 on 1 March 1942, the *Isabel* was the last U.S. Navy ship to leave Tjilatjap. Taking with her twenty-one late arrivals from Admiral Glassford's staff, she eluded Japanese warships and aircraft, weathered a typhoon in the Indian Ocean, and arrived, somewhat the worse for wear but safe, in southern Australia.

# 7

# MINECRAFT

Six minesweepers were assigned to the Asiatic Fleet. Two of them, the *Bittern* and *Finch*, comprised Mine Division 8. The four other ships, the *Quail* (AM-15), *Tanager* (AM-5), *Lark*, and *Whippoorwill*, made up Mine Division 9. These sturdy vessels were more than 187 feet in length, had a top speed of 14 knots, and a ship's company of 72 officers and men. All were armed with one 3-inch gun, several .30-caliber machine guns, and as many .50-caliber machine guns as their crews could beg, borrow, or steal.

The first minesweeper to perform with distinction in the face of war's chilling realities was the *Whippoorwill*, commanded by Lieutenant Commander Charles A. Ferriter. During the systematic destruction of Cavite Navy Yard by Japanese bombers on 10 December 1941, the destroyer *Peary*, moored to a wharf with her boilers cold, was hit by a bomb which killed nine of her crew and wounded several others, including her commanding officer. Fires sweeping over the wharf were about to spread to the ship herself when Ferriter, with great daring and skill, maneuvered the *Whippoorwill* alongside and towed the *Peary* to safety.

Two days later, the *Whippoorwill* and *Lark* were ordered to steam south to Surabaja, Java. The voyage was made without incident and, upon arrival, both ships operated with the Royal Netherlands Navy in conducting local patrols and sweeps.

During the latter part of February, when Japanese bombing attacks on *Surabaja* intensified and enemy invasion armadas were approaching

Java's north coast, the *Whippoorwill* and *Lark* were moved to the port of Tjilatjap on the south coast. On 27 February the big aircraft tender *Langley* was sunk by Japanese bombers about 130 miles south of Tjilatjap, and the *Whippoorwill* was ordered to search for survivors. She found a large oil slick, but no sign of the *Langley*'s crew. They had been rescued by the destroyers *Edsall* and *Whipple*, but no one bothered to inform either the *Whippoorwill* or the gunboat *Tulsa*, which also had been ordered to search.

Just before dawn the following day, however, lookouts reported a pulsating fire on the horizon. With battle stations manned, the *Whippoorwill* steamed at full speed to investigate. It turned out to be a British merchant ship, the *City of Manchester*, which had been torpedoed and shelled by a Japanese submarine. She was on fire and sinking, but the *Whippoorwill* arrived in time to rescue 126 survivors.

By this time, the Battle of the Java Sea had been lost, and the Japanese were landing in force on Java. The *Whippoorwill* and *Lark* made their way safely to Exmouth Gulf, Australia, to continue fighting the war, but the four minesweepers left in the Manila Bay area were not so fortunate. The *Bittern*, in the navy yard at the time of the bombing with her essential engine-room machinery undergoing repair ashore, was hit by bomb fragments and set on fire. Although she was pulled to safety by the submarine rescue vessel *Pigeon* and her fires were rapidly extinguished, her irreplaceable engine parts were lost and she had no means of propulsion. She was towed to Mariveles Harbor where, when Bataan fell, she was scuttled.

The three operational minesweepers were based at Corregidor and, during the early weeks of December 1941, actively patrolled off the entrance to Manila Bay and swept the minefield channels. By the first of January, however, the only traffic through the minefields was an occasional submarine bringing supplies to the "rock," or a night sortie by the motor torpedo boats. This lack of traffic, coupled with enemy bombing attacks against which they were helpless, and the shortage of fuel, reduced minesweeper activities to a minimum. As a result, minesweeper crews were reduced by two-thirds, and the men no longer assigned to them were ordered to join defense forces on Bataan or Corregidor.

After the fall of Bataan, the vessels still in the Corregidor area had more to worry about than bombing and strafing attacks—artillery fire from the hills of Bataan. For this reason, shipboard personnel spent the daylight hours ashore, unless, for some pressing reason, a sweep was required. But the inevitable end was fast approaching. On 10 April 1942, the *Finch* was sunk at her moorings off Corregidor's eastern point. On 4 May the *Tanager* went down, and on the sixth the *Quail* was scuttled by her crew even as the white flags of surrender were raised over Corregidor and her forts.

Many men of the minesweepers who survived the fighting died in Japanese prisoner-of-war camps, but two officers and sixteen enlisted men evaded capture by taking a desperate gamble. Incredible as it may seem, these men escaped from Corregidor in a 36-foot motor launch, traversed hundreds of miles of waters dominated by the Japanese, and eventually arrived safe and sound in Darwin, Australia.

# 8

# TORPEDO BOATS

---

The arrival of Motor Torpedo Boat Squadron 3 in Manila, on 28 September 1941, was not, as far as the Asiatic Fleet was concerned, a breathtaking event. With the threat of war growing each day, the crying need was for more cruisers, submarines, and destroyers, not for a handful of PT boats whose merits had never been tested in combat and for which no standard employment doctrine had been established. Nevertheless, when World War II began, these novel weapons of naval warfare existed and, although there were only six of them, their usefulness and combat effectiveness, coupled with the daring and skill of their crews, made sudden believers of even the most skeptical.

Commanded by Lieutenant (jg) John D. Bulkeley, MTB Squadron 3 boasted eleven officers, sixty-eight enlisted men, and PT boats *PT-31*, *PT-32*, *PT-33*, *PT-34*, *PT-35*, and *PT-41*. Six additional PT boats and their crews, awaiting transportation from Pearl Harbor to Manila when World War II broke out, never arrived. It should be noted that at the time there were only three MTB squadrons, and no more than thirty-six PT boats in the entire U.S. Navy.

These unarmored plywood boats were 70 feet long and powered by three 1,250-horsepower, Packard gasoline marine engines. They were designed to carry a crew of two officers and seven men. For armament, PTs mounted four torpedo tubes and four .50-caliber machine guns firing in pairs from power-driven turrets. To give themselves more

Note: Motor Torpedo Boat Squadron 3 was the only seagoing segment of the Asiatic Fleet that operated continuously as a unit. For that reason, the entire history of MTB-3 in World War II is included in part I of this book.

firepower, the crews mounted two .30-caliber Lewis guns on the forward deck.

The PT boats of Squadron 3 first went into action on 10 December 1941, when Japanese bombers attacked and destroyed their operating base, the Cavite Navy Yard. Forewarned, all six boats moved smartly out into Manila Bay with guns manned and ready for action. In concert with the attack on the yard, Japanese dive-bombers, ignoring many larger ships lying helplessly at anchor in the bay, concentrated their fury on the PT boats. This was a costly mistake, because the speedy, highly maneuverable PT boats dodged and raced away unscathed while enemy bombs were wasted on open water. To add insult to injury, the *PT-31* shot down two of the attackers and the *PT-35* splashed another. When the raid was over, the boats returned to the bomb-devastated yard to transport the wounded to the naval hospital at Cañacao.

Destruction of the navy yard forced Squadron 3 to move to Sisiman Bay, a cove on the southern tip of the Bataan Peninsula, where a small fishing dock and a few nipa shacks were their only accommodations. From this base they were immediately pressed into service making nightly patrols along the coast of Bataan, north of Manila Bay, and south along the Batangas Peninsula to Verde Island. They were also effectively used to make high-speed dispatch runs between Fort Mills, on Corregidor, and Manila.

On the night of 17 December 1941, an inter-island steamer, the SS *Corregidor*, attempting to take 700 evacuees from Manila to Australia, hit a mine off Sisiman Bay and sank like a rock. Lieutenant Bulkeley immediately ordered the only boats available, the *PT-32, PT-33,* and *PT-35*, to get under way. When they did so, they could see flashing lights at the edge of the army minefield protecting the entrance to Manila Bay and hear screams for help. As they neared the lights, they saw hundreds of people struggling in the oil-coated water. Operating in the dark in the midst of a minefield was not exactly preferred duty, but the men of Squadron 3 saved 282 men, women, and children. Had it not been for the courageous efforts of their rescuers, most of these people assuredly would have perished, because no other boats, probably for fear of the mines, came to help them.

On 26 December, following the departure of Admiral Hart to his new command post in Java, Rear Admiral Francis W. Rockwell took command of all naval forces in the Manila area. This unimposing collection of ships consisted of three river gunboats, three minesweepers, five tugs, a submarine rescue vessel, a submarine tender, and the PT boats of Squadron 3. The MTB Squadron, however, now cast in the role of the navy's first line of defense in the Philippines, was down to only four boats. The *PT-33*, investigating lights believed to be those of a submarine near Point Santiago on the night of 24 December, went hard aground. When three attempts to pull her off failed, she was stripped and destroyed to prevent her being captured. Earlier, the *PT-32*, which had already suffered an accidental gasoline explosion in her engine room, was shot up in a strafing attack as a result of which she was out of action for several weeks.

The loss, at the very beginning of the war, of almost all MTB spare parts in the Cavite Navy Yard hamstrung the squadron's operations. Fortunately, a few engines had been dispersed outside of Cavite, but the effort to keep boats in operating condition soon became a tedious around-the-clock chore. In addition, on 16 December 1941, all naval personnel were restricted to two meals a day and, as time passed, both the quantity and quality of the rations deteriorated. The overworked, undernourished crews became so run-down physically that, by the end of December, Rockwell had been forced to discontinue most of the nightly patrols.

Compounding the squadron's problems was the dwindling supply of gasoline. Large quantities of it stored in and around Manila had to be burned to prevent its being captured. For the same reason, gasoline spared in the bombing of Cavite and of the Sangley Point Naval Air Station was also set to the torch. Before this happened, however, the squadron had the foresight to load two large barges with drums of gasoline and oil and tow them to Sisiman Bay. This action was all the more fortunate because on 29 December one of the two gasoline dumps on Corregidor was destroyed by Japanese bombers.

To add to the woes of Squadron 3, much of the gasoline and oil then available to it had been sabotaged. The gasoline was found to contain large quantities of soluble wax, which clogged gas strainers and carburetor jets so badly that they had to be cleaned hourly. It took the men a while to discover that they could get rid of most of the wax by straining the gasoline through an army felt hat. The lubricating oil also had to be carefully strained before it could be used because it had sand in it.

On 18 January 1942, MTB Squadron 3 got its first crack at enemy surface forces. The army reported that there were four Japanese ships, one of which was thought to be a destroyer and one a big transport, lying in Binanga Bay, a narrow little indentation on the Bataan Peninsula, off the southwestern entrance to Subic Bay. They were said to be reinforcing the Japanese Army already ashore and lobbing 5-inch shells into positions held by the Philippine and American forces. Bulkeley was ordered to take two boats and attack the ships between dusk and dawn.

*PT-31*, one of six torpedo boats operated by Motor Torpedo Boat Squadron 3 in Philippine waters. James C. Fahey Collection, U.S. Naval Institute

With Bulkeley riding in her, the *PT-34*, commanded by Ensign Barron W. Chandler, and the *PT-31*, commanded by Lieutenant (jg) Edward G. DeLong, proceeded to the entrance to Subic Bay, where they separated. The *PT-34* was to reconnoiter the western entrance to the bay, then cross over to the mouth of Binanga Bay. The *PT-31* was to scout along the eastern side and rendezvous with the *PT-34* for the attack.

It was 0030, and darker than a witch's cave, when the *PT-34* eased into the western reaches of Subic Bay to be promptly challenged by a light from land a mile off her port beam. Ignoring it, but immediately slowing the boat from 18 knots to 10, Bulkeley stealthily kept going.

Suddenly, from the other side of the bay, the booming of field pieces broke the stillness of the night. Bulkeley wondered if the *PT-31* was in trouble. Soon afterwards a small boat, probably a picket boat, which was hardly discernible in the darkness, flashed a light challenge. In order to lose the pesky boat in the night and also to keep his rendezvous, Bulkeley turned to a southeasterly course. As he made his way to the entrance to Binanga Bay, two more lights—one on Grande Island, a mile to the north, and the other from a point just south of Binanga Bay—flashed their probing fingers seaward and were joined by rattling volleys of machine-gun fire. This, coupled with the fact that the *PT-31* was not at the rendezvous point at the determined time, added to Bulkeley's concern. He idled the *PT-34* in lazy circles and waited. When a half hour passed and there was still no sign of the *PT-31*, he decided to "go it" alone.

The *PT-34* had penetrated about 500 yards into Binanga Bay when the silhouette of a two-masted freighter loomed up dead ahead. The ship's signal light challenged the intruder. The *PT-34* replied by firing two torpedoes. One, a "hot run," hung up in the tube. Bulkeley promptly ordered the *PT-34* out of the area. A minute later there was a loud explosion and crewmen reported a flash of fire followed by two larger flashes. There was no time to assess actual damage because, not

only were shells from shore batteries bursting perilously close, but the
*PT-34* was faced with something more terrifying. The "hot run" torpedo, sticking halfway out of its tube, roared and hissed as its propellers
raced unchecked. The casings around the torpedo's runaway turbines
glowed white hot, and threatened to disintegrate with deadly force at
any moment.

Without hesitation, Chief Torpedoman's Mate John Martino, fully
aware of the danger, hurried to the awesome metal monster and shut
the air-line valve to its combustion chamber, thus ending the "hot run."
But this brave man did not stop there. With each dip of the bow, the
choppy sea washed over the torpedo's warhead and turned its impeller
blades. It would take only a few more turns for the warhead to be fully
armed and no more than an 8-pound force to detonate it. Sitting
astride the protruding torpedo, Martino worked his way out to its
warhead and, to prevent its blades from turning, jammed toilet paper
between them. It took four hours for the rogue torpedo to shake loose
and fall into the water without damaging the boat.

On the return run to base, Bulkeley and his crew searched for signs
of the *PT-31*, but to no avail. She had vanished. This sad fact Bulkeley
reported to Rear Admiral Rockwell. He also reported that the *PT-34*
had probably scored a hit on a merchant ship in Binanga Bay. The
admiral informed him that army observers on Mariveles Mountain had
seen the ship explode and sink. Through 20-power binoculars, they
judged it to have been a 5,000-ton armed merchant ship that had been
shelling army positions in western Bataan with 5.5-inch guns.

All hands in Motor Torpedo Boat Squadron 3, still mourning the
loss of their squadron mates, were ecstatic when, at 1730 on 20 January
1942, nine bedraggled crewmen from the *PT-31* arrived back at the
base. It was distressing, however, to learn that Ensign William H. Plant
and two other men were missing.

It seems that, as the *PT-31* began her slow patrol along the eastern
shore of Subic Bay, wax deposits in the gasoline clogged strainers on
both wing engines, which stopped cold. Soon afterwards the center
engine's fresh-water cooling system became airbound and it too ceased
to function. Unable to maneuver, the boat drifted with wind and tide
onto a reef. When the engines were once again operable, Lieutenant
DeLong walked out anchor and tried desperately to back off. After
three hours of effort, the boat's reverse gears burned out and, to make
matters worse, a Japanese 3-inch gun ashore, alerted by the sound of
roaring engines, began firing in their direction. Dawn was not far off,
and DeLong had no choice but to abandon ship.

After destroying all important equipment, Ensign Plant and eleven
crewmen shoved off in a raft, leaving DeLong to drain the gas tanks

into the boat and set it on fire. While his boat burned and finally exploded, DeLong swam like a scalded dog for the beach. At dawn, he saw tracks in the sand and followed them to a clump of bushes, where he found nine of his men. Ensign Plant and two of the men, not being strong swimmers, chose to stay on the raft when the others decided to swim for the beach. Their fate was not known until after the war; it was then learned that they were taken prisoner, and died when the transport taking them to Japan was bombed by American planes.

The survivors who swam ashore found themselves in a precarious situation behind enemy lines. Blocking their escape route to the south were Japanese troops and planes attacking positions near the village of Moron, on Bataan. The only way they could get back to American lines was by sea, and, as soon as the enemy planes left the area, two men slipped down to the beach to look for a means of transportation. They returned an hour and a half later to report that they had found two seaworthy bancas, or canoes, one large and one small.

With Japanese soldiers all over the place and some only 200 yards away, the men waited until dark before sneaking down to the bancas. They picked up two rusty shovels and a board to augment the two paddles already in the bancas. It was close to 2100 when they shoved off from the beach. A hundred yards from shore, both boats capsized in the heavy surf, and the two shovels were lost. After considerable effort the men righted their boats and tied them together. Then with the larger one towing the smaller and the men who had no paddles scooping with their hands, they set course for Napo Point, Bataan, about 12 miles to the south.

It was tough, slow going against wind and waves, and by 0300 the men were too exhausted to make it around Napo Point. DeLong decided to attempt a landing to the north, and in the lee of the point, while it was still dark. Fortune smiled on them and, at about 0330 they beached the bancas without mishap; they were behind friendly lines. Confronting them, however, were barbed-wire entanglements, through which they painfully worked their way, only to find their passage blocked by sheer cliffs. At dawn, some Filipino soldiers spotted them and guided them up a dangerous trail to safety.

The *PT-34* was again prowling the coastline of Bataan looking for enemy ships on the night of 22 January. This time she was commanded by Lieutenant (jg) Robert B. Kelly who, because he had been hospitalized on Corregidor with a seriously infected finger caused by shrapnel, was making his first patrol. His second officer, Ensign Chandler, and Lieutenant Bulkeley were also on board. It should be noted that Lieutenant Bulkeley, as squadron commander, regarded it as his responsibility to go along on patrols whenever possible.

About 25 miles up the coast, friendly shore batteries, thinking they were seeing an enemy boat, opened fire, forcing the *PT-34* seaward out of range. Soon after that, the PT boat sighted a dim, moving light close to the water, and closed in on it. The light came from a Japanese landing barge loaded with elite troops on their way to make a landing behind Allied lines. A savage fire fight ensued, in the course of which the landing craft was sunk, but Ensign Chandler was wounded in both ankles. Since, the boat could not transit the minefields guarding the approaches to Manila Bay until daylight, he was given first aid, and the *PT-34* continued her search for enemy craft.

It was almost dawn and the *PT-34* was heading home when it discovered another landing barge, this one heading away from the beach. With all guns blazing, the *PT-34* bore in for the kill. Enemy fire was light and was soon silenced. When the boats closed to within a few yards of each other, Bulkeley, to make certain no tricks were played, lobbed two hand grenades into the barge, which was on fire and sinking when the *PT-34* pulled alongside. With his .45 automatic in hand, Bulkeley jumped on board the enemy craft and saw among the dead two soldiers who were alive but wounded. One of them was an officer. The wounded prisoners were quickly hoisted on board the *PT-34*, and Bulkeley, whose search of the craft turned up a dispatch case containing a muster list of the infiltration force and the operation plan, scrambled off just as the barge sank.

Two nights later, Lieutenants Bulkeley and DeLong went hunting in Subic Bay in the *PT-41*. Sneaking along on one throttled-back engine, they came upon a large Japanese ship anchored close to shore in a cove west of the bay's entrance, near Sampaloc Point. Cautiously and as silently as possible, the *PT-41* eased ever closer. At 2,500 yards, the order was given, "all engines ahead full speed," and the boat, her 3,750 horses roaring in deadly earnest, shot forward. The range closed fast. At 1,000 yards, the first torpedo leaped eagerly into the water. Simultaneously, a pom-pom on the enemy ship opened fire. As the *PT-41* raced to within 400 yards and launched a second torpedo, her four .50-caliber machine guns and two Lewis guns raked the enemy's decks. The tail of this second "fish," however, hit the deck as it left the tube, throwing it off course.

Having released his last torpedo, Bulkeley ordered a fast reversal of course to get the boat out of the cove. Seconds later, there was a violent explosion, and debris from the enemy ship was flying in all directions. Fires generated by the blast gave the crew of the *PT-41* their first good look at their victim, which was judged to be a modern, streamlined ship of about 6,000 tons—perhaps an aircraft tender. By this time, 3-inch shore guns were banging away furiously at the elusive *PT-41* as she darted about, missed by a scant 20 feet a wire-mesh net that could have stopped her cold, and "high-tailed it" to safety in the China Sea. Motor Torpedo Boat Squadron 3 chalked up another kill.

Since the latter part of December 1941, the boats of Squadron 3 had deteriorated considerably. The machine shops in the submarine tender *Canopus* fully extended themselves in manufacturing or repairing parts that had failed. Japanese bombing attacks, however, made it impossible for them to work during the hours of daylight and, because of backlogged work orders, only two PT boats of the four remaining were in operating condition on 1 February 1942. That is why the *PT-32*, which had suffered an engine-room explosion in December and was now held together by braces and wires and running on only two engines, was called upon that night to patrol along the west coast of Bataan.

On board the *PT-32* with her skipper, Lieutenant (jg) Vincent E. Schumacher, was Lieutenant DeLong. It was almost 2100 when gun blasts were seen several miles ahead. The *PT-32* increased speed, as she went to investigate. At 2130, a large ship was sighted about 3 miles distant, which suddenly speeded up and headed north toward Subic Bay. The *PT-32* was unable to overtake the vessel because, on two engines, her best speed was about 22 knots. Nevertheless, and even though the strange ship steadily pulled way, the little boat continued to give chase, for about a half hour. Then persistence paid off. All at once, for no apparent reason, the stranger turned eastward toward the shore of Bataan, and the range rapidly closed.

At 5,000 yards the enemy ship's powerful searchlight snapped on, fixing the *PT-32* in its blinding beam. A few seconds later, what were believed to be two 6-inch shells, screaming like lost souls, exploded in the water 500 yards ahead. Blinded by the searchlight, the boat had no choice but to head directly into it to fire her starboard torpedo. Another salvo of shells landed 200 yards ahead, almost immediately followed by one 200 yards astern. Undeterred, the *PT-32* kept boring in and, at 3,000 yards, launched her port torpedo directly at the searchlight. With this, Schumacher executed a fast 180-degree turn to escape from what was now determined to be a light cruiser.

No longer burdened by the weight of her torpedoes, the *PT-32* was making 25 knots, but that was hardly enough to outdistance the onrushing cruiser, whose four 6-inch guns were belching salvos in pairs. The situation was growing more desperate by the second when, suddenly, there was a loud explosion in the vicinity of the cruiser. Smoke and debris could be seen rising in the beam of her searchlight, and her guns fell strangely silent. One of the torpedoes must have scored a timely hit. The cruiser's speed slowed noticeably, and the *PT-32* began drawing away. The fiendish searchlight, however, still held the boat in its glare and, before long, the firing began again. Bursting shells churned the water around the boat but, as she raced on, the light fell farther and farther astern until she made an abrupt hard turn to starboard and threw it off completely.

The following morning, the army informed Squadron 3 that the *PT-32* had foiled a 7,000-ton cruiser's attempt to land a party near Moron. Although there is no evidence that this cruiser was sunk, nobody in the *PT-32* had the slightest doubt that she was at least damaged.

Late in the afternoon of 18 February, Ensign George E. Cox, Jr., was directed to take an army major in the *PT-41* to reconnoiter the south shore of Manila Bay, where the Japanese were reported to be placing heavy guns to bombard Corregidor. The object of this risky mission was to entice the Japanese to open fire, so that the major could plot the positions of the guns. Corregidor's big guns would then be able to zero in on them.

No guns were found but, while running close to the beach a few miles east of Ternate, the *PT-41* happened upon a company of Japanese soldiers stripped to their underwear, ready to go swimming. Instead of running away, they crowded to the water's edge and laughed and jeered at the men in the boat. With a chance at last to retaliate for all the hell they'd been through, the boat crew laughed and jeered back with .50-caliber machine-gun bullets. Spies later reported that eight of the enemy soldiers were killed and fourteen wounded.

Motor Torpedo Boat Squadron 3 made its last foray into Subic Bay on the night of 17 February 1942. By this time the Japanese had ringed the entrance with guns, and it was considered suicidal to penetrate the bay. Bulkeley, however, had a plan that might bag one of several destroyers reported to be anchored there.

The *PT-35*, commanded by Ensign Anthony B. Akers, in which Bulkeley was embarked, followed by the *PT-34*, commanded by Lieutenant (jg) Kelly, arrived off the entrance to Subic Bay at 2240. According to plan, Kelly hid his boat in the shadows of a small cove near the eastern entrance while the *PT-35* moved to the mouth of the bay. Here, Bulkeley intended to create a disturbance by firing machine guns into the bay, or by any other means, in the hope of enticing a destroyer to give chase. If a destroyer swallowed the bait, she would have to pass the hidden *PT-34*, which would slip a "fish" or two into her guts.

As luck would have it, a patrol vessel, judged to be between 200 and 300 tons, and was sighted entering the bay on the east side of the channel, by Grande Island. The *PT-35* raced to short range and fired a torpedo which apparently passed beneath the vessel but did not explode. Soon, a larger ship was discovered east of Grande Island, near an Olongapo pier, and a torpedo was launched at her. With that, the *PT-35*, which had penetrated dangerously far into the bay, immediately retired. Since no enemy ships followed them, the two MTBs made a sweep past Sampaloc Point, at the western entrance to Subic Bay, and sprayed the 3-inch batteries there with .50-caliber machine-gun bullets before continuing on their patrol.

A large fire was observed at Olongapo, but its cause was not known and no torpedo explosions had been seen or heard. The next day, army observers reported that a large tanker at the pier had sunk after burning all night. Bulkeley, however, did not claim this ship as a "kill."

Since late December, Bulkeley had been planning what to do when he ran out of gasoline and torpedoes. His first idea was to take what boats were left and make a break for the Netherlands East Indies. Patrol Wing 10 had cached gasoline on various islands along the route, and Admiral Rockwell told him where to find it. As time passed, however, the Japanese got control of most of the areas to the south, and the plan died.

Determined to get his officers and men out of the Philippines when the time came, Bulkeley decided that their best chance lay in making a dash for the coast of China, where they would burn their boats and move inland to join the forces of General Chiang Kai-shek. With the utmost secrecy and the help of Colonel Wong, a Chinese military observer assigned to MacArthur's staff, plans for the operation were formulated. At a given time, Chinese soldiers would rendezvous with the squadron on the China coast south of Swatow, where the Japanese were spread thin, and help them to Chungking. The rest would be easy. However, with Japanese task forces roaming the China Sea, not to mention their aircraft, traversing more than 600 miles of open sea was an extremely hazardous venture. Nevertheless, all hands in Motor Torpedo Boat Squadron 3 were determined to take the risk. By the end of February, gasoline supplies were almost exhausted, and only eight torpedoes were left. The time had come. The boats were being readied for departure when there was an abrupt change of plans.

With the situation in the Philippines deteriorating and no reinforcements able to breach the enemy's blockade, it was apparent by mid-February that the men on Bataan and Corregidor were doomed. On 22 February, President Roosevelt directed General MacArthur to leave the Philippines as soon as possible and go to Australia, where he was to assume command of all Allied land and air forces. Accordingly, the submarine *Permit* (SS-178) was scheduled to arrive off Corregidor on

15 March to evacuate the general and his party to Mindanao, where they would be met by army B-17s, which would then fly them on to Australia. For security reasons, this was a closely guarded secret.

On 1 March, Lieutenant Bulkeley was surprised to receive a directive to take General MacArthur for a ride in one of his MTBs. During the short cruise the general formally presented to Bulkeley the Army Distinguished Service Cross, which he had been awarded several weeks before. This was to mask the real reason for the ride, for, after swearing Bulkeley to secrecy, the general informed him that he, the general, would soon be leaving Corregidor. The clincher came when he said the MTBs of Squadron 3 were going to take him and his party to Mindanao.

During the first week in March, radio broadcasts and prominent newspapers in the United States began calling for MacArthur to be placed in command of Allied forces in Australia. No doubt these pleas were intended to prepare the defenders of Bataan and Corregidor for the departure of their leader in such a manner as to allay fears that he considered the situation hopeless and was deserting them. These pronouncements were not lost on the Japanese, who could be counted upon to do everything possible to prevent the escape of such a prize.

Why the general chose to have his party travel through Japanese-controlled waters in four, run-down torpedo boats instead of in a submarine is anybody's guess, especially since nine days after he made his choice, a Japanese destroyer division was sighted in the southern Philippines heading north at high speed, and there was a marked increase in the activity of enemy surface craft off Corregidor.

An elaborate plan was formulated. The boats, having embarked their passengers at different points so as not to arouse the curiosity of enemy spies, were to rendezvous off the entrance to Manila Bay at 2200 and proceed south in company. Traveling only at night, they were to go first to Tagauayan, in the Cuyo Island group, about 50 miles west of Panay Island, and 250 miles south of Corregidor. Hiding there overnight, they would depart on the last leg of their journey at 1700 on 12 March to reach Cagayan, on the north coast of Mindanao, by 0700, 13 March. The boats were to avoid enemy ships like the plague but, if they should sight any and come under attack, the *PT-41*, carrying General MacArthur, was to attempt to escape while the others engaged the enemy.

Should a boat break down, her passengers would be transferred to another and the cripple would either continue independently or, if necessary, be scuttled. Alternate rendezvous points and hideaways were designated in case any boat was unable to reach Cagayan, and, as an escape hatch, the *Permit* was ordered to stand by at Cuyo Island at daybreak on 13 March to take on passengers, if the situation warranted.

History records 11 March 1942 as the day General Douglas MacArthur escaped from the island fortress of Corregidor. It was also the day on which some thirty-two officers and men of Motor Torpedo Boat Squadron 3, for lack of space, were left on the "rock" to become part of the U.S. Army fighting the Japanese on Bataan and Corregidor. At 1930 that night, Bulkeley in the *PT-41* went alongside Corregidor's North Dock to pick up his passengers, who included General and Mrs. MacArthur, their young son, a Chinese maid, and Major General Richard K. Sutherland, MacArthur's chief of staff. Lieutenant Kelly in the *PT-34* and Ensign Akers in the *PT-35* embarked their passengers in Sisiman Cove. Included in this group was Rear Admiral Rockwell on board the *PT-34*. The fourth boat, the *PT-32* commanded by Lieutenant Schumacher, picked up her passengers at Quarantine Dock, Mariveles. In all, there were twenty-three passengers: twenty-one in MacArthur's party, and two naval officers, Admiral Rockwell and his chief of staff, Captain Herbert J. Ray.

While Philippine MTBs staged a diversionary raid off Subic Bay, to give the impression that Squadron 3 was still on the prowl, all four boats met as scheduled and headed out on course. Just before they left, however, a disquieting air reconnaissance report told of a Japanese destroyer being sighted in Apo East Pass, about 80 miles west of Mindoro, and a cruiser to the southwest of Mindoro. Both ships directly threatened the boats' escape route.

Traveling in column, the *PT-41* leading, the boats sailed southwest for 50 miles. They hoped to slip unseen past some Japanese-held islands, but a fire that suddenly blazed up on one of them in the deepening twilight led to the fear that their movement had been detected and word of it was being signaled to the mainland. If so, they could expect enemy bombers and, possibly, destroyers to come after them at dawn.

Turning south Bulkeley hugged the west side of Mindoro Strait, hoping to steer clear of the destroyer and cruiser reported to be patrolling there. A strong easterly wind sprang up and the boats, heavily burdened with drums of gasoline lashed to their decks, pitched and rolled to the extreme discomfort of their landlubber passengers. Darkness and the turbulent seas made it difficult for the boats to stay together, a problem that was complicated when one of them had to stop to repair some trouble she was having with her ignition. Before long the boats were hopelessly separated.

At dawn, Schumacher, in the *PT-32*, which had not run satisfactorily since the explosion in her engine room and was still operating on two engines, saw what he believed to be a Japanese destroyer overhauling him. In a frantic effort to increase speed, he jettisoned his deckload of gasoline. Although that helped him to pick up a few knots, the stranger continued to close. Unable to run for it, Schumacher decided to stand and fight it out. Just in time, however, he realized that it was not a Japanese destroyer he was seeing, but the *PT-41* strangely magnified in the pale early light.

The *PT-34* arrived at Cuyo Island at 0930, two hours behind schedule, and Kelly was distressed to discover that none of the other boats was there. Passengers and crewmen alike passed long, anxious hours until late that afternoon when the *PT-41* and *PT-32* eased into the cove. Fearing enemy aircraft, just after dawn they had taken refuge at another island in the Cuyo group and waited there until it seemed safe to make the rendezvous. The *PT-35*, however, was still missing.

The *PT-32*, having dumped all 600 gallons of her reserve fuel, could go no farther. Besides, only one of her engines was working and, some of her struts having come loose, she was leaking. Accordingly, her passengers were transferred to the two other boats. Schumacher was instructed to wait in the cove until the *Permit* and the *PT-35* arrived and inform their commanding officers that the general and party had departed for Cagayan. He was then to try to make the island of Panay, where he would be able to get fuel, and go on from there.

At about 1830, the *PT-34* and *PT-41* left the cove, the former in the lead so that General MacArthur could ride more comfortably in the smoothest part of the other's wake. Fifteen minutes later, a Japanese cruiser was sighted. She was hull down on the horizon, but her masts and superstructure were plainly visible. If the PT boats continued on course, they would cross the bow of the enemy ship. Kelly ordered hard right rudder and full speed ahead, and the two boats raced away without being seen. At 1900, when the sun went down, they returned to course.

The moonless night was very dark. A strong wind sprang up and lightning flashes ahead portended trouble. Navigating entirely by dead reckoning, the boats crossed sealanes in the Sulu Sea without incident and, hugging the coast of Negros Island, groped their way toward Silino Island, which marks the entrance to the Mindanao Sea. From about 0100 until dawn, the boats were battered by heavy seas and blinding rain squalls. They made landfall on Silino Island around 0200 and turned east into the Mindanao Sea. Neither Bulkeley nor Kelly had ever before sailed in this part of the Philippines, which is laced with hundreds of reefs and small islands, but, although they did not have proper charts, they pushed on at a good speed. Unable to define their exact position throughout the entire trip, they miraculously brought the two boats to Cagayan in northern Mindanao at 0700, 13 March 1942, the precise time designated by the plan, before this remarkable 560-mile odyssey began.

Later that same day, the *PT-35*, which had been plagued with engine trouble, straggled into Cagayan and disembarked her passengers. For everyone involved it had been an exhausting and, at times, nerve-racking experience. But all the passengers, especially General MacArthur, were high in their praise of Lieutenant Bulkeley and Motor Torpedo Boat Squadron 3. Four days later B-17 bombers flew the general and his party to Australia.

Directed to keep his boats hidden near Cagayan until the general had left, Bulkeley worried about the fate of the *PT-34* and spent many fruitless hours in a dilapidated army plane searching for her. Weeks passed before he learned that she had been scuttled at Tagauayan because, with two engines out of commission and the third threatened by sea water leaking into the engine room, she was no longer sea-worthy. The *Permit* took her crew back to Corregidor, but Schumacher was more fortunate; he stayed in the *Permit* and arrived safely in Australia.

On 18 March, the day after General MacArthur and his party left for Australia, Bulkeley was called to army headquarters and informed that, for reasons of safety, President Quezon, his family, and several members of his cabinet had moved to Negros Island from Panay, where the submarine *Swordfish* had taken them less than a month before. Now, with Japanese forces drawing a deadly steel ring ever tighter around the Philippines, it was imperative that he be moved again. If the president could be brought to Mindanao, the army air forces would fly him to Australia. The route that would have to be traversed to carry out this mission was only a matter of 200 miles; however, seven Japanese destroyers were reported patrolling the southern approaches to Negros in an effort, no doubt, to prevent President Quezon's escape. Without hesitation, Bulkeley volunteered to go.

That night at 1900, the *PT-41* with Bulkeley and Cox, followed by Akers in the *PT-35*, departed Cagayan bound for Dumaguete on Negros Island. To even the odds against seven destroyers, Bulkeley could have taken the *PT-34* along, but she had run hard aground on a coral reef and damaged her propellers, shafts, and struts.

Near their destination, they sighted a Japanese destroyer off Apo Island. Fortunately, she did not see them, as they dodged around the island to lose her in the night. While the *PT-35* patrolled off the entrance to Dumaguete to engage any hostile ship that might threaten to cut off President Quezon's escape route, Bulkeley cautiously took the *PT-41* into the harbor. The night was pitch-dark. Town and harbor were blacked out, and he had no chart of the area, but he managed to find the pier and moor his boat.

The president's aide, Major Andres Soriano, met the boat. He said that Quezon was at his temporary residence in the mountains, about 30 miles up the coast, and he would take Bulkeley to him. The president, who was awake and dressed when they arrived, told Bulkeley that he had just received a message from General Jonathan M. Wainwright suggesting that the number of Japanese warships in the waters south of Negros made the venture much too dangerous, and it should be canceled. He questioned Bulkeley at length, and must have been favorably impressed by the forthright answers he got, because he decided to entrust not only his own life, but those of persons very dear to him, to Bulkeley.

Meanwhile, Akers in the *PT-35* ran into a submerged object, which put a 20-foot gash in his bow. Water poured in but the crew formed a bucket brigade and kept the boat afloat. Akers realized his boat was in no condition to return to Mindanao, but he hoped he would be able to maintain his patrol until Bulkeley returned with the president. When he saw dim car lights approaching the dock, he figured it was time for him to go into the harbor.

The *PT-41*, with President and Mrs. Quezon, their two daughters, Vice President Osmeña, Major General Basilio Valdes, Major Soriano, nine members of the president's cabinet, and a large amount of luggage, pulled away from the dock and almost immediately encountered the *PT-35*. By this time, the latter's crew was exhausted from bailing, and the boat was rapidly sinking. All hands quickly climbed on board the already overburdened *PT-41*, which towed the *P-35* near shore and cut her loose to beach herself.

At 0320, 19 March 1942, the *PT-41* left Dumaguete for Oroquieta on Mindanao, a distance of not more than 60 miles, but the sea became ugly. At 0400 a huge wave slammed into the boat snapping the shear pins of her two after torpedoes. Jarred halfway out of their tubes, the torpedoes started "hot runs." The hissing of compressed air and the grinding of runaway propellers made a fearful sound. Trouble with the firing mechanism prevented the torpedoes from being jettisoned, and, if the propellers could not be stopped from turning within a very short period of time, the torpedoes would explode with disastrous consequences.

Realizing the seriousness of the situation, Chief Torpedoman James D. Light and Torpedoman First Class John L. Houlihan ran to the torpedoes, which by this time were sticking so far out of the tubes they seemed about to fall off, stood on them and, while holding on to the forward part of the tubes, tried to kick the "tin fish" loose. Hanging out over the surging sea in such a fashion was extremely dangerous, but the efforts of these courageous men failed to budge the runaway torpedoes. Happily, the firing mechanism was made operable, and the torpedomen stood clear while both torpedoes were ejected safely into the sea. Aside from the pounding waves, the rest of the journey was uneventful. At dawn, the *PT-41* entered the harbor at Oroquieta and disembarked her passengers. In saving President Quezon, his family, and leading members of the Philippine government from capture by the Japanese, Bulkeley and his Motor Torpedo Boat Squadron 3 performed another invaluable service.

Bulkeley desperately wanted to get the crippled *PT-35* and *PT-34* back in operating condition. No less determined were their crews. As soon as possible, he returned to Negros with the crew of the still-beached *PT-35*. A temporary patch was put on her hull and she was towed to Cebu City, where the Opan Shipbuilding & Slipway Corporation had a small marine railway. This outfit belonged to a 71-year-old American known to all as "Dad" Cleland. Dad was a true patriot with a can-do attitude, and went to work immediately on the *PT-35*.

Returning to Mindanao, Bulkeley found that the *PT-34*, which was considered by all but her crew to be finished, had been refloated and towed by army tug to a primitive machine shop at Anaken. Her crew had dipped into their own cash reserves to pay native workers to dig her out of the coral. Working like dogs, they repaired her well enough to allow her to make 12 knots without shaking to pieces and to accompany the *PT-41* to Cebu City for more permanent repairs. While at Cebu, the boat crews worked for three nights helping to load two submarines with supplies for Corregidor. In return for this work, the submariners gave Bulkeley two torpedoes to replace those lost by the *PT-41*.

On the afternoon of 8 April the *PT-34* went back in the water ready for combat, but repairs on the *PT-35* still had a long way to go. When Dad Cleland was asked by Bulkeley how much all this work was going to cost, he refused payment saying, "You fight 'em and I'll fix 'em." That same afternoon Bulkeley learned that two Japanese destroyers, sighted heading south through Tanon Strait, which runs between Cebu and Negros, should be off the southern tip of Cebu by midnight. To the east of the destroyers, a Japanese cruiser carrying four seaplanes had been sighted. This was chilling news for a small convoy of inter-island steamers, packed with supplies for Corregidor, which was scheduled to get under way. Apparently this enemy force was heading for Cebu to intercept the convoy. An army general told Bulkeley that American bombers that were to arrive the next morning could be counted on to polish off the cruiser, but it would be helpful if he attacked the destroyers. Bulkeley and company needed no second invitation.

That night, Bulkeley with Cox in the *PT-41*, followed by Kelly in the *PT-34*, moved down the eastern side of Cebu to its southernmost tip, where they waited in the shadows close to shore for the destroyers to enter the strait. It was almost midnight when an enemy ship was sighted, but this one, looming large and dark against the moonless sky, was no destroyer. She was a light cruiser easing along at about 10 knots. Idling into attack position, the *PT-41* moved undetected to within 500 yards of the cruiser's port beam and fired two torpedoes. Both missed. Increasing speed, the boat circled to the right and fired her last two torpedoes. They were seen to run true, one to the bow, the other beneath the bridge, but there was no explosion.

Kelly meanwhile brought the *PT-34* into firing position on the starboard side and fired two torpedoes, which also missed. By this time the cruiser had increased speed, and her powerful searchlight, sweeping the sea, picked up the *PT-34* as she crossed astern to come up on the cruiser's port quarter. Immediately, .50-caliber and 40-millimeter guns opened up sending continuous streams of bullets whistling overhead as Kelly, whose boat had fallen 2,500 yards behind the cruiser, attempted to close the range. The *PT-41*, out of torpedoes, circled on the cruiser's starboard side to strafe her decks in an effort to draw fire away from her companion boat, which was firmly fixed in the searchlight's beam and was now being fired on by the ship's main battery. The cruiser, however, continued to concentrate on the *PT-34*.

Kelly, determinedly pressing home his attack, ordered one of his .50-caliber turrets to fire at the searchlight, which was blinding him, and the other to sweep the cruiser's decks. He closed within 300 yards. Shellfire was intense. Chief Commissary Steward Willard J. Reynolds, Kelly's port gunner, was shot through the throat and shoulder. The boat's mast was shot away, and bullets ripped into her. To stay there any longer might be fatal. Drawing the *PT-34* out to the port quarter, Kelly fired his last two torpedoes, then ordered hard right rudder to retire. Streams of tracers were flying all around the boat when Kelly suddenly realized that two ships were firing at them. The second was a destroyer whose searchlight also fixed them in its glare.

The cruiser was turning to give chase and the destroyer closing to port to prevent the *PT-34* from escaping when two detonations were heard and two columns of water, one amidships of the cruiser the other about 30 feet aft of that, spouted high in the air. The cruiser's searchlight dimmed and went out, and all her guns ceased firing. At first, Kelly thought shells from the destroyer firing on him from starboard had hit the cruiser, but Chief Torpedoman's Mate Martino saw the hits and reported that they were torpedoes.

No longer burdened by four torpedoes, the *PT-34* was able to make 38 knots and, after some harrowing minutes of violent maneuvering to avoid shells from the destroyer, was once again out of danger. Kelly's chief concern was to get Reynolds to a doctor at Cebu. Moving along at high speed in the dark, without a chart, and only a compass by which to navigate was hazardous enough, but there were more than rocks and shoals to be reckoned with that night. Belief that they were in the clear was shattered when a searchlight beam, less than a mile ahead, snapped on. It came from another Japanese destroyer, which was steaming at about 30 knots and heading directly at them. Kelly had hardly time to order hard left and hard right rudder when the two ships scooted past each other close aboard at a relative speed of more than 60 knots. Holding her searchlight on the *PT-34*, the enemy destroyer, all guns firing, smartly turned to give chase. Shells chewed up the water around the boat, but Kelly again zigzagged and miraculously escaped. Ten miles from Cebu City, he misjudged the course and ran his boat aground on a pinnacle of coral. Unable to back free, he sent Ensign Iliff D. Richardson ashore in a rowboat to get an army doctor and an ambulance for Reynolds and a tug for the *PT-34*.

For the next four hours, in futile efforts to back off the pinnacle, the crew rocked the boat while her propellers churned. Finally, the *PT-34* broke free, but without proper charts, Kelly was forced to wait until daylight before attempting to navigate the narrow channel to Cebu. Dawn brought fog, and Kelly was forced to wait some more. At 0730 the fog vanished and he began working his way up the channel on two engines, one screw having been damaged on the coral. Suddenly, a 100-pound bomb exploded 10 feet off the boat's port bow, blowing a large hole in the crew's washroom, tearing the port machine gun off its stand, shattering windshields, and covering the entire boat with mud.

This air attack, coming after Bulkeley had been informed by the army that American planes would be in the area that day to work over the Japanese, was a shock. For a half-hour or so, the *PT-34* was bombed by four cruiser-based seaplanes. Twisting and turning in the restricted channel, Kelly was able to evade all the bombs, none of which fell more than 30 feet away. When their bombs were expended, the planes began diving low to strafe the boat. On the first run, Torpedoman's Mate Second Class David W. Harris, manning the starboard .50-caliber machine guns, was killed, and his guns knocked out. Quartermaster First Class Albert P. Ross shot down one of the enemy planes, but on the next run he was hit in the leg and his guns were disabled. Now, the *PT-34* had no guns with which to fight back. Riddled with holes, she was sinking, and Kelly had no alternative but to beach her and try to save his crew.

While enemy attacks continued, the boat ground to a halt about 1,200 yards off Cauit Island. Kelly and two others were the only ones on board who had not been wounded. Getting the wounded ashore while the enemy planes strafed was a difficult task, but it was done. Then Kelly and his radioman returned to carry the body of Harris ashore so he could receive a proper burial.

Filipino soldiers in the vicinity helped to carry the wounded to the other side of the island, and from there they were taken by motor launch to a hospital. Soon after the launch shoved off, a banca, which Ensign Richardson had dispatched, arrived with a doctor. Kelly rode the banca back to Cebu City, where he was grieved to learn that Reynolds had died of his wounds.

After the *PT-41* had fired her last torpedoes, Bulkeley was helpless to assist the *PT-34*. The best he could do was race his boat in various directions and fire his machine guns in the hope of creating the illusion that there were many MTBs around and of drawing some of the cruiser's fire. He did not succeed. The men in the *PT-41* saw the *PT-34* deliver her attack and turn away, only to be simultaneously engaged by a Japanese destroyer. They, like the crew of the *PT-34*, saw the thick, yellow smoke rising from the cruiser, saw her searchlight dim and go out, and were aware that her guns ceased firing.

As the *PT-34* raced off into the night with the destroyer in hot pursuit, Bulkeley headed in for a closer look at the cruiser, only to find three destroyers bearing down on him with searchlights blazing and guns spewing hate. Under full power, the *PT-41* turned sharply to evade this new threat, but not before the light of a destroyer briefly illuminated the cruiser. She appeared down by the stern and frantic sailors were dashing about her decks. Bulkeley positively identified her as a *Kuma*-class light cruiser. There was no doubt but that she had been torpedoed and was in serious trouble. Although some natives Bulkeley met later on Mindanao witnessed the fight and reported that the cruiser sank, Japanese documents uncovered after the war failed to confirm this.

Shells ripped up the water all around the *PT-41* as Bulkeley zigzagged and raced her full-out to escape the enemy "cans." The chase continued for almost 90 miles, with the boat slowly outdistancing her pursuers. Near Port Misamis, Mindanao, Bulkeley headed into an area where 6 miles of shallow water prevented further chase and, with the *PT-41* hidden under a pier, a very tired crew spent the day sleeping.

Motor Torpedo Boat Squadron 3 had arrived at the end of the line. The *PT-34* was finished, having been completely destroyed by enemy aircraft after she beached on Cauit Island. The *PT-35*, still undergoing repairs at Dad Cleland's slipway, was burned by Lieutenant (jg) Henry J. Brantingham on 12 April 1942, when the Japanese advanced on Cebu City. Only the *PT-41* was in operating condition, but there were no more torpedoes and what little gasoline was left was needed by the army. An attempt to move the *PT-41* overland to Lake Lanao on Mindanao for use as a patrol boat was unsuccessful, and she too was destroyed to prevent her being captured.

Lieutenant (jg) Bulkeley's last orders, given to him by MacArthur's chief of staff, Major General Sutherland, before the latter departed for Australia, concluded: "Upon completion of the offensive mission, due to destruction of material or lack of essential supplies, Lieutenant Bulkeley will proceed to Mindanao, reporting upon arrival to the Commanding General, Mindanao Force." Accordingly, Bulkeley reported to Brigadier General William F. Sharp for duty, and, on 13 April 1942, by order of General MacArthur, was flown to Australia.

When the end came, the twelve officers and sixty-eight enlisted men of Motor Torpedo Boat Squadron 3 were widely dispersed. Five had been lost with the *PT-31* and *PT-34*. By order of MacArthur, Lieutenant (jg) Kelly, who made a miraculous escape to Mindanao after the Japanese landed on Cebu, Ensign Akers, and Ensign Cox were flown to Australia to join Lieutenant Bulkeley. Two or three, including Lieutenant (jg) Schumacher, escaped to Australia by submarine. Of those who remained in the Philippines, two officers and twenty-nine enlisted men manned beach defenses on Corregidor, while others joined guerrilla forces to fight on Mindanao, Leyte, and Cebu. When the war ended, it was learned that thirty-eight officers and men, most of whom were on Corregidor, were captured by the Japanese, and nine of them died in Japanese prisoner-of-war camps.

The record shows that the officers and men of Motor Torpedo Boat Squadron 3 literally fought their hearts out. Constantly handicapped by lack of spare parts, proper maintenance facilities, and sabotaged fuel, these ingenious men worked long, exhausting hours to keep their boats in the fight. Without air support or ships-of-the-line to back them up, time and again they unhesitatingly attacked superior enemy forces and, in so doing, exhibited great daring, courage, and skill.

Motor torpedo boats were new in the navy's inventory and untried, but the performance of only six of them during those terrible, early days of World War II in Asia, more than proved their worth. By the end of the war, the navy had 212 PT boats, 11 tenders, and numerous PT bases throughout the southwest Pacific. But the courageous men of Motor Torpedo Boat Squadron 3 became legendary and achieved so much with so little that theirs was a tough, if not impossible, act to follow.

# II
# BATTLE REPORTS

# 9

# THE DOOMED DESTROYER—USS *PEARY* (DD-226)

When unopposed Japanese bombers destroyed it, the Cavite Navy Yard was jammed with ships frantically being readied to fight an all-too-sudden war. One of them was the old four-stack destroyer *Peary*, flagship of Destroyer Division 59, which several days earlier had been in a near-fatal collision with the destroyer *Pillsbury*. Both ships were moored at Central Wharf. The next pier over, Machina Wharf, was so crowded that two fleet-type submarines, the *Seadragon* and *Sealion*, were tied up side by side, the *Seadragon* being next to the dock. Hull to hull with the *Sealion* lay the minesweeper *Bittern*. At the head of Machina Wharf was moored the big submarine tender *Otus*.

Several vessels, including the minesweeper *Whippoorwill*, the submarine rescue vessel *Pigeon*, and the yacht *Isabel*, sometimes referred to as a gunboat, were anchored off the navy yard. A few hundred yards beyond them, navy PBY seaplanes rode serenely at their moorings. Anchored in the harbor off Manila were more than forty merchant ships and the submarine tenders *Holland* and *Canopus*, around which were nested numerous submarines. The time was 1245 on 10 December 1941.

Suddenly, the mid-day calm was shattered by the gut-shrinking wail of air-raid sirens. This, coupled with the word that bombers were heading for the yard, sent all hands racing to battle stations. Ships with steam up immediately got under way to seek maneuvering room in Manila Bay. Submarines, at four-engine speed, moved from their tenders to find deep water in which to hide. The seaplanes, as quickly as crews could be put on board, scrambled to get out of the area.

Marines unlimbered their nine, vintage 3-inch antiaircraft guns and a
few .50-caliber machine guns, and stood by to defend the yard.

Twenty minutes after the alarm sounded, fifty-four enemy bombers
with fighter escort circled over Cavite. Guns boomed and black puffs of
smoke from bursting shells pockmarked the sky, but it was all in vain.
Not a gun in the area could reach the planes flying at 19,000 feet.
Unruffled, the Japanese pilots casually selected their targets. With
murderous accuracy, tons of bombs rained down on the yard, which at
once erupted into an inferno of death and destruction. Ruptured oil
tanks belched raging yellow flames and black smoke. As machine
shops, warehouses, barracks, and buildings of all descriptions crumbled, they were engulfed in flames. Even the docks were afire. In less
than an hour, all of Cavite Navy Yard was reduced to a molten pile of
rubble. More than 500 civilian workers and military personnel lay dead
or wounded.

Soon after the first bombs fell, the *Pillsbury* got under way and found
relative safety in Manila Bay. But the *Peary*, her boilers decommissioned and fires dead, had no choice but to remain at the pier and take
it. Her small-caliber guns were useless. Bombs from the first two waves
of attackers burst close by, but did not damage her. The third wave
straddled her with bombs. Some exploded on Central Wharf, others in
the water alongside. One slammed into the fire-control platform on
her foremast and detonated. Instantly, the mast jackknifed into three
sections. White-hot shrapnel flew in all directions, gouging holes in her
navigation bridge, torpedo directors, galley deckhouse, and stacks, and
ignited small fires from stem to stern. The *Peary*'s commanding officer,
Lieutenant Commander Harry H. Keith, struck down by shrapnel, was
seriously wounded in both legs. Many of his crew were dead or
wounded.

Adding to the terror of bursting bombs were exploding air flasks in
the blazing torpedo-overhaul shop on Machina Wharf. The *Peary*,
powerless to move away from the holocaust, was doomed. Lieutenant
Commander Charles A. Ferriter, commanding the minesweeper *Whippoorwill*, realizing the destroyer's desperate situation, bravely took his
ship to the rescue. With all hoses streaming water to help counter the
intense heat, he maneuvered the "Whip" in between Central and
Machina Wharfs, and nosed her bow against the *Peary*'s stern. A 6-inch
hawser was passed to the *Peary* and made fast. Slowly, the "Whip"
backed down. The heavy line stretched taut. When the *Peary* did not
budge, Ferriter signaled the engine room for more turns. With a retort
like the crack of a 3-inch gun, the line parted. Disheartened but not
discouraged, Ferriter once more braved the mounting inferno on the

dock. Another hawser was made fast, and again the "Whip" backed down. Again the line parted.

Flaming debris rained down on both ships. Heat and smoke from the ever-mounting fires made breathing painful. Ferriter could not understand why the *Peary* did not move. He was inclined to attribute the parting of the lines to the searing heat. If that was the cause, he couldn't possibly get the destroyer out. His own ship was in one hell of a dangerous spot, and he was torn between abandoning the *Peary* to a horrible fate and risking the loss of the *Whippoorwill* and his crew.

Defeat, however, did not come easy to Ferriter. Like a boxer gamely struggling to his feet after a second knockdown, he headed the "Whip" back for one last, desperate attempt. All at once it occurred to him that the *Peary* might still have lines secured to the dock. As he closed her, he shouted for the *Peary*'s crew to check her mooring lines. Sure enough, in the confusion that reigned in the destroyer, two lines had been overlooked. This time, the "Whip" backed down pulling the *Peary* clear of the danger zone.

At the same time, a similar magnificent rescue effort was under way. The big fleet-type submarines alongside Machina Wharf had not escaped the fury of Japanese bombs. The *Sealion* had been sunk and the *Seadragon*'s conning tower slashed by flying fragments of steel. The minesweeper *Bittern*, outboard of them, was on fire. There were dead and wounded men in all three vessels. The *Bittern*, her fires not yet under control, moved out into Manila Bay. But fires on Machina Wharf, fed by oil from ruptured storage tanks, threatened to reduce the *Seadragon* to a cinder, wedged, as she was, to the wharf by the sunken *Sealion*. Fate, however, had not sounded her death knell. She was destined to put to sea and avenge this day by taking a heavy toll of Japanese shipping.

Lieutenant Hawes, commanding the *Pigeon*, seeing that the *Seadragon* was trapped, unhesitatingly went to the rescue. Although severely handicapped by a faulty rudder that seamen had to work with a hand winch, Hawes maneuvered the *Pigeon* close to the big boat. Despite the fierce heat, which scorched the *Seadragon*'s superstructure and blistered the *Pigeon*'s bridge and hull, a line was passed to the submarine. With the *Seadragon*'s engines pounding full ahead and the *Pigeon*'s full astern, the submarine was slowly worked into the channel, just as volumes of burning oil rolled over Machina Wharf.

Once the *Peary* was clear of the navy yard, men from the *Whippoorwill* went aboard her to help extinguish fires and tend the wounded.

Five of the *Peary*'s eight officers had been wounded, one mortally. Eight of her 126 enlisted men had been killed and 15 wounded. Fifteen men were missing, and presumed to have been killed in the navy yard while making their way to the dispensary either in search of medical attention or carrying wounded buddies. Lieutenant Commander Keith, although grievously wounded, refused to be taken to the hospital until he was convinced his ship was safe and his dead and wounded men had been removed.

To make emergency repairs and get ready for sea, the destroyer put into a small shipyard in Manila that belonged to the Atlantic Gulf and Pacific Company. Facilities there were marginal at best, but the *Peary*'s engineering force, led by Lieutenant (jg) Arthur L. Gustafson, worked around the clock to do in two weeks what many considered could not be done in less than a month.

On 23 December 1941, the *Peary* carried out her first assignment of the war—patrolling for enemy submarines between Mindoro Island and the southwest coast of Luzon. By this time, casualties had been replaced and a new commanding officer, Lieutenant Commander John M. Bermingham, had reported on board.

The day after Christmas, the *Peary* was lying at anchor off Corregidor, not far from two merchant ships, as she waited for her captain to return from a conference on the "rock." The first indication anyone had of enemy planes zeroing in on her came at about 1230 with the droning of motors high overhead. The wild clamor of the general alarm sent all hands scurrying to battle stations just as the first bombs landed. Nine of them exploded between the *Peary* and the two merchantmen, narrowly missing all three. The *Peary*'s executive officer, Lieutenant Martin M. Koivisto, immediately ordered up anchor and, at flank speed, headed the destroyer toward the center of Manila Bay. For the next two hours, she was subjected to attacks by twin-engine bombers flying high above the range of her guns. Only excellent shiphandling by Koivisto saved her from destruction. He needed all the cunning he had to outwit the enemy by slowing, backing, abruptly turning, and racing at full speed. Bombs exploding close to the *Peary* cut one of her signal halyards, severed a forestay, and threw water over her decks, but she suffered no serious damage and no casualties. For men whose nerves had not yet recovered from the navy yard ordeal, this was an especially harrowing experience. They were angry and depressed because their inadequate antiaircraft weapons did not give them a fighting chance against bombers.

At 2030, the *Peary* was ordered to proceed south at once and report to commander, Task Force 5, who was based in Java. This was welcome news. Everyone was delighted to get out of Manila Bay, where the

Japanese had seemingly selected them for extinction. Not only that, but the thought of joining other ships of the Asiatic Fleet and operating under skies controlled by the Allies was exhilarating.

Early the next morning, Bermingham nosed the *Peary* into remote Campomanes Bay on the west coast of Negros Island. He planned to hide out during daylight hours because Japanese bombers were known to be combing the Philippines for Yankee targets. Deep water at Campomanes permitted him to run the ship close inshore and moor her, parallel to the beach, with fore and aft lines out to trees. As soon as she was secure, the crew went to work covering her with palm fronds and painting everything on her topside green. That done, they prayed the ship would be overlooked by enemy aircraft. There were many anxious moments on board the *Peary* that day as several flights of Japanese bombers passed directly overhead. But the ship, looking like a mere bulge on the shoreline, was not spotted. At dusk, she was once again under way.

Bermingham planned to steam along the western edge of the Sulu Archipelago and make his way to Java through Makasar Strait separating the east coast of Borneo and the west coast of Celebes Island, but reports received during the afternoon indicated that would be much too hazardous. That way he would have to pass the heavy concentration of enemy ships lying in Jolo Harbor. Several Japanese cruisers were known to be patrolling off the northeast coast of Borneo, and a minelaying submarine had been seen working at the entrance to Makasar Strait. Faced with no happy alternative, Bermingham was forced to take a longer route down the east coast of Celebes.

Near midnight, the *Peary*, with no lights showing, sliced at full speed through the Sulu Archipelago into the Celebes Sea via Pilas Strait, a mere 30 miles north of Jolo. By dawn of the twenty-eighth, the destroyer was well into the Celebes Sea, and all hands relaxed in the thought that, having eluded the Japanese at Jolo, their troubles lay behind them.

Hopes of an uneventful day at sea were shattered at 0810, when distraught lookouts reported an enemy, four-engine seaplane 8 miles off their port quarter and heading toward them. "Battle stations" sounded and seamen hustled to unlimber machine guns they knew were useless. Tensely, the crew waited. The big plane approached as though on a bombing run, but, at the last moment, turned away. Several times the plane seemed to be coming in on a bombing run and the *Peary* took evasive action. Still no bombs were dropped. At 1000 another four-engine seaplane joined up with the first, and for the next five hours the two of them kept up the pretense of making bombing runs. As long as this deadly game of cat and mouse went on, it was impossible for anyone in the *Peary* to relax; any one of the approaches might be the real thing. Bermingham drafted a dispatch reporting his position and the harassing of his ship by enemy bombers, but was unable to raise an Allied station to receive his message. The men of the *Peary* were somewhat reassured at 1400, when two PBY seaplanes were sighted flying about 5 miles to the west of them. At this time, the enemy planes were shadowing the destroyer some miles to the east. Although the PBYs remained in the area for almost an hour before flying off to the south, the destroyer's efforts to exchange light signals with them were not successful.

After the PBYs had left, one of the Japanese bombers attacked the *Peary* from an altitude of 5,000 feet. She kept up continuous machine-gun fire, as Bermingham took evasive action, and the bombs exploded harmlessly 500 yards astern. When the second plane attacked from an even lower altitude, the *Peary*'s .50-caliber machine guns seemed to be finding their mark, and the plane aborted the run.

At this point, two twin-engine torpedo planes joined the seaplanes. As though to divide attention on board the *Peary*, they circled ominously out of gun range while the seaplanes made two more bombing runs. Some bombs fell close, but none of them did any damage. Now the torpedo planes attacked. The first, flying 50 feet above the water, approached the *Peary* from her port bow. Immediately, the destroyer's machine guns trained on this new threat. Bullets seemed to be getting closer to their mark, but the plane came to within 500 yards, launched two torpedoes, and zoomed out of range. Bermingham, with a wary eye on the second torpedo plane attacking from his port quarter, backed down full on the starboard engine, and these deadly tin fish sped harmlessly past his bow. But there was no respite. Two more torpedoes were on their way and, to avoid them, Bermingham had to swing his stern clear and stop.

Simultaneously, one of the seaplanes made a run from the stern of the *Peary*, which, lying dead in the water, appeared to be an easy victim. Just as the torpedoes missed, a scant 2 feet to starboard, Bermingham ordered all engines ahead flank speed. The engine room responded magnificently. The *Peary*'s propellers churned and, faster than anyone believed possible, she moved out from standstill to 15 knots. It was just enough. The seaplane's bombs erupted harmlessly where only moments before the destroyer looked like a sitting duck. Having expended sixteen heavy bombs and four torpedoes, the enemy planes withdrew.

This was a trying nine-hour ordeal but morale in the *Peary* was exceptionally high. All she had to do now was steam under the protective cover of night, which was rapidly approaching, and in the morning, she would be in friendly territory.

The northern tip of Celebes Island was passed at 1745, and Bermingham tried to radio the shore station there to ask whether the waters
leading into the Molucca Sea had been mined. He received no reply
but, preferring to risk traversing a minefield to being subjected to
more hell from the air, he continued on his way. Twenty minutes later,
as dusk was descending, three twin-engine planes were seen
approaching from the stern. Once again, his exhausted crew hurried to
their battle stations, there to wait in grim silence. The lead plane,
maneuvering to pass ahead, crossed the *Peary*'s course from starboard
to port. Joy ran through the ship when it was determined from her
markings that the plane was an Australian—a Lockheed Hudson
bomber. The Anglo-Dutch-U.S. recognition challenge was flashed on
the *Peary*'s signal searchlight, and the pilot appeared to wave. The
destroyer men waved back. A few cheered.

Joy turned to dismay when one of the planes went into a glide-
bombing approach from astern. Bermingham ordered the machine
guns to hold their fire but, taking no chances, at flank speed he
abruptly changed course to starboard. A bomb exploded 100 yards off
the *Peary*'s port beam. During this evasive action, as the ship heeled to
hard rudder, Seaman First Class Billy E. Green, stationed at one of the
.50-caliber machine guns, lost his footing and fell overboard. A life
jacket was thrown to him, and, when last seen, he was swimming
toward Sunakeng Island a mile away.

The Lockheed Hudsons made two more bombing attacks, each time
dropping a single 250-pound fragmentation bomb and machine-
gunning the ship. All the bombs missed, but the last one exploded 10
yards off her port propeller guard, sending showers of shrapnel slamming into her. Seaman First Class K. E. Quinaux, manning a machine
gun, was killed instantly. Chunks of shrapnel pierced the after engine
room, and a steam line to the steering engine was ruptured, making it
necessary to shift to hand steering. Shrapnel also split open three
depth charges and set fire to a 4-inch shell in the ready racks aft. Before
it could explode, Fireman Third Class G. A. Fryman courageously
unstrapped the burning cartridge and threw it overboard.

It was dark when the bombers departed. The cruel attack left the
men of the *Peary* dumbfounded. Again and again they had tried to
signal the Australians that they were friendly, and certainly, it was
agreed, they should have recognized the American flag flying from the
mast. With one man lost overboard, another killed, and three wounded, the dispirited crew had every reason to be apprehsensive about
what lay ahead.

Aside from the bomb damage, the *Peary* was in serious trouble. Her
starboard engine's Kingsbury thrust bearing was overheating, and she
could maintain headway only with her port engine. Both fuel and feed

water were in short supply. For these reasons, Bermingham headed for the small island of Maitara, near Ternate Island, in the Moluccas, where, according to his navigational information, there was an ideal harbor for hiding his ship while he made temporary repairs. He sent a message detailing the day's attacks, the condition of his ship, and his immediate destination to commander, Task Force 5, and received an acknowledgement. Now that his ship's whereabouts were known, Bermingham had every reason to believe that Allied aircraft would leave them alone.

With the captain steering from the after deckhouse, the crippled destroyer managed to reach the harbor at Maitara at dawn of the twenty-ninth and anchor close to shore, with bow and stern lines out to trees. As they had done before, the crew used palm fronds to camouflage the ship's sides and superstructure.

That day and the next were spent in efforts to make the *Peary* seaworthy. In the interim, Bermingham took the ship's motor launch and visited the Dutch military commander at Ternate, from whom he obtained a good supply of potable water, bread, and native fruits. No fuel oil was obtainable, but it was determined that the *Peary* would be able to reach the Dutch base at Ambon, 325 miles to the south, on the 19,000 gallons she had left, if she used them carefully.

At sunset on the thirtieth, the *Peary* shed her palm fronds and got under way for Ambon. It soon became apparent that, despite the temporary repairs, her starboard thrust bearing was overheating to an unacceptable degree, and Bermingham was forced to continue the passage on only the port engine. Without further incident, the *Peary* arrived in Ambon Bay in the early afternoon of 31 December 1941. With Japanese air and sea armadas pressing every closer to the Netherlands East Indies, men of the *Peary*, having suffered so many tragedies, found little of good cheer in this particular New Year's Eve. Most of them were content to down a few warm Dutch beers and turn in for a peaceful night's rest—the first in a long time.

While the destroyer was at Ambon, she got an explanation of the attack on her by Allied planes. It seems that Manado, on Celebes Island, had been heavily bombed by the Japanese a few days earlier, and it was believed this would soon be followed by a landing force. When the American PBY pilots saw the *Peary* making high speed in the general direction of Manado and apparently convoyed by Japanese four-engine bombers, they mistook her for an enemy light cruiser. This information, radioed to Ambon, brought the Australians to the attack.

The *Peary* was ordered to proceed to Darwin, Australia, and arrived there on 3 January 1942. Everything possible was done to put her in operating condition, but the overhaul facilities there being inadequate, no major work could be done. Because the Allies were desperately short of combatant ships, on 17 January the *Peary* was pressed into convoy duty, even though her meager armament could not be augmented.

On 18 February, she was ordered to accompany the heavy cruiser *Houston* to Java, where a last-ditch attempt would be made to forestall Japanese landings on that capital island of the Netherlands East Indies. The two ships cleared the minefields protecting Darwin Harbor at dusk and, as they did so, the *Peary* made sonar contact with an ememy submarine. The *Houston* steamed on out of the area, leaving the *Peary* to continue searching and, it was hoped, destroy the submarine. Several hours later, after dropping depth charges with undetermined results, the destroyer returned to Darwin to top off her fuel supply. This, she found, could not be done until the next morning.

When the sun's sultry eye first leered through the haze at Darwin on the morning of 19 February 1942, to most people it was just the beginning of another hellishly humid day. This would be a hellish day all right, but a man-made one, which those who survived it would always recall with horror.

No one had the slightest inkling that Japanese land-based bombers had moved up to newly acquired bases within striking range of Darwin, or that the most powerful enemy strike force to be assembled since the

The USS *Peary* (DD-226), sinking in Darwin Harbor, Australia, on 19 February 1942, a victim of Japanese bombers. Courtesy Royal Australian Navy Historical Section

attack on Pearl Harbor—two battleships, three heavy cruisers, and four aircraft carriers—had penetrated the Malay barrier and was in the Arafura Sea, a scant 200 miles away. An enemy attack on Darwin, at this time, was unthinkable. Its harbor was jammed with more than twenty merchant ships, an Australian hospital ship, several Australian corvettes, the seaplane tender *William B. Preston*, three PBY seaplanes of Patrol Wing 10, the *Peary*, and several lesser naval vessels. At 1030, the *Peary* completed refueling and Lieutenant Commander Bermingham was about to get under way for Java when, with the stunning suddenness of a lightning bolt, 188 carrier-based fighters and dive-bombers, in concert with 54 land-based bombers, struck Darwin.

In a matter of minutes the airfield was gutted, its few fighter planes shot down or destroyed on the ground. Barracks, warehouses, the town itself lay shattered and engulfed in flames. Ships in the harbor attempted to get under way to escape the planes swarming over them. Many did not escape. The British ammunition ships *Neptuna* and *Zealandia*, unloading at the docks, disintegrated amidst horrendous explosions. In short order, bombs and air-launched torpedoes sank the U.S. Army transports *Mauna Loa* and *Meigs*. A bombed-out Norwegian tanker, vomiting orange flames and dense black smoke, went down. The freighter *Admiral Halstead*, loaded with drums of high-octane gasoline, burst into a gigantic fireball and sank. Two Australian corvettes, shattered by bombs, went to the bottom. The *William B. Preston* was badly damaged, and the three PBYs were sunk at their moorings. When the enemy planes finally departed, thirteen ships lay on the bottom of Darwin Harbor and nine others were damaged. The number of casualties on land and afloat was staggering, and tons of supplies, desperately needed by the Allies, were demolished.

Immediately after the first bombs exploded, Bermingham had the *Peary* under way, zigzagging as best he could in a harbor cluttered with wildly maneuvering ships. It seemed as though every ship was under attack at the same time. The sweeping volleys of machine-gun fire that the *Peary* directed at enemy planes did little to stay the relentless onslaught. Shrapnel from innumerable near-misses gouged holes in the *Peary*'s hull and superstructure, while strafing planes raked her decks. All at once, the little destroyer shuddered from stem to stern as two bombs in rapid succession burst on her fantail. They demolished her depth-charge racks, sheared her propeller guards, and flooded her steering engine room. Moments later, incendiaries slammed into her galley creating an infernal fire. In the face of continuous attacks, the *Peary*'s crew sprang to the awesome jobs of extinguishing the flames, which threatened to consume the ship, repairing bomb damage, and attending to numerous casualties.

In a matter of minutes the galley fire was under control, but the nauseous breath of death and destruction shrouded the *Peary*. A bomb exploded in her forward magazine, and violent concussions from near-misses threatened to rip her apart at the seams. Next, an incendiary wrecked her engine room. She was all but done for but, somehow, the flaming, battered hulk kept fighting back. Finally, with her decks steeped in the blood of dead and wounded, the *Peary*, smashed by one bomb too many, broke up, and vanished beneath the waves.

Eighty officers and men, including Lieutenant Commander John M. Bermingham, her commanding officer, perished with the ship. One ship's officer, Lieutenant W. J. Catlett, survived, only because he was ashore in the hospital at the time. Forty enlisted men, many of them wounded, miraculously escaped.

So ends the saga of the USS *Peary* (DD-226) and the magnificent Americans who manned her. Hopelessly outgunned, but always tenaciously fighting back, they exhibited a raw courage and steadfast devotion to duty that should constitute an inspirational chapter in our navy's history. Yet, when the smoke of battle cleared, the little four-stack destroyer USS *Peary*, without so much as a "well done" for her heroic crew from the Navy Department, was summarily scratched from the lists, to be forgotten by all but a handful of survivors and the loved ones of those who died fighting for their country.

# 10

# THE OLD LADY—USS *CANOPUS* (AS-9)

Old China hands referred to her as "the Old Lady." Actually, she was the *Canopus*, one of three tenders assigned to Submarine Squadron 20 of the U.S. Asiatic Fleet. Built as a passenger liner, she was purchased from the Grace Line in 1921 and converted by the navy into a tender—a mother ship for S-type submarines, or pigboats, as those squat, cramped, ungodly hot, undersea boats commissioned in 1923 and 1924 were disparagingly called.

To pigboat sailors, the tender was a floating home away from home. Her sleeping accommodations and chow-line fare beckoned like a Ritz Carlton to submariners eager for a respite from the austere life they led in their own boats. But the Old Lady was much more than that. She was a seagoing miniature navy yard. She was so well equipped with machine shops, forges, and spare parts of all kinds that there were few things her top-flight crew of artisans couldn't do to keep an S-boat in operating condition. To replenish her brood, she carried fuel oil, food, and ammunition—including torpedoes. Little wonder, therefore, that rock-hard S-boat crews regarded her as their Old Lady. The *Canopus*, with a division of six S-boats, arrived on the China Station in 1925 and was still there in December 1941, when all hell broke loose at Pearl Harbor. Her only armament was four 3-inch antiaircraft guns and an assortment of .50-caliber and .30-caliber machine guns—hardly a warship to strike terror into the hearts of Japanese bomber pilots. Nevertheless, she had been keeping her guns manned and ready from dawn to sundown for a week prior to that fateful day.

96

That first day of the war, the *Canopus*, whose commanding officer was Commander Earl L. Sackett, lay at anchor off the Cavite Navy Yard, across the bay from Manila. Japanese planes ignored Manila and ships in the bay, but, around noon, 108 twin-engine bombers escorted by 84 Zero fighters pulverized the U.S. Army Air Forces base at Clark Field—60 miles north of Manila. The rumble of exploding bombs and giant pillars of oily black smoke smearing the distant sky grimly testified to the fact that great damage was being inflicted.

More bombers came that night. Guided by flares ignited by fifth-columnists, they attacked Nichols Field on the outskirts of Manila. Flames from burning fuel dumps vaulted into the sky, weirdly illuminated the city and the bay, making a ghoulish mockery of the night. Rolling volumes of dense smoke shrouded the countryside, while high overhead the sky was brilliantly punctured by bursting antiaircraft shells and crisscrossed by the fiery tails of tracer bullets, all of which sought in vain to bring down the attackers. This ghastly spectacle, accompanied by thunderous explosions, brought to the men of the *Canopus* the sickening reality that war had in fact come to the Philippines and they were helpless even to defend themselves. Frustrated and fighting mad, they swore violent oaths that somehow they would strike back.

For the defenders of the Philippines, that first day of the war was a depressing one. Before midnight tolled, the smouldering debris of more than half the bombers and two-thirds of the fighters in MacArthur's small Far East Air Force littered the gutted airfields. From then on, the Japanese ruled the skies over the entire Philippine Archipelago and the contrails of their warplanes spelled defeat.

The message delivered by Japanese bombers came in loud and clear—ships in Manila Bay were sitting ducks. At dawn the *Canopus* moved from her anchorage to moor alongside a dock in the port area of Manila, where she had less then 4 feet of water under her keel. Here, if holed by a bomb, she would simply rest on the bottom, her decks above water. It was hoped that this would permit the salvage of valuable equipment and stores needed to keep submarines of the Asiatic Fleet operating. To minimize losses, many torpedoes and spare parts were hurriedly off-loaded and sent by barge to Corregidor for safekeeping; other stores were put aboard a small inter-island steamer. To disguise the *Canopus*, bluejackets painted her superstructure to match the docks and spread camouflage nets overhead. Her exposed fuel tanks were filled with water in order to reduce the danger of fire if she should be hit by a bomb. In a word, everything possible was done to ready her for the worst.

On 10 December 1941, Japanese bombers, flying beyond the range of the defenders' antiaircraft batteries, demolished Cavite Navy Yard, the navy's only ship-repair and supply facility in the Far East. The important role that the *Canopus* instantly assumed became vital the following day, when the *Holland* and *Otus*, the only other submarine tenders in Asia, were ordered out of Manila Bay to safer ports in the Netherlands East Indies. From the bombed-out navy yard, battered ships limped to the "Old Lady" for help, and her crewmen responded like surgeons in an emergency room. Night and day they toiled to ready these ships for sea while, at the same time, equipping their regular submarine brood for offensive patrols. When the doleful wailing of air-raid sirens interrupted work, the submarines sought refuge on the bottom of Manila Bay and all hands aboard the *Canopus* manned battle stations until the sounding of "all clear."

After two weeks of sporadic fighting to stem the Japanese advance on Manila, General MacArthur conceded that without air support the effort was futile. To spare the city from certain destruction, he abruptly declared that, effective midnight 24 December 1941, Manila would be an "open city." MacArthur had not discussed such an eventuality with Admiral Hart, commander in chief, Asiatic Fleet, and this sudden directive, delivered to the admiral just before noon on the twenty-fourth, caught him totally unprepared. Vital naval supplies were scattered throughout the waterfront of this Manila base, from which the admiral had planned to conduct submarine warfare until forced by the enemy to withdraw. Given just twelve hours to close down his headquarters and move ships, supplies, and personnel to Corregidor and Bataan, Hart was understandably furious. The decision meant that he would no longer be able to sustain submarine operations from the Philippines, and the short notice he was given meant an appalling loss of precious supplies that could not possibly be moved in the time available.

That night, Christmas Eve, Japanese bombers attacked Manila. One bomb hit the headquarters of Captain John Wilkes, commander, Submarine Squadron 20, which had been established in the newly completed Enlisted Men's Club near the dock area, showering fragments and debris on the decks of the *Canopus*. The ship immediately got under way for the Corregidor area. As she steamed down the bay, she could see large fires in and around Manila, some caused by bombs, but most of them purposely set to prevent fuel and other valuable supplies from falling into enemy hands. Early on Christmas morning, the *Canopus* arrived in Mariveles Bay, at the southern tip of the Bataan Peninsula. Lying just across a narrow stretch of water from the guns of Corregidor, this bay had been considered relatively safe from air attacks but, as the tender nosed into the harbor, she was greeted by a depressing sight. A bombed and burning merchant ship, victim of the previous night's raid, bore mute testimony to the fact that no place in the Philippines could now be considered safe.

With great hopes of hiding from the enemy, Sackett moored his ship close to the shoreline in a small cove partially protected by high hills. To help blend her with the adjacent jungle, the crew spread camouflage nets over her decks, applied lavish quantities of green paint topside, and lashed branches of trees to her masts and upper works. Unfortunately, a nearby rock quarry caused a large white gash in the cliffs forming a backdrop that, viewed from one direction, was impossible to match. They would have to live with this chink in the camouflage and pray that no enemy plane photographed the area from that direction.

Whether enemy agents, who haunted Bataan, or "Photo Joe," a Japanese plane that made daily reconnaissance, disclosed her presence is not known, but on 29 December the *Canopus* was unmasked. During most of that day, Japanese bombers, contemptuous of the small-caliber antiaircraft guns defending Corregidor, hammered the island fortress. The *Canopus* lay ignored until the last group of nine, twin-engine bombers wheeled in from the exposed quadrant and bracketed her with a perfect pattern of thirty-six bombs. Moored to the beach as she was, her guns unable to reach the high-flying attackers, she was struck, amazingly enough, by only one of the closely bunched missiles. But that one, armor-piercing bomb ripped through all her after decks, exploded atop the propeller shaft, blew open her port after magazine, and started fires that could detonate the ammunition. The *Canopus* shuddered violently with this near-fatal rendering of her vital parts, while rocks, gouged from the hills by exploding bombs, slammed down on her decks. Smoke pouring from ammunition scuttles leading from her magazines, coupled with muffled secondary explosions below decks, were grim reminders that her magazines could blow at any second. These, however, served only to speed all hands to rescue wounded shipmates and to fight the fires which threatened to destroy their beloved ship. It took four grueling hours to extinguish the fires and permit examination of the magazines, where seventy-five crushed and exploded 3-inch powder charges were found. It was a miracle that the general magazine did not explode when the bomb set off those charges. To the men of the *Canopus*, it was indeed a miracle that bomb fragments severed water and steam pipes near the magazines, and the resulting deluge automatically isolated them from the flames.

The *Canopus* was grievously hurt. Six of her crew were dead and six seriously wounded, but she was far from being out of action. At dusk, when enemy bombers no longer haunted the sky, it was "business as usual" on board the Old Lady. While repair parties, spurred on by the ardent hope that they would soon be steaming south to join the fleet, were hard at work patching up the damage, other crew members were busily servicing submarines for their war patrols.

The bomb completely wrecked the supply officer's compartment and cindered all his accounts. From that day forward there would be no supply accounting. Whatever was aboard the ship could be had without the usual red tape. Since there was nothing for which men could spend money, pay days were abolished. Ice cream and canteen supplies were free. Clothing became community property and was allocated to those considered to be in the most naked condition. As Sackett wrote:

> This Utopian state inevitably welded us all into a great family working and fighting in a common cause, with only one aim—to do our damndest to lick the Japs.
>
> Curiously enough, the boys who had been the worst troublemakers in time of peace, became our most shining examples in wartime. Perhaps they had just too much restless energy for their own good when things were normal, but this same quality enabled them to perform prodigies [sic] when the chips were down.
>
> Ordinary methods of discipline of course failed, since the men got no liberty or pay anyhow, and what would normally be extra duty was now only the usual stint for everyone. But punishments were fortunately unnecessary, as the spirit of the community would tolerate no shirkers, and the men themselves saw to it that no one was derelict in his duty.*

Two days after the bombing, the last of the submarines pulled out of Manila Bay, bound for new operating bases in the Netherlands East Indies, leaving the crew of the *Canopus* feeling depressed and abandoned. To a man, they desperately wanted to do their share in the war against Japan. They argued strongly that a submarine tender without submarines to tend was a waste of talent and equipment, and the *Canopus* should, therefore, be permitted to go south. Although fully aware of the many dangers inherent in such a voyage through areas now dominated by Japanese sea and air forces, the crew was eager to take the risk. The high command, however, had other ideas and the tender was ordered to remain in Mariveles Harbor.

It did not take long for the word to spread that the *Canopus*, with her well-equipped machine shops and talented craftsmen, was looking for work. The submarine rescue vessel *Pigeon*, several minesweepers, motor torpedo boats, and other auxiliary vessels also left behind were constantly in need of repairs, and soon came to the Old Lady for help. But those were not her only "customers." When army and army air

*Sackett, "The History of the USS *Canopus*," p. 8.

forces units got the message, they too came to her in droves to have their damaged ordnance and transportation equipment put back in operable condition. Suddenly, the men of the *Canopus*, finding themselves busier than ever, realized that they were very important to many people, especially those on Bataan, and readily adapted to their new mission—to help hold Bataan.

The magnificent efforts of the *Canopus*'s men were attested to by the fact that, besides dealing with a constant stream of repairs, they manufactured 150 machine-gun tripods, improvised mounts for naval guns to be used in coastal defense, and made mounts for more than 40 .50-caliber machine guns for use in antiaircraft defense. They charged torpedoes for the motor torpedo boats and even put structural steel plates on many an army motorized unit to protect it against small-arms fire. There seemed to be no limit to what the ship's company could do.

The first bombing attack made everyone realize that daylight hours aboard ship were not conducive to longevity, and it became doctrine to send most of the crew ashore to sleep during the day and bring them back to work all night. Only the gun crews remained on board ship during the hours of danger.

On 5 January 1942, the Japanese tried again to eliminate the *Canopus*. Flying out of gun range, as usual, seven heavy bombers dropped twenty-eight bombs. Again, luck was with the *Canopus*, because only one of the bombs scored a direct hit. It struck the side of her towering smokestack and literally sprayed her upper decks with small chunks of metal. The gun crews ducked behind their splinter shields just before the bombs landed, but that gave them little or no protection from shrapnel coming from above, and fifteen men were wounded. Fortunately, no one was killed. In a matter of minutes, the sailors ashore raced out to their ship with stretchers for the wounded and quickly went to work repairing damage.

Damage to the ship was superficial. The bomb started several minor fires, which were soon extinguished, and some of the upper works, where hundreds of fragments had punctured the light plating, looked a bit like Swiss cheese. The near-misses, though, had left their marks. Both sides of the ship were pierced above the waterline by shrapnel thrown up by the bombs that exploded on contact with the water. Other bombs exploded deep underwater and dished in her hull two or three inches, cracking plates and causing heavy leakage through loosened rivets.

Since the *Canopus* had to remain moored to the beach in Mariveles Harbor and the Japanese knew she was there, something had to be done to keep her alive and well. There being no antiaircraft protection, Sackett decided that survival lay in making the enemy think that his ship had been polished off by the most recent bombing attack. To that end, all hands worked throughout the night to prepare the Old Lady for the arrival of Photo Joe, whose pictures would show an abandoned hulk in all but sinking condition. They flooded empty fuel tanks in order to give the tender a starboard list. They made her cargo booms look forlornly askew, and blackened large areas to look like bomb holes from which smoke, derived from burning oil-soaked rags in strategically placed smudge pots, would ooze skyward for several days. Photo Joe's pictures would not disclose that, every night, the "abandoned hulk" hummed with activity, forging weapons for the beleaguered forces on Bataan.

Realizing that by firing her futile antiaircraft volleys at enemy planes, the *Canopus* was only attracting attention to herself, Sackett had all .50-caliber machine guns removed and mounted in the surrounding hills. Two of her four 3-inch antiaircraft guns were damaged in the bombing and, since there was little ammunition left for the other two, they were dismantled to provide spare parts for similar guns that the marines were manning at the head of Mariveles Bay.

When it was decided that the ship would be abandoned during daylight hours, her company took over a large, recently completed storage tunnel near Mariveles, in which they built bunks, fitted out office spaces, hospital accommodations, a telephone communications center, and a makeshift galley. Although more than a hundred men were living in this shelter and many of the repair force slept there during the day, most of the men scorned the tunnel's dank atmosphere and took their chances beneath the shade of tropical trees in the hills, leaving a lookout to warn them in time to dive into foxholes whenever marauding planes appeared.

*Canopus* sailors who were not in the "night owl" group of workers, manned machine guns on the hilltops surrounding Mariveles and waited impatiently for a chance to get an effective crack at any Japanese plane foolish enough to venture within range. Others manned lookout and signal stations on the same hilltops. Equipped with telephones removed from the ship, wires for which they strung throughout the entire system, these men continually searched the skies for enemy planes.

Mariveles Harbor was generally considered well defended against surprise attack from the sea. Although enemy naval forces were always hovering off the coast of Bataan, the big guns on Corregidor forced them to stand their distance, and, 20 miles to the north, the army had stabilized the front on the China Sea side of the heavily jungled Mariveles mountains. One man, Commander Francis J. Bridget, a naval aviator in command of the remnants of Patrol Wing 10 that had not been able to fly out of the Philippines with their squadron mates, took issue with the prevailing belief that the area was safe unless the front lines failed to hold.

The seacoast between Mariveles and those lines was not defended because treacherous, rock-strewn beaches, crouching before sheer cliffs backed up by seemingly impassable jungles were not regarded as likely places for Japanese landings. Bridget noted that in several areas, the only road to those front lines ran close to the sea. If the Japanese succeeded in making a landing, they could cut the road to prevent reinforcements and vital supplies from moving up. Such a maneuver could spell disaster, and Bridget was determined to forestall it. The army, hard-pressed, could ill afford men to defend such unlikely landing areas, but the navy could. To start with, Bridget had under his command about 150 aviation ratings and a few officers. After describing the situation as he saw it to others, he was able to augment his force with 130 men from the *Canopus*, about 80 from the navy's ammunition depot, and 100 or so marines. Thus was formed the Navy Battalion on Bataan, with Lieutenant Commander Henry W. "Hap" Goodall of the *Canopus* second in command to Bridget. A few marine and naval aviation officers became company commanders.

It has long been an adage in the navy that you can't make a soldier out of a sailor. No way! Bridget, however, was determined to try. Equipment posed a serious problem. The marines were ready for field duty but the sailors did not have even the bare essentials. Rifles and ammunition were begged, borrowed, or stolen. Some shotguns turned up and arguments ensued that, according to international law, they could not be used. However, those who had them stoutly maintained that it didn't matter a damn what you killed Japs with, they'd still be dead, and rather than go unarmed, they kept the weapons. Perhaps two-thirds of the sailors knew which end of a rifle to point at the enemy and had even practiced on a target range, but none of them had the slightest concept of how to act in the field. Experienced marines were spread thinly throughout each company in the hope that their example would help the sailors to shape up. White naval uniforms were hardly suitable for jungle fighting, and attempts to dye them khaki by boiling them in coffee resulted in their being a sickly mustard yellow. Only one canteen could be rounded up for every three men, so the great American tin can was pressed into service to make up the deficiency.

In late January, when the Navy Battalion, a rag-tag outfit if there ever was one, had been together only a few days, it was decided that, to harden them up, a hike along the coast road was in order. With spirits high and considerable wisecracking filtering through the ranks, the men sallied forth on what might be considered their first training exercise. They had gone only a few miles when, at the base of Mount

Pucot near the China Sea, they came across a group of soldiers who were highly agitated because they had just been rudely ejected from their signal station atop the mountain by Japanese soldiers. Commander Bridget's worst fears were confirmed when it was discovered that the enemy, having landed at nearby Longoskawayan Point, was working inland toward the vital communications road.

It suddenly became "field training" with a vengeance for the fledgling infantrymen. At Bridget's command to "go get 'em," men of the battalion, equipped with little more than enthusiasm and determination, moved out. Up various mountain trails they went, soon to be swallowed in an all-but-impenetrable jungle. With no means of communicating, units became separated and, in the next five days, some of the weirdest jungle fighting of all time ensued. It wasn't long before the men in the van made contact and the sound of gunfire resounded through the jungle. It was apparent that the Japanese had landed in force and the Navy Battalion had a "bear by the tail." Nevertheless, they succeeded in driving back the enemy's advance patrols, then dug in to plot their next move. They were not equipped for sustained warfare, and no thought had been given to logistics. But when the *Canopus* received a hurried call to send plenty of everything, all work was dropped and food, water, ammunition, blankets, and stretchers were rushed to the new battle zone.

What little contact the units of the Navy Battalion were able to maintain with each other during daylight hours went completely by the board at nightfall. Trails through the jungle, difficult to follow in daylight, were impossible to find in the dark. The Japanese, however, were masters of night jungle-fighting and put their famous infiltration tactics to good use. This, however, did not produce the expected results. The sailors, not having been indoctrinated in the time-honored army principle that it is fatal to be outflanked, simply held their ground and, at dawn, sent back detachments to clear out the pesky intruders.

The Japanese landing party consisted of picked men, larger and stronger than the average, and well equipped for jungle fighting. Had they made a determined assault, they might have wiped out the ragged but resolute Navy Battalion. However, being well versed in the precepts of war, they refrained from making such an assault until they knew the location of the strong reserve, which they assumed was backing up the small force they had encountered. Little did they suspect that the Americans didn't have a reserve anywhere.

After two days of hard fighting in the snake- and mosquito-infested jungle, the Navy Battalion was still holding out, but Japanese mortars were adding to the unpleasantness of their situation. To counter this enemy advantage and help to delude the Japanese as to the size and composition of the force pitted against them, sixty marines equipped with mortars were brought over from Corregidor. Strangely enough, the inadequacy of the Navy Battalion's communications facilities helped to fog the Japanese estimate of the situation. Several times, rumors somehow reached pockets of *Canopus* men that their ship was getting under way to join the fleet and their presence on board was required. Eagerly, they made their way to Mariveles, only to learn the rumor was someone's pipe dream and be immediately ordered back to man their positions. The noisy scurrying along the jungle trails that these trips to Mariveles entailed led the Japanese to believe that reinforcements were moving up. A diary later found on the body of a Japanese officer confirmed that the enemy was completely bewildered by the conduct of the Navy Battalion. He described the men as "the new type of suicide squads, which thrashed about in the jungle, wearing bright-colored uniforms and making plenty of noise. Whenever these apparitions reached an open space, they would attempt to draw Japanese fire by sitting down, talking loudly, and lighting cigarettes."

On the fifth day, the 57th Regiment of Filipino Scouts relieved the battered and hard-pressed Navy Battalion. In three days, these tough jungle fighters, assisted by the murderous fire of huge mortars on Corregidor, literally tore the enemy to pieces. Hundreds of Japanese dead littered the jungle, and the remnants of a once-elite force retreated over the cliffs. Holed up in deep crevices and caves which honeycombed the sheer cliffs, these desperate men could be expected to fight to the death. To shoot it out with them from the land side would not only be intensely difficult but would exact an unacceptable price in dead and wounded Filipino Scouts. Yet, the Japanese presence posed a serious threat that could not be ignored.

Acutely aware of the Scouts' dire situation, *Canopus* men contrived an ingenious way of helping them out. They would attack the enemy from the sea. Even as the plan was being approved, shipfitters were hard at work converting three of the tender's 40-foot motor launches for combat. Thus was spawned what was to be pridefully known as "Uncle Sam's Mickey Mouse Battle Fleet." Armed with .50-caliber machine guns and a light field piece with protective boiler plate around the engine and gun positions, the first of the "Mickey Mouse battleships" was soon ready for action. Manned by Hap Goodall and a crew from the *Canopus*, the little craft put to sea. It was an 8-mile cruise to Longoskawayan Point, where the Japanese were holed up, and, on her first operating day, this unorthodox naval weapon made two round trips, blasting scores of Japanese from their caves. As evidence of her success, the "battleship" brought in two live but dazed enemy prisoners and the corpses of three others who had been wounded but failed to survive the trip.

The second midget man-of-war was completed the following day, whereupon both sallied forth to continue the mopping-up. This time, only four of the enemy were found and, in short order, dispatched to the land of their ancestors. Thorough reconnaissance of the area revealed that it had been swept clean of Japanese troops, and the *Canopus* sailors at last felt avenged for seven shipmates killed in the land fighting and the six who died in the first bombing attack on their ship.

Goodall's "Mickey Mouse fleet" was not about to be mothballed, for within a matter of days a large Japanese force tried to land on Quinauan Point, several miles north of the site previously used. This landing met with fierce opposition: boats of Motor Torpedo Squadron 3 viciously attacked the landing craft and escorting destroyers, while three P-40 fighters, the last in the army's inventory, doggedly bombed and strafed the invaders. Although thirteen troop-laden barges were sunk and a destroyer was crippled by a torpedo, a sizable force managed to get ashore, which meant more work for the Filipino Scouts. The Japanese made persistent efforts to reinforce their beachhead and air-dropped supplies to the men ashore. It took the scouts and other army units more than a week of hard fighting to drive the remnants of this contingent back to the cliffs. Then, once again, Hap Goodall was called upon to clean out the caves.

By this time three midget men-of-war were available for the attack. They shot up everything in sight and when the dead enemy soldiers were laid out for inspection, the count ran to thirty-three. Mission accomplished, the little task force headed for home, but en route it was attacked by four Japanese dive-bombers. As the boats scattered and took evasive action, a salvo of bombs bracketed the lead boat, blowing a hole in her bottom, killing three of her crew, and wounding four, one of whom was Goodall, who was hit in both feet. It was an uneven battle which they could not hope to win, so Goodall ordered the two remaining boats beached, permitting the survivors to scramble for safety among the rocks.

After shooting up the beached boats and making several unsuccessful strafing runs on the survivors, the enemy planes flew away. Once the danger had passed, the *Canopus* men improvised crude stretchers and carried their wounded comrades over the rugged jungle terrain until the exhausted little group eventually came to the west coast road. There, they were able to flag down an army truck and get a ride back to Mariveles.

The "Mickey Mouse fleet" was no more, and, with the army having mounted guns along the exposed China Sea side of Bataan to hold off any more landings, the Navy Battalion was designated "T" Company and incorporated into the Fourth Marines. On 16 February 1942, "T" Company, along with their "leatherneck" fighting mates, was moved to Corregidor to man guns defending the beach approaches to the island fortress. There were 130 *Canopus* sailors in "T" Company, all of whom still had visions of the Old Lady steaming south to join the fleet. As they boarded boats, Corregidor-bound, they threatened their shipmates with dire consequences, should they steam off leaving them behind.

Very little bombing of the Corregidor and Mariveles area occurred between 11 February and 23 March 1942, and it was generally believed that the enemy had changed tactics from seeking a clear-cut military victory to one of starving the Filipino and American troops into submission. Actually, the lull resulted from the stinging reverses suffered by the Japanese on Bataan early in February, coupled with their diverting men and equipment from the Philippines for the all-out offensive to capture Singapore and the Netherlands East Indies. In any event, throughout that period, the machine shops on board the *Canopus* never ceased to hum with activity during the hours of darkness.

With her amply-stocked refrigerators in operating order, the Old Lady served up ice cream and sandwiches to any Filipino Scout, soldier, sailor, or marine who managed a half-way plausible excuse to come on board. Until near the end, when the food ran out, the ship was a haven and, as Commander Sackett wrote:

> Nearly every evening, Army officers and nurses who were able to snatch a few hours of leave from their duties, gathered on board the *Canopus*. We had refrigeration, excellent cooking facilities, and decent living quarters, which seemed heaven to them compared to their hardships in the field. To enjoy a real shower bath, cold drinking water, well-cooked meals served on white linen with civilized table ware, and the greatest luxury of all, *real butter*, seemed almost too much for them to believe. When these favored ones returned to their primitive surroundings and described these "feasts" topped off with ice cream and chocolate sauce, they were often put into the same "dog house" as the optimists who claimed to have seen a fleet of transports steaming in.*

During the last week of March, the Japanese launched an all-out offensive against the exhausted, half-starved defenders of Bataan and, every day, wave after wave of bombers dropped their deadly loads on Corregidor and the Mariveles area. Singly and in pairs, they kept up

*Sackett, "The History of the USS *Canopus*," pp. 17–18.

the pressure with nightly nuisance raids. Most of the navy's oil supplies, dispersed in small caches throughout the underbrush around Mariveles Harbor, were destroyed. Bombed-out water lines and power and communication lines required constant repair. The Old Lady herself was subjected to four more attacks, but she led a charmed life and the salvos exploded harmlessly around her.

The ferocious tempo of these attacks was maintained and it was hardly a surprise to men of the *Canopus* when, on 6 April, word came that the front lines were in serious trouble. Following days of murderous artillery fire, exhausted Philippine Army troops in the center of the line had given way, exposing to capture the crest of Mariveles Mountain. Unless the lost ground could be recaptured and that commanding position denied the enemy, the entire peninsula would be at the mercy of Japanese artillery fire. All available reserves were frantically thrown into the breach but the men, weakened by dysentery, malaria, and hunger, could not stem the onrushing enemy hordes. On the eighth it was learned that army forces on the eastern flank were in full retreat toward Mariveles, destroying ammunition dumps and stores of all kinds as they came.

To avoid certain capture or death, everyone on Bataan wanted desperately to fall back to Corregidor, which was considered impregnable. The rock, however, was overcrowded, and General Jonathan Wainwright, commanding all American and Filipino forces in the Philippines, issued orders which strictly limited the number of those on Bataan who would be permitted on Corregidor. About 2,000 persons, including all of the nurses and most of the navy personnel on Bataan, managed to reach Corregidor.

The evacuation had to be completed before dawn, when Japanese bombers could be expected to attack anything attempting to cross the 3-mile strip of water between Mariveles and Corregidor. It was a fiendish night. The ground constantly shook from the violent explosions of ammunition dumps, which hurled flaming showers of bursting shells high in the sky. Burning supply dumps for miles around cast a weird yellow glow over the slopes of Mariveles Mountain and, above all this madness, the rolling thunder of artillery fire coming ever closer grimly tolled Bataan's death knell.

Spurred on by thoughts of impending disaster, the men of the navy worked fast. They dynamited all tunnels to prevent their use by the enemy, blew up the Dewey Floating Dry Dock, which had served the Asiatic Fleet for so many years, and sank minor vessels that could play no part in the defense of Corregidor. All night long, they lugged to evacuation boats large quantities of machine guns, rifles, ammunition, food, and fuel urgently needed on Corregidor.

The submarine tender USS *Canopus* (AS-9), scuttled by her crew on 10 April 1942 to avoid capture when Bataan fell to the Japanese. National Archives, 1014614

In the midst of this feverish activity, a skeleton crew boarded the *Canopus* with the unhappy assignment to scuttle her and, in so doing, end forever her valiant crew's dream of steaming south to join the fleet. The proud Old Lady, whom the Japanese had not been able to finish off, was able to back out under her own power to anchor in 14 fathoms of water off Lilimbon Cove. Working with desperate abandon, the crew wrecked all her machine tools and valuable equipment to ensure that any enemy efforts to salvage her would prove futile.

When the wrecking crews had done their work and doors to all below-decks compartments had been opened to permit water unhindered access to all parts of the ship, the sea valves were opened. With volumes of water rushing into her guts, the USS *Canopus* soon took on a 10-degree list to port, whereupon the crew abandoned her. From a safe distance, the men sadly watched the slow death of their beloved ship. Lower and lower she settled until, with a final convulsive shudder racking her from stem to stern, the grand Old Lady vanished beneath the sea.

It was almost dawn when the last of the evacuation boats, three motor launches filled with weary *Canopus* men, pulled away from the docks at Mariveles. Hardly had they set for Corregidor when they were numbed by shock waves from a tremendous explosion. Undoubtedly, what had happened was that gasoline drums stored in one of the hillside tunnels broke open when the entrance was dynamited earlier, causing fumes in the corked-up tunnel to build to a massive explosive charge, which somehow ignited. When it blew, the entire hillside was engulfed in sheets of raging flame, and huge boulders ripped from the craggy slopes were hurled a half-mile out into the bay. Torrents of rocks and debris churned the calm waters into frothing, angry waves, and the three motor launches were caught in the midst of this diabolic barrage.

Boulders crashed down on two of the boats. One, her entire stern sheered off, sank instantly. Miraculously, no one on board was injured. The other lost an officer and three enlisted men when a boulder crashed through her canopy, and nine enlisted men were wounded. Although seriously damaged, this launch was still able to run, and her crew, overburdened with dead and wounded shipmates, assisted in the rescue of all hands from the sunken boat. A long hour later, both boats arrived at Corregidor.

The Old Lady was no more, and the savage battle for Bataan had been lost. For nearly four months the crew of the *Canopus* had fought with marked ingenuity to stave off a Japanese victory. The shattering of their cherished dream of joining the fleet so that they could more effectively use their skills in the war against Japan in no way dulled their determination to produce "beyond the call" when the chips were down. Now, they were faced with another last-ditch battle. The Battle for Corregidor.

Oddly enough, these *Canopus* sailors had come to be considered "seasoned troops" and, as such, were thrust into the outer defenses where, with the marines, they manned machine guns and automatic rifles to defend the beaches. When Corregidor's big guns and defensive positions were finally blasted into bloody rubble and the Japanese launched their decisive assault on the "rock," men of the *Canopus* were in the thick of the fighting. Many were killed or wounded. The survivors, captured by the Japanese, spent three and one-half terrible years in prisoner-of-war camps, where more died of disease and malnutrition.

For navy men, particularly submariners, the stirring saga of the USS *Canopus*, like the star of the first magnitude for which she was named, will shine forever in the galaxy of naval history, a proud beacon for all to see.

# 11

# THE *S-38* IN LINGAYEN GULF

On 21 December 1941, the submarine *Stingray* sounded the alarm. A massive Japanese invasion force, under cover of fighter planes, was landing on the shores of Lingayen Gulf, midway up the west coast of Luzon. From the very beginning of the war, a landing in that area, about 100 miles from Manila, had been anticipated. However, Japanese dominance of the skies over the Philippines having driven the PBY seaplanes of the Asiatic Fleet's Patrol Wing 10 south to the Malay barrier and destroyed the army's Far East Air Force, any hope of air reconnaissance had been eliminated. For this reason and because the submarine *S-36*, detailed to patrol the area, was having trouble with her radio transmitter and had to be recalled, the Japanese were able to hit the beach unmolested.

Had this enemy force of about eighty ships, which included cruisers and destroyers, been detected earlier, a strong pack of American submarines could have been mustered to intercept and harass it en route. But, with its faulty torpedoes, how much effect such a pack would have had on the first Japanese landing in force on Luzon is a matter of conjecture.

The *Stingray* did not arrive on the scene until after the enemy ships were safe within the confines of the gulf. Nevertheless, in a last-ditch effort to attack, the submarines *S-38, S-40, Saury,* and *Salmon* were rushed to the Lingayen area to join the *Stingray.*

It was practically impossible to attack the invasion fleet because, although the mouth of the gulf is some 25 miles wide, treacherous reefs protect almost half of it and numerous destroyers and patrol boats were guarding the rest. More than that, the overall shallowness of the gulf and its poorly charted depths made submarine operations extremely dangerous. A foray into it by the three big fleet-type boats would have been suicidal. Consequently, four of the submarines lay off the entrance to attack the only targets available—Japanese destroyers, while the fifth, the little *S-38*, commanded by Lieutenant Wreford G. "Moon" Chapple, entered the gulf.

"Moon" Chapple, a heavyweight boxing champion at the U.S. Naval Academy, was well aware of the dangers confronting him in Lingayen Gulf, but he was determined to get a crack at the enemy. His best hope of entering the gulf undetected lay in going through the area the Japanese believed no submarine would dare to venture—over the reefs. If the *S-38* was caught on the surface in waters too shallow for her to dive, it would be the end for her. Nevertheless, Chapple and his gung-ho crew decided to take the risk.

In the dark, early hours of 22 December 1941, Chapple, ably assisted by his navigator, Lieutenant (jg) Robert C. Fletcher, commenced working the *S-38* over the reefs. For three and a half tension-packed hours they cautiously maneuvered the boat through the perilous area and, just before dawn, she submerged in the no-less-dangerous waters of Lingayen Gulf.

Then at 0615, Chapple brought her up to periscope depth and, as the first rays of sunlight shattered the night, he surveyed the situation. He did not mask his delight at what he saw. The entire east side of the gulf was alive with Japanese ships. Unconcerned that two destroyers and numerous patrol boats armed with depth charges were patrolling like fierce watchdogs near the transports, Chapple slowly, ever so silently, inched his boat closer to his targets. It took him close to an hour to get into firing position, and all the while tension mounted as the crew, eager to score a kill, prayed they would get there without being detected. At last the moment of truth arrived. Chapple selected four fat targets and fired four torpedoes.

Seconds ticked by and, as the time for impact came and went, Chapple and his men looked at each other in shocked disbelief. How could it be? All four torpeodes had missed. Now, instead of the sound of torpedoes striking home and the noises of sinking ships breaking up, there was the ominous pounding of a destroyer's propellers racing every closer as she traced tell-tale torpedo wakes to their source.

Chapple dove the *S-38* as deep as he dared and headed east to escape the destroyer, whose exploding depth charges reverberated throughout the submarine and sounded somewhat like a boiler being pounded with a sledgehammer. With luck and canny maneuvering on his side, it took him only forty-five minutes to outwit the kill-bent destroyer and, while depth charges ripped up a far-removed area of the gulf, the *S-38* was stalking other prey.

To Chapple and his crew it seemed incredible that all four of their torpedoes could have missed. The range was easy, the targets were moving slowly. In all respects, the circumstances were ideal. What none of them knew or suspected was that their Mark-10 torpedoes ran several feet deeper than set. Believing he had miscalculated the draft of the targets, Chapple set his remaining "tin fish" to run at a depth of 9 feet instead of 12.

It was 0758. The *S-38* was within easy range of an enemy transport at anchor. Through the periscope, as he made ready to fire, Chapple could see enemy troops massed on the decks ready to disembark. In quick succession he fired two torpedoes. The first ran ahead of the target, but the second ran true. Fascinated, Chapple watched panic-stricken Japanese soldiers pointing to the approaching torpedo. All at once, a violent explosion jarred the *S-38*, as the 5,445-ton transport *Mayo Maru* blew apart and vanished into a watery grave.

The *S-38* spotted two enemy destroyers charging toward her. Chapple ordered a crash dive and had the boat rigged for depth charging. She went down until she hit bottom. In a matter of minutes, all hell broke loose around her as the avenging destroyers unleashed a furious barrage of depth charges. The old S-boat and her crew took a terrible beating as Chapple desperately maneuvered in one direction and another to escape the "pinging" destroyers. This was a dangerous game of blindman's buff because the submarine, having no sonic depth-finding gear, was forced to grope her way through the gulf's unknown depths.

All at once, for some mysterious reason, the *S-38* slowly began rising toward the surface. Her auxiliary tanks were flooded and she stopped just short of breaking into the clear, with 47 feet showing on her depth gauge. The tanks continued to fill and the submarine sank back to the bottom but, as she coasted forward, her nose plowed into a mud bank and she stopped.

With the waters above teeming with destroyers and patrol boats all dropping depth charges, some nearby, some far away, Chapple did not dare take the risk of giving his position away by making the noise involved in attempting to back out of the mud. He had no alternative but to order all machinery, except the motor generator on the lighting circuits, stopped. Lying silent in the deep, with the sound of depth charges hammering in their ears, all hands wondered to themselves whether they would eventually be able to break free of the mud or whether this was to be their final resting place.

The noise of high-speed propellers—probably destroyers or patrol boats on the hunt—continually approaching and receding could be heard on the sound gear and was so nerve-racking that Chapple ordered the sound man to turn his gear off and stow it. There was not a single thing anyone could do about it and, if they were going to die, what was the use of knowing exactly when?

Chapple called all his officers and chief petty officers together to discuss the situation. They decided that their best chance of survival lay in remaining absolutely silent until moonset, then attempting to break free. Accordingly, the whole crew removed their shoes, spoke in whispers, and were careful not to drop so much as a spoon for fear the give-away sound would be picked up by the enemy overhead.

Almost all day long, they heard depth charges exploding in various parts of the gulf, some too close for comfort. The noise of small boats passing overhead at regular intervals was judged to be caused by landing barges going to and from the beach. When larger ships passed over, the heavy pounding of their propellers reverberated throughout the boat. Their passing nearby caused the *S-38*, lying in shallow water, to rock back and forth and, when that happened, the sound of water sloshing in the control-room bilges seemed to mock the tomb-like silence in the boat. Chapple, faced with the prospect of many painfully long, anxious hours of waiting, broke out a deck of cards and started a game of cribbage in the control room. He hoped thereby to relieve tension and allay fears that he might be seriously worried about how he was going to get the *S-38* free of the mud, which he was.

Having no air-conditioning, the submarine soon became as hot as an oven. Men and machines began to drip and the decks became slimy with sweat and condensed moisture. Humidity thickened to an almost visible fog. From stem to stern, the boat reeked of perspiration, warm oil, and battery gases. Gasping for air, men sprawled on decks or moved like zombies to perform little tasks which suddenly became tedious. Soda lime was sprinkled throughout the boat to absorb carbon dioxide, but it did little to freshen the foul air.

After twelve punishing hours of lying on the bottom, Chapple decided it was dark and safe enough to attempt to surface. Exhausted men, reeling at the end of their physical tethers, manned their stations. Ballast was blown and, when the engines hummed in reverse, the old S-boat shuddered a bit then slowly pulled free. All hands were overjoyed by the ease with which they had come out of the mud but, as she backed, the *S-38* took a sudden steep angle down by the stern, and her port propeller hit bottom, knocking it off center. This unhappy turn of events caused the propeller to make a rasping noise as it turned, which jeopardized the submarine's chances of evading enemy destroyers.

No Japanese ships were in sight, and Chapple took the *S-38* to the surface. Hatches were flung open to air the boat and, with this new lease on life, the crew's flagging spirits were rejuvenated. For two hours the *S-38* slowly cruised westward on the surface using one engine for propulsion and the other for charging batteries. Then it happened again. A lookout sighted a destroyer heading their way at high speed. Chapple dove his boat in a hurry and the enemy ship passed without sighting or detecting them. One hour later the *S-38* again surfaced to continue charging her batteries. Anchored off Hundred Islands at dawn, Chapple made a stationary dive to remain on the bottom during daylight hours and give his crew a much-needed rest.

The S-boat surfaced at dusk on 23 December, and remained at anchor to complete the charging of her batteries. Once during the night she was forced down by a roving patrol boat which, fortunately, failed to sight her. By 0500 on 24 December, her batteries were fully charged and the *S-38*, although crippled, was again ready for battle. At 1127, Chapple sighted six large auxiliary-type ships some distance away and maneuvered so that he would be able to get among them when they anchored. Twenty minutes later, when he was at periscope depth and slowly closing in on his targets, a bomb or shallow mine exploded forward of the conning tower. The shock threw crewmen off their feet and knocked out both depth gauges in the control room. Instantly, Chapple dove to 90 feet and headed north, puzzling over the source of the explosion because the only destroyers in sight were several miles away.

The *S-38*, one of six S-class submarines assigned to the Asiatic Fleet's Submarine Squadron 20. Naval Institute Collection

Ten minutes later, the sound man reported one or more destroyers bearing down on them. Chapple stopped all machinery except that to the bow planes, which were used for depth control. At 1205, three depth charges exploded to port. Three minutes later, five more hammered the boat from starboard. At 1223, four more of the devils burst to starboard, followed three minutes later by another.

The *S-38* was taking a terrible beating, and the deadly depth charges were coming ever closer. Chapple, fearing that any second might be their last, took a desperate chance to escape and rang up full speed ahead on all motors. With her noisy propeller, the *S-38* did not have a snowball's chance in hell of eluding the Japanese. No sooner were her engines started than four more depth charges exploded to starboard. Instantly, Chapple ordered all engines and machinery stopped, and the *S-38* silently sank to the bottom. As she did, eleven more depth charges, in rapid succession, bracketed her. The crew, trapped in the cigar-shaped, iron hull, literally sweated it out and fearfully wondered just how much more punishment their old boat could take. Within a period of forty-eight minutes, twenty-eight depth charges had burst dangerously close to her, but her hull was still intact and her crew, although shaken both physically and mentally, was not about to say die. The Japanese destroyers and patrol boats seemed to have lost track of the submarine, for they could still be heard moving about in other areas.

By 1720, propeller noises had died away and, to the men silently waiting in the stifling heat as they had done the day before, it seemed as though once again they had outfoxed the enemy. No depth charges had been dropped on them for more than four and a half hours. From the control room came the word that all was clear. Just then, six depth charges exploded terrifyingly close, and battered submarine and crew unmercifully.

There having been no sound of propellers overhead for several hours, the *S-38* assumed that the Japanese, believing they had finished her off during their earlier massed attacks, had left a patrol boat anchored in the area to listen for signs of life. Hearing none, that boat dropped these depth charges for good measure as she secured for the night. A present from Santa Claus that Christmas Eve was nowhere in evidence. In fact, it was probably the most depressing Christmas Eve any of the men on board the *S-38* were ever likely to experience. At 2230, while the boat was submerged and running slowly on the west side of the gulf, there was an abrupt jolt, which all hands knew only too well meant they were aground.

The submarine was worked clear and Chapple, finding no Japanese in sight, surfaced near Hundred Islands, but the submarine's troubles were far from over. When she was riding high, Chapple gave the order to ventilate the hull outboard and the battery room into the engine room. No sooner had this started than there was an explosion in the after battery room. Chapple, who was on the bridge, raced below to find thick smoke pouring from the after battery compartment and yellow flames quivering in its gloomy interior. Two men had bad burns and a third, Chief Machinist's Mate E. C. Harbin, a broken back. Electrician's Mate Third Class Howard L. Buck, Chief Machinist's Mate Ross, and Chapple, quickly donned rubber boots and raincoats and went into the compartment to fight the fires and remove the injured men.

The explosion, thought to have been triggered by a spark when someone started the blowers before air had time to circulate and freshen the gaseous atmosphere, cracked several battery cells. As soon as the fires had been extinguished, electricians went to work to cut the damaged cells out of the circuit. By dawn of the twenty-fifth that work had been completed, but the S-38 had lost half of her submerged power. That loss, coupled with her damaged propeller, was going to make it exceedingly difficult for her to evade enemy destroyers. During the night, however, a happy note had been struck: a radio message ordered the S-38 to leave the gulf and return to base.

With daylight breaking and Chapple about to submerge, it was discovered that some of the gaskets on the engine-room hatch, which had been opened to air the boat, had rotted and the hatch would not close tight. While the hatch was being dogged down, a Japanese destroyer squadron came into view, heading their way. With speed spawned of desperation, the hatch was secured just in time for the S-38 to crash dive before she was sighted.

Not long after the destroyer menace was over, a pesky patrol boat picked up the sound of the S-38's defective propeller, and once again she became the target of deadly "ash cans." Chapple managed to avoid them and threw the enemy off his track by taking his boat deep but, for the third time, she ran aground. This time she was hung up on a mud bank with her bow angled 50 feet higher than her stern. Although it was very hazardous to move along the slippery, tilted decks to operate controls, every effort was made to break the submarine free. However, the slimy mud, with the suction of a giant octopus, seemed reluctant to relinquish its victim. After what to the men was an eternity of frustrating work, the S-boat slowly began sliding backwards.

Jubilant smiles of relief soon turned to brows furrowed in anguished disbelief. As though the crew of the S-38 had not been through enough hell for a lifetime, the old boat began to slip faster and faster down into the depths. With electrical power reduced by the battery casualty, it was impossible to stop the downward movement. When pressure gauges indicated that the boat was at 300 feet, 100 feet below her tested depth, and she was showing no signs of leveling off, all hands feared that the tremendous pressure to which she was being subjected would crush her like an eggshell. At 325 feet, her ballast tanks compressed, causing the battery-room decks to buckle, a terrifying signal that the end was near. At 350 feet, her steel plates groaning under the intense pressure and threatening imminent collapse, her downward movement suddenly stopped and she headed back up.

With her new-found buoyancy, the *S-38* moved ever faster toward the surface. Chapple did everything in his power to level off at periscope depth, but he could not stop her and, to the consternation of all on board, she broke the surface like a harpooned whale. He knew that, had this action been spotted by the enemy, every destroyer and patrol boat in the gulf would soon be on top of them, and he doubted his crippled boat's ability to survive much more depth-charging. A 360-degree periscope sweep of the gulf disclosed that, miraculously, there was not an enemy ship in sight. This being the happy case, Chapple kept the *S-38* on the surface and headed out on his projected escape route to the northwest.

An hour later, with the afternoon still young, lookouts reported what appeared to be two Japanese destroyers cruising about 12 miles distant on the seaward side of the reef. To avoid being detected, Chapple promptly "pulled the plug." The boat was barely submerged when she hit heavily on the bottom. Then, moving forward, she rammed into an underwater obstruction. The force of the collision shook the *S-38* from stem to stern, knocking crewmen in all directions, smashing the outer glass on gauges, and splintering paint on bulkheads. This was too much for Chapple. Neither he, nor his crew, nor his boat could stand any more of this underwater punishment. In spite of the two destroyers, he decided to battle-surface and, if he had to, make a running fight for deep water on the seaward side of the reef. This was a fortunate decision, because the "destroyers" turned out to be small auxiliary craft which did not even see the *S-38*.

Several hours later on that eventful Christmas Day, Lieutenant W. G. "Moon" Chapple and his courageous crew, having successfully worked the *S-38* over the reefs and out of Lingayen Gulf, were safe and Manila-bound. As darkness descended and cloaked them from prying enemy eyes, all hands were firmly convinced that the proverbial cat with nine lives had nothing on them.

The experiences shared by the officers and men of the *S-38* during the four torturous days they spent in Lingayen Gulf, welded them into a closely knit group and, as Rear Admiral W. G. "Moon" Chapple proudly stated, "We will all be like brothers to the end of our days."

# 12

# DISASTER AT JOLO

One hour before midnight on 26 December 1941, six U.S. Navy PBY seaplanes of Patrol Wing 10 took off from the seadrome at Ambon, in the Netherlands East Indies, as two, three-plane sections of "Vs." Each plane carried one and a half tons of demolition bombs and enough fuel for a sixteen-hour flight. Their mission—to bomb a concentration of Japanese cruisers and transports anchored off Jolo, in the Sulu Archipelago. It was to be a surprise attack at dawn.

The first section to climb into the darkness was led by Lieutenant Burden R. Hastings, the second by Lieutenant John J. Hyland. They were to fly independently during the night and rendezvous near their objective just before dawn. Throughout the 600-mile flight, they navigated, of necessity, by star sights. Radio silence was imposed, and no communication between planes was permitted. During the long moonless flight, the second section passed the first, and arrived at the rendezvous point ten minutes ahead of schedule. As they waited for the first section to come on and lead the attack as ordered, they circled, and the heavy drone of their engines alerted the Japanese, who quickly manned antiaircraft guns and scrambled land-based fighters that had recently arrived.

When the first section reached the rendezvous, Hastings led his planes straight toward the target area. The sketchy intelligence available led the Americans to believe that they would encounter resistance only from ship-based antiaircraft guns. Little did they know that the Japanese had ringed the hills surrounding the city with similar guns. As the lumbering, practically defenseless PBYs approached Jolo Harbor, the sky around them was suddenly pockmarked with puffs of black smoke from bursting shells and enemy fighter planes were boring in for the kill.

Hyland, flying his section at a prescribed long interval behind the first, watched with horror the cruel fate of his squadron mates. When he saw Hastings's lead plane plummet earthward trailing black smoke and orange flames and his two wingmen being attacked by Zero fighter planes, he correctly concluded that the mission could not possibly be completed. More Zeros, circling overhead, were about to attack and, to escape certain destruction, Hyland wheeled his section and headed, full-throttle, for home. To put it in the best possible defensive position, he dove his section to within 50 feet of the sea. This forced the Zeros to fight uncomfortably close to the water, but they nevertheless pressed home their attacks. Concentrated machine-gun fire from the PBYs shot down one of the fighters and several others appeared to be damaged. Bullets ripped into all three of the seaplanes, but they managed to fight off the attackers until, by a stroke of good fortune, they became enveloped in a blinding rain squall. Ten minutes later Hyland and one of his wingmen broke into the clear to discover the enemy planes were nowhere in sight, nor was the PBY piloted by Ensign Leroy C. Deede. Attempts to contact him by radio proved fruitless. Apparently Deede's plane had been shot down but, having no way of knowing where, Hyland had no alternative but to keep going back to base.

It was a disheartening day. Only two of the six PBYs returned to Ambon, and they reported little likelihood of there being survivors from the downed planes. Patrol Wing 10 was composed of a group of officers and men who had shared many agonizing experiences together, and this was a crushing blow. Every man among them had lost at least one close friend in the disastrous raid.

Just as the second section neared the sanctuary of the rain squall, the Japanese fighters attacked the plane piloted by Ensign Deede. Projectiles tore large holes in his fuselage and wings, knocked out his port engine, and damaged his radio. But he kept the crippled "big boat" flying long enough to plunge into the squall and shake off the fighters. Then, his starboard engine, whose oil line had been severed, froze up. In the midst of a blinding rain, Deede skillfully made a rough, but safe, dead-stick landing in angry, wind-whipped seas. Instantly, all hands ripped up blankets, life jackets, and clothing, and plugged the numerous bullet holes in the hull. When it became apparent that the plane was not going to sink immediately, they turned their attention to repairing the radio.

The following morning, when Ensign Duncan A. Campbell was out on patrol, he intercepted faint distress signals on the wing's operational frequency. Upon making contact, he found that the signals came from Deede, who gave him a rough estimate of the downed PBY's position. He told Deede, who was 300 miles to the north in waters controlled by the enemy, not to transmit any more but to guard the frequency. Next, Campbell asked wing headquarters for permission to discontinue his patrol and go to the rescue. Dangerous as this mission was, permission was instantly granted. Campbell then headed north and instructed Deede to transmit the letters *MO* for one minute every twenty minutes. This would permit Campbell to get a homing fix and, he hoped, prevent the Japanese from doing the same.

On board Deede's plane things were going to hell. Water was seeping through the plugged holes. All seven crewmen had been bailing without letup for almost thirty hours and, with the sea slowly getting the better of them, were on the verge of complete exhaustion. Water, 3 feet deep, sloshed around inside the hull and the battered "big boat" was about to capsize when, to the elation of all hands, they sighted Campbell's PBY approaching at wave-top level.

While Campbell landed and taxied alongside, Deede's crew fired their .50-caliber machine guns into their plane's hull and, as she settled into her watery grave, dove over the side to be hauled on board the rescue plane. The joys of rescue, however, were short lived. No sooner was the heavily burdened seaplane airborne than six Japanese fighters came into view several miles away. All eyes were anxiously fixed on the enemy until, interminably long minutes later, the planes flew off over the horizon. The rest of the flight to Ambon was routine.

When Lieutenant Hastings headed his section of three PBYs toward the target area at Jolo and unexpectedly ran into heavy antiaircraft fire from land-based guns and bullets from attacking fighter planes, he must have known it was all over. He was trapped. It was too late to turn back. With grim determination, he led his section toward the targets. Just as he released his bombs, Hastings's battered PBY burst into flames, and flipped over into a steep, spiraling dive to destruction. With their leader gone, Ensign E. L. Christman and Lieutenant (jg) Jack B. Dawley were strictly on their own. Beset with troubles of the devil's making, both pilots frantically maneuvered to complete their mission and, at the same time, survive.

Christman's first indication that he was being attacked by fighters was the sound of his own .50-caliber machine guns firing back in the waist hatches. Over the intercom he learned that two Zeros had singled him out. When one of them zoomed past his cockpit, rolled over, burst

PBY seaplanes similar to those flown by pilots of Patrol Wing 10, in "V"
formation. Naval Institute Collection

into flames, and spun out of control to the ground, Christman could
have yelped for joy with the thought that his gunners were shooting
true. But there was no time for that, with the antiaircraft barrage
threatening to blast his plane out of the air at any moment.

Well aware that to continue on the slow, horizontal bombing run
would be suicidal, Christman pushed the PBY over into a sharp dive
toward the ships in Jolo Harbor. His "big boat" shuddered as its
air-speed indicator moved past the red line. At 5,000 feet, he salvoed
all his bombs on a Japanese cruiser, then pulled out of the dive to head
for home. He did not have time to assess results or to look for Dawley
because a persistent Zero was still hounding him.

The Zero made all its firing runs from the port side, and Christman,
by manhandling the unwieldy seaplane in turns toward his attacker,
managed to break up several of them. Dogfighting was the last thing in
the world for which any pilot would consider using a PBY. Christman,
however, managed to hold his own for about twenty minutes, until a
projectile ripped a hole in one of his fuel tanks. Raw gasoline, which all
on board feared would explode at any given second, gushed into the
mechanic's compartment and out along the length of the fuselage.
Another projectile burst in the radio compartment, igniting gasoline in
the main body of the plane. The PBY was doomed. Could they land
before she blew up?

With precious seconds evaporating, Christman dove for a landing
on the Sulu Sea. Flames and heat forced Radioman Second Class Paul

H. Landers and Aviation Machinist's Mate Second Class Joseph Banquist, manning the machine guns in the waist hatches, to jump for their
lives. This was a risky thing to do because the plane was in a steep dive
at an altitude of 300 feet and there was no assurance their parachutes
would open quickly enough to save them. The third man in the waist
hatch area, Aviation Machinist's Mate First Class Andrew K. Waterman, could not join them. He was killed on the Zero's last firing run.

The fire raged through the plane, spewing searing heat forward
into the navigator's compartment and the cockpit. Christman, his
co-pilot Ensign William V. Gough, the navigator Chief Aviation Machinist's Mate Don D. Lurvey (who was also a pilot), and Radioman
First Class Robert L. Pettit were trapped. Although there was a hatch
above the cockpit, anyone attempting to use it in flight would be
chopped to pieces by the propellers directly aft of it. The four men
were forced literally to sweat it out.

With his plane blazing like a meteor and destined to explode, God
only knew when, Christman cut the engines and stalled it in for a
landing. With their clothing on fire, the men scrambled through the
cockpit hatch and dove into the sea. Ensign Gough's life jacket was so
badly burned, it was useless. When Chief Don Lurvey realized this, he
unhesitatingly swam back to the blazing plane, climbed on board, and
returned with a life ring. Moments later, the PBY blew up and sank.

All were burned to some extent, but Pettit was the only one in serious
condition; he had severe burns on his hands, face, and neck. There was
nothing to indicate any of the three men stationed in the after section
of the plane had escaped, so the little band of survivors struck out for
the only land to be seen, a small island about 14 miles away.

To make swimming easier, they discarded their bulky flight suits
and shoes, but their progress was hampered by Pettit who, because of
his painful burns, was forced to swim on his back. The others took
turns keeping him headed in the right direction. After swimming for
several hours, they seemed to have made little headway. Realizing
Pettit was in critical condition, Christman suggested that Gough, a
strong swimmer, go it alone for land and try to find a boat to rescue
them. From the sun, they judged it was about 1500 when Gough left
them. He was soon lost to sight, and the others continued their labor-
ious swimming.

Toward sunset, Pettit, concerned about impeding the progress of
his friends, tried swimming on his stomach from time to time. Soon
after dark, however, he vanished. Christman and Lurvey called out to
him, but got no answer. When they found his empty life jacket, they
surmised that the pain and exhaustion had become too much for

Radioman First Class Robert L. Pettit to bear, and that he had slipped off his life jacket and drowned.

Throughout the long night, as the two men swam on, Christman's burns became increasingly painful, forcing him on occasion to swim on his back. The following morning, with the tropical sun beating down on them, they became badly sunburned and very thirsty. The island was still many miles away and Christman, nearing the end of his physical tether, told Lurvey to go on without him. Lurvey, however, refused to desert his friend, and encouraged Christman to keep swimming.

The situation, as far as Christman was concerned, was hopeless, and he was about to end it all when Lurvey had an idea. He began to talk about women, beautiful women back in the States. He stoutly maintained that Christman and he had not yet enjoyed their rightful share of thousands of sexy, beautiful women eager and ready for love. This idea hit a responsive chord and crowded all other thoughts out of Christman's mind. He began swimming again with renewed strength.

Not long afterward, with the sun past the meridian to indicate they had been swimming for more than thirty hours, Christman and Lurvey were overjoyed to see sailing toward them a large outrigger canoe. The vinta, as the natives called it, was manned by several fierce-looking Moros, but the weary swimmers would not have cared if it carried the devil himself. Unsmiling and appearing anything but friendly, the Moros fished the two men out of the sea, and took them to a small island about 3 miles from Siasi Island. The Moros, convinced their captives were Germans, wanted to kill them, because there was a rumor that Germans, masquerading as American sailors, had gone ashore in Jolo and, before anyone knew what was happening, captured all strategic areas. This ruse, it was said, paved the way for Japanese troops to land.

Shoeless and unimpressively clad in their GI underwear, Christman and Lurvey had a difficult time trying to convince the sullen-faced Moros that they were indeed Americans. Tactfully, but forcefully, they argued for their lives. Finally, the chief of the village decided to check out their story with the Philippine constabulary on Siasi Island.

Escorted by armed Moros, Christman and Lurvey arrived at the constabulary post on Siasi late in the afternoon of 28 December. It was deserted except for a handful of soldiers who had remained because their families lived in the area. The others, fearing death at the hands of the Japanese, had scattered. The acting post commander, Lieutenant Fernando Brilliantes of the Philippine Army, soon identified them as Americans, and the Moros departed.

Lieutenant Brilliantes had some cheerful news for Christman and Lurvey. Word had come that there were some American airmen on two other islands. He did not know how many or who they were, but said they would all be brought to the post the next day. He then did whatever he could to treat his guests' burns and make them comfortable. After a meal of rice and boiled chicken, the two exhausted men lay down on army cots and fell into a deep sleep.

When Lieutenant (jg) Dawley, piloting the third plane in Hastings's section, began the bombing run, his plane was hit several times by flak, but damage was minor and none of his crew was injured. On the first attack by fighters, however, his two waist gunners, Aviation Machinist's Mate Second Class Earl B. Hall and Radioman Third Class James M. Scribner, were killed. The relief gunner, Aviation Machinist's Mate Second Class Evern C. McLawhorn, then manned both guns to fire whichever one would bear on a target.

The instant Dawley saw his section leader shot down, he, like Christman, realized that his plane too would be destroyed before completing the horizontal bombing run, and he dove the unwieldy PBY on targets in the harbor. He salvoed bombs on the largest ship he could find, a Japanese cruiser. Because of attacking fighters, Dawley was unable to assess damage to the cruiser or determine Christman's fate. Cannon and machine-gun bullets were ripping into his plane. Gasoline streamed from its ruptured tanks, rudder control was lost due to severed cables, and the starboard engine, hit by a cannon projectile, stopped running. Destruction of the plane by fire or explosion was only moments away, and no one could parachute to safety for they were only a few hundred feet off the water. Dawley's only hope was to land immediately while he at least had aileron control. He managed to put the PBY down about 200 yards off the south shore of Jolo, and, as he did so, it burst into flames. It was impossible to remove the bodies of Hall and Scribner, for the crew barely had time to dive over the side and swim clear before the fighters bore in to strafe the burning plane. It blew up and sank in a matter of minutes.

The survivors found themselves directly in front of a small Moro village, later identified as Lapa. As they swam toward shore, natives armed with spears and bolo knives rushed to meet them in dugouts known as bancas. The sight of this fierce mob prompted the survivors to resort to shouting, "Hello, Joe," a greeting commonly exchanged among natives and Yankee sailors throughout the Philippines. Once they had convinced the natives they were Americans, not Japanese, they were pulled into the bancas and taken ashore.

On the beach injuries were checked. Dawley, his co-pilot Ensign Ira Brown, and the third pilot, Aviation Machinist's Mate First Class Dave W. Bounds, were not hurt. Radioman First Class "N" "T" Whitford had a bullet nick in his back and one on his wrist. McLawhorn had bullet creases in both arms and legs, and a metal splinter imbedded in his left eye. The Moros produced a small first-aid kit to help the wounded, but they were sullen and uncommunicative, and the Americans were worried about what fate was planned for them. Their concern increased when Dawley's trousers, which he had shed to make swimming easier, were carried ashore by a native and returned to him—minus his watch, twenty dollars, a knife, and some papers. At the same time, he was told he would be killed if he did not surrender his .45 automatic.

They had been in the village no more than twenty minutes when a band of savage looking Moros arrived: their heads were shaved, teeth filed to points, and they were armed with spears and krises. Without hesitation they grabbed hold of the Americans and hustled them out of the village. They followed a jungle trail for about a quarter of a mile until they came to a large nipa house. Here they met a Mr. Namli Indangi, a school teacher who had evacuated his family from Jolo to this safer part of the island. With his limited command of English, Indangi acted as an interpreter. He informed the Americans that they would remain in the house until word of their presence could be taken to the deputy provincial governor who was in hiding somewhere on the island. He would decide what to do with them.

About noon, the attitude of the Moros changed noticeably for the better. They brought the Americans cool water to drink, and mats to rest on, and gave them some rice with broiled chicken. Because food seemed to be in short supply, the killing of a chicken meant quite a sacrifice for its owner, and this tended to assure them that the natives were not interested in harming them—otherwise, why waste a valuable chicken.

The mayor of Lapa arrived at the hut during the afternoon. He had conferred with a representative of the deputy governor, who informed him that Japanese patrols were working their way toward the village and were less than a day's march away. It was imperative that the Americans leave the island quickly. A vinta and crew would be provided to sail them to Siasi, a village 50 miles to the south on Siasi Island, where a constabulary post was located. Such a move fit perfectly into Dawley's plan. Their best chance of escaping the Japanese, he knew, lay in working their way south through the Sulu Archipelago to Borneo, where the Dutch would undoubtedly help them return to the wing's headquarters in Surabaja. They gratefully accepted the mayor's offer, and Dawley told him that to avoid detection by enemy aircraft, they would depart at dusk.

Just as the Americans were about to head for the boat, excited natives raced past the house shouting, "The Mundos are coming. The Mundos are coming." The Mundos, a savage, outlaw band of Moros, lived in the hills, but came down periodically to raid villages, kill, and plunder. With no time to lose, the Americans, accompanied by the three vinta crewmen, made a dash for the boat. Before reaching the beach, however, the crewmen deserted them to return to the village to defend their families. Dismayed but undaunted, Dawley and his crew continued along a small trail through a thick tropical jungle. Presently they came to the shore where they saw a small pier with a vinta tied up alongside. The vinta apparently belonged to a Moro fruit peddler who was about to get under way. As the Americans approached a small nipa house on the pier they were delighted to see the school teacher, Mr. Indangi, come out to greet them. When he learned of their predicament, Indangi quickly made arrangements for the peddler to take them to Siasi en route to his own island.

During the night the vinta drifted on a practically windless sea, and sunrise of 28 December found them no more than a precarious 20 miles from Jolo Island. With little or no wind throughout the morning, their progress continued to be negligible, but soon after mid-day a brisk, favorable wind sprang up. By late afternoon, they were only a few miles from Siasi when a vinta, larger and faster than theirs, was seen approaching. Up to this time, they had steered clear of other boats, because of the uncertainty of who might be in them. Now, they had no choice but to continue on course. As the two vintas passed close aboard, a man dressed in a khaki uniform jumped to his feet and began tooting on a police whistle and motioning for them to stop. As their vinta hove to, the unarmed Americans waited apprehensively. When the larger vinta drew alongside, however, they were elated to see a soldier of the Philippine constabulary, who greeted them with, "Thank God, you are alive."

Information had been received at the constabulary post on Siasi that some American aviators were in a native village not far away, and the soldier was on his way to pick them up. Now, he believed he had found them. But Dawley convinced him that they could not possibly be the aviators in question because they had come straight from Jolo. It was exciting to think that other squadron mates might have survived the raid, so, eager to find out who, the navy men transferred to the larger vinta and headed for the village.

Upon reaching the village they learned that two Americans had been there, but only two hours before, had been taken to Siasi. As it was getting late, the soldier suggested they sail to a larger village, named Laminusa, to spend the night. They reached Laminusa just after dark, and the Americans were escorted to a large nipa house in the center of the village. There they were cordially greeted by Arasid Alpad, a first lieutenant in the Philippine Army, Isaoani Chanco, a first lieutenant in the Philippine Army Medical Corps, and Judge Yusup Abubakar from Jolo. Doctor Chanco treated McLawhorn's and Whitford's wounds with the limited medical supplies available. He said the dispensary at Siasi was well stocked, and he would take them there the next day to do a more professional job.

The Americans gorged themselves on rice, mangoes, and scrambled eggs, their first real meal since they left Ambon two days before. The village was jammed with evacuees from Jolo, but sleeping quarters were prepared for them in the local schoolhouse. While they slept on grass mats on the floor, two soldiers of the Philippine constabulary stood guard outside. The next morning, Dawley and his co-pilot Ira Brown, using the school's globe and maps in a geography book, drew a chart of the Sulu Islands and the coast of Borneo. The chart would come in handy when they had to navigate those waters. Then, accompanied by Doctor Chanco and Judge Abubakar, they sailed for Siasi.

At Siasi's constabulary post, Dawley's group was elated to find Ensign Christman and Chief Lurvey. Although both men were very weak from their long ordeal and suffered painful burns, they struggled to their feet to greet their friends. Doctor Chanco wasted no time in opening the small dispensary and treating the wounded. He could not remove the metal splinter from McLawhorn's eye because he did not have the proper instruments, but he gave him some drops that eased the pain.

The Americans were quartered in an annex to the main constabulary barracks, where they enjoyed the luxury of bunks. At dusk, Lieutenant Brilliantes, the acting post commander, went off to spend the night with his family who, like all other villagers, had taken refuge from the Japanese in the center of the island. Three armed constables, Doctor Chanco, and Judge Abubakar stayed with the Americans.

They had been asleep no more than an hour when all were brought to their feet by natives shouting, "Americanos, Americanos." Hurrying to the main gate, they were amazed to see Ensign Gough and Radioman Third Class Landers being escorted to the post by Moros. Like Christman and Lurvey, they were suffering severe burns, mainly from the sun. While Chanco applied medication, the new arrivals recounted their experiences.

After striking out for help, Ensign Gough swam for more than twenty-seven hours before he was picked up by Moros. He was taken to an island where he tried to get the natives to go look for his friends, but they refused to do anything, saying the Americans had been picked up and were known to be on another island.

Landers, who was in the after section of Christman's plane, told how he and Banquist had been forced to jump from the burning plane and how Andrew K. Waterman had been killed by machine-gun fire. Banquist was badly burned and did not live long, but Landers, after many hours alone, was pulled from the sea by Moros and taken to an island where he found Gough.

Once the excitement occasioned by the new arrivals had subsided, everyone tried again to get some much-needed rest. A half-hour later, Dawley, the senior American officer, was awakened by Judge Abubakar shaking his arm. The judge excitedly told him that a sentry had just reported the landing of five vintas carrying thirty armed Moros whom he thought had come to plunder the stores and burn the constabulary buildings. Dawley awakened the others and gave them the disquieting news. Just then another sentry reported that there were actually fifty Moros.

The constabulary barracks, a large building with many windows, seemed too difficult to defend, so it was decided to make a stand in the dispensary, a smaller structure some distance away. Since no one had firearms, the Americans picked up clubs of wood and pipe, determined to fight rather than stand passively by and be murdered. En route to the dispensary, they heard that their three armed guards had taken off for the jungle.

When they arrived at the dispensary they found it locked, and Doctor Chanco suddenly remembered that Brilliantes had the key. With no place else to go, the group returned to the barracks, placed the injured on cots in the center of the room, and extinguished all lights. The able-bodied men took stations at windows and doors, determined to bash in the head of anyone trying to take them by surprise. All was silent. The Americans stood tense and ready.

An hour passed and nothing happened. Then three figures were seen approaching from the main gate. They walked straight up to the barracks door where Dawley and Dave Bounds stood ready. If the doctor had not recognized two of the figures and let out a shout, their skulls would have been pulverized the minute they entered the building. The two men recognized were Mayor Iman Lakibul Dugasan, and ex-Mayor Idris Dugasan, Moro headmen of Tapul Island who had brought Gough and Landers to the post.

Somehow the headmen had heard that the Americans were concerned about the fifty armed Moros, and had come to tell them not to worry as these men were from their own village. They had come to protect their mayor. For further reassurance, the headmen offered to spend the remainder of the night with them. But the Americans were suspicious. This could be a "Trojan horse" trick to get inside, but since they had brought Gough and Landers safely to the post, it seemed logical to assume they meant no harm. On the other hand, if trouble came, the headmen would make good hostages, so it was decided to let them stay.

The next morning, 30 December, Dawley and the others were anxious to get under way before the Japanese blocked their escape route. Their plan was to go to Tarakan in northeastern Borneo, where Dutch troops were still positioned. To get there required sailing some 300 miles southward along the Sulu Archipelago and Borneo's east coast. Although a vinta was put at their disposal, finding a crew took considerable searching and coaxing. This was understandable because throughout the archipelago the natives were in terror of the Japanese invading their villages.

Early that morning, Lieutenant Brilliantes sent out a call for contributions of food and, throughout the day, chickens, coconuts, canned food, and cigarettes trickled into the post. The canned food and cigarettes were, as Brilliantes slyly put it, "squeezed" from the Chinese merchants who owned the only food supplies. By late afternoon all was in readiness. Equipped with food, water, and medical supplies, which included burn ointment, the Americans boarded the vinta and departed Siasi, with the best wishes of their native friends who urged them to return with more planes and bomb the Japanese.

The journey's first leg would take them to the village of Batu Batu, about 70 miles to the southwest on the island of Tawitawi. Before putting to sea, however, they stopped at a nearby village to get additional rice. The village consisted of no more than fifty nipa shacks but, among the crowd that gathered when they tied up to a small dock, there was, surprisingly, one native who spoke good English. He introduced himself as Mr. Jesus, a Protestant preacher who had spread the Christian doctrine throughout the village, an extraordinary accomplishment in a region predominantly inhabited by Moslems.

Just before they shoved off, Mr. Jesus asked the helmsman to take the Americans past the chapel. Night had fallen. Not a breath of wind rippled the glassy, moonlit surface of the sea, as the outgoing tide drifted them slowly past the nipa hut which was the village chapel. All at once, those in the vinta were astounded to hear a chorus of voices singing a hymn to the accompaniment of a trumpet. The villagers had gathered to say good-bye with a song and a prayer. Although only three or four of the natives could carry on a conversation in English, the words of the long hymn were sung in perfect English. The warmth of this friendly gesture left nine very solemn American navy men adrift on the sea that night.

Dawn of 31 December found them with no wind, and a head tide. Since the native crewmen refused to paddle in the hot sun, the impatient Americans took turns trying to make headway. After four hours of strenuous effort with little gain to show for it, they conceded that the natives were right, rest in the daytime whenever winds and tide were unfavorable, and paddle at night. Accordingly, the vinta was anchored near a small island to await a change of tide.

In the afternoon the vinta got under way again and made good speed, thanks to a fair breeze and a following tide. By midnight, the Americans were many miles at sea, but were not unprepared for the advent of the new year. Before they left Siasi, Lieutenant Brilliantes managed to "squeeze" four small bottles of so-called brandy from the Chinese, and included them in their provisions. The stuff, a synthetic concoction, had a rancid taste, but it would do for the occasion. Having no way of telling time exactly, the men arbitrarily decided that, when the moon could be seen by sighting up the mast, it would be midnight. When that moment came, they drank to their loved ones, their shipmates, and the hope they would all be around to toast again in 1943. Then, in accordance with time-honored custom, they "dropped the hook" for 1941, and "weighed anchor" for 1942 by singing "Auld Lang Syne."

When dawn broke on New Year's Day, the vinta was off the south shore of Tawitawi. Approaching from the opposite direction was a lipa, an open sailboat somewhat larger than a vinta and with outriggers. The Americans hastily covered themselves with grass mats and lay still. As the lipa drew near, someone on board her hailed them in a native dialect. The Americans' one English-speaking crewman quietly reported that a man in the lipa was asking for news of Jolo. Peering from beneath his mat, Dawley saw a white man standing in the lipa. Figuring he was friendly and wanting to warn him against going to Jolo, Dawley told his helmsman to go alongside.

The white man was Father C. B. Billman, a Catholic priest stationed in Batu Batu, whom Brown and Landers had met there during prewar, advanced base exercises. Upon learning of the dangerous situation in Jolo, Father Billman wisely canceled his trip. He was eager for news and asked if he might ride the few remaining miles to Batu Batu in the vinta. The Americans, interested in sharing the priest's stateside cigarettes, welcomed him on board.

In Batu Batu, where they arrived in mid-morning, Father Billman's assistance was invaluable. He arranged for beds in the public hospital for McLawhorn and the three men suffering from burns. Everything possible was done to make them comfortable. Then the priest found room for Gough and Bounds in the home of the local judge, and took Dawley, Brown, and Whitford to his house to rest.

Dawley learned that Major Alejandro Suarez of the Philippine constabulary, the provincial governor of Sulu, was due to arrive that night. Believing the governor might have important news concerning the Japanese, and wanting the injured men to get what much-needed rest and medical attention they could, Dawley decided to await his arrival.

During the afternoon, Father Billman and a Filipino civil engineer took Dawley and Whitford on a food-foraging expedition into the interior of Tawitawi. Bouncing over dirt roads in an old truck, they told natives along the way to gather coconuts, bananas, papaya, and whatever food they could find, and deliver it to Batu Batu. They were especially fortunate to purchase from a farmer a "lanchon," or fat young pig, which was destined to be barbecued soon. Upon returning to the village, however, Dawley learned the bad news. The vinta and boatmen from Siasi had gone home without so much as a word to anyone in authority.

Governor Suarez and two of his officers, Captain J. Celis, Jr. and First Lieutenant R. L. Flores, arrived at the village that evening. The governor had been shot in the arm by the Japanese during the invasion of Jolo and had come to Batu Batu for medical treatment. Before evacuating Jolo, he was able to obtain detailed information concerning Japanese activities there, and was anxious to pass it along to Dawley, who provided the governor's first opportunity to get this news to the outside.

The governor stated that the defenders of Jolo consisted of 200 Philippine Army troops, only 120 of whom had rifles, and these were old Enfields many with missing or broken parts. From midnight until 0300, these men heroically resisted the landing of several thousand Japanese, armed with machine guns, mortars, and hand grenades, before being forced to retire to the hills. There, they were ambushed by the Mundos, who inflicted more casualties on them than the Japanese. Although the Mundos did not harm the governor, they robbed him and his officers of their valuables, and most of their clothing. Governor Suarez was positive that the PBY raid on 27 December sank one transport and left a warship burning.

When they awoke on the morning of 2 January, Dawley and his squadron mates were faced with a serious problem. None of the natives in Batu Batu could be persuaded to sail them to their next objective, the village of Sitankai on Tumindao Island, the southernmost island of consequence in the archipelago. The voyage was considered too dangerous. Besides, the men wanted to stay to protect their families. The Americans would have attempted to sail themselves, but no one would part with a vinta even though the governor personally offered to pay a good price for one.

When the only white man on Tawitawi, apart from Father Billman, heard of the Americans' plight, he came to the rescue. He was an old-timer named Stratton, reputed to be a former soldier who arrived in the Philippines with the U.S. Army in 1899 and stayed there. Stratton immediately set sail for a nearby island, where relatives of his Filipino wife lived. They, he said, would be willing to make the trip. He returned just before dusk with a fine big lipa and a reliable crew, and plans were made to depart at high tide the following morning.

On the morning of 3 January, while the lipa was being loaded with provisions, including eight live chickens, Dawley and Governor Suarez talked over plans for the trip. The best way to reach their destination, it was decided, was to sail at night directly across Sibutu Passage, the main shipping route between the Sulu Sea and the Celebes Sea, to the northern tip of Sibutu Island. The darkness would help them evade the prying eyes of any Japanese in the area. Then, following the west coast of Sibutu Island, they would proceed south to Sitankai. The governor gave Dawley a letter addressed to Deputy Governor Amirhamja Japal at Sitankai ordering him personally to make certain the Americans were safely taken to Borneo. He also gave Dawley fifty pesos to use in the event the deputy governor required additional persuasion.

The injured men were carefully placed on board and, just as the lipa was about to set sail, Father Bellman presented each man with a small wooden cross and said he would pray for their safety for the next thirty days. A large crowd, including the governor and others who had been so kind to them, gathered to see the Americans off. When the lipa pulled away from the dock the natives waved and the good father made the sign of the cross.

Stratton, who insisted on accompanying them, directed the crew to put into the village of Bongao, about 2 miles east of Batu Batu. Here he hoped to find an experienced native to guide them across Sibutu Passage, and south to Sitankai. They reached Bongao about noon, and the usual crowd of natives gathered to stare at the Americans.

Dawley and Stratton went looking for a navigator and, if possible, to buy some canned food. They stopped at a small Chinese store and, when the owner learned that Americans who had been fighting the Japanese were on board the lipa, he did everything possible to please them. Out of the dark interior of his store came cigars, cigarettes, canned beef, sardines, beans, crackers, cookies, and a case of beer. A table was set and, while the Patrol Wing 10 guests ate their fill, natives stood behind them fanning away the flies. To the Americans it was a delightful meal, and the Chinese owners of the store, who refused to accept a single peso, seemed overjoyed to be helpful.

Stratton succeeded in engaging a navigator, a shriveled-up old man who came from a small tribe of Bagio fishermen. Once warlike but now rather timid people, the Bagios live in their vintas, shunning the land as they move from one fishing ground to another. They are excellent seamen, and Stratton said the man he had found was one of the best.

They departed Bongao at twilight. When the lipa moved out of the bay's sheltered water, their Bagio navigator suddenly jumped to his feet and demanded silence from everyone. Although Dawley and his comrades thought the old man had gone bananas, they obeyed him. When all was quiet, he walked to the mast. Facing the wind, he waved a brightly colored cloth and, in a loud bleating voice, called upon his gods to send them a favorable wind. To ensure a safe voyage, he continued his weird ritual by leaning over the gunwale, patting the waterline, and giving the inside of the hull a resounding kick with his bare foot. He repeated this performance at the stern. Then, while sitting as far back on the stern as he could without falling overboard, he once again asked for absolute silence and forbade anyone to create disturbing influences while he chanted a long, eerie sounding prayer for good fortune.

Whether or not the ancient Bagio was crazy, no one ever determined. But, when he had finished his incantations, he took over the tiller and, with no navigational aids, steered a beeline course for five hours through the dark of night, heavy seas, and a strong wind to the north end of Sibutu Island, which could not be seen until they were practically upon it.

On the morning of 4 January the lipa put into the village of Sitankai, half of which was built out over the water. In spite of the early hour, word of their approach had spread. Most of the male villagers, armed with bolos and Moro krises, were congregated along a small dock ready to defend their village from foreign intruders. One brave lad paddled a small banca out to see whether or not they were Japanese. Upon learning they were Americans, weapons were sheathed and shouts of "Hello, Joe" were exchanged.

With their arrival in the southernmost island of the Philippine Archipelago, the Americans' primary concern was to get to Borneo. Their friend Stratton, having made good his promise to deliver them safely to Sitankai, would set out for home in a few hours. The old ex-GI's courageous assistance had been invaluable, and would never be forgotten. In fact, his action probably saved Dawley and his friends from falling into the hands of the Japanese.

Deputy Governor Japal was among the first to greet them, and Dawley immediately tried to negotiate with him for a boat. Although the atmosphere was cordial and Japal was sympathetic, he was not the least bit encouraging. He said no vintas or lipas were available, let alone crewmen willing to sail them to Borneo. With this disheartening news, Dawley asked whether they might be able to use a customs service launch which he heard was in Sitankai. Mr. Dias, the customs agent, was sent for, and he soon arrived with Judge Dominador, which put Dawley in company with the village's three leading citizens.

Mr. Dias explained that the customs launch, a 50-foot, diesel-powered cruiser, was available, but the Philippine Maritime Commission had condemned it after an inspection showed the hull to be more than 75 per cent rotten. He was expecting a letter authorizing him to destroy the boat, but it had not yet arrived. Dias was more than willing to let them look it over, and decide for themselves. The boat's engineer was called to take Dawley, Brown, Bounds, and Whitford on an inspection. True enough, the hull was rotten, but the vessel was afloat and, there being no alternative, they decided to make it do.

The Chinese storekeepers in Sitankai were even more lavish in their hospitality than those at Bongao. Only one of the three Chinese stores in the village was open, but the owners of all three contributed generously to the cause of feeding hungry Americans. As a result, having been provided with an ample breakfast, the nine survivors were also treated to a sumptuous noon meal of duck, rice, strange but tasty vegetables, fish, and a variety of sauces.

The contentment generated by a filling meal followed by cigars and coffee was cut short, however, when Mr. Dias returned with news that use of the launch was out of the question because its compressed air tank, essential for starting the engine, had holes in it and would not hold pressure. With this depressing news, Dawley once again approached Japal and pleaded for a vinta. Even when offered fifty pesos, the deputy governor insisted there were no boats of any kind to be had. Dawley then thought of stealing a vinta but, after considering the many risks involved, quickly discarded that idea. It had to be the launch, or nothing.

At about 1330 Dawley, Bounds, Brown, and Whitford went to inspect the launch again, this time to determine what, if anything, could be done. To get it started, the engine had to be turned over by 150 pounds of pressure built up in the compressed air tank. However, not only did this tank have five small holes in it, but it was crusted with rust. At hand were brass tacks, screws, solder, and a blow torch but, try as they might, the Americans, assisted by Mr. Dias, could not get the solder to adhere to the rust. They had hoped to have made repairs before 1730, the latest that day when tide and current would permit departure. But the deadline came and went with the holes still not plugged, and the tired men stopped work for the night. After they enjoyed another epicurean treat provided by the Chinese merchants, floor space for sleeping was found for them in various houses.

Early in the morning of 5 January, the Americans and the launch's three-man crew went to work trying to patch the tank. All morning long schemes were suggested and tried, but not until noon was the most likely fix ready for test. Wooden pegs, coated with white lead, were hammered into the holes and covered with pliable rubber from the soles of native shoes. On top of each rubber pad a wooden block was placed and secured by metal straps wrapped over them and around the tank. Wedges were driven between the tank and the straps to give maximum pressure on each block. It was a "jury rig," but it had to work—or else.

When the air pump was activated, anxious eyes were riveted on the pressure gauge. Everyone knew it had to register 150 pounds before the engine could be started. The gauge slowly began to climb. It passed 30 pounds, and was looking good. Hopes were running high when it passed 70, but they sagged when the gauge failed to rise above 80 pounds, and several of the plugged holes began spewing air.

The pump was shut down, and more wedges driven under the metal straps to hold the plugs more firmly in place. Again the pump was started. The pressure gauge rose to 100 pounds, and continued climbing. When it reached 140 pounds, all hands prayed the rusty tank would go the route without blowing up. The air pump labored as the needle on the gauge worked its way to 150 pounds. With fingers crossed, they tried to start the ancient engine. It emitted a few heavy wheezes, coughed, kicked over twice, and stopped. Far from discouraged, the men made minor adjustments to the engine, and built up pressure for another try. This time she wheezed, coughed, and continued to run as though glad to be alive again. A shout went up from numerous bystanders as the Americans, with smiles of joy smearing their bearded faces, congratulated each other.

Food and water were hastily brought on board and the entire village population assembled to watch the launch cast off. Carefully nursing the engine to a moderate speed, the little group of survivors, assisted by the three Filipino crewmen, headed their craft out of Sitankai Harbor, Borneo-bound. Their main concern was that the leaky, rotten hull would not hold together until they reached their destination, 160 miles away. Not the least of their worries was the fact that Japanese air and naval units were operating near northern Borneo preparatory to invading that oil-rich land. For that reason, they decided to make a dash for Tawao, roughly 60 miles north of Tarakan, in British northeast Borneo. This would minimize the number of daylight hours they would have to spend on the open sea. Furthermore, they suspected there were minefields in Tarakan Harbor, and information concerning the approach to them might also be obtained at Tawao.

Using the chart Dawley and Brown had sketched back at the Laminusa schoolhouse and the antique compass with which the launch was equipped, they chugged steadily on through the night. With the first rays of the sun, all hands were delighted to see the Borneo coast lying dead ahead. When they were able to make a landfall, they had to change course only slightly to the south; crude as their navigational equipment was, they were not far off course.

The small town of Tawao existed only to serve several rubber plantations in the surrounding area. As the launch approached the dock, its occupants saw three white men and a handful of natives awaiting their arrival. It was impossible for those on shore to know what to expect of the people in the vessel, for a wilder-looking gang of white men had never before descended upon Borneo. The nine survivors, dressed in cast-off Moro clothing, their faces obscured by scraggly eleven-day-old beards, and their wounded arms and legs patched up, were enough to make the so-called Wild Man of Borneo look like a boy scout. Realizing how grotesque they looked, Dawley hailed the white men on the dock and told them that, believe it or not, they were officers and enlisted men of Uncle Sam's navy.

Two of the men turned out to be English managers of rubber plantations, the third, a refugee German doctor. They were most cordial and quite amused at the appearance of the Americans. While the doctor examined and treated McLawhorn and the other wounded men, the plantation managers gave Dawley a chart and navigational advice for his journey to Tarakan, and cautioned him not to arrive at the minefield entrance before daylight because he might inadvertently hit a mine. After calculating how long it would take to reach Tarakan, Dawley planned to delay departure for about four hours. The plantation managers, however, grimly told him to leave Tawao as soon as possible, for a Japanese landing party was expected at any time.

News of the impending approach of Imperial Japanese forces was disquieting, to say the least, and the Americans decided to leave immediately. During the time the launch was at dockside, natives bailed large quantities of water out of the leaking hull, making her as seaworthy as she would ever be. When the pump was started, pressure built up nicely to 130 pounds, then it stopped. A plug was leaking. It took fifteen precious minutes to hammer more wedges beneath the strap and build up the required pressure. All the while wary eyes were kept on the harbor entrance for signs of the anticipated enemy. But the engine started on the first try, and the launch headed out to sea.

The voyage down the coast went smoothly as long as there was light enough to take bearings, but with darkness came trouble. Dawley decided to anchor off Bungu Island, which was as far south as they could safely venture before nearing the minefield. He calculated they would arrive at the anchorage at about 2200. However, there were indications that a strong current was moving the launch south faster than believed, and Dawley, not wanting to take any chances, now chose to anchor near the Borneo shore. Consequently, at 2000 he changed course.

With no navigational aids and riding fickle tides, it was impossible to determine in the dark, moonless night how far they were from the coast. Cautiously they groped their way southwest and occasionally west for about an hour until soundings indicated they were moving into shallow water. Soon thereafter, the low silhouette of the Borneo coast could be seen, and they dropped anchor in calm seas about a mile off shore.

Dawley stood the first watch until midnight, when he was relieved by one of the Filipino crewmen. The man was instructed not to let Dawley sleep more than an hour, but fell asleep himself. Sensing something wrong, Dawley awakened at 0300 to find the launch aground. Having planned to be under way well before that time, Dawley was furious. Now, nothing could be done but wait several hours for an incoming tide to refloat them. To add to their troubles, a rock or piece of coral had punched a hole in the launch's bottom. Although they plugged the hole with pieces of cloth, it continued to leak and compound the bailing problem. Three hours passed before the launch was refloated and under way.

The seventh of January 1942 was one day the nine survivors would never forget. At 1100 they came alongside the lightship marking the entrance to Tarakan Harbor and identified themselves. Much too exhausted to shout, they had to let their bearded faces, wreathed in grins, express their joy at being safe at last. The lightship master, a very cordial fellow, gave them American cigarettes, up-to-date war news, which they could have done without, and a pilot to steer them through the minefield. He also radioed Dutch officials in Tarakan to report their arrival.

When the little band landed at Tarakan, it was met by the senior Dutch Army officer in the area, who announced that arrangements had already been made to fly the Americans south to Balikpapan the next morning. After enjoying the luxury of a long-needed bath and shave, the survivors, dressed in clothing contributed by Dutch residents of the city, relaxed in easy chairs on the veranda of Tarakan's only hotel drinking gin and tonic. Somehow it was difficult for any of them to believe that what they were experiencing was real.

On the morning of 8 January, the Americans boarded a Dutch Dornier flying boat for the trip to Balikpapan, 300 miles to the south. Before taking off, they were informed that during the night the motor launch had sunk at her moorings. It saddened them to think of their old boat lying on the harbor's bottom, for she had served them well.

With one exception, the flight to Balikpapan was uneventful. Right after takeoff, just as they were comfortably settled in their seats, short bursts of machine-gun fire reverberated through the plane. This all-too-familiar sound instantly brought nine of the passengers to their feet. Other passengers, aware that it was only the bow gunner testing his machine gun, were amused at the Americans' knee jerk reaction.

Soon after arriving in Balikpapan, Dawley sent a message to Patrol Wing 10's headquarters in Surabaja, Java, requesting transportation. A quick reply advised that one of the wing's PBYs would pick them up the following morning.

On 9 January 1942, fifteen adventure-packed days after leaving their base at Ambon, the last survivors of the disastrous Jolo raid arrived at the Dutch military airfield at Surabaja, where happy officers and men of Patrol Wing 10 welcomed them back from the land of "missing in action."

# 13

# THE LITTLE
# GIANT-KILLER—
# USS *HERON* (AVP-2)

Three weeks after Pearl Harbor, when defeat after bitter defeat shrouded in gloom the spirits of Asiatic Fleet sailors, some sort of victory was urgently needed to bolster morale. On 31 December 1941, the most unlikely ship in the fleet, the little 900-ton seaplane tender *Heron*—all 175 feet of her—produced that victory.

Commanded by Lieutenant William K. Kabler, the *Heron* was stationed at Ambon in the Dutch Moluccas, when, on 29 December, came the news of another depressing setback: the destroyer *Peary* had been seriously damaged by bombs. In order to hide while making emergency repairs, the destroyer had put into a remote cove 300 miles to the north of Ambon, near Ternate in the Moluccas. Being the closest available ship, the *Heron* was ordered to go to the battered vessel's assistance.

Late the following afternoon, the *Heron* reached Ternate via the south passage only to learn that the *Peary*, made seaworthy by a supreme effort of her crew, had departed for Ambon via the north passage. On receipt of this information, Kabler immediately headed back to Ambon.

It was 0930 on 31 December 1941. The *Heron*, on a southerly course, was steaming in the Molucca Sea at 10 knots when a four-engine seaplane was reported approaching at low level. General quarters sounded and all hands instantly manned battle stations. Because the plane resembled a Sikorsky VS-42, a type flown by the Dutch, Kabler ordered his gunners to hold fire until positive identification had been made. With guns loaded and ready, all eyes strained to ascertain whether the big plane barreling in on them was friend or foe. A few hundred yards from what he judged to be the bomb-release point, Kabler detected red "meatballs" painted under the wings, and gave the order to open fire.

The *Heron's* two obsolete 3-inch antiaircraft guns and her four .50-caliber machine guns opened up with a blistering barrage, and some of the .50-caliber guns found their mark. Such an unfriendly welcome from what probably looked like a defenseless merchant ship must have stunned the Japanese, for the bomber abruptly veered away. After climbing much higher, it began a run from the port beam. While his gunners hammered away, Kabler steamed his ship at maximum speed—slightly more than 11 knots—and cannily maneuvered so that the bombs, two 100-pounders, exploded harmlessly 1,500 yards off the port beam. When the enemy circled to attack from the port bow, he again outfoxed the bombardier, and two more bombs fell 300 yards off his starboard bow.

For more than an hour the bomber harassed the *Heron* with real and fake bombing runs until a rain squall suddenly came up and blanketed the ship, giving all hands a welcome respite. But the squall ended at 1120, and the *Heron* broke into the clear to find the pesky flying boat sitting on the water a few hundred yards off her starboard quarter. As soon as they could be brought to bear, all guns opened up on the bomber, which took off like a scared duck and was soon out of range.

As were the commanding officers of all seaplane tenders, William "Bill" Kabler was a naval aviator. Furthermore, he was a qualified bomber and torpedo-plane pilot. When he saw the big seaplane circling his ship at a safe distance instead of flying off, he correctly guessed that reinforcements had been called to the scene and the *Heron* was about to be subjected to more determined attacks. Although he knew no planes were available to come to the rescue, he radioed his situation to commander, Patrol Wing 10. The *Heron* must face alone whatever fate had in store. For four hours she continued on course, all the while being shadowed by the enemy plane. Then, at 1520, Bill Kabler's fears materialized: six more four-engine bombers, flying in two three-plane sections of "Vs," appeared. One section moved directly in to attack from his port quarter. Kabler fixed it with a steady eye and, when it reached the bomb-release point, abruptly maneuvered his ship from her projected course, as twelve 100-pound bombs burst 200 yards astern.

Immediately, the second section attacked from his starboard bow and dropped six 100-pounders, all of which fell more than 200 yards to starboard. This time, as the bombers bored in for the kill, a shell from one of the *Heron's* 3-inch guns scored a direct hit on the outboard

The seaplane tender USS *Heron* (AVP-2), as she looked in the 1920s. National Archives, 80–G–466184

starboard engine of the right-hand plane in the formation. The sight of the big bomber, trailing black smoke, falling out of formation and retiring to the northwest brought a cheer from the *Heron*'s crew.

In a determined effort to finish off the little ship, the two remaining planes of the section wheeled and charged back from her port bow to drop four more 100-pound bombs. Although these fell uncomfortably close, they did no damage.

It was nearly 1600 when the seaplanes, their bombs expended, winged away. Just as it appeared that a terrifying encounter had at last been terminated, five twin-engine, land-based bombers came swooping in from the *Heron*'s port bow at a fairly low altitude. Until this moment the ship's .30-caliber machine guns had been outranged. Now, every gun on board went into action. Their fire was so intense and the *Heron*'s maneuvers so erratic that the attack was aborted, but not before several of the planes were stung by bullets.

For fifteen minutes or so, these planes licked their wounds as they circled at a safe distance, then made a medium-level attack again from the ship's port bow. As they came within range, the *Heron*'s gunners took up the fight. Although the .50-caliber bullets seemed to be scoring hits, the planes sped ever closer to the bomb-release point, posing a horrendous dilemma for Kabler. The ship's slow speed precluded his making the sharp turns and sudden speed changes required to throw off this determined attack. When he saw the bomb bays open and the ominous black projectiles tumbling toward his ship, Bill Kabler knew there was nothing he could do. Screaming like tormented souls, twenty

100-pound bombs rained down on the hapless little *Heron*. Miraculously, most of them missed, but three exploded 15 yards off her port bow and a fourth hit directly on top of her mainmast. Sickening tremors ran through the ship as she heaved and rolled with the force of the explosions. Death and destruction stalked her decks. Her port 3-inch antiaircraft gun was knocked out and every man in its crew was wounded, as were the crews of the port side machine guns. A lookout was killed instantly and another seaman mortally wounded. In all, the crew suffered twenty-eight casualties, almost half the ship's complement.

Damage to the *Heron* was considerable, but it was nothing compared to what might have happened had the bomb that hit atop her mast instead exploded in her guts. Twenty-five shrapnel holes, varying in size from 1 to 10 inches, pockmarked her port side forward from the waterline to the main deck. All three of the ship's boats were studded with holes and the engines of two of them were damaged. The emergency radio was knocked out, and there was considerable minor damage topside, including a stubborn fire in a forward storeroom which smouldered and resisted all efforts to put it out for nearly three hours. The battered *Heron* was still seaworthy and her sadly mauled crew was grimly determined to fight her to the death.

The harrowing task of tending the wounded got under way, while wary eyes kept track of the bombers circling the ship out of gun range. All hands dreaded another attack, but stood ready to meet it if it came. That eventuality, however, failed to materialize and, with intense relief, the *Heron*'s beleaguered crew saw the bombers suddenly turn and fly away. But their ordeal was not yet over. At 1645, even as the five land-based bombers diminished to specks in the distant sky, three more four-engine seaplanes were spotted streaking toward the ship at wavetop level. This was a torpedo attack, one plane coming in on each bow, and the third on the port quarter. All operable guns were manned on the double, some by wounded seamen who refused to stay out of the fight. Angry, rattling bursts of machine-gun fire and the rhythmic, sharp crack of the remaining 3-inch gun greeted the onrushing seaplanes. Bill Kabler, as he had done throughout the day, maneuvered his ship to take evasive action. This time, however, he was grimly aware that to avoid three torpedoes launched simultaneously from three directions was going to take more than skill. What is known in the navy as the "J," or Jesus, factor had to be cranked into the problem in a big way.

As luck would have it, the Japanese planes did not coordinate their attack and launched their torpedoes several seconds apart. Kabler turned, stopped, and backed his ship. The three torpedoes missed. They had come frightfully close, but the miracle was—they missed.

During the attack, the seaplane that approached on the port quarter was shot up by the *Heron*'s guns and forced to land. Thereupon, the pilots of the two remaining planes, their common sense probably overcome by anger and frustration, made strafing runs on the *Heron*. Their light machine guns did only superficial damage to the ship but, for their efforts, both planes were hit repeatedly by the *Heron*'s .50-caliber guns. One of them appeared to be seriously damaged, and both beat a hasty retreat westward.

When the sky was clear of enemy planes, Kabler maneuvered the *Heron* close to the sinking seaplane, which had been abandoned by its crew, and, with deliberate gunfire, blew it to bits. He then tried to pick up the plane's eight-man crew swimming in the sea, but they stubbornly refused to grasp the lines thrown to them. His ship being overburdened with casualties, most of whom were in dire need of shore-based medical treatment, Kabler had no time to spare. After making several earnest attempts to rescue the Japanese, he left them to their own devices and headed the *Heron* full speed for Ambon.

After eight punishing hours, the sky was at last clear of enemy planes and, with darkness enveloping her, the *Heron* was safe. A little giant-killer, if there ever was one, she had survived ten attacks by fifteen planes which unleashed forty-six bombs and three torpedoes. In the process, she had shot down one four-engine patrol bomber and so severely damaged several other planes that their ability to make the long flight back to base was doubtful. Overall, the outcome was a glorious tribute to the *Heron*'s crew and to her commanding officer, Lieutenant William L. Kabler, who, throughout the long torturous day, kept his cool and maneuvered his ship superbly.

The USS *Heron*'s battle against fearful odds was but a straw in the tumultuous winds of war, yet, to the anguished men of the Asiatic Fleet, it was a victory of magnificent proportions.

# 14

# A FIRST FOR THE NAVY

During the early weeks of World War II an unheralded adventure occurred in the remote Molucca Sea. Documentation of this strange affair is justified, if only to provide the exponents of "Navy Blue and Gold" with another "first" for the record books.

Lieutenant (jg) Frank M. Ralston was the pilot of a PBY seaplane that departed the seadrome at Ambon, in the Netherlands East Indies, at 0255 on 11 January 1942. His plane, with its crew of seven, was in company with three other PBYs of Patrol Wing 10 ordered to bomb Japanese transports anchored off Manado, on the northern end of Celebes Island. These slow-flying PBYs, woefully lacking in defensive armament, were being used as bombers because the Allies had nothing else available. To help them survive, this was to be a surprise attack at dawn.

During the 370-mile flight in the pitch-dark of a moonless night, the planes became separated. At daybreak, Ralston found himself 10 miles south of the target area with one of his squadron mates flying a half-mile off his starboard wing and the other two planes not in sight. While circling, in the hope the others would soon join up, the two PBYs spotted six Japanese fighter planes rapidly approaching. Before the Japanese could maneuver into attack position, both pilots dove their planes into the protective cover of a nearby cloud bank. By this action, they not only eluded the enemy, but also lost contact with each other.

Ralston and his crew soon had another problem. Without warning, their port engine sputtered, stopped, and could not be restarted. Unable to maintain altitude on one engine, the heavily loaded plane slowly sank earthward. At 5,000 feet, they broke out into the clear and found the Japanese fighters waiting, like hound dogs after a treed coon. To lighten ship for a climb back into the clouds, Ralston jettisoned his bomb load. The plane, however, continued its agonizing descent, as the enemy headed in for the kill.

On their first firing run, the Japanese slammed the lid on the coffin by shooting out the starboard engine. Although bullet after bullet ripped through the fuselage and wings, no one was wounded. Faced with disaster, Ralston dove his PBY for a dead-stick landing on the sea and managed to put the cumbersome seaplane down roughly, but in one piece. Without hesitation, the crew dove over the side, and frantically swam away from the plane, which the Japanese began riddling with machine-gun bullets.

One hundred yards from the PBY, the seven men, alone in a vast sea, watched with alarm as bullets chewed their plane to pieces. Fortunately, no attacks were directed at them. Nevertheless, they were in a most precarious position. They were many miles from land and had not the slightest chance of surviving unless they could retrieve the inflatable life rafts still in the plane. Miraculously, the PBY did not catch fire, and the Japanese, apparently convinced it was sinking, all at once flew away. This fortuitous turn of events enabled the crew to return to their plane.

Back on board, they found that they could not call squadron mates for help because their radio had been shot to pieces. One of their two life rafts had been shredded by bullets, but the other one was in perfect condition. While some of the men inflated and launched the raft, others hurriedly threw the secret bomb sight over the side and destroyed all classified material. With the plane rapidly sinking beneath them, the seven men crowded into the five-man raft and pushed away, bringing along a 10-gallon breaker of water and whatever canned rations they could find. They had gone no more than 20 yards, when the seaplane vanished beneath the waves.

From a chart they had salvaged, they determined that the plane had gone down about 60 miles east of Manado in the Molucca Sea. That meant they were about 90 miles north of the equator and a good 370 miles from their base in Ambon. The Japanese were to the west, and two small atolls about 30 miles to the east were the nearest possible sanctuary. Without debate, they headed east. All that day and night they paddled, striving to put as much distance as they could between themselves and the Japanese. At noon on 12 January, when there was no sign of the atolls, they stopped. They deduced that, despite their best efforts, wind and current were taking them to the southwest. The exertion of paddling under the equatorial sun made them so thirsty that they made no effort to preserve their water supply. Alarmed at how little water was left and pessimistic about how long they might have to be at sea, they began rationing both water and food. Each man was permitted three sips of water a day, and the daily ration of food was one can of brown bread and one can of baked beans divided among them all.

Someone had had the foresight to bring along a parachute, which they cut up to make a small jury-rigged sail and an awning. The latter, however, did little to prevent all of them from becoming badly sunburned.

The little raft drifted with the current through the twelfth, thirteenth, and fourteenth of January. Jammed together like sardines in a can, the men grew weaker by the hour. Whenever they saw Japanese aircraft in the distance, they camouflaged themselves by draping their blue dungarees over the raft to make it blend with the sea. Not the least bit encouraging, though, was the occasional sighting of a shark swimming in lazy circles around them.

The morning of the fifteenth found them without food or water. They began to pray for rain. They could live a few more days without food but, parched as they were, they could not survive much longer without water. Their prayers were answered in mid-afternoon, when they were struck by a cyclonic squall that lasted for several hours. By the time it subsided they had trapped almost 5 gallons of precious water. It had a strong rubbery taste, but it would sustain life.

At sundown excitement ran at fever pitch because they thought they saw land on the western horizon. All eyes strained to verify the sighting, but darkness came before they could be certain. Encouraged with the thought they were drifting in the right direction, they manned the sail continually and raised it at the slightest whisper of a friendly breeze. Around midnight, ominous black clouds blotted out the stars, and they were struck by an even more violent storm than the one that afternoon. Gigantic waves, some of them more than 20 feet high, crested over the raft and torrential rains, driven by screeching winds, drenched and chilled them. Clinging for dear life to the sides of the raft, the men fervently prayed that it would not capsize, as it crazily lurched and dipped in the churning sea. This terrifying ordeal lasted several hours until, just as suddenly as they came upon them, the wind and rain vanished and stars once again twinkled in the heavens.

At dawn on the sixteenth, land was sighted definitely many miles to the west, but treacherous winds were determined to drift them to the southeast. Despite their weakened condition, they paddled without letup all that day and night in one last attempt to survive. On the morning of the seventeenth, the weary men were overjoyed to discover their efforts had been successful, for they were no more than 10 miles from the shore. Not until mid-afternoon, however, after more paddling with hands that were blistered and raw, did the little rubber raft grate to a stop on the sandy beach. Having been packed together for almost six unbelievable days, the seven survivors stumbled ashore to find they were too weak to stand for more than a few minutes at a time. Gradually, they made their way up the beach where, beneath the shade of coconut palms, they lay down on the good earth to regain their strength.

From the chart, they figured they had landed on the north shore of Mangoli, one of the Sula Islands, about 100 miles south of the equator. This meant they had traversed a straight-line distance of nearly 200 miles in their little raft. However, the magnitude of their accomplishment did not dawn on them for some time.

As soon as the famished Americans felt able, they began walking eastward along the shore, and soon arrived at a small native village whose inhabitants gave them a hearty meal of rice, fish, and fruit. The natives confirmed that this was, in fact, the island of Mangoli, and advised the men to go to the town of Sanana, on the nearby island of the same name, where they could expect to get help from the Dutch. As night was falling, the tired men wisely decided to rest in the village overnight before setting out on the next leg of their journey. Just after sunrise on the morning of 18 January, they began to make their way across the island toward its south coast, where they hoped to find boat transportation to Sanana. The natives casually suggested the distance was no more than 10 miles, which was probably true as the crow flies, but it turned out to be closer to 20 on land, much of it over a 5,000-foot mountain. Only four of the crew had managed to keep their shoes. The others wrapped pieces of torn-up life jackets and flight suits around their feet. Walking over the rough terrain was difficult, and twelve hours of superhuman effort had passed when they staggered into a small native village on the south coast.

The village mayor was very friendly, did everything possible to make them comfortable, and promised that, the next day, there would be a boat to take them to Sanana, a distance of only 3 miles. After eating an ample meal, the exhausted men flopped down on the dirt floor of a native hut and fell asleep. They arrived at Sanana in a large native sailing canoe about noon on 19 January 1942. The Dutch controller, a Mr. De Santy, greeted them warmly and provided them with the good things of life—a place to stay, hot baths, shaves, haircuts, clean clothing, hot food, and cool beer. After sending a radio message to Patrol Wing 10 headquarters requesting transportation, Ralston and his crew relaxed in carefree comfort to await its arrival.

The next morning, the jubilant survivors were picked up by a PBY and flown back to their base at Ambon, where they were accorded a hero's welcome. Not until then did Lieutenant Ralston realize the significance of their adventure.

For centuries, men have been acclaimed and recorded in history for achievements beyond the ordinary—first to jump off the Brooklyn Bridge, first to sit atop a flagpole for thirty-three and one-half days, first to eat twenty live goldfish, and so forth. Ralston and his crew claimed to be the first seven men to cross the equator in a rubber life raft—at least in the Molucca Sea.

# 15

# THE BATTLE OF BALIKPAPAN

On 11 January 1942, Tarakan, in oil-rich northeastern Borneo, became the first Dutch city to fall to the Japanese. Targeted next was the more important port city of Balikpapan, 350 miles to the south, where, it was said, one had only to drive a stick into the ground to strike oil. The ease with which they had captured Tarakan, led the Japanese to assume that they would be able to overrun Balikpapan in similar fashion. They were in for a surprise.

Five days later, the Dutch Army informed Admiral Thomas C. Hart, commander of ABDA's naval forces (ABDAFLOAT), that a Japanese force of sixteen transports escorted by a cruiser and twelve destroyers was heading for Makasar Strait, apparently bound for Balikpapan. At the time, Hart's inadequate naval forces were thinly spread in three directions: British and Australian ships were operating from the Singapore-Palembang area westward to Ceylon; Dutch naval forces were committed to the Java Sea, or center position; and the Americans were responsible for defending the eastern flank, which encompassed the island of Bali and eastward to Australia. Because Balikpapan lay north of Bali, Admiral Hart called on units of his Asiatic Fleet to put a crimp in this enemy operation.

His strike force, consisting of the heavy cruiser *Houston*, light cruisers *Boise* and *Marblehead*, and eight destroyers of Destroyer Squadron 29, rendezvoused on 18 January 1942 in Kebola Bay, Sumbawa Island, to refuel from the tanker *Trinity* and to familiarize the ships' commanding officers with the operational plan. As outlined by Rear Admiral William A. Glassford, the force commander, the plan called for the

*Marblehead* and the eight destroyers to steam as fast as their tired boilers permitted and intercept the Japanese fleet off the northern coast of Celebes Island. They were to make a night attack with torpedoes. The role of the *Houston* and *Boise* was to steam 50 miles astern of the strike force, in order to cover the cruiser and destroyers if enemy pursuit should force them to withdraw.

American surface forces had not yet engaged the Japanese. Having been forced to stomach nothing but enemy victory claims since the war began, men of the Asiatic Fleet were tired of running away and of tedious convoy duty, and were spoiling for a fight. While they were refueling, a report received from the submarines *Pike* and *Permit*, which were scouting the northern entrance to Makasar Strait, indicated the Japanese invasion force was not moving toward the strait, as anticipated. This sour turn of events caused cancellation of the operation, and sent the assembled ships on their various ways.

Four days later, the Japanese moved toward Balikpapan, and once again Admiral Hart ordered offensive action. By this time, however, it was a whole new ball game. Instead of a strike force of three cruisers and eight destroyers as originally planned, only the *Boise*, *Marblehead*, and six destroyers were near enough to the scene of action to participate. But disaster struck this little force before it could go into action. The *Boise*, heading for the rendezvous through Sapeh Strait, hit an underwater rock, which slashed a long hole in her hull. With compartments flooding and salt water in her fresh water lines, *Boise* was forced to retire to the nearest port for repairs. In so doing, a destroyer was assigned to escort her.

Next, the *Marblehead* suffered a turbine casualty, which slowed her speed to 15 knots. To protect her from falling prey to enemy submarines, another destroyer was detached. It was now up to only four old "cans" of World War I vintage, the *John D. Ford*, *Pope*, *Parrott*, and *Paul Jones* to attempt the seemingly impossible. Confronting them in their effort to sink the transports were twelve modern destroyers, a light cruiser, and an undetermined number of armed auxiliaries. There was little solace in the thought that the *Marblehead* would now wait some 50 miles south of Balikpapan to fight off possible pursuers.

Although Glassford on board the *Marblehead* was in overall command of the operation, it was up to Commander Paul H. Talbot, commander, Destroyer Division 59 in the *John D. Ford*, to lead the attack. During the afternoon of 23 January 1942, as the four destroyers sped through the Flores Sea toward Makasar Strait, Talbot issued his orders for battle: "Initial weapons will be torps. Transports chief objective. Cruisers as required to accomplish mission. Launch torps at close range if unsighted by enemy. Each tube set for normal spread torps. Fire single shots if size of targets warrants. . . . Will try to avoid action en route. . . . Attack independently when targets located if necessary. When all torps fired, close with all guns. Use initiative and determination."

Talbot proceeded like a fox sneaking up on a chicken coop. During daylight hours, he steamed his destroyers at 25 knots toward Mandar Bay, Celebes, lying to the east of Borneo. His intent was to throw passing Japanese reconnaissance planes off the scent. Fortunately, the only plane encountered was a PBY from Patrol Wing 10. One hour after sunset, Talbot increased speed to 27 knots, and changed course to the northwest across Makasar Strait toward Borneo. The *Marblehead*, unable to make 27 knots, proceeded independently.

At 2200, in a move calculated to bring the flotilla in contact with the enemy off Balikpapan at about 0300, Talbot took a more northerly direction. Near midnight, lookouts reported that, many miles ahead, a light was stabbing into the starless sky like a beam from a ship's searchlight. It was seen for only a few seconds, then vanished. Some minutes later, the *John D. Ford*'s foretop spotter reported strange orange fires on the water about 30 miles ahead. They appeared to flicker and blaze up from time to time. When they became visible to Commander Talbot, who was on the bridge, he noted the sky in the general direction of Balikpapan was taking on a weird yellow glow.

While the darkened column of destroyers surged ever closer to the enemy, officers and men manning torpedo tubes and guns checked and rechecked their weapons to ensure readiness for instant action. Thirty minutes later, it was discovered that the flickering lights on the water were the burning hulks of several Japanese ships blasted hours before by American and Dutch bombers. To avoid detection, Talbot kept his flotilla well clear of them.

At 0230, on 24 January, the American destroyers were abreast the port of Balikpapan, where raging fires were clearly visible. The Dutch, it was presumed, were destroying oil tanks and other installations to prevent their capture. Thick black smoke hung throughout an area extending 20 miles into the strait, hampering visibility and hiding the onrushing four pipers from enemy eyes.

Suddenly, at 0245, when the destroyers were only minutes away from the reported position of enemy transports, a large Japanese warship burst out of the smoky darkness heading on an opposite course. Although the ships passed close aboard, they were moving so fast that no action was possible before they lost each other in the night. No doubt, the enemy mistook them for their own destroyers, for they certainly never suspected American ships would dare attack in that area.

The USS *John D. Ford* (DD-228), with Commander Paul H. Talbot on board, led the destroyer attack on Balikpapan, Borneo, the night of 24 January 1942. Shown here in August 1942. James C. Fahey Collection, U.S. Naval Institute

Minutes later, four Japanese destroyers crossed ahead of the American column from port to starboard. One of them blinked a challenge. Without replying, Talbot ordered an immediate change of course, and these ships too passed without incident. The Americans, ready to open fire at the least provocation, breathed sighs of relief because they were after more succulent targets. Another change of direction put them back on course to their objective. All at once, before anyone could believe their good fortune, Talbot and his destroyer captains found themselves in the midst of a pack of Japanese transports anchored about 5 miles off the entrance to Balikpapan Harbor.

Torpedo tubes had been trained out and ready for several hours. Now, torpedomen zeroed in on targets, and eagerly awaited the order to fire. The *Parrott* was the first to launch torpedoes. At close range, she sent a spread of three toward a large transport. All hands waited tensely for the expected explosion. Seconds ticked by. Nothing happened. Two minutes later, she fired five torpedoes at a sitting-duck target 1,000 yards to starboard. Again nothing happened. Simultaneously, the *John D. Ford* fired one torpedo at an anchored transport. It missed. The *Paul Jones*, the last ship in column, fired a torpedo at a cruiser or a destroyer that briefly loomed out of the night. It too missed.

Launching ten torpedoes against easy targets and not getting one hit was as infuriating as it was frustrating. Here were the first torpedoes fired in anger in the Pacific by highly trained destroyermen, and the scoreboard read zero hits. The destroyermen were not at fault. They, like their comrades-in-arms, the submariners, were plagued with faulty torpedoes.

The all-important element of surprise had been lost. Torpedoes missing or slamming against ships' sides without exploding sounded the alarm. Signal lights flashed, and enemy destroyers came racing to the scene. By this time, 0300, the Americans had passed through the pack of anchored transports. Undaunted, Commander Talbot turned his column back for another run. As the *Parrott* steadied on course, she launched three torpedoes at a target on her port bow. This time there was a mighty explosion, and the 3,519-ton transport *Somanoura Maru* went to a watery grave. Two minutes later, the *Pope*, *Parrott*, and *Paul Jones* fired torpedoes at another ship. Again there followed a tremendous explosion, and down went the 7,000-ton transport *Tatsukami Maru*.

Upon reaching the southern end of the anchorage, Talbot turned his flotilla for another run to the north. This time the destroyers were to proceed parallel to an inner line of transports. As they turned, the *Pope* and *Parrott* fired at what looked like a destroyer to port. Their torpedoes sank a large patrol boat.

By now the enemy force was thoroughly demoralized. The light cruiser *Naka* and the twelve destroyers, which could have chopped the four pipers to bits, misled into thinking they were being attacked by submarines, charged bone-in-teeth into Makasar Strait on a wild-goose chase.

The *John D. Ford* and *Paul Jones* launched single torpedoes at a good-sized transport, which was under way. These missed, but the next one fired by the *Paul Jones* struck home, and to the bottom of the deep went the 5,000-ton *Kuretake Maru*. When course was changed for a final dash through the transports, the *Pope, Parrott,* and *Paul Jones* reported "all torpedoes expended," and were directed by Talbot to resort to gunfire. The *John D. Ford* unleashed her last torpedoes at a group of three transports but was not able to determine the results. Then she, too, opened fire with her deck guns.

Like tigers slashing for the jugular, at point-blank range the old "cans" pumped shell after shell into Japanese ships with murderous results. Sinking and burning ships were all around, and hundreds of Japanese soldiers and sailors were swimming for their lives. According to Lieutenant William P. Mack, the *John D. Ford*'s gunnery officer, some of the sinking ships looked as though they were "covered with hundreds of flies," as Japanese soldiers swarmed in panic down their sides.

During this part of the engagement, shells from the *John D. Ford* seriously damaged and set afire the transport *Asami Maru*. Others tore into the 7,000-ton *Tsuruga Maru*, which exploded with a thunderous blast, sending deck plates and debris flying in all directions. The three other four pipers were wreaking havoc on enemy transports, which suddenly realized they were being attacked not by submarines but by surface ships, and directed their fire toward the destroyers' gun blasts.

Enemy shells erupted in the water around the four pipers, but the *John D. Ford* was the only one hit. A shell wrecked her after deckhouse and set fire to some ammunition. Courageous sailors rushed to throw the burning ammunition over the side and extinguish the flames. In less than a minute the fire was out. Unfortunately, four men had been wounded.

With a squadron of furious Japanese destroyers and a no-less-disturbed light cruiser about to descend on them, Commander Talbot ordered his destroyers to get out of the area. To put it mildly, the flotilla of American "cans" raced southward like the proverbial "bat out of hell." They hit the amazing speed of 32 knots, a speed at which their screws had not turned since their trials in 1917 and 1918. Behind them, what was left of a badly shot-up Japanese landing force, was outlined against the smoke-filled sky by fires burning on many ships.

When dawn broke, thirty minutes after the engagement ended, all eyes anxiously strained to pick up the first signs of the pursuit that was deemed inevitable. Enemy ships, however, were conspicuous by their absence. Confounded beyond reason by the devastating fury of this unexpected attack, and hard pressed to rescue the mass of soldiers and sailors floundering in the water, the superior Japanese naval force was compelled to forego hunting the phantom four pipers.

Throughout the battle a Dutch submarine commander was a silent witness. Lying off Balikpapan Harbor at periscope depth, biding his time to score a fat kill, he gleefully reported that, in a little over an hour, the American destroyers sank thirteen ships. Much too engrossed in fighting the battle to keep tally, the Americans claimed only six ships sunk. It is interesting to note that, before he left the area the next day, the Dutchman torpedoed a Japanese cruiser at such close range that the resulting explosions damaged his own boat, forcing him to remain motionless on the bottom until nightfall.

The four pipers scored an incredible victory. They were officially credited with sinking five ships for a total of 23,496 tons, but there is little doubt that they seriously damaged and probably sank several more. This daring and potentially suicidal attack, executed to perfection, was the first surface action by U.S. naval forces in the Pacific war. Though it only temporarily slowed the Japanese advance, the Battle of Balikpapan, fought by the men of the *John D. Ford*, *Pope*, *Parrott*, and *Paul Jones*, stands as one of the U.S. Navy's most valiant victories.

# 16

# THE MIRACULOUS
# SURVIVAL OF
# COMMANDER GOGGINS

The light cruiser *Marblehead* dropped her hook in Bounder Roads, a broad expanse of sheltered water that washes the northeastern shores of Java, on the morning of 3 February 1942. From the ships already lying at anchor, even a landlubber could discern that something of major proportions was in the wind. The heavy cruiser *Houston*, the Dutch light cruiser *De Ruyter*, the Dutch destroyer leader *Tromp* with three of her destroyers, and nine vintage American four pipers, with which the *Marblehead* rendezvoused, were virtually the only Allied fighting ships available to defend the Netherlands East Indies. There were, of course, a few other cruisers and destroyers, but they were stationed far to the west, in the Sumatra-Singapore area.

These were perilous times, and it was no scuttlebutt that massive Japanese air and sea armadas were gathering for an all-out assault on Java. In a forlorn effort to stave off the inevitable, this little striking force was ordered to make a surprise attack the following night on the transports of a large invasion fleet assembled at Makasar, on the southwest coast of Celebes Island. Because four American destroyers, blessed with incredible luck, had made a successful night attack on transports at Balikpapan, Borneo, less than ten days earlier, the Allied high command in Java calculated that a carbon-copy attack, with a larger force, would bring even more spectacular results.

Supporting Allied air power was nonexistent. Nevertheless, this "go-for-broke" operation was based on the premise that, if it was launched under cover of darkness, enemy bombers could be eluded. Completely ignored, however, was the fact that, to reach their objective, the ships would have to steam for a whole day without being detected by Japanese air patrols. If successful, this suicidal mission might delay Nippon's invasion plans by several weeks. If not—the consequences were not subject for discussion.

That night, under the command of Rear Admiral Karel Doorman of the Royal Netherlands Navy, the little fleet got under way. At 0930 the following day, it was moving through the Flores Sea when lookouts on the *Marblehead* shouted, "Japanese bombers approaching off the port beam!" Air defense and general quarters were immediately sounded.

At the time, Commander William B. Goggins, the *Marblehead*'s executive officer, was on the bridge with Captain Arthur G. Robinson, the commanding officer. In compliance with the air defense plan, Goggins left the bridge to take cover below decks, where he would be available to assume command should Robinson be killed or wounded. Upon reaching the main deck, he hurriedly inspected the starboard and port sides to make certain the stations were properly manned and men not actively engaged were lying down. By then, the *Marblehead* was maneuvering at full speed, and Goggins could see antiaircraft shells from the *Houston* bursting in the sky. The *Houston* was under attack by nine twin-engine bombers, and another nine-plane formation was zeroing in on the *Marblehead*, whose 3-inch antiaircraft guns opened fire. Goggins waited until the last minute, then scurried down to his station in the wardroom, where the muffled explosions of bombs that missed shook the bulkheads. He hated to be cooped up below decks because he desperately wanted to take part in, or at least witness, the action.

Lieutenant Edward M. Blessman, the *Marblehead*'s senior aviator, and Ensign C. H. Coburn were with him in the wardroom. The three men drank black coffee and chain-smoked cigarettes, as they listened to the crisp, seemingly endless, banging of antiaircraft guns overhead and felt the ship heel sharply in wild evasive maneuvers that made her old plates creak and groan. Occasionally, bombs landed dangerously close and sent violent tremors coursing through the ship, while fragments bouncing off her underwater hull made strange crackling sounds. Goggins was frustrated beyond description. For one agonizing hour, he sweated out the battle. Then word was passed that almost all the ammunition at the guns had been expended. Thereupon, in the vicinity of the wardroom, an ammunition party was formed to bring up shells from the forward magazine. Leaping at this opportunity to help remedy a serious situation, Goggins pitched in with the men to ensure that shells were passed along to the guns as fast as possible. The magazine was almost empty when all gunner's mates were ordered topside to help the exhausted gun crews set fuses.

All but one or two men had barely cleared the area when the *Marblehead* was violently jolted by a bomb hit on her stern. Sensing serious damage had been sustained, Goggins started to go aft. But, immediately on the heels of the first, another bomb crashed through the upper deck, then penetrated the main deck, and exploded 15 feet abaft the wardroom. The lights went out, and Goggins had a weird feeling that the entire after end of the ship was coming right at him. Nerve-numbing shock dulled his senses and permitted him no awareness of noise associated with the explosion. Something hurtling through the air struck him heavily on the left hip, knocking him to the deck.

Darkness, veiled in pungent smoke, made it impossible to see, yet Goggins was vaguely aware that the wardroom was cluttered with wreckage. As he staggered to his feet, intense heat, caused by the combustion of superheated gases, enveloped his body. Clothed in shorts and a short-sleeved shirt, he stood helpless as the skin on his exposed arms and legs blistered and burned. The searing gases made the paint on bulkheads and the linoleum on the deck sizzle and smoke. Fortunately, for some unexplained reason, his clothing did not ignite. All he could see was Signalman Douglas Murch, who was between him and the wardroom door. The doorway was choked high with debris, but Murch, followed by Goggins, clawed his way through it. Behind them the wardroom was a mass of flames.

Dazed and insensible to his condition, Goggins hurried to the bridge. He had to learn whether the captain was all right, and what damage the ship had suffered. He found the captain unharmed, but the ship in serious trouble. The bomb, which hit on the stern, had smashed the steering gear and jammed the rudder full left. With steering control gone, the *Marblehead* was steaming at 22 knots in a circle. Most Allied ships were keeping well clear of her, but the *Houston* moved in close to help fend off attacking bombers with her antiaircraft guns.

The ship's interior communications system had been knocked out, and it was impossible for the captain to learn what, if anything, could be done to regain steering control. Goggins took it upon himself to go aft and find out. On the main deck, he passed corpsmen desperately striving to relieve the suffering of burned and wounded men, and he noted with satisfaction that damage-control parties were hard at work extinguishing fires. A corpsman asked what had happened to the back of his neck. Goggins was not aware that shrapnel had gouged out a chunk of flesh just above the collarbone and his shirt was steeped in blood. Waiting impatiently as the wound was dressed, he vaguely noted that his arms and legs, from which cooked skin hung down in folds, were raw. For the moment, he was insensitive to pain. His own condition did not matter. All that mattered was the *Marblehead*. She had to be saved.

The corpsman urged him to lie down, but Goggins, insisting he was all right, refused. Working his way aft, he learned from a sailor that the steering engine room, adjacent to the hand steering room, was flooded with sea water and oil from a ruptured tank. It would be extremely difficult for anyone to get in there to attempt repairs.

Enemy bombers were still attacking as Goggins climbed the ladder to Battle 2 (the secondary command center just forward of the after 6-inch gun mount), where he hoped to communicate with hand steering. The power phones were out, but there was a voice tube from Battle 2 to hand steering. Goggins repeatedly called through it, but there was no reply. He soon learned why. The bomb hit on the stern had exploded in the hand steering room and all hands there were dead.

Goggins then went down number 3 hatch to determine what could be done to solve the steering problem. At the foot of the ladder, he came upon Dr. T. C. Ryan, who was dressing the wounded. When the doctor saw the executive officer's massive burns, he immediately began to spread tannic-acid jelly over them, but Goggins, stubbornly insisting that others were in more pressing need of medical attention, made him stop. Ryan tried to give him a shot of morphine, but Goggins, wanting to remain as alert as possible, would not permit it. The doctor then insisted he take at least two morphine pills to help relieve the pain. Reluctantly, Goggins consented, because feeling was returning to his seared flesh and he was in intense pain.

It was impossible for Goggins to examine the below decks damage in the stern because there were fires in the chief's quarters, and considerable debris was blocking the narrow passageway along which seamen were feverishly working to get at and extinguish the flames. Realizing that he would only be in the way, Goggins returned to the main deck, where his knees gave way, forcing him to sit down to regain strength. After a short rest, he slowly made his way forward and climbed to the bridge to report the situation aft. Dr. F. F. Wildebush, the ship's senior medical officer, happened to be on the bridge. He took one look at Goggins and recommended that he lie down. The commander vehemently objected, but Captain Robinson interceded and ordered his executive officer to go below and lie down. Dejected, Goggins retreated one deck down to the conning tower, where he would be on hand if needed.

As he arrived outside the conning tower, men of the forward damage-control party were coming out on deck from central, located just aft of the bridge and below the waterline. A near-miss on the port side had sent water flooding into several compartments, including central. Unable to exit through the regular hatch because of a fire above them, the men found their only means of escape was through a leg of the tripod mast that led up from central to an opening in the charthouse. Originally the hollow mast leg was large enough to permit easy passage, but it gradually became cluttered with wires and tubing, leaving barely enough room for a man to squeeze through. Some men didn't believe they could make it, but it was try or die. Fortunately, all of them managed to worm their way to safety. The last one out was Joe DeLude, the ship's corpulent tailor, who insisted on going last for fear he might be stuck and block the escape route for others. There were smiles of relief when DeLude, somewhat scraped up, tumbled out on deck.

Goggins entered the conning tower and sat down. His burns were beginning to pain him severely. To keep the sleeves of his shirt and legs of his pants from rubbing against his raw flesh, he trimmed several inches off both garments. Murch, the signalman who escaped with him from the wardroom and had also been badly burned, brought him a can of gun grease. This, Murch conceded, was not the prescribed remedy for burns, but it would at least reduce pain by keeping air away from them.

By this time, Japanese bombers, having expended their bombs, no longer harassed the ships. The *Marblehead* still steamed in a great circle and heeled over, while all hands worked frantically to save her. The fire over the steering engine room had been extinguished but the hatch to it, jammed shut by the bomb blast, could not be opened. Repair crews finally got into it by using acetylene torches to cut a hole in the deck. A hasty inspection of the flooded steering engine room revealed that both men on watch had been killed. Power lines had been cut, and oil transfer lines and steering motors were damaged beyond repair. It was then decided to drain the oil from the steering engine's starboard ram, a job that had to be done before the rudder could be brought back amidships. The drainage plug to the ram, under oil and water, had to be located and then turned by a large, heavy wrench. Men, working in relays under the ram, succeeded in removing the plug shortly after noon. Then, using chain falls rigged to the rudder yokes, the rudder was gradually swung amidships and locked in position. Once that was done the *Marblehead* could be steered by varying the speed of her engines.

The *Marblehead* was all but finished. Thirteen of her crew, including Lieutenant Blessman, who was standing only a few feet from Commander Goggins in the wardroom, had been killed, and more than thirty were badly wounded. The bomb hit forward on her main deck showered shrapnel over the entire length of the ship, and hot gases burned men from the vicinity of the explosion all the way back to number 3 hatch. Men taking shelter near number 2 hatch were burned and wounded by bomb fragments that hurtled 100 feet down the deck and turned the corner. Even a heavy safe in the post office was blasted open. Several decks in the forward part of the ship were flooded, and all officers' rooms on the lower level were inundated with oil and water.

Worst of all the damage were holes in the ship's hull. One of them, below the waterline, was about 10 feet by 13 feet. Through this hole, *Marblehead*'s forward compartments shipped great quantities of water, causing the bow to sink dangerously lower and lower. Her forecastle was barely riding above the waves and she was teetering on the verge of capsizing when exhausted sailors and their gushing pumps finally managed to restrain the rising water.

One other ship in the strike force, the heavy cruiser *Houston*, had been damaged. A 500-pound bomb destroyed her number 3 turret, killing forty-eight of her crew and wounding more than fifty. Although the bombers had gone, more attacks were a distinct possibility, and, since the element of surprise had been lost, the mission was terminated. The two damaged cruisers were ordered to Tjilatjap, on Java's south coast, to make emergency repairs.

It was a tribute to Captain Robinson's seamanship and inspirational leadership and his crew's superhuman efforts that two days later, the *Marblehead* arrived off the entrance to Tjilatjap Harbor. For forty-eight hours she had been kept afloat by pumps and bucket brigades. Steering the unwieldy, down-by-the-bow cruiser required absolute concentration. One false move and she would have gone under. This had been accomplished by slowing or speeding up port or starboard propellers on orders from the bridge, given over jury-rigged sound power lines to the engine room.

Tugs slowly towed the battered ship through the minefield and up the narrow channel to the dock. As she passed the *Houston* close aboard, a spontaneous, lusty cheer went up from the heavy cruiser's crew. In return, sailors on board the *Marblehead* cheered their counterparts in the *Houston*.

Commander Goggins had been immobilized since he first sat down in the conning tower. The terrible burns on his arms and legs became so taut that making the slightest move caused him excruciating pain. When the *Marblehead* docked, the most seriously wounded were placed on board a waiting hospital train and taken inland to a Dutch hospital. Although he fitted the "most seriously wounded" category, Goggins insisted on returning to the States with his ship. In deference to his rank, his wish was granted. He and several of the less serious cases were moved ashore to a small dispensary, where they were to wait until the

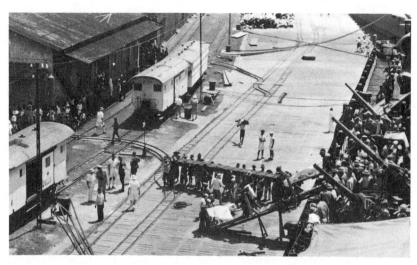

Casualties from the USS *Marblehead* (CL-12), bombed 4 February 1942 in the Battle of the Flores Sea, are carried ashore in Tjilatjap, Java, to a waiting hospital train. James C. Fahey Collection, U.S. Naval Institute

ship was ready to sail. Later, however, it was determined that the *Marblehead* was so badly damaged that it would be impossible to provide proper medical care for any of these men.

At 0800 the following day, Goggins and the other wounded were loaded into three field ambulances and taken to a Dutch hospital in Jogjakarta, 125 miles away. The nine-hour ride over rutted dirt roads in stifling equatorial heat was a miserable experience. Throughout the day, the ambulances rattled and bounced along, stopping only occasionally to give the wounded men a drink of water or a sandwich.

They arrived at the Petrinella Hospital in Jogjakarta late that afternoon. Formerly a mission hospital run by churches of the Netherlands, it had been taken over by the Dutch Army. Doctors and nurses were waiting and, as quickly as possible, the patients were taken inside for treatment. Before his wounds were dressed, Goggins was given a shot that mercifully put him to sleep.

When he awoke the next morning, 8 February 1942, Goggins found he was the sole patient in a pleasant room and was being attended by a Javanese nurse. Soon afterwards he was visited by Lieutenant Commander Croyden M. Wassel, a doctor sent by Admiral Hart to care for the wounded Americans. In the course of his conversation with Wassel, Goggins learned that all the *Marblehead*'s wounded, along with a few from the *Houston*, making a total of forty-one, were in the same hospital. What Goggins did not learn was that his condition was so critical that his chances of living more than a few days were considered slim. It was believed that at best, he might be able to walk only after many weeks.

During the days that followed, Doctor Wassel, who had taken up quarters in the local hotel, spent most of his time at the hospital with his patients. He was ably assisted by the Dutch medical staff of the Petrinella Hospital. These fine people, who were destined to be captured by the Japanese, did everything humanly possible to care for the Americans. That only one man died is a tribute to the effectiveness of their treatment. To the astonishment of everyone but himself, Goggins passed the crisis stage in a little less than two weeks and was on his way to recovery.

Singapore fell to the Japanese on 15 February, and, by the twenty-third, it was evident that Java would be next. From Dutch Army sources, Wassel learned that some Allied staff officers and as many important civilians as possible were about to be evacuated to Australia. He also learned from U.S. Navy headquarters in Surabaja that all American staff members there and at Bandung were preparing to move to Tjilatjap should the situation deteriorate.

Using Java's telephone system, with its native operators, was a mind-blowing experience for anyone who spoke only English. A lesser man might have given up, but Doctor Wassel hung on the line for several hours until he finally contacted the senior American naval officer in Tjilatjap. When the doctor explained that he had to get his patients out of Java, he was told to bring them to Tjilatjap as soon as possible, but to bring only those capable of withstanding a rough deck passage. The others, he was told, would have to remain in Java. Wassel had other ideas. He was not about to leave even one of his patients to the mercy of the Japanese.

On the morning of 25 February, the forty wounded men were put on a train for Tjilatjap. Ambulatory patients rode in a coach. The ten stretcher cases, including Commander Goggins, were placed in a small hospital car. All were jubilant at the prospect of going home. Not wishing to dampen their spirits, Doctor Wassel told no one that ten of them might not make it.

It was late that afternoon when the train rattled into Tjilatjap. No hospital facilities being available in the town, the doctor took his patients to a large house that was being used by American navy men stationed in the area. The stretcher cases were bedded down on cots placed on the porch. Wassel soon learned that the thirty ambulatory patients had been assigned to the tanker *Pecos*, which would sail for Australia on the twenty-seventh. His pleas to evacuate the stretcher cases were emphatically denied on the grounds that facilities on board available ships were inadequate to care for them properly. He was ordered to return these patients to Jogjakarta. When he was finally forced to break this disheartening news to the unfortunate ten, Doctor Wassel told them not to lose hope, for he would do everything possible to get them out of Java.

A train was leaving for Jogjakarta the following morning, but no hospital car was available. Since his patients could not ride in a coach, Wassel induced the Dutch to add a small freight car into which the men on their cots were loaded. The train arrived in Jogjakarta in mid-afternoon of the twenty-sixth. The next morning there were several air raid alerts. At the siren's doleful wail, hospital personnel put the patients under their beds, because it was impossible to carry them to the distant shelter. It was then that Commander Goggins realized he had little chance of escaping Java if he could not walk. With extremely painful effort he struggled to his feet and, to everyone's amazement, staggered a few yards before collapsing. In the few remaining days at the hospital, Goggins continued to take short, agonizing walks, which inspired others to do the same.

Doctor Wassel relentlessly pursued every possible avenue of escape for his patients and, on the twenty-eighth, was given a glimmer of hope. The U.S. Army Air Forces still had a few planes left in service and were evacuating senior civilians from a nearby airfield. A colonel promised that the patients would be taken out that night—if there was room for them. The doctor was instructed to remain by the phone so he could be notified the minute space became available. He alerted the patients to be ready to move at a moment's notice, and all hands waited expectantly. Throughout the long night the sounds of planes landing and taking off could be heard, but no call came. With the dawn, the last plane departed, leaving behind some very tired and disconsolate Americans. The patients appeared to be doomed to slaughter or capture, for now no trains were running, Japanese bombing and strafing attacks had seen to that. Additionally, the Dutch had blown up the airfield, and other means of transportation were said to be impossible to obtain. The situation brightened a bit, however, when Doctor Wassel fell heir to a Ford sedan abandoned by the U.S. Army Air Forces.

On the morning of 1 March, Wassel raced into Goggins's room and told him to get out in front of the hospital on the double, and not to ask any questions. There was no time to lose. When he had assembled all his patients, the doctor loaded as many as possible into his newly acquired sedan and drove them to the local hotel. He then returned for the others. This happened so fast that none of the men had taken time to put on clothes. Everyone wore hospital pajamas. Most had no shoes. This did not matter when they learned that the Japanese, having decimated the Allies' sea and air forces, had landed on Java. Land defense forces were said to have been routed.

Doctor Wassel's untiring efforts to find transportation for his charges had paid off at last. Near his hotel he had flagged down a British mobile antiaircraft unit which was en route to Tjilatjap hoping to be evacuated, and persuaded the captain in charge to take his patients with them. Space in two trucks was found for six of the patients considered to be in the best condition. Three others were placed on the back seat of the Ford sedan, and Commander Goggins sat up front with the doctor, who was driving.

The convoy set out about noon, moving along at no better than 20 miles an hour. Considerable distance separated the trucks to prevent too many of them being knocked out by a bombing or strafing attack. Bringing up the rear was the Ford sedan. To keep from being easily spotted by enemy aircraft, the convoy traveled along roads well hidden by trees. These back roads, rutted and rough, made travel exceedingly painful for the wounded. Occasionally, a truck broke down. If it could not be repaired, it was pushed off the road, doused with gasoline, and set afire so it could not be used by the enemy.

The convoy stopped for tea and food at about 1700, but Doctor Wassel, concerned that time was running out and determined to find a way to evacuate his patients from Java, kept going. He arrived at Tjilatjap at about 2230 and went directly to the Grand Hotel, which had temporarily housed Admiral Glassford's headquarters. Only the Dutch liaison officer, Lieutenant Schmidt, remained, and he told the doctor that he was too late. All the American ships had gone. He also mentioned that the British captain in charge of the battery had arrived a few hours earlier. With him was one of Wassel's patients who had somehow fractured his arm. This man was lucky to be taken on board the USS *Isabel*, just as she was getting under way.

Wassel was able to place three of his patients in a small Dutch dispensary for the night and, with the help of Schmidt, he obtained a room in the Grand Hotel for Goggins and himself. The hotel's name was a gross misnomer, for its facilities were more primitive than grand. Nevertheless, they were very fortunate to find room there, because Tjilatjap was jammed with civilian refugees and military personnel, all frantically trying to escape the Japanese, and most of them had no place to sleep.

Dawn the next day brought the fearful wailing of air-raid sirens. Enemy planes were seen overhead, but no bombs were dropped. Suddenly, outside the hotel there was a great commotion. Then several excited Dutchmen dashed into the lobby shouting that enemy para-

troopers had landed and everyone would have to fight. Goggins and
Wassel, having no weapons, were deeply concerned about this new
threat to their escape from Java. However, when the all clear sounded
an hour later, it was learned that the report of Japanese paratroopers
was false.

Doctor Wassel spent the morning trying to obtain space for his
patients on board a ship. He had no luck. Even worse, he learned that,
during the night, two ships loaded with evacuees had been torpedoed
off the harbor entrance, and only a handful of their passengers had
been saved. Now, with Japanese submarines lying in wait, the chance of
escaping by ship, provided they could get on one, appeared grim
indeed.

The British convoy, with the rest of the Americans, arrived at noon,
but one man, Hopkins, was missing. He had become very sick during
the trip and, unable to continue, was placed in a small Dutch hospital
35 miles away. Nothing could be done about it, but the British convoy
commander promised to get the man out, if it were at all possible.
Doctor Wassel gathered his eight charges in his hotel room and, at
about 1300, brought them some rice and stew. He then left with a
Dutch sailor named Gelarins, assistant to the Dutch liaison officer, in a
last desperate effort to obtain ship passage, perilous as it might be.

That afternoon Wassel returned to the hotel with exciting news.
The captain of a small inter-island vessel, the *Janssens*, had agreed to
take them along. How the doctor performed this seemingly impossible
task, while hundreds of people were begging and offering huge sums
of money to be evacuated, is not known, but his powers of persuasion
and unrelenting determination must have had something to do with it.
In short order the wounded men were put into a small bus and driven
to the dock. Before leaving the hotel, however, Gelarins gave them
three mattresses which he had thoughtfully confiscated, stating that, if
thrown overboard, they would float. Goggins had the impression that
the man honestly believed they would be needed for that dismal
purpose.

The *Janssens*, a 300-ton diesel-powered vessel, was overburdened
with refugees. On board were Dutch officers who had blown up the
naval base at Surabaja, British seamen from sunken ships, Australian
soldiers, prominent civilians, women, and children—in all, more than
600 pitiful souls. No bunks being available for the Americans, the
mattresses were placed under an awning on the refugee-packed after
deck, where the five seamen, four of whom were still stretcher cases,
were made as comfortable as possible. Doctor Wassel and the three
wounded officers, Commander Goggins, Lieutenant Arthur A.
Goodhue, and Ensign Coburn, were assigned space in a little combina-
tion smoking and dining room along with many more persons than it

could comfortably accommodate. No one, however, was disgruntled with his lot; all were thankful to have this chance to escape the hell descending on Java.

Soon after dark, the little ship got under way. As she headed out through the minefield protecting the harbor, the ugly prospect of being torpedoed was foremost in everyone's mind. There were not enough lifeboats, but everyone on board had been issued a life jacket. Off the harbor entrance, instead of submarines, they encountered a severe thunderstorm. The *Janssens* pitched and rolled sickeningly in the violent, wind-whipped sea, but the deluge of rain was a godsend. It lowered visibility to almost zero and helped hide the ship from the prying eyes of enemy submarines.

When dawn broke, Commander Goggins was alarmed to discover that, instead of being well south of Java, the ship was steaming eastward along the Java coast. He immediately questioned the captain about the advisability of continuing on such a course, and the captain replied that the Dutch Admiralty had advised him to proceed 800 miles to the east before heading south. By so doing, he would have a better chance of evading Japanese warships known to be lying in wait. The commander, keenly aware of what Japanese bombers could do, argued that because of the ship's proximity to land-based aircraft, her chances of getting through were not good. The captain thought otherwise, and the *Janssens* continued on course.

At 0930 everyone on board the *Janssens* was terrified to sight a large formation of Japanese bombers flying toward them. These planes passed directly overhead as they continued due west toward Tjilatjap without attacking. At this juncture, Goggins was more apprehensive than ever. True, the ship had not been attacked but, in all probability, its position had been reported to other flyers, who would be only too willing to do her in. One hour later, Goggins's fears were confirmed. As he and Doctor Wassel sat talking in the little dining room, an earsplitting racket brought everyone to his feet. Three enemy fighter planes had swooped in undetected and were machine-gunning the ship with explosive 20-mm. and .30-caliber bullets. Those who could, made a wild dash to find shelter below decks, where some protection was offered by the ship's steel hull. In the resulting confusion, Wassel tried unsuccessfully to bull his way aft to reach his litter patients. Later, he was relieved to learn that the men had been pulled beneath the protective cover of the overhanging upper deck. Goggins, whose arms and legs still caused him great pain with only the slightest movement, managed to drag himself down a ladder to the deck below.

Dutch sailors, manning the ship's two .30-caliber machine guns, fired away at the enemy planes. Fortunately, the attack was short-lived, but when the planes departed, eight refugees lay wounded, two of them critically. No Americans were hit, but the dining room where Goggins and Wassel had been sitting was riddled by bullets. All topside cabins and the bridge were damaged, but not seriously enough to put the ship out of commission. For many, the attack was the last straw in a long series of nerve-racking experiences. Some were hysterical and demanded to be put ashore. To accommodate them and to lie hidden for the rest of the day, the captain put into a small bay about 70 miles east of Tjilatjap, where he anchored the ship as inconspicuously as possible close to shore.

The most responsible persons on board met and decided that the *Janssens* should make for Australia, and that those not willing to take the risk would be sent ashore immediately. If any of the patients had wanted to go ashore, the doctor and Commander Goggins were prepared to go with them. However, all hands voted to go for broke and head for Australia. About 160 other passengers, convinced the ship was doomed, chose to take their chances ashore.

At nightfall the *Janssens* got under way. The captain, anxious to avoid encounters with Japanese land-based aircraft, now ignored the Admiralty's advice and put his ship on a southerly course away from Java. Yet, everyone on board knew only too well that, no matter what course they took, long odds were against them. The Indian Ocean, through which they steamed, was known to be crawling with Japanese submarines, destroyers, cruisers, and at least two aircraft carriers. Since the little ship, with only one diesel engine, could make no more than 7 knots, it was a waste of time to zigzag in order to evade submarines. Throughout the night, a brilliant tropic moon did nothing to allay fears of being detected by the enemy.

By the third day of steaming, the *Janssens* was almost 500 miles south of Java, and no enemy ships or aircraft had been sighted. An air of optimism prevailed for, if the ship could make it safely through the next 200 miles, she would be relatively safe from everything but submarines. All at once, however, there was serious trouble when the *Janssens*'s steering gear broke down. For two anguished hours the ship steamed in circles while attempts to repair the damage failed. The captain had no recourse but to shift from power to hand steering, a difficult and strenuous job for the crew.

On 11 March, when they were well down the west coast of Australia, lookouts shouted that an aircraft was approaching. All eyes were fixed upon the plane coming ever closer, and a joyous cheer went up when it was recognized as an American PBY seaplane. The first friendly plane anyone had seen in weeks, it circled the *Janssens* several times, then dipped its wings in salute and flew away.

The following day, Commander Goggins was sitting in the little dining room mulling over the past and contemplating the ship's impending arrival in Australia when his thoughts were interrupted by turmoil on deck. Alarmed, he hobbled out to see what was happening. Half a mile astern, a large black submarine had surfaced and was following the ship. To be sunk now, after surviving so much and with the escape trail's end so near, was an unbearable thought. The suspense was intolerable and the captain, determined to learn the intentions of the ominous black terror that seemed to be stalking him, abruptly changed course to the south. The submarine did not follow, but remained on course. Neither did it submerge when, a short time later, an Australian light bomber arrived on the scene and flew directly over it. That was all the proof those on board the *Janssens* needed; the submarine had to be a friendly one.

To some, Friday the thirteenth is an unlucky day. But to those on board the little *Janssens*, Friday, 13 March 1942, was a gloriously lucky day, one none of them would ever forget. On that day, the *Janssens* anchored, safe at last, in the harbor of Fremantle, Australia, having accomplished what many others had died attempting to do. Far behind them lay all the terrors of Japanese aggression and, for this, Commander Goggins and his men fervently thanked the good Lord and the indomitable Doctor Wassel.

# 17

# DELAYED REPORT OF A "ROUTINE PATROL"

It was a cruel joke to call scouting patrols conducted by PBY seaplanes of Patrol Wing 10 "routine." Hell, anything could happen on these flights, and generally did. On board the PBY-4 that took off from Saumlakki Bay, on Jamdena Island in the Netherlands East Indies, at dawn 5 February 1942, the crew of two officers and six enlisted men entertained no happy illusions. They had survived these routine patrols before. What's more, from the opening guns of World World II, they had seen the woefully inadequate air arm of the Asiatic Fleet chopped down from forty-four to a mere seventeen PBYs.* Little did they know that when this day was done Nipponese pilots would chalk off five more, including theirs.

Once airborne, the command pilot, Lieutenant (jg) Richard Bull, announced their patrol would take them 300 miles north to the southeastern tip of Ceram, then 350 miles west to Buru Island. From there they would beeline it home. Between Ceram and Buru they would pass over the former ABDA base at Ambon, on Amboina Island, now occupied by the Japanese, and unload bombs on a few transports reported anchored there. Opposition from fighter aircraft was not anticipated.

More than four hours passed to the monotonous, but reassuring drone of motors. Few words were spoken as all eyes incessantly searched for the enemy. Nothing had been seen even to suggest that Japanese forces existed in this part of the Banda Sea. Now, 40 miles out

*The original twenty-eight PBYs were augmented by eleven more from VP-22 and five from the Dutch.

of Ambon, tensions mounted as the engines, responding to increased power, droned louder, and the PBY laboriously climbed to 17,000 feet. At that, their maximum altitude, they would be beyond the range of antiaircraft guns normally carried by merchant ships.

Lieutenant Bull moved forward to work the bombsight in the nose section, and Ensign William Hargrave slid over into the first pilot's seat. Chief Aviation Machinist's Mate Oliver, also a naval aviator, assumed the duties of co-pilot. Minutes dragged by until breaking waves gave the first indication of a shoreline. The first ship sighted, a Japanese cruiser patrolling off the entrance to Ambon Harbor, was considered no cause for alarm. In fact, it was a good indicator that the transports they sought were lying at anchor inside.

Soon the entire harbor unfolded below them. To their astonishment, it was cluttered with ships—more than twenty of them, including two aircraft carriers and several cruisers. Merchant ships were forgotten as targets. Although they were bound to be within range of the cruisers' antiaircraft guns, the thought of knocking off an aircraft carrier was an exhilarating challenge Lieutenant Bull elected to accept.

The enemy contact report was quickly transmitted to commander, Patrol Wing 10, and Ensign Hargrave steadied the PBY on course to the target selected by Bull. Midway to the aircraft carrier, the surrounding sky erupted with black puffs of smoke from exploding flack, and shock waves buffeted the seaplane. It seemed as though every ship in the harbor was firing at them, but steadfastly the course was held.

Suddenly a more dangerous threat than flack was observed. Fighter planes, scrambling from an airfield, were racing to intercept them. Realizing that to continue on would be sheer suicide, Bull yelled at Hargrave to get the hell out of the area and into the protective cover of a large cloud bank to the east at 12,000 feet.

Hargrave immediately responded by manhandling the heavy-on-the-controls PBY into a violent, diving turn. Seconds away from sanctuary in the clouds, Zeros, approaching to port, opened fire. In a frantic effort to throw them off, Hargrave slipped the cumbersome flying boat toward and under the attackers. This surprising, unorthodox maneuver prevented the plane from being shot out of the sky on the spot, but as it entered the clouds, streams of bullets chewed jagged holes in the port wing and tail section.

They were no sooner safely hidden in clouds than the port engine, damaged by bullets, quit, and was quickly feathered. In an effort to maintain altitude and remain in the clouds, all bombs were jettisoned, but the altimeter continued to unwind. Now gasoline from a severed fuel line commenced streaming into the hull; its acrid fumes permeated the plane. Fearing an explosion at any moment, Hargrave shut

PBY seaplane of the type flown by pilots of Patrol Wing 10. National Archives 80–G–1791

down the remaining engine and turned off the radio transmitter to
prevent sparking. Long, anxious moments followed as Hargrave grimly dove the PBY beyond redline speed for a water landing.

They broke out of the clouds at 5,000 feet over the north coast of
Amboina Island. Fortunately, no enemy aircraft were in sight while
Hargrave made a dead-stick landing a half mile off the beach near the
native village of Hila. Safely down, all hands quickly prepared to
abandon ship. The pilots then learned that Aviation Machinist's Mate
Third Class Sharp had either jumped or been shot and fallen over the
side during the engagement. The tailgunner, Radioman Third Class
Cusack, was bleeding profusely from wounds in his right arm and left
leg.

While Lieutenant Bull destroyed the secret bomb sight and classified
codes, Hargrave administered first aid to Cusack, but was unable to
stanch the flow of blood. Because of the urgency of getting the wounded man to a doctor, a rubber life raft was hurriedly inflated and
launched. Cusack was lowered into it, then Hargrave, Radioman First
Class Nelson, and Aviation Machinist's Mate Second Class Muller
climbed on board. Lieutenant Bull ordered them to head for the
beach, saying he and the two men with him would follow in a second
raft as soon as they finished scuttling the plane.

The men in the raft were just shoving off when the unmistakable
high-pitched whine of a plane diving at great speed was heard. Looking up, the men were dismayed to find a Japanese Zero bearing down
on them. All at once, yellow flames erupted from its machine guns.
Deadly bullets, reaching for the target, kicked up a chain of nasty little

geysers in the sea, and then, with an awesome clatter, ripped into the PBY fore and aft. The three men on board never had a chance.

During the initial shock, the men in the life raft took refuge beneath the seaplane's starboard wing. As the fighter circled for a second pass, Hargrave, Nelson, and Muller dove into the water, and, towing Cusack in the raft, swam for their lives. They were not more than 50 yards away when bullets again ripped through the plane. This time there was a violent explosion. A hellish fireball shot high in the air, and the PBY vanished.

Where the plane went down, burning gasoline covered the surface of the sea and was rapidly spreading. Muller, who lagged 10 yards behind the others, was suddenly trapped in the flames. Hargrave and Nelson, towing the raft, managed to keep beyond the fire's reach. While the hapless men struggled to gain the beach, the heroic Japanese pilot, thirsting for more Yankee blood, made two strafing runs on them. This time his aim proved poor.

Hargrave and Nelson, who had escaped with only minor cuts and bruises, carried Cusack ashore. Then, hearing Muller's shouts, they raced back into waist-deep water to save him from drowning. Though he had severe burns all over his body and was in a state of shock, Muller somehow had managed to swim more than a quarter of a mile. Anxiously searching seaward, Hargrave and Nelson found no signs of their squadron mates. Only the diminishing fire, which still spewed oily black smoke into the sky, gave mute testimony to the mission's tragic end.

Friendly natives from the village of Hila gathered around the survivors, trying to help. Through one who spoke some English, the men learned there was no doctor available. The village "head man" offered them food and a small grass hut, and brought bandages and coconut oil to treat the injured. Cusack's wounds stopped bleeding and there was hope that he would recover, but Muller was in constant agony and unable to move.

Two days later, on 7 February, the natives found a body in the water which Hargrave sadly identified as Oliver, the third pilot. The natives buried him at sea. The next day they found another body, identified by Nelson as Aviation Machinist's Mate Bean. He too was buried at sea. Lieutenant (jg) Bull's body was never sighted.

Although everything possible was done to make Muller and Cusack comfortable, their failure to improve after four days was a matter of deep concern. It was imperative that all of them escape to the south, but the wretched condition of the sick men made this impossible. Neither Hargrave nor Nelson could stomach the thought of moving out, leaving their comrades to an uncertain fate, but something drastic had to done and quickly. On the word of natives that there were a few Australian soldiers somewhere down the coast, Nelson set out to find them in the hope that they had the urgently needed medical supplies.

During Nelson's five-day absence, Hargrave had the forlorn task of tending the wounded, who grew progressively worse. Muller was delirious most of the time, forcing Hargrave to be with him day and night. It was a heartrending task to stand helplessly by while comrades moved to the end of the line. Nelson's arrival did nothing to alleviate the situation. He had encountered and returned with a lone Australian soldier who had escaped a Japanese massacre at Ambon. The man had no knowledge of other soldiers or of medical supplies.

The situation was now desperate, not only from the standpoint of the wounded, but also in terms of the safety of the others. Japanese planes continually flew over the village, and the "head man" was apprehensive that he and his people would be caught sheltering them. Japanese reprisals for such activities were well known, and the results were ugly. Left with no alternative, Hargrave explained to the wounded men that their only chance lay in finding help at the Japanese Army hospital at Ambon. It was a long shot, but Cusack and Muller agreed to go and, that afternoon set out for Ambon in a canoe manned by natives.

Early the next morning, Hargrave, Nelson, and the Aussie began walking along the coastline hoping to find a village with a boat large enough to take them to Ceram. The Japanese had not yet landed on that island, and the Dutch were known to have several radio stations there which were still in contact with ABDA forces. If they could get a message to Patrol Wing 10, a PBY would be dispatched to pick them up. At least that was the hope which motivated them.

Two days later they came upon an Australian soldier lying in the shade of palm trees alongside a fresh water stream. He too had escaped from Ambon, but was suffering the chills and fevers of malaria. He begged to go with them, but his condition and the distance to be hiked made that out of the question. Hargrave and Nelson knew that powerful Japanese forces would soon overrun the lightly defended Dutch East Indies, and feared time was running out. Nevertheless, they decided to remain with the man until he gained enough strength to continue. Fortunately, when they left Hila they had obtained, along with food, a small supply of quinine pills, which they started administering to the stricken man. In four days he was back on his feet and ready to go.

Tired and hungry, the four men shuffled into a large Moslem village on the morning of 23 February, to be greeted by a friendly rajah who not only ordered food brought to them, but also promised transportation to Ceram. The men were anxious to continue on without delay, but the rajah insisted they rest during the day and travel at night to avoid enemy eyes. While they were resting, natives from Hila arrived by canoe with the sad news that Muller had died en route to Ambon. He had been buried by the Japanese who, it was believed, took Cusack to the hospital.

They headed out to sea at midnight in a large canoe manned by two natives. Everyone took turns paddling, and by dawn they had crossed 15 miles of open sea to land at a nondescript village on the southwestern tip of Ceram. The natives told them that no Japanese had landed on the island. The only radio transmitter they knew about was operated by the Dutch controller at Piru, about 100 miles to the north. Undeterred by the prospects of a long, hard trip through sparsely inhabited jungle, the little band of survivors was soon headed for the transmitter at Piru, with visions of rescue paramount in their minds.

They worked their way from village to village, walking long, sweltering miles and sometimes persuading natives to move them by canoe, and arrived in Piru three days later. Anxious to radio for help, Hargrave hurriedly contacted the Dutch controller, only to learn that the transmitter had been knocked out by Japanese bombers the previous week. Their best bet, he advised, was to go to Geser on Ceram's south coast where, if the local controller's radio was not working, they could probably obtain a sailboat. This meant a journey of well over 300 miles, part of it retracing their route. Dispirited but determined to escape, Hargrave and his three companions rested in the controller's house throughout the following day.

They left Piru on 26 February in a sailing canoe provided by the controller, who also gave them food, money, and a note addressed to all village head men instructing them to provide all possible assistance. They were put ashore 50 miles down the coast. Again they moved from village to village either on foot or in native canoes.

During this time Hargrave contracted malaria and a bad case of dysentery, which made the miserable journey all the more so. Late in the evening of 2 March, they arrived in the sizable town of Amahai. The nearly delirious Hargrave, who had lost all track of time, suddenly remembered it was his sister's birthday, and was concerned for fear she might be worrying about him.

The Dutch controller at Amahai took the men into his home and fed them well. He bolstered their spirits too by telling of a transmitter in the town of Saporua, a half day's journey inland. The following day, while the others rested, Nelson, who was the strongest, volunteered to go to Saporua and try to contact the wing. He arrived only to learn that the transmitter there had been blown up the previous day. But his trip was not entirely in vain, for he returned with money given him by the controller, and several large bottles of Dutch beer.

To regain strength, the men rested two days at Amahai. During this time they learned that most of the Netherlands East Indies, including Java and Sumatra, had fallen to the Japanese. To avoid capture or death, their only chance lay in heading for northern Australia, more than 1,000 miles to the south. They still hoped to be rescued, if only they could contact the wing. What they did not know was that Patrol Wing 10, with only three PBYs left, had been sent to southern Australia and radio contact was impossible.

The men left Amahai on the morning of 5 March in a canoe paddled by two natives. Carrying with them a fair amount of canned food and rice they had purchased, they were put ashore 20 miles down the coast at the next village to continue the journey on foot. Traveling along jungle trails and primitive roads proved slow going, for all of them became sick with malaria, dysentery, or both. On several occasions they were helped along the way by natives in canoes. It took nearly two weeks to cover the last 100 miles of the journey, a feat the men accomplished through sheer guts and a fierce determination to survive.

When Hargrave, Nelson, and their two Aussi companions finally slogged into Geser, twenty-one days after leaving Piru, they were at the absolute end of their physical endurance. They had existed mainly on rice and wild fruits. Their shoes were worn out, and their clothing dirty and torn. With long, matted hair and shaggy beards, their skin seared dark brown by the unrelenting sun, they were a sight to behold.

Twenty miles from Geser Hargrave and his companions had been joined by three more Australians who had escaped from a nearby island recently overrun by the Japanese. The seven men were welcomed by the Dutch controller who dejectedly answered their first question by reporting that his radio station had also been knocked out. This was disheartening news, but in other respects, their fortunes took a turn for the better. Although short of meat and other staple foods, the controller fed the famished men plenty of fish and rice. After bathing and donning clean clothing donated by the controller and the villagers, the men again found life bearable.

Fortunately, there was a native doctor in Geser who tended their blistered feet and ulcerous sores, gave them shots to cure dysentery, and quinine for malaria. Without this medical attention it is doubtful that Hargrave and some of the others could have continued. Capping their good fortune, the controller put at their disposal a fine 40-foot lugger manned by four native crewmen, saying they could keep it for as long as required, and the crew would sail it back.

With Japanese forces coming ever closer to Ceram, there was no time to relax, and the next morning the seven survivors sailed away from Geser for a 180-mile trip to Tual in the Kai Islands. There was reason for optimism, since a radio station at Tual was said to be still operating, making the prospect of rescue more promising than ever.

En route to Tual, they occasionally put into small island villages for fresh water and provisions. At one of these nameless places, a Chinese shopkeeper invited them into his home and served up a chicken dinner which they all agreed was better than anything they ever had tasted. Wherever they went the natives were friendly, and went out of their way to be accommodating.

They reached Tual on 27 March 1942 after a relaxing, uneventful voyage. The radio transmitter was in operating condition, but unfortunately the controller could communicate only with nearby islands. On the brighter side, the controller said, there was a ship in Dobo Harbor on Aru Island some 140 miles further south which was there to pick up Allied soldiers. He suggested they sail immediately, and he would radio ahead to hold the vessel until they arrived.

With reasonable winds, the trip to Dobo should have taken but two days. Instead, they ran afoul of contrary winds and high seas, and it took five days. At one point the winds shoved the lugger over a reef into a shallow channel where several times she ran aground on jagged coral. Holes were punched in the hull, and hand pumps had to be manned around the clock to keep from foundering. By the time they arrived in Dobo they were out of food and water. Worse than that, on the previous day the troop ship had sailed for Australia.

Dobo was a fairly large town where food and medicine were in good supply, but it had no radio contact with Allied forces. The men's only hope now lay in sailing through the Arafura Sea to Merauke in Dutch New Guinea, 500 miles to the southeast. Compounding their problem was the fact that following the ABDA defeat in the Java Sea battle, the Japanese had gained complete mastery of the air and sea throughout the entire Netherlands East Indies. A Japanese invasion of Dobo, considered inevitable, was likely at any time.

Holes in the lugger's hull were readily patched, and preparations were being made to get under way when a radio message came from Tual requesting they wait for six more soldiers already en route. To delay was dangerous, but all agreed to wait for the poor devils, whose objective was the same as their own. Two days were anxiously sweated out. On the morning of 3 April, an outrigger canoe finally sailed into the harbor with the six men on board. Four of them were Australian soldiers who had escaped from a Japanese prison camp at Ambon. The other two were Dutch soldiers from an abandoned outpost; they had joined the Australians at Tual. As soon as the new arrivals were on board sails were hoisted and the lugger headed out of Dobo Harbor, Merauke bound.

This leg of the escape route was calculated to last from ten to fourteen days. On board was sufficient food, on a two-meal-a-day basis, and water to last two weeks. Hargrave was elected navigator, a responsibility he assumed equipped with a hand-held compass and a small map he had found in a school house. Spirits were high as the lugger headed into the open sea, for the winds were perfect for a speedy and direct trip to their destination.

Two days out of Dobo their troubles commenced. The wind dropped off to a mere zephyr, and for the next two days the boat drifted with the whims of the sea. On the fifth day, fresh winds sprang up, but these came out of the southeast, the direction in which they wanted to sail. On top of that, one of their two 40-gallon cans of water was discovered to have sprung a leak and was empty. With only 30 gallons of drinking water remaining, it was immediately rationed to permit only two drinks of coffee or tea per man per day—one in the morning, one in the evening.

At the time, none of them realized the monsoon winds had changed for good. Hargrave suspected as much, but kept the notion to himself, hoping he was wrong. With the winds continuously blowing from east around to south, Hargrave set the course as near to east as they could possibly sail, confident this would bring them to the New Guinea coast, though well north of Merauke.

On the tenth day they ran into heavy rain squalls and high, surging seas. Although many were miserably seasick, the storms were a blessing, for water, cascading down the sails, was caught in every available receptacle, putting an end to that problem. Food now became their main concern. To conserve it, each man was allotted two handfuls of cooked rice daily. Everyone was out of tobacco; not to be denied, some men smoked cooked tea leaves and coffee grounds.

The wild New Guinea coast was joyously sighted on 17 April, but due to having been forced to tack on numerous occasions and storms that had blown them all over the sea, Hargrave hadn't the foggiest idea where they were. He reasoned, though, that by following the coastline south they would eventually arrive at Merauke.

The second morning of sailing along the coast, six canoes loaded with fierce looking savages approached close aboard. The natives were naked, and armed with spears and dart guns. They said nothing, but grimly paddled to keep up with the lugger, apparently assessing their chances of capturing it. About fifteen tense minutes passed with both sides silently eyeing each other. Fortunately, several of the soldiers still had their guns, and these were prominently displayed. Finally tiring of the game, two shots were fired over the bow of the lead canoe, and the natives, later identified as headhunters, abruptly turned away. This activity quickly eliminated any thoughts of putting into a native village in that area for food.

Hugging the shoreline, with no way of determining depth of water, the lugger occasionally ran around. Whenever this happened most everyone would jump out of the boat and push it off the bottom. One night about 2300 they ran aground and, before the lugger could be pushed free, the ebb tide went further out making their efforts in vain. When dawn broke they found themselves high and dry, with the shore more than 1,000 yards away.

When the tide started to flood, the boat was suddenly surrounded by schools of small fish, followed by swordfish 3 to 4 feet long. One of the native crewmen dove after them with a knife, bagging eight swordfish and a shirt full of smaller fish. Although others tried, not one of them caught a fish. That day and the next all hands feasted on flesh from the deep.

At high tide the lugger was finally freed, and on 22 April sailed into the Straits of Marianna, which run for over 100 miles along the southwest coast of Dutch New Guinea. Under normal conditions this stretch of water could be transited in a day, two at the most—but not this time. Soon after they entered the straits, the wind died to less than a whisper, and the men found themselves adrift on a glassy sea. Worse yet, a strong tide was pushing them back to the north. To prevent this, the boat was anchored to await a favorable wind. No wind came, but when the tide turned the anchor was hauled in to permit the lugger to drift southward with it. For five agonizing days, the last two without food or water, they were becalmed. Nevertheless, by drifting with favorable tides and anchoring when they weren't favorable, the men succeeded in moving the lugger through the straits at last to pick up a spanking breeze.

Parched, hungry, and desperate in the knowledge that to continue under such conditions was impossible, the survivors ran the lugger up on a sandy beach near the first native village they saw. Headhunters or not, they were determined to get food and water even if it meant a bloody fight. No sooner had they landed than a mob of practically naked natives rushed from the village toward them. Those with rifles held them ready for instant use, but, to everyone's relief, the natives were friendly. The natives brought them plenty of fresh water and sold them an ample supply of fresh fruit and rice. In addition, one native, dressed in the best tribal fashion—a large shell covering his manhood—agreed to guide them through the treacherous shoals en route to Merauke.

Two days later, on 29 April 1942, the lugger sailed into the harbor of Merauke, and a more ecstatic group of bearded, rag-tag men could hardly be imagined. There was even more joy in their hearts when the Dutch controller told them he was in radio contact with Allied forces on Thursday Island, off the northeast tip of northern Australia, a mere 140 miles away. He wasted no time in transmitting a message requesting transportation. Hargrave also sent a message addressed to commander, Patrol Wing 10, to which there would be no reply.

The cutter *Ran Paloma* picked up the hardly little band of survivors on 5 May, and two days later put them ashore on Thursday Island. On 9 May, Hargrave and Nelson went by boat to nearby Horn Island, where a Royal Australian Air Force plane flew them to Townsville, 500 miles down the northeastern coast of Australia. At U.S. Army Headquarters there, it was recommended that they report to U.S. Navy Headquarters in Melbourne, 1,200 miles further south. Although air transportation was promised them, no one could say when. Hargrave and Nelson waited for two frustrating days, and finally decided to hitch a ride in a four-engine bomber to Brisbane, where transportation to Melbourne was readily accessible. This was almost their undoing.

Midway to Brisbane, over wild, mountainous terrain, the bomber lost an engine. This was no cause for alarm as it was flying well on three. But ten minutes later, a second engine quit. Everyone on board immediately cinched up their parachutes, and nervously waited for the word to jump. Having survived so much, it seemed ironic to Hargrave and Nelson that they might meet their end in the mountainous wilds of Australia. Fuel was dumped to lighten the plane, which maintained altitude until a safe forced landing was made at Rockingham, 250 miles out of Brisbane.

Two more days of fretful waiting followed with prospects of a continuing military flight none too bright. Impatient with the uncertainty and anxious to get going, Hargrave took matters into his own hands. He had no money, but in Rockingham he talked a commercial airline into giving them seats on a flight to Brisbane simply by signing a voucher.

At Brisbane the two survivors learned the U.S. Navy staff of commander, Task Force 42 had recently set up headquarters there, and quickly reported in. Officers and enlisted men they had never known before welcomed them as heroes, and made both men feel like long lost cousins. The next day, dressed in new uniforms and with money in their pockets, Hargrave and Nelson, happy as clams, were en route by train to Melbourne.

Ninty-five days after taking off from Saumlakki Bay on that disastrous flight, and after traveling several thousand wild and arduous miles the hard way, Hargrave and Nelson reported in to U.S. Navy Headquarters at Melbourne, Australia, on 22 May 1942. Following a complete medical checkup and several days of much-needed rest, Hargrave set down to write the official report of their incredible adventures. In a bland, matter-of-fact manner, Hargrave began, "On 5 February 1942, as prescribed by Commander Patrol Wing 10, we took off on a routine patrol." BROTHER!!

# 18

# THROUGH HELL AND HIGH WATER

During the dark early hours of 19 February 1942, the most powerful striking force to be sent by the Imperial Japanese Navy on a single mission since Pearl Harbor sneaked undetected into the Timor Sea. Objective: to destroy military installations in and around Darwin, the Allies' only air and sea base in northern Australia. This armada, commanded by Vice Admiral Nobutake Kondo, comprised two battleships, four aircraft carriers, three heavy cruisers, and numerous destroyers. One hour after daybreak, 188 fighters and dive bombers roared from the carriers' decks and headed south, hell-bent for Darwin. Close behind followed 54 land-based bombers, stealthily deployed to newly captured airfields within striking range of the strategically important objective.

At 0800 that same morning, a lone U.S. Navy PBY seaplane scooted across the placid waters of Darwin Harbor, lifted gracefully into the air, and climbed out on a northerly heading. For the pilot, Lieutenant Thomas H. Moorer, and the seven members of his plane's crew, this was supposed to be a routine scouting mission in the vicinity of Ambon, on Amboina Island, about 600 miles to the north. Japanese fighters might be encountered near the former ABDA base at Ambon, but there was no reason to believe the first few hours of their flight over the Timor Sea would be anything but peaceful. Little did they suspect they were on a collision course with disaster.

Co-pilot was Ensign W. H. Mosley, and the third pilot was Chief Aviation Machinist's Mate J. J. Ruzak. The following men made up the remainder of the crew: Aviation Machinist's Mate Second Class A. P.

Fairchild, Radioman First Class R. C. Thomas, Aviation Machinist's
Mate Second Class J. C. Shuler, Radioman Third Class F. E. Follmer,
and Aviation Ordnanceman Second Class T. R. LeBaron. This crew
had flown together on many occasions, and were highly skilled, battle-
hardened men of proven courage.

At 0920, a previously unreported merchant vessel was sighted about
140 miles north of Darwin. Moorer, who had been flying at 2,000 feet
altitude, immediately descended and leveled off at 600 feet to challenge and identify the stranger better. During the approach, all eyes on
board the PBY peered down, anxious to determine whether or not the
ship was armed. If she happened to be an enemy raider, hidden
antiaircraft guns could open fire at any moment. The last thought in
anyone's mind, however, was the possibility of their being attacked
from the air.

The ship was still several miles away when the low, steady drone of
the plane's engines was suddenly blotted out by a monstrous noise that
sounded like giant hailstones slamming down on a tin roof. These were
not hailstones, but deadly exploding bullets ripping through the aircraft's metal skin. Over the intercom from the after station came the
frantic report, "Nine Zeros attacking out of the sun."

The port engine was instantly destroyed. Gaping holes appeared as
though by magic in the wings and throughout the fuselage. Gasoline,
streaming from ruptured tanks, burst into flames, engulfing the
plane's port side from the trailing edge of the wing, aft to the tail. The
ungainly seaplane swerved dangerously into the dead engine. Instinc-
tively, Moorer killed power on both engines, and battled the suddenly
heavy controls with all his strength to pull the mortally wounded PBY
back on an even glide path. Time was running out. Fuel tanks could
explode momentarily. To save their lives, the plane had to be landed
quickly, and every second was crucial.

Moorer glanced at his co-pilot, and noticed Mosley trying to stanch
the flow of blood from a wound on the left side of his head. He wanted
to help, but that was impossible. He could hear bursts from the .50-
caliber machine guns back in the port and starboard waist hatches, as
LeBaron and Fairchild strove to shoot down fighters bearing in for the
kill.

It was impossible to turn into the wind. Most of the fabric on the
control surfaces had been shot or burned away. The best Moorer could
hope to do was to keep the plane in a shallow dive and level off for a
downwind landing which, under the best conditions, was extremely
dangerous.

At 50 feet above the sea, Moorer yelled for Mosley to lower the wing
tip pontoons. Still bleeding, Mosley reached over and flipped the

switch. Nothing happened. The activating mechanism had been destroyed. Now the landing was going to be even more hazardous, for without pontoons a wing tip could easily dig into a wave and cartwheel the plane to oblivion.

Bullets continued to slam into the plane. The noise was deafening. Moorer ventured a quick look over his shoulder. Exploding bullets, appearing as small balls of fire, were bounding around inside the radio and navigation compartment. At that instant, Moorer felt a sharp stinging sensation in his left hip. He was hit, and could feel the warm blood oozing down the seat of his pants. But that was the least of his worries. They were only seconds away from landing, and the discomforting problem of downwind contact with the sea was yet to be solved.

The starboard engine was restarted and, while Mosley gingerly manipulated the throttle to help stabilize the cumbersome plane, Moorer strained to work what was left of the controls. Traveling at 125 knots, the PBY struck the sea with great force, and bounded high in the air. The two pilots teamed up to keep the wings level as it slammed twice more into the sea and bounded high into the air before settling dead in the water. Miraculously, the PBY was still intact, but there was no time for congratulations. She was burning furiously and sinking. All hands quickly prepared to abandon ship, but were alarmed to find pools of flaming gasoline spreading over the surface of the sea. As though they didn't have enough trouble, Japanese fighters continued to strafe them. Then, abruptly, the Japanese flew off to rejoin comrades winging on to Darwin. Moorer noted the direction of their flight and was heartsick that he had been unable to alert the Allied forces at Darwin. In the initial attack his radio had been shot out.

With fire engulfing the after portion of the plane, an explosion was imminent. The men moved rapidly to launch an inflatable rubber life raft. Ruzak, Thomas, Shuler, Fairchild, and Follmer lugged one forward from the plane's center section and heaved it over the side. To their dismay, it was full of bullet holes. With complete disregard for their own safety, the men returned to the PBY's oven-like interior and brought forward the second raft. Fortunately, it was intact and inflated easily.

Pools of blazing gasoline surrounded all but the forward section of the plane where the men were going over the side. Once in the water, they piled into the little raft and paddled furiously to put as much distance as possible between themselves and the roaring inferno. They were barely 100 yards away when a tremendous explosion vomited skyward a mass of yellow flames and oily black smoke. In an instant the PBY vanished, leaving in its place a sea of burning gasoline.

Fortunately, there had been no serious casualties. Moorer had a slight flesh wound in his left hip, Mosley a scalp wound, Thomas a scalp wound and either a broken or severely sprained right ankle, and Follmer a painful wound in his left knee. Flight suits and undershirts were ripped up to provide makeshift bandages. When the wounds were cared for, the men assessed their situation.

The merchant ship was still in sight, although a considerable distance from them, and steaming away. Moorer decided their best chance lay in paddling on a southerly course in the hope that they could land on sparsely populated Melville Island and work their way overland to Fort Dundas. The situation was critical, for they had no food and, worst of all, no water.

After the men had paddled for about thirty minutes, they noticed that the merchant ship had changed course and was heading toward them. Uncertain of her nationality and unable to outrun her, the men stopped paddling and waited anxiously. When the small vessel came close, the men were elated to find she flew the American flag. They were helped on board and welcomed by the captain who, like his entire crew, was a Filipino. The wounded were given medical aid, and everyone was treated to dry clothing, food, and cold beer.

In his conversation with her captain, Tom Moorer learned that the *Florence D* was under charter by the U.S. Navy to transport munitions and other supplies from Australia to the beleaguered fortress of Corregidor, a virtual suicide mission through Japanese-controlled waters. Although his ship had been unsuccessfully attacked by several Japanese bombers the preceding day, the courageous captain had decided to proceed as directed. He would put Moorer and his men ashore at his next port of call, Surabaja, Java. Such a voyage was not particularly appealing, but it beat the tar out of bobbing around in the lonely sea jam-packed into a little rubber raft and without food or water.

The survivors had been on board the *Florence D* for about an hour when they were brought to their feet by wild shouts and ringing of the ship's bell. Rushing out on deck, they encountered Filipino crewmen excitedly pointing skyward. High overhead, sixty Japanese carrier-based aircraft were counted flying in a northerly direction. Fortunately, they continued on to disappear over the horizon. Minutes afterwards, an SOS was intercepted from the steamer *Don Isidore* stating she was under continuous air attack, on fire, and there were many casualties on board. The captain of the *Florence D* immediately changed course, and proceeded to the aid of the *Don Isidore*, which gave her position as 30 miles north of them.

The ship had no sooner steadied on her new course than the nerve-racking alarm sounded again. A small aircraft was sighted approaching from the stern. It was identified as a twin-float, single-engine seaplane of the type carried by Japanese ships of the line for scouting. This was a bad omen. It meant only one thing. Somewhere over the horizon enemy surface units were operating, and once this plane reported their position, they, in all probability, would be subject to attack. In spite of this danger, the captain of the unarmed *Florence D* did not turn tail and run, but continued on to offer whatever assistance he could to the stricken *Don Isidore*.

The unarmed *Florence D* was helpless against any kind of assault and, with a top speed of only 10 knots, she was incapable of taking effective evasive maneuvers against bombers. Thus, it had become doctrine, whenever the ship was under air attack, to anchor immediately and have all hands take shelter beneath the steel main deck. When it became apparent that the seaplane intended to attack, the anchor was quickly dropped, and everyone took shelter as prescribed. The intrepid pilot from Nippon flew toward the ship and, at a very low altitude, dropped two 100-pound bombs, which exploded harmlessly several hundred feet short. Then, as though to vent his anger for failing to score a hit, he strafed the *Florence D* several times from extreme range with a small-caliber machine gun, causing no damage. He then flew away to the west, and was seen no more.

About an hour and a half later, lookouts reported dead ahead on the horizon a ship which turned out to be the *Don Isidore*. Recognition signals were exchanged, but without slowing down, the damaged ship with her dead and wounded sped on past to the south. At this juncture, the captain of the *Florence D* decided too many Japanese ships and aircraft were in the area to suit him, and he changed course for Darwin. This of course made Moorer and his men happy, but not for long.

The alarm sounded again thirty minutes later as twenty-seven carrier-type dive bombers were observed heading for the distant *Don Isidore*. Moorer was standing on the bridge, peering through binoculars, when directly overhead he heard the all-too-familiar whine of an attacking dive bomber. Without stopping to look for the plane, he raced in vain for the protected portion of the ship. He didn't make it. A thunderous explosion on the bow slammed him flat on deck. On the heels of the initial blast came violent secondary explosions in the forward cargo hold where 4-inch, .50-caliber shells, intended for Corregidor, were detonating.

Bruised but otherwise uninjured, Tom Moorer reached the protected deck area just as a second 500-pounder burst amidships, plunging the ship's interior into absolute darkness. Groping his way aft amidst burned and wounded sailors Moorer searched for his plane crew. Those he could find he ordered over the side, for the ship was finished.

When Moorer jumped into the sea, the *Florence D* was down by the bow with her propeller out of the water. Accompanied by most of his men, Moorer swam as fast as he could away from the ship, which was still under attack. They were several hundred yards away when two 500-pound bombs missed the ship and landed in their vicinity. Great columns of water shot into the air to cascade down upon them. The underwater shock waves caused excruciating pains in the testicles, stomach, back, and chest. Tom Moorer and several others coughed up blood. As they floundered in the water, Japanese bombers continued to blast the *Florence D*. In all, nine 500-pound bombs were dropped, four of which were direct hits, and five were near misses.

Having expended their bombs, the dive bombers flew off to the north. Then Moorer, clinging to a piece of driftwood, paddled around among the survivors looking for his men. He rounded up all but Shuler, who, it was sadly determined, had been killed when a bomb exploded in the water close to where he last had been seen.

The nearest land was Bathurst Island, 60 miles to the east. Without life jackets, the little band of Americans struck out for it, determined to help each other survive what would be a long swim in shark-infested waters. They had been swimming only a short time when, to their great joy, they discovered that crewmen of the *Florence D* had managed to lower away two lifeboats and were heading for them.

Once he and his men were in the lifeboats, Moorer found the captain of the *Florence D* to be badly wounded and quite helpless. He immediately assumed command of the boat he was in and put Ensign Mosley in charge of the other. The area was thoroughly searched for survivors and, when that was completed, Moorer's boat contained twenty-three survivors, and Mosley's seventeen. Although many were burned or wounded, only Shuler and three of the ship's company were unaccounted for.

It proved exceedingly difficult to get the Filipino seamen to row properly. Most of them did not understand English, and after two days of harrowing air attacks their nerves were on the ragged edge. Just as the lifeboats were leaving the area, the Japanese planes that had been attacking the *Don Isidore* swooped low overhead to strafe the burning hulk of the *Florence D*. In a panic, most of the native crewmen jumped over the side. Although the enemy pilots ignored the lifeboats, it was only with great difficulty that the Filipinos were persuaded to get back into them.

Moorer decided that, all things considered, they should get ashore as quickly as possible. He set a course for the nearest land, the uninhabited coast of Bathurst Island. There they would be free to rest and plan their next moves.

A check of the injured showed ten Filipinos suffering from major burns or wounds and five more slightly injured. Thomas had injured his sprained ankle further when he jumped from the sinking ship. He was in considerable pain and running a fever.

The lifeboats were poorly stocked. There was a small supply of water, but that was quickly consumed by the Filipinos, over whom Moorer had no control. He was unable to use force since he had lost his pistol in the plane crash. There were no medical supplies and no blankets, but they were blessed with large quantities of condensed milk and crackers.

The survivors had rowed about 10 miles when they spotted a plane approaching the *Florence D* from the south. It circled her several times, then headed for the lifeboats. Again the Filipinos panicked, but this time the more levelheaded among them succeeded in preventing anyone from jumping over the side. To their great relief, the plane was a Lockheed Hudson of the Royal Australian Air Force. For several minutes the aircraft circled the boats at a low altitude, attempting unsuccessfully to communicate with a blinker light. When the plane departed the survivors at least were relieved that their location was known and that attempts probably would be made to rescue them.

During the afternoon a breeze sprang up, and good headway was made by rigging the small sails with which both boats were equipped. Just before nightfall land was sighted dead ahead, and calculated to be Bathurst Island's west coast. Although the wind suddenly fell off to a whisper, all hands, with spirits high, took to the oars with renewed vigor, and by midnight they approached the shoreline. Thanks to a flood tide and gentle breakers, the boats were easily beached.

A quick search of the island showed no signs of habitation or water. The wounded were made as comfortable as possible on the beach, using the sails for windbreakers. Sleep was impossible, for everyone's clothing was wet from beaching the boats. It was cold and there were no blankets. The few hours until dawn seemed interminably long.

During the sleepless night, Moorer and Mosley discussed their situation. Their only food, canned milk, was practically exhausted. Bathurst Island was known to be an arid wasteland, and it probably would be difficult to find potable water. The seriously burned and wounded desperately needed medical attention, without which some would soon die. Days, possibly weeks might elapse before friendly forces located them, and by that time they could all be dead. Their one chance for survival lay in reaching a small mission located on the southern end of the island where they could obtain help, and possibly send a message to Darwin requesting rescue.

Moorer calculated the distance overland to the mission at about 40 miles. With luck they could make the trip in less than two days. Such a hike would be grueling, but Moorer and Mosley chose this route rather than risk the hazardous longer one by sailboat through shoal waters, without charts, and at the mercy of fickle winds. Besides, after their experiences of the preceding day, they had little desire once again to find themselves in the open sea, helpless and exposed to attacks by enemy aircraft or warships.

At dawn Moorer explained the plan to the captain of the *Florence D*, suggesting that he and all other seriously wounded men remain behind in the vicinity of the boats until rescued. To this the captain agreed. Thomas and five Filipino crewmen were unable to walk, so Ruzak and LeBaron volunteered to remain behind to take care of them.

When it was light enough to see, on 20 February 1942, Moorer, Mosley, Follmer, and Fairchild, each carrying two cans of condensed milk, started walking south along the shoreline. Those remaining behind were given the last of the biscuits and enough milk for seven days. The Filipino seamen, over whom no one had any control, helped themselves to canned milk and independently headed for the mission. Although some were too badly burned or wounded to attempt such a trip, Moorer found it impossible to dissuade them, especially when, for some unexplained reason, their captain suddenly changed his mind and began hobbling down the beach. The fit Filipinos took a faster pace and soon outdistanced the Americans, while the pathetic wounded straggled along far behind.

Moorer and his three companions were barefoot, having shed their shoes soon after abandoning their plane. Walking at first was easy on the damp, soft sand, but as they progressed they were forced to detour inland to circumvent mangrove swamps and sheer cliffs. Jagged rocks and rough underbrush cut and bruised their feet. They were without water, and the equatorial heat was torturous. The condensed milk did little to quench the thirst, for it was hot and made their tongues feel like they were coated with cotton. Earlier in the day they had passed a small brackish stream, but fearing it was contaminated had decided against drinking the water. As time passed they would have given their souls to discover another such stream.

About 1400, having clawed their way through almost impassible terrain, the four men slumped exhausted to the ground beneath the shade of a large tree. It was now apparent that they could not continue on to the mission, especially without water. Moorer made the undisputed decision to retrace their steps and attempt the trip again, but by boat. There were no signs of the Filipino crewmen who had preceded them, and no way of recalling them. The Americans seriously doubted that the Filipinos could reach the mission, but if they did—so much the better.

It was almost dark when Moorer and his men finally arrived at the brackish stream they had passed up earlier. Here they found the captain of the *Florence D* and most of the wounded who had attempted the trip. These men were in pathetic condition, and none were able to travel. There was little or no greeting between the two groups, for the dehydrated Americans instantly flopped down alongside the stream and sucked up quantities of water, figuring it was better to risk sickness than die of thirst. They were physically incapable of walking the remaining miles back to the boats that night, so Moorer and his men simply sprawled on the ground and fell asleep.

The next morning, after ascertaining that none of the wounded Filipinos could accompany them, Moorer and his men departed. With muscles stiff and aching from their 25-mile trek the previous day, they walked the remaining miles on feet that were blistered, cut, and swollen.

At the makeshift camp, the wounded were suffering intensely from lack of water and medical attention, and there was no way to help them. Their only recourse was for all of them to go as soon as possible in one of the boats, and attempt to reach the mission. That meant sailing 140 miles in an open boat without water or food, and with no charts to guide them along a coastline strewn with treacherous rocks and shoals. Then too, there were the Japanese to worry about. The odds against any of them surviving such a voyage were appalling, but to wait much longer in that waterless wasteland could mean certain death.

With speed spawned of desperation, they readied one of the sail-boats and were about to place the wounded on board when they heard the drone of aircraft engines. A twin-engine land plane was sighted approaching from the south. Fearing it was the enemy, all hands took cover and prayed it was friendly. Flying low along the shoreline, the plane passed directly overhead. To their great joy, it was a Hudson bomber of the Royal Australian Air Force. Those who could, immediately jumped to their feet and raced into the open, shouting and wildly waving their arms. The plane continued down the beach for a few hundred yards, then banked sharply and came zooming back overhead.

Moorer lost no time. He grabbed a piece of driftwood, and wrote a message in the wet sand telling who they were and that they urgently needed water, medicine, and food. The Aussie pilot circled the little band of survivors several times, then waggled his wings to let them know he got the message, and flew off to the south.

Throughout the hot afternoon they waited, hoping it would not be too long before they were rescued, for they were completely out of water. Near sundown the sound of motors heralded the approach of another Hudson bomber, which flew over the little group once. On the second pass three parachutes blossomed in the sky carrying to earth the urgently needed supplies. Attached to one of the parachutes was a note stating that a ship would rescue them the following morning.

With darkness setting in, it was impossible to attempt to locate the captain and the other wounded Filipinos who remained by the brackish stream about 7 miles away. Had they complied with Moorer's suggestion and remained with the boats, they would have been in better physical condition, and able to share the food, medicine, and water they so urgently needed.

Soon after sunrise the next morning, a small ship was seen approaching from the north. The rescue vessel was expected to come from the south, so everyone remained out of sight until it was identified as an Australian subchaser. A cutter was launched and, hoisting a sail, easily made it to the beach. The sublieutenant in charge identified his ship as the HMAS *Warrnambool*, commanded by Lieutenant E. J. Barron, Royal Australian Navy Reserve. He stated his instructions were to bring them all back on board ship without delay.

Moorer told of the *Florence D*'s captain and the wounded men with him, as well as the other seamen whose whereabouts was not known. In view of his orders, the sublieutenant insisted they return to the ship and discuss the matter with his commanding officer. They left the remaining supplies near one of the lifeboats in the event any of the Filipino seamen returned, then Moorer, his six crewmen, and the five wounded men from the *Florence D* boarded the cutter.

Midway to the *Warrnambool*, as the rescued men were congratulating themselves on their good fortune, a Japanese four-engine seaplane was sighted flying in their direction. The cutter quickly put about and headed toward the beach, for fear that the low-flying plane might strafe and sink them.

The *Warrnambool*, armed only with small-caliber machine guns for air defense, was helpless to drive off the attacker, even though the big plane circled the ship several times at a very low altitude. With despair, those on board the cutter watched as the subchaser maneuvered wildly to foul up the bombing runs. After several unsuccessful attempts, the Japanese pilot, figuring he had the ship squarely in his bomb sight, dropped two bombs. Both were near misses. The *Warrnambool* commenced making smoke, whereupon the Japanese pilot, not to be denied, steadied on another bombing run. Those in the cutter saw two more bombs dropped, but with the dense smoke screen were at a loss to determine the results.

The Japanese plane, apparently out of bombs, suddenly flew away to the north. For what seemed an interminable period, the men in the cutter waited. All at once, they saw the *Warrnambool's* bow slash through the smoke and head for them at high speed.

In short order the cutter was hoisted on board. While the wounded were being taken to sick bay for treatment, Tom Moorer went to the bridge to meet the ship's captain and inform him that there were still crewmen from the *Florence D* somewhere ashore. Lieutenant Barron stated that time did not permit his sending a search party ashore and he was heading back to Darwin at once. He assured Moorer, however, that another vessel would return the next day to search for survivors.

At 1300 on 23 February 1942, the *Warrnambool* put into Darwin Harbor, which had been devastated by the Japanese air raid four days earlier. Nine ships had been sunk, including the destroyer *Peary* and the 12,568-ton U.S. Army transport *Meigs*, and eleven others seriously damaged. Only a handful of Allied aircraft survived the attack on the airfield, whose hangars and repair shops had been bombed to rubble. Three PBY seaplanes of Moorer's squadron, the only ones in the area, had been sunk at their moorings. The docks and tons of military stores intended to support the war effort in the Netherlands East Indies were destroyed; little in the town of Darwin was left standing.

On being apprised of the carnage, Tom Moorer candidly commented, "Hell, it's lucky we weren't around here during the attack. We could have been killed."

Lieutenant Moorer capped a distinguished naval career as Admiral Thomas H. Moorer, chairman of the Joint Chiefs of Staff.

# 19

# THE HEAVY CRUISER USS *HOUSTON* (CA-30)

The Japanese claimed to have sunk the heavy cruiser USS *Houston* (CA-30), flagship of the United States Asiatic Fleet, so many times during the first three months of World War II that she was nicknamed "The Galloping Ghost of the Java Coast." On several occasions she had come perilously close to fulfilling those pronouncements, but it was not until the night of 28 February 1942 that her luck ran out and, off the northwest coast of Java, *Houston* vanished with all hands. The mystery shrouding the cruiser's fate persisted until the war's end, when groups of half-dead survivors were discovered in Japanese prison camps scattered from the Netherlands East Indies, through the Malay peninsula, the jungles of Burma and Thailand, and northward to the islands of Japan.

Of *Houston*'s 1,087 officers and men, 721 went down with the ship and 366 escaped, only to be captured as they floundered helplessly in the sea or attempted to penetrate the wilds of Java. Of the original survivors, 76 died, but 290 somehow managed to live through the ordeal of filth, starvation, and brutality meted out to them during three and one-half years as Japanese prisoners of war.

What happened to the *Houston* that night is a nightmare of many years standing, yet each incident lives in my mind as though it occurred only yesterday. Near sundown of that fateful evening of 28 February 1942, *Houston*, in company with the Australian light cruiser *Perth*, steamed out of Tandjungpriok, the port for Batavia, Java, heading for Sunda Strait. I stood alone on the *Houston*'s quarterdeck contemplating the placid green of the Java coast as it slowly fell astern.

Often I had found solace in its beauty, but this time it seemed only a mass of coconut and banana palms that had lost all meaning. Like the rest of the *Houston*'s crew, I was physically and mentally exhausted from four nerve-racking days of incessant bombings and battle, and was deeply preoccupied with the question that gnawed at every man on board, "Will we get through Sunda Strait."

True, Captain Rooks of the *Houston* and Captain Waller of the *Perth* had visited the British Naval Liaison Office in Batavia, where by telephone to Supreme Allied Naval Headquarters at Bandung they had been informed that a Dutch navy reconnaissance plane had reported as late as 1500 that no Japanese sea forces were within ten hours steaming time of Sunda Strait. That was a pleasant thought, but what about the Japanese cruiser planes which had shadowed us throughout the day? The ships from which they had been launched could not be far away, and certainly they were well aware of our movements. There was also the possibility that enemy submarines would be stationed throughout the length of Sunda Strait, between Java and Sumatra, to intercept Allied ships attempting to escape from the Java Sea into the Indian Ocean.

Although there appeared to be little room for optimism, there had been other times when the odds had been heavily stacked against us, and somehow we had managed to battle through. Perhaps I was just a plain damn fool, but I could not bring myself to believe the *Houston* had run her course. With a feeling of shaky confidence, I turned and headed for my room. Having just been relieved as officer-of-the-deck, I found the prospect of a few hours rest most appealing.

The wardroom and interior of the ship through which I walked was dark, for the heavy metal battle ports were bolted shut, and white lights were not permitted within the darkened ship. Only the eerie blue beams of a few battle lights close to the deck served to guide my feet. I felt my way along the narrow companionway, and briefly snapped on my flashlight to seek out the coaming of my stateroom door. As I stepped into the cubicle that was my room, I quickly scanned the place and switched off the light. There had been no change. Everything lay as it had for the last two and a half months. There had been only one addition in all that time. It was Gus, my silent friend, the beautiful Bali head I'd purchased six weeks before in Surabaja.

Gus sat on top of my desk lending his polished wooden expression of absolute serenity to the cramped atmosphere of the room. In the darkness I felt his presence as though he were a living thing. "We'll get through, won't we, Gus?" I found myself saying. And, although I could not see him, I thought he slowly nodded.

I slipped out of my shoes and placed them at the base of the chair by my desk, along with my tin hat and life jacket, where I could reach them quickly in an emergency. Then I rolled into my bunk and let my tired body sink into its luxury. The bunk was truly a luxury, for the few men able to relax lay on the steel decks by their battle stations. I, being an aviator, with only the battered shell of our last seaplane left on board, was permitted to take what rest I could get in my room.

Although there had been little sleep for any of us during the past four days, I found myself lying there in the sticky tropic heat tossing fretfully and yearning for sleep that would not come. The hypnotic hum of blowers thrusting air into the bowels of the ship, the *Houston*'s gentle rolling as she cleaved through a quartering sea, and the occasional groaning of her steel plates combined to parade through my mind the mad sequence of events that had plagued us during the past few weeks.

Twenty-four days had elapsed since that terrifying day in the Flores Sea, yet there it was haunting me again as it would for the rest of my life. From my vantage point on the signal bridge I saw ahead of us the Dutch light cruiser *De Ruyter*, on board which was the striking force commander, Rear Admiral Karel Doorman. Behind the *Houston* steamed the only other American cruiser in all of Southeast Asia, the old light cruiser *Marblehead*. She was followed by the Dutch light cruiser *Tromp*. Screening our line of ships were the Dutch destroyers *Van Ghent*, *Piet Hein*, and *Bankert*, along with the American destroyers *Bulmer*, *Stewart*, *John D. Edwards*, and *Barker*. We were en route to attack an enemy convoy in the vicinity of Makasar Strait. This was to be the *Houston*'s initial engagement with the Japanese, and all hands were excited with the prospect of battle and victory. But the doughty little fleet would never reach its objective.

Suddenly and unexpectedly, enemy planes were sighted in the distant sky heading in our direction. The shrill bugle call "air defense" immediately sounded in raucous concert with the clanging gongs of "general quarters." All hands rushed to battle stations as 54 twin-engine bombers, flying in six nine-plane formations, circled out of gun range to commence their attacks.

On the first bombing run by a nine-plane section, the planes appeared to be within easy reach of our 5-inch antiaircraft guns. The batteries opened fire. Wide-eyed we watched, anticipating the blasting of enemy planes from the sky. But something was wrong. Although our gunners rapidly fired shells into the sky, we were appalled to see most of them failed to explode at altitude. The *Houston* was cursed with faulty ammunition. A bursting shell staggered the lead plane, but all of them continued on course. Bomb bays opened and down tumbled the black projectiles of death and destruction.

The bombs, large armor-piercing ones, straddled the *Houston*. Detonating well beneath the surface, they spewed up great volumes of water as high as the main director atop the foremast. The force with which they exploded lifted the big cruiser, as though by some giant hand, and tossed her yards away from her original course. Men were dashed to the decks, but there were no casualties. Our principal antiaircraft director, however, was wrenched from its track, rendering it useless, and the *Houston* was taking on water from sprung plates in the hull.

The attacks continued to be concentrated on the *Houston* and *Marblehead*. Even with faulty shells it was only the steady barrage from our antiaircraft guns and the skillful shiphandling by Captain Rooks that kept the *Houston* from the realms of Davy Jones. For over two hours we successfully evaded the bombs and, in the process, even knocked down three planes and damaged others. But our luck was running out.

All at once, bombs dropped on the *Marblehead* sent geysers of water leaping into the air, engulfing the old cruiser from stem to stern. When the curtain of water settled back into the sea, there were fires amidships and near her after turret. She suffered two direct bomb hits, one of which jammed her rudder hard to port, and she could take evasive action only by steaming in a circle. Near misses gouged holes in her forward hull, and she was shipping water at an alarming rate. Captain Rooks rushed the *Houston* close to the stricken ship, hoping to fend off the attackers with our guns. But now it was the *Houston*'s turn.

"Stand by for attack to port," bellowed from the ship's loudspeakers, and immediately all eyes shifted from the smoking *Marblehead* to the sky. There they came again, nine more of the bastards. Guns commenced tracking the oncoming enemy, then opened fire. Salvo after salvo sped from their flaming muzzles, but the determined attack was pressed home. When the bombs were seen falling, over the speakers came the command, delivered in cool, matter-of-fact tones, "Take cover. Take cover." Those who could sought cover, others hit the deck. But the men on the 5-inch guns amidships stood fast and, as they had done throughout all other attacks, unflinchingly fired away. They were magnificent in their resolute performance of duty.

All but one of the bombs burst harmlessly in the sea off our port quarter, but the stray, released a fraction of a second late, nearly finished the *Houston* on the spot. There was a tremendous explosion aft. The big ship lurched and trembled violently. Crashing through the searchlight platform on the mainmast, the bomb cut a foot-long gash in a mast leg, ripped through the radio shack, and exploded at main deck level just forward of number 3 turret. Chunks of white-hot shrapnel slashed through the turret's armor plate as though it were paper, igniting powder bags in the hoist. In one blazing instant, all hands in the turret and in the handling rooms below were dead. Where the bomb spent its force, it blew a gaping hole in the deck beneath which the after repair party had been stationed. They were wiped out almost to a man. The damnable battle ended with forty-eight of our shipmates killed and another fifty seriously burned or wounded.

Desperately I strove to rid myself of that gruesome picture—the blazing turret, the bodies of the dead sprawled grotesquely in pools of blood, and the numb, bewildered wounded staggering forward seeking medical aid—but I was forced to see it through. I heard hammers banging, hammers that pounded throughout long hours as weary men steadily worked building coffins for their shipmates lying in covered little groups on the fantail.

The following day we put into Tjilatjap, that stinking, fever-ridden little port on the south coast of Java. The bomb-damaged *Marblehead* limped in behind us several hours later with thirteen men killed and more than thirty wounded. When the *Marblehead* passed the *Houston* close aboard, the crews of both ships lined the rails and cheered in spontaneous acknowledgement of mutual admiration and respect.

Sadly, we unloaded our wounded and prepared to bury our dead. In the hum of the blowers, I detected strains of that mournful tune the ship's band had played when we carried our fallen comrades through the heat of those sunbaked, dusty streets at Tjilatjap. I saw again the silent, sarong-clad natives who watched as we placed our dead in the little Dutch cemetery bordering the sea, and wondered what they thought of all this.

The scene shifted. Only four days had elapsed since we steamed through the minefields protecting the beautiful port of Surabaja. Air raid sirens whined throughout the city and lookouts reported bombers in the distant sky. Large warehouses along Rotterdam Pier were burning, and a sinking merchant ship lay on its side vomiting dense black smoke and orange flames. The enemy had come and gone, but left his calling cards. Anchored in the stream a few hundred yards from the docks, we silently watched soldiers of the Royal Netherlands Indies Army methodically work to extinguish the fires.

Six times during the next two days we experienced air raids. Lying at anchor, we were as helpless as a duck in a rain barrel. That the men of the 5-inch gun crews did not collapse is a tribute to their sheer guts and brawn. Resolutely they stood by their guns, beneath the searing equatorial sun, slamming shell after shell into the sky while the rest of us sought what shelter was available in that bull's-eye of a target.

Time and again bombs, falling with the deep-throated swoosh of a giant bullwhip, exploded all around us spewing water, shrapnel, and even fish over our decks. Docks not far away were demolished and a Dutch hospital ship was hit, yet "The Galloping Ghost of the Java Coast" still rode defiantly at anchor.

When the siren's baleful wail sounded the all clear, members of the *Houston*'s band came from battle stations to the quarterdeck, where all hands gathered to clap and stomp as they played swing tunes. God bless the American sailor, you can't beat him.

Like Scrooge, I continued to be haunted by ghosts of the past. I saw us in the late afternoon of 26 February 1942, standing out of Surabaja for the last time. In tactical command of our small striking force was Rear Admiral Karel Doorman of the Royal Netherlands Navy. His flagship, the light cruiser *De Ruyter*, was in the lead followed by the heavy cruiser *Exeter* of *Graf Spee* fame. Next in line came the *Houston*, whose bomb-shattered number 3 turret was beyond repair. The light cruisers *Perth* and *Java*, in that order, were last in the line of ships. Nine Allied destroyers; four American, three British, and two Dutch; comprised the remainder of our force. We slowly passed gutted docks where small groups of old men, women, and children had gathered to wave tearful goodbyes to their loved ones, most of whom would never return.

Our small, hastily gathered force had never operated together as a unit. Communications among ships of three different navies was poor at best. Orders from Vice Admiral Conrad E. L. Helfrich, commanding the American, British, Dutch, and Australian naval forces (ABDAFLOAT) for defense of the Netherlands East Indies,* were vague. We had no battle plan, only the grim directive from the ABDA naval command, "Continue attacks until enemy is destroyed." We knew only that we were to do our utmost to break up one of several Japanese invasion fleets bearing down on Java—even though it might mean the loss of every ship and man. This was a last-ditch attempt to save the Netherlands East Indies, which were doomed regardless of the outcome.

All night long we searched for the enemy convoy, but it seemed to have vanished from its reported position. At 1415 the next afternoon we were still at battle stations and about to return to Surabaja when

*Helfrich relieved Admiral Thomas S. Hart as commander, ABDAFLOAT, on 14 February 1942.

reports from air reconnaissance indicated that the enemy we sought was south of Bawean Island and heading south. The two forces were less than 50 miles apart.

A hurried but deadly serious conference of officers was immediately held in the *Houston*'s wardroom. Commander Arthur L. Maher, our gunnery officer, explained that our mission was to sink or disperse the protecting enemy fleet units, then destroy the convoy. My heart pounded with excitement, for the battle, to be known as "The Battle of the Java Sea," was only a matter of minutes away. I wondered if the sands of time were running out for the *Houston* and all of us who manned her. At that moment, I would have sold my soul for the answer.

In the darkness of my room the Japanese came again, just as I had seen them from my duty station on the bridge. At 1615 a British destroyer in the van signaled, "Two battleships to starboard." With this, my heart froze, for battleships, with their huge guns, could stand off beyond our range and blast us all to bits. A minute later, this awful thought was dispelled by a correction to the report which read, "Two heavy cruisers."

The *Houston*'s foretop spotter reported the enemy ships bearing 30 degrees relative to starboard. I strained my eyes and finally made out two small dots on the far horizon. With each passing minute they grew larger until their ominous, pagoda-shaped superstructures became clearly visible. They were *Nachi*-class heavy cruisers, each armed with ten 8-inch guns in five turrets, and eight 21-inch, long-range torpedoes in addition to powerful secondary batteries.

I watched, transfixed, as sheets of copper-colored flame erupted from the enemy ships, and black smoke momentarily masked them from view. My heart pounded and cold sweat drenched my body as I realized the first salvos were on the way. Somehow those big guns all seemed aimed at me. I wondered why our guns did not open fire, but when the shells fell harmlessly 2,000 yards short, I understood that the range was still too great.

Suddenly, masts were reported dead ahead. These, we anxiously hoped, were the transports. They rapidly developed into a forest of masts and then into ships which climbed in increasing numbers over the horizon. To our dismay, they were identified as two flotillas of destroyers, six in one, seven in the other, and each led by a light cruiser. Now the situation had taken a drastic change. Because the *Exeter*'s after turret was malfunctioning and could not be brought to bear on the enemy, and the *Houston*'s number 3 turret was destroyed, we had only ten 8-inch guns between us against twenty for the Japanese. We were both outnumbered and outgunned.

At 30,500 yards, the *Exeter* opened fire, quickly followed by the *Houston*. The sight of the *Exeter*'s big guns firing and the attending heavy booms so fascinated me that I was caught unprepared when the *Houston*'s main battery let go. Concussion from our gun blasts knocked me against a bulkhead and tore off my helmet, sending it bounding along the deck. Although shaking with excitement, I recovered my helmet to discover that the tensions induced by waiting for the battle to begin had magically vanished. It was heartening to hear a battle-phone talker relay a report from spot 1, "No change in opening range." The *Houston* was close to target.

The range closed rapidly and soon all cruisers were joined in a furious battle. The *Houston*'s fire was directed at the rear enemy heavy cruiser. The *Exeter* and our light cruisers seemed to be engaging the Japanese light cruisers, which by now were broad on our starboard beam. For the first fifteen minutes, the enemy completely ignored the *Houston*, concentrating their fire on the *De Ruyter* and the *Exeter*. After their initial salvos, their shells were falling dangerously close to our lead ships.

From the onset, the *Houston*'s shells had landed close to her target. She was the only ship firing shells with dye in them to mark their fall. When they exploded in the water, they kicked up blood-red splashes. There was no mistaking where the *Houston*'s heavy shells were landing. Following our sixth salvo, spot 1 reported, "Straddle." On the tenth, the *Houston* scored her first effective hit, and a brilliant fire broke out in the vicinity of the heavy cruiser's forward turrets. In succeeding salvos, additional hits were observed. By 1655, the cruiser was aflame both forward and amidships. She ceased firing and turned away under dense smoke from the fires and her funnel. The *Houston* had drawn first blood.

Enemy cruisers were concentrating fire on the *Exeter*. To give her relief, the *Houston* engaged the remaining heavy cruiser. Spotters reported hits, but there was no visible damage. The *Exeter*, meanwhile, scored a direct hit on one of the light cruisers, forcing it, smoking and on fire, out of the action. Despite the loss of two cruisers, the fall of enemy shells did not seem to diminish, and salvo after salvo ripped into the sea around us. I was mesmerized by the savage flashing of enemy guns, and the sight of their deadly shells flying toward us like flocks of black birds.

Suddenly, we were in a perilous position. A salvo of 8-inch shells exploded close to our starboard side, quickly followed by another to port. This was an ominous sign that the Japanese had at last zeroed in on the *Houston*, and the next salvo could spell disaster. Fearfully we waited. With high-pitched screams the shells came hurtling down to explode all around us. It was a perfect straddle, but not a hit was sustained by the *Houston*. Four more screaming salvos followed, but miraculously we remained unscathed. At the same time, the *Perth*, 900 yards astern, was straddled eight times in a row, yet she too continued to fight without so much as a scratch.

About ten minutes later, enemy destroyers attempted a torpedo attack. The two flotillas raced toward us, but gunfire from our light cruisers turned them back. The *Perth* claimed one destroyer sunk and another damaged in this abortive effort. But the Japanese were not to be denied. They re-formed and, with a light cruiser leading, charged in again as a single coordinated group. This time, instead of thirteen destroyers, there were only twelve. They were heavily engaged by the *Exeter* and the light cruisers, while the *Houston* continued dueling with the remaining heavy cruiser. Hits were observed on enemy destroyers, but they pressed on. At 17,000 yards they launched torpedoes and immediately retired under heavy smoke. It was estimated that it would take almost fifteen minutes for those deadly "tin fish" to reach us.

At this juncture, the heavy cruiser previously damaged by the *Houston* returned to attack the rear of our column. Whatever damage she sustained evidently was under control, but her rate of fire was considerably reduced. The light cruiser *Java* was hit by a 6-inch shell, but there were no injuries and it did little damage. An 8-inch projectile ripped into the *Houston*. Passing through the main deck, aft of the anchor windlass, it penetrated the second deck and exited through the starboard side just above the waterline, without exploding. Another ruptured an oil tank on the port side aft, but did little damage as it too failed to explode.

It was not about 1725, and the vicious tempo of the battle was stepping up. Heavy shells exploding in the sea often threw water over the *Houston*'s decks. Accuracy of the Japanese gunfire left no doubt that someone was going to be hit seriously. Throughout this madness, all hands were uncomfortably aware that those damnable torpedoes were knifing through the sea toward us, yet Admiral Doorman gave no orders for evasive action.

Suddenly, a billowing white cloud of steam was seen venting amidships from the *Exeter*. She had been hit by an 8-inch shell which killed the four-man crew of her S2 4-inch gun, slashed through several steel decks, and exploded in number 1 boiler room. Six of her eight boilers were instantly knocked out of commission, and around them lay ten dead British seamen. The seriously crippled *Exeter*'s speed rapidly fell off to 7 knots.

In a desperate attempt to avoid the oncoming torpedoes, Captain Oliver L. Gordon immediately turned the crippled cruiser to port.

Captain Rooks, believing he had missed a signal from Admiral Door-man for a simultaneous turn of ships from line ahead to line abreast, turned the *Houston* with the *Exeter*. And when Captain Waller of the *Perth* and Captain Van Staelen of the *Java* saw the two ships ahead of them turn, they too swung to port. Instant confusion reigned in the Allied fleet. Without orders, the three groups of American, British, and Dutch destroyers made off in various directions. Left no alterna-tive, Admiral Doorman quickly ordered the *De Ruyter* turned to port, thereby joining in a logical defensive maneuver he should have ordered in the first place.

Before the *Perth* had completed her turn, Captain Waller realized the *Exeter*'s predicament and abruptly pulled his ship back out of the line. With volumes of thick black smoke pouring from her funnels, the *Perth* raced around the *Houston* to screen the *Exeter* from the Japanese. Then, to add to the confusion, lookouts reported three additional enemy cruisers with six destroyers on the horizon to starboard.

At that moment, the water became alive with torpedoes, which seemed to be running in all directions. A seaman standing near me shouted, "Jesus Christ, look at that!" I whirled to look in the direction he was pointing and could hardly believe my eyes. Immediately off our starboard bow a gigantic pillar of water was rising to a height of more than 100 feet. Directly beneath it, with only small portions of her bow and stern showing, was the Dutch destroyer *Kortenaer*. She had been racing to change stations when a torpedo aimed at the *Houston* blew her guts out. With her back broken, she rolled over and jackknifed. When the water pillar slumped back into the sea, only the bow and stern sections of the ship's keel remained above water. A few hapless men could be seen scrambling for their lives to cling to her barnacled bottom while her twin propellers, in their dying propulsive effort, slowly turned over in the air. In less than a minute, the *Kortenaer* had vanished beneath the Java Sea. No ship stopped to look for survivors, for any one that did could have easily shared the same fate.

Now all Allied ships were making black smoke to hide the *Exeter* from the enemy. The sea for miles around was so heavily curtained with smoke that to determine accurately who was where, or what Admiral Doorman had in mind for his next maneuver was impossible. Occasionally a Japanese scouting plane circled out of gun range to relay our fleet's disposition, course, and speed back to his flagship. The confused mass of Allied ships steaming in various directions must have produced some wild and perplexing reports.

Eventually, through the smoke, the *De Ruyter* was spotted flying her usual "follow me" signal. The *Houston* and the other cruisers attempted to fall in line while firing on enemy ships to prevent their closing on the

*Exeter*. To further complicate the situation, the sea still bubbled with torpedo wakes, and it took extreme vigilance to avoid them. Throughout this period, the waters around us occasionally erupted with strange explosions. These, it was finally determined, were caused by enemy torpedoes self-destructing at the end of their runs.

Foretop spotters reported many enemy ships moving to penetrate the smoke screening the *Exeter*. Only the British destroyers *Electra*, *Jupiter*, and *Encounter* were in position to meet this attack. With traditional British courage, they resolutely charged to intercept this numerically superior force.

The *Electra*, first to make contact, broke through the dark curtain of smoke into the brilliant sunshine and was immediately engaged by Japanese destroyers, the tail end of a force consisting of seven destroyers led by a light cruiser. The fight grew to savage proportions when the cruiser, followed by the other destroyers, wheeled back to do battle. The *Encounter* and *Jupiter* arrived on the scene just as the *Electra* was blasted into a flaming hulk. But, before she went under, *Electra* scored hits on the cruiser and a destroyer.

The *Encounter* and the *Jupiter* exchanged fire with the Japanese until our cruisers moved into position to take up the fight and permit them to move back behind the protective smoke screen. The Japanese, realizing they were outgunned, hightailed it out of range. The attack was broken up and the *Exeter* saved, but it was depressing to know that the *Electra* and her valiant crew had been lost.

The action continued to be extremely confused. The *Houston* was maneuvering to fall in line behind the *De Ruyter* when a Japanese destroyer broke through the smoke not 2,000 yards dead ahead. Our main battery, alert and ready, fired a salvo of 8-inch shells which virtually tore the ship apart. She was there one moment and gone the next.

By this time, the *Exeter* had managed to build up speed to 10 knots, and the Dutch destroyer *Witte De With* was ordered to escort her back to Surabaja. Then, with his column once more assembled, Doorman returned to the attack. At a range of about 20,000 yards, the ships continued the engagement. Hits were observed on several enemy ships, but with no telling effect, and the Allies suffered no more than near misses. This part of the battle lasted less than fifteen minutes and the admiral, to conserve ammunition for use against transports, turned his force to the south in an effort to break off the engagement.

As his cruisers steadied on course, Doorman signalled to the American destroyers, "Counterattack." He quickly followed that with, "Cancel counterattack—make smoke." A few minutes later he signalled, "Cover my retirement." By this time the American destroyer captains were thoroughly confused and far from certain what the man had in mind. It was determined, however, that the last directive meant they should attack the enemy cruisers, which were following uncomfortably close. Braving heavy enemy fire, the old four pipers *John D. Edwards*, *Alden*, *Paul Jones*, and *John D. Ford* pressed to within 10,000 yards. To move in further would have been sheer suicide and, at extreme range, they launched torpedoes. At times, enemy shells splashed dangerously close, but the courageous destroyermen brought their ships back unharmed.

During the attack, the *Houston*'s main battery fired on what appeared to be two heavy cruisers not previously encountered. The *Perth* also fired on them, and the Japanese warship was engulfed in flames fore and aft. With that, Commander Maher shifted his attention and the *Houston*'s guns to other targets. Though Maher could not confirm this ship sunk, observers on board the *Houston*, *Perth*, and other Allied ships reported seeing a violent explosion, following which the enemy cruiser disappeared stern first beneath the sea.

The daring torpedo attack failed to damage any enemy ships, but it forced the Japanese to turn away, terminating the engagement. It was then 1830. The battle had lasted for over two hours. Such a time span was contrary to the thinking of most naval strategists, for it was believed gunnery and torpedo fire had been developed to such a fine point that a naval engagement would be decided in a matter of minutes. Perhaps the assumption was sound, provided the battle was conducted in accordance with the book, but the likes of this fouled up fight were not contained in any book.

The afternoon had been filled with blood-boiling tensions, and the brief lull, during which hastily prepared sandwiches and coffee were served, was a godsend. Although there was a modicum of comfort in knowing we were still alive, all hands were haunted by the agonizing question, "How much longer can our luck hold out?" Admiral Doorman, we knew, was determined to intercept the transports and, if necessary, die in the attempt. That he might kill us all in the process was not a pleasant thought.

We checked our losses. The destroyers *Kortenaer* and *Electra* had been sunk. The crippled *Exeter*, escorted by the destroyer *Witte De With*, had retired to Surabaja. The four American destroyers, out of torpedoes and running low on fuel, also had withdrawn to Surabaja. Only the two British destroyers, *Jupiter* and *Encounter*, remained with us. The cruisers *Houston*, *Perth*, *De Ruyter*, and *Java*, showing the jarring effects of continuous gunfire, were still in the fight.

Our main battery was in sad shape. The guns of both turrets were less than 40 rounds away from their designed life expectancy of 300 rounds per gun. Even then their accuracy was questionable. That afternoon they had fired so rapidly for such a sustained period of time that the liners in the gun barrels crept out an inch or more. The casings were so hot that it would be hours before they could be touched. To add to the *Houston*'s predicament, only 50 rounds of 8-inch shells per gun remained.

The ventilating system in the magazine areas had proven totally inadequate. Men on the shell decks passed our during the battle from the oppressive heat and the physical exertion required to keep the guns supplied with ammunition. Adding to the hardships of the gun crews, melted grease from the gun slides lay 2 inches deep in the pits, making the platforms treacherously slippery. A 1-inch deep pool of water and sweat in the powder circles made footing extremely hazardous, especially with the ship maneuvering at high speed, and caused the wetting of trays and the dampening of powder. The situation was no better in the bowels of the ship, where the chief engineer reported his force, which had suffered more than seventy cases of heat prostration during the battle, was on the verge of complete exhaustion.

After sunset, Admiral Doorman led his remaining ships on a northerly course. At 1930, enemy warships were reported to port. At the same instant, the darkness was shattered when the *Perth* fired a spread of star shells. We strained our eyes, but could see nothing. To elude enemy ships lurking in the darkness, we abruptly changed course to the east. Twenty minutes passed without a sign of the enemy. Then, all of a sudden, night became day as a parachute flare burst above us. Blinded by the brilliant, greenish light, and helpless to defend ourselves, we stood by, fearful that the unseen enemy was closing in for the kill.

One after another the flares burst in the sky, burned, and slowly fell into the sea. On board ship, men spoke in hushed tones, as though their very words might expose us to the enemy. Only the rush of water, as our bow knifed through the Java Sea at 30 knots, and the continuous roaring of blowers from the vicinity of the quarterdeck, were audible. Death stood by, ready to strike. No one talked of it, although all thoughts dwelt upon it.

Following the eighth flare, we tensely awaited the next. It failed to come, and once again we were cloaked in darkness. No attack materialized and, as time passed, it became evident that the unseen plane which dropped the flares had gone. How wonderful the darkness, yet how terrifying to think that the enemy was aware of our movements, and was merely biding his time to strike.

The flares caused Admiral Doorman to change course to the south. When the dark mountains of Java were seen silhouetted against the star-flecked sky, a westward course was set paralleling the coast. Some miles west of Surabaja, we headed into a large bay where it was anticipated the Japanese might attempt a landing. Our charts showed that these waters were not very deep, and when a large stern wave started to build up on either side of the fantail, Captain Rooks became alarmed, for this indicated the ship was endangered by shallow water. Suddenly, the *Houston* commenced vibrating violently and losing speed. Aware that his ship was running aground, Rooks instantly turned the *Houston* out of the formation and headed for deeper water away from the coast. Soon afterward, Doorman apparently realized his mistake, and led the other ships out of the bay, where the *Houston* rejoined the column.

Coincident with Doorman's change of course, the British destroyer *Jupiter*, covering our port flank on the landward side, exploded in flames. "I am torpedoed," she reported.* We were appalled, for there were no enemy ships in sight. Leaving the doomed destroyer to her fate, we raced away and continued blindly searching for the transports.

The moon, sometimes obscured by scudding clouds, aided our search, but for an hour we saw nothing of enemy warships. I climbed up on the forward antiaircraft director platform and sprawled out for a bit of rest before the inevitable shooting began. Hardly had my eyes closed when the sounds of whistles and shouting men jerked me to my feet. The water to starboard was dotted with men who hailed us in a foreign tongue. They were Dutch survivors of the destroyer *Kortenaer*, torpedoed during the day action, and the British destroyer *Encounter* was ordered to rescue the poor devils and take them to Surabaja.

Stripped of destroyers, all that remained of our little fleet were three light cruisers and one crippled heavy cruiser. On we steamed through the eerie night. Suddenly, six water-borne flares mysteriously appeared paralleling our line of ships. Aghast, we stared at these insidious lights, which resembled those round pots that burn with an oily yellow flame alongside road construction sites. No one could tell how they got there or what they were. Some thought they were mines, others thought their purpose was to mark our course for the enemy. Either possibility was disquieting.

As fast as we left one group of lights astern, another popped up alongside. As we continued on we could see behind us the unnerving lights, spread out for several miles, clearly defining our track. In zigzag lines, on the rolling surface of the Java Sea, they bobbed and glowed like fiendish jack-o'-lanterns. It was stupefying to know the enemy was following our every move. Then, as suddenly as they appeared, the

---

*Unknown to Doorman, he was leading the Allied ships into a newly laid minefield. The *Jupiter* was sunk by one of those mines.

lights stopped. Apprehensively, we continued on, searching for the elusive transports. When the enemy failed to strike, and the mysterious lights vanished in the night, we were grateful once again for the cloak of darkness.

The nerves of all hands were as taut as a hunter's bowstring. There could be no relaxing. We were in an area charged with hostility. From our ships, hundreds of eyes peered into the night, seeking the enemy convoy we hoped would momentarily be within our grasp. The battle was bound to begin soon, and men wondered if these were their last living moments on earth.

At about 2300, lookouts reported two cruisers to port, moving on an opposite course. No friendly ships sailed within hundreds of miles of us, and all hands, standing keyed-up and ready at battle stations, knew this was the enemy. The sharp cracking of 5-inch guns ravaged the silence as the *Houston* attempted to illuminate the enemy with star shells. The first spread, fired at a range of 10,000 yards, was short. Rapidly, two additional spreads were fired at a range of 13,000 yards. Although they brilliantly illuminated the area, these too were short and served only to blind both sides temporarily. As the enemy ships drew away in the darkness, the *Houston* fired one main battery salvo with undetermined results. The shortage of 8-inch shells prevented firing more. The Japanese, however, fired three salvos, one of which straddled our stern. The encounter was brief, and both sides lost each other in the night as Admiral Doorman continued the wild, blind hunt for transports.

During the night, the order of ships in column was changed. The *De Ruyter* still maintained the lead, followed by the *Houston*, *Java*, and *Perth*, in that order. A half-hour passed without incident. It was almost midnight. The moon, partially obscured by clouds, was of little help in our search. All hands desperately wanted to end this mad game of blindman's buff and settle the issue one way or another. All at once, our senses, numbed by fatigue and unrelenting tensions, were shocked back to terrifying reality. With the quickness of a lightning bolt, a savage explosion shattered the oppressive silence and the *Java*, 900 yards astern of the *Houston*, was instantly enveloped in flames which leaped high above her bridge.

At the same time, torpedo wakes foamed in the water around the *Houston*. Where they came from no one could tell, for the enemy remained invisible. The *De Ruyter* abruptly changed course to starboard. The *Houston* was about to follow when another tremendous explosion racked the *De Ruyter*. Monstrous, crackling flames licked over her bridge and spread like wild-fire over the ship's entire length. We passed within 100 yards of this terrifying inferno as ammunition, detonated by the intense heat, sent white-hot fragments rocketing into the sky.

During the last precious moments he had left on earth, the courageous Admiral Doorman, who had resolutely carried out the directives from higher authority until the end, ordered the *Houston* and *Perth* not to stand by for survivors, but to retire to Batavia.

Captain Rooks, in a masterpiece of seamanship and quick thinking, maneuvered the *Houston* to avoid torpedoes that zipped past us 10 feet on either side. Then, joined by *Perth*, we raced away from the striken ships, and the killer enemy which still remained unseen. How horrible and depressing to leave our valiant comrades-in-arms to die in such a manner, but we were powerless to assist them.

With Admiral Doorman gone, Captain Waller in the *Perth* assumed command, for he was senior to Captain Rooks. We now faced the unsavory prospect of being the only Allied cruisers, other than the damaged *Exeter*, in all of Southeast Asia. Both of us, low on fuel and ammunition, were pitted against the entire might of the Japanese Navy and Air Force. Our only hope was somehow to elude enemy forces and escape into the Indian Ocean through Sunda Strait, which lay between Java and Sumatra.

Throughout the night, we followed the *Perth* as she zigzagged along at 28 knots. All hands stood at battle stations and all eyes sought to penetrate the darkness, looking for ships they prayed they would not find. With the dawn, it seemed a miracle to watch the sun come up, for there had been many times during those past fifteen hours when I could have sworn we never would.

The *Houston* was a wreck. During the battle, turrets 1 and 2 each had fired 101 salvos for a total of 606 8-inch shells. The concussions from those big guns, coupled with the shock waves from firing them, played havoc with the ship's interior. Every unlocked desk and dresser drawer had been torn out and the contents spewed all over. In lockers, clothing was wrenched from hangers and dumped in muddled heaps. Pictures, radios, books, in fact everything not bolted down, had been jolted from normal places and dashed about.

The admiral's cabin, once the shipboard home of President Roosevelt, was a deplorable sight. Broken clocks, overturned furniture, cracked mirrors, charts ripped from the bulkhead, and large chunks of soundproofing jarred loose from overhead added to the rubble underfoot.

The ship too had suffered. Steel plates along the *Houston*'s sides, weakened by near hits in previous bombing attacks, were badly sprung and shipping water. Glass windows on the bridge were shattered. Fire hoses, strung along passageways for emergency purposes, were leaking and caused minor flooding. The *Houston*, for sure, was battle-scarred and battle-weary, but there was still plenty of fight left in her.

Morale remained high, but the physical condition of the crew was poor. Most had not had a chance for anything one might call rest for more than four days because battle stations had been manned more than half that time, and freedom from surface contacts or air alerts had never exceeded four hours. This had caused meals to be irregular and inadequate. Nevertheless, the exhausted crew shrugged it off, for every man considered himself lucky to be alive, and was determined to give every last ounce of strength to bring the *Houston* through.

These events, and qualms about what lay in store, tortured my mind until at last my senses numbed and I relaxed in the arms of Morpheus. While I slept, Captain Rooks was on the bridge along with Lieutenant Harold S. Hamlin, Jr., the officer-of-the-deck, who was busy keeping station 900 yards astern of the *Perth*. Turrets 1 and 2 were manned with powder trains filled. The 5-inch battery was divided with the flight deck guns on the forward director, and the boat deck guns on the after director. The sea was calm, the night windless. A full moon silhouetted the foreboding, volcanic mountains of western Java. Saint Nicholas Point light, marking the entrance to Sunda Strait, was sighted, and the quartermaster noted that the time was 2315. All hands on deck were elated, for it seemed as though the *Houston* and *Perth* just might make it. But, at that moment, lookouts reported surface vessels dead ahead. Tensions mounted. At first it was hoped these were Dutch patrol boats known to be operating in the strait. Captain Rooks and Lieutenant Hamlin examined them closely through night glasses and concluded they were maneuvering much too fast for an ordinary patrol. Captain Rooks immediately ordered general quarters sounded and Hamlin, who was officer in charge of turret number 1, made a mad dash for his battle station.

Clang! Clang! Clang! Clang! Clang!, the nerve-shattering general alarm burst my wonderful cocoon of sleep. Through nearly three months of war, that gong calling all hands to battle stations had rung in deadly earnest. It meant only one thing, danger. So thoroughly had the bitter lessons of war been taught to the brash, heartless clanging of that gong that I found myself in my shoes before I was fully awake.

Clang! Clang! Clang! Clang! Clang! The alarm resounded along the steel bulkheads of the *Houston*'s deserted interior. I wondered what kind of deviltry now confronted us and felt depressed. Strapping on my steel helmet, I hurried from the room. As I did, a salvo from the main battery roared out overhead. The shock flung me against the barbette of number 2 turret. We were desperately short of those 8-inch bricks. I knew the boys were not wasting them on mirages. I groped my way through the empty wardroom and into the passageway at the after end.

At the base of the ladder leading to the deck above, a group of stretcher bearers and corpsmen was assembled. I asked what we had run into. They did not know. As I quickly climbed the ladder heading for the bridge, the 5-inch guns joined with the booming of the main battery. This was getting to be one hell of a fight. I paused on the communication deck where the pom-pom guns were getting into action. Briefly, I watched their crews working swiftly, mechanically in the dark as their guns pumped out shell after shell. I glimpsed the fiery streaks of tracers hustling out into the night. How beautiful, I thought, these emissaries of death.

Before I reached the bridge, every gun on the ship was in action. Their murderous melody was magnificent, reassuring. At measured intervals the thunderous crash of the main battery joined the sharp, random cracking of the 5-inch guns, and the steady pom, pom, pom of the 1.1s, while above it all, from platforms high in the foremast and mainmast, came the sweeping volleys of the .50-caliber machine guns, placed there to fight off low-flying aircraft but now finding themselves engaging surface targets.

My arrival on the bridge was greeted by a blinding flash and a thunderous boom as a salvo from number 2 turret raced out into the night. My eyes had just begun to refocus when a salvo from number 1 turret shattered the darkness, blinding me again. I wanted desperately to know what we were up against, but to ask would have been absurd. On the bridge, from the captain to the sailors manning the overburdened battle phones, everyone was grimly absorbed in fighting the ship. Eventually, by the bright flashes of her guns, firing on all sides, I distinguished the *Perth* several hundred yards ahead of us. Continuous gun flashes from many directions indicated that the *Houston* was the target for numerous men-of-war.

Outgunned as we obviously were, it would have made little difference to any of us to know we had rammed into the very midst of the largest amphibious landing operation yet attempted by the Japanese. Targets were on all sides and there was little room to be selective. Lining the shores of Bantam Bay, where most of the battle was fought, were sixty transports readying to unload troops and materials of war for the conquest of Java. Between us and the transports was a squadron of destroyers, led by a light cruiser and augmented by motor torpedo boats. A few miles behind us steamed two heavy cruisers, an aircraft carrier, and an unknown number of destroyers. Blocking the entrance

to Sunda Strait were two heavy cruisers, a light cruiser, and ten destroyers. The *Houston* and *Perth* were trapped.

In attempting to fight through the encircling warships, the *Houston*
and *Perth* were forced to make radical and violent maneuvers to evade
torpedoes launched by destroyers from every conceivable direction.
The dark waters of the Java Sea glowed with their phosphorescent
wakes. At one point, two torpedoes were reported approaching the
*Houston* to port. The ship then was maneuvering to avoid others; to do
more was impossible. Awestruck, my eyes frozen to the onrushing "tin
fish," I braced myself for whatever might come. Then, miracle of
miracles, both torpedoes passed directly beneath the *Houston* without
exploding.

As the battle progressed, the evasive maneuvering of both ships and
the constant blinding flashes of gunfire made it difficult, and at times
impossible, to keep track of the *Perth*. A few minutes past midnight, she
was observed dead in the water and sinking, but with her guns still
firing. When Captain Rooks realized that the *Perth* was finished and
escape impossible, he turned the *Houston* toward the transports, determined to sell his ship dearly. From then on, every ship in the area was
an enemy, and we began a savage fight to the death.

The Japanese desperately fought to protect their transports. Like a
wolf pack closing in for the kill, destroyers fearlessly raced in close to
illuminate the *Houston* with powerful searchlights so their cruisers' big

The light cruiser HMAS *Perth*, sunk near Sunda Strait, Java, during the
early hours of 1 March 1942 by Japanese naval forces. James C. Fahey
Collection, U.S. Naval Institute

guns could find the range. Undaunted by the blinding glare, the *Houston*'s crew battled back. No sooner were the lights snapped on than our guns blasted them out. One destroyer attempting to illuminate the *Houston* was torn apart by a main battery salvo, and instantly disappeared. Another, victimized by the port side 5-inch guns, had its bridge shot away. Several times, confused destroyer crews mistakenly illuminated their own transports close to the beach, and the *Houston*'s gunners quickly seized the opportunity to pump shells into them.

The *Houston* had no difficulty selecting targets, but the Japanese were hard-pressed at times to distinguish their own ships. On one occasion, we watched in amazement while the enemy, for a short time, fired heavily at each other and no shell so much as splashed near us.

For almost fifty minutes the *Houston* led a charmed life. The enemy had scored not a single hit of consequence. A salvo of heavy shells had even passed completely through the wardroom, from starboard to port, without exploding. But the *Houston*'s luck had run its course. A shell, bursting on the forecastle, started a fire in the forward paint locker, pinpointing our location for the enemy. While men of the forward repair party raced to extinguish the fire, Japanese gunners, shooting at point-blank range, scored several more hits on the forecastle. Shrapnel and debris flew in all directions, wounding several in the repair party. It seemed like an eternity, but within a few minutes, the fire was out.

The *Houston* now was overtaken by the inevitable. At about 0015 the great ship was rocked by a torpedo crashing through the port side. Everyone in the after engine room was killed instantly, and the *Houston*'s speed was reduced to 23 knots. Thick smoke and hot steam from the engine room inundated the boat deck, driving men from their guns and rendering the after 5-inch gun director useless. When the smoke and steam subsided, gun crews returned to battle stations and fired independently. Power to the shell hoists was knocked out, stopping the flow of 5-inch ammunition from the almost-empty magazines. Men tried to go below to bring shells up by hand, but debris and fires blocked their way. Lacking service ammunition, the crews attacked enemy ships with star shells, all they had left in the ready ammunition boxes.

Close on the heels of the first, a second torpedo smashed into our starboard side, just below the communications deck. Bursting shells started fires throughout the ship, and frantic efforts to extinguish them failed in the face of intensified enemy gunfire. Suddenly number 2 turret, penetrated by a direct hit, blew up sending flames soaring above the bridge. The intense heat buckled steel deck plates, driving everyone out of the conning tower and off the bridge. Communications to other parts of the ship were completely disrupted.

Within a few minutes the fire was out, and turret 2 lay silent and dark. The shortage of ammunition had forced turrets 1 and 2 to use a common magazine. When that was flooded to prevent an explosion, it deprived turret 1 of ammunition. The *Houston*'s big guns were now silent forever, but a few 5-inch guns, along with the pom-poms, and .50-caliber machine guns continued the fight.

Confident the *Houston* was finished, the enemy sent in several motor torpedo boats to rake the decks with gunfire. One, caught in the murderous cross fire of the *Houston*'s .50-caliber machine guns and number 1 pom-pom, disintegrated. Another was sliced in half by the same guns; it sank 50 yards off our port quarter, but not before launching a torpedo, which exploded in the *Houston*'s guts forward of the quarterback.

The *Houston* was shipping great quantities of water through gaping holes in her hull and listing slowly to starboard. Her speed fell off making it impossible to maneuver. Ships were attacking from all sides, and enemy planes flew overhead. It was impossible to determine whether we were being blasted by shell, torpedo, or bomb. Like a groggy fighter, the *Houston* was all but knocked out.

The time had come for Captain Rooks to give his last command. I was standing next to him on the bridge when he summoned the young marine bugler and, in a strong, resolute voice ordered, "Bugler, sound abandon ship."

As the bugle notes rang out, I decided not to wait to go down the already crowded ladder. Instead, I climbed over the rail and lowered myself to the deck below. This was a fortuitous move, for just as I landed a shell burst on the deck above. I made my way to the starboard catapult tower where, in the gloom, the battered hulk of our last seaplane spread its useless wings. It contained a two-man life raft and a bottle of brandy, both of which I figured would come in handy on such a night. But I was too late. Others were there ahead of me.

About this time, Ensigns Charles D. Smith and Herbert Levitt, looking for wounded shipmates to help over the side, found Captain Rooks lying on the communications bridge. His head and chest were covered with blood. Barely conscious, he was unable to speak. The ensigns gave him a shot of morphine to ease his pain then, seconds later, he died. They covered him with a blanket and were about to abandon ship when, looking back, they saw someone sitting cross-legged on the deck cradling the captain's body in his arms. They returned to find it was the captain's rotund Chinese steward, good-

Captain Albert H. Rooks, commanding officer of the heavy cruiser *Houston*.

naturedly known to all hands as "Buda." They urged him to leave the sinking ship before it was too late, but he ignored them. Rocking back and forth, he held Captain Rooks as though he were a little boy asleep and, in a voice overburdened with sorrow, repeated over and over, "Captain die, *Houston* die, Buda die too." He went down with the ship.

Although the *Houston* continued to be pounded by shells and was sinking slowly, there was no panic or confusion. Men quickly went about the job of abandoning ship. Fear was nowhere apparent, perhaps because the one thing we all had feared most had become a reality.

Enemy ships closed in to rake the weather decks systematically with machine-gun fire. In spite of the order to abandon ship, and the fact that the *Houston* was plagued with fires and dangerously listing to starboard, a few stouthearted sailors and marines refused to discontinue the battle. Several .50-caliber machine guns, and one 5-inch gun continued to fire. Their diversionary fire served to disrupt the gunning down of many men attempting to get over the side. They undoubtedly saved the lives of shipmates but, in all probability, not their own. Who these heroic men were, will never be known.

I dropped from the catapult tower to the quarterdeck, where several men were sprawled grotesquely. Sadly, I examined each one. I knew them all, and they all were dead. Time was running out. I saw men of the "V" Division struggling to drag a large seaplane pontoon and two wing-tip floats from the starboard hangar. These had been filled with food and water in anticipation of just such an emergency. Joined together in the water as designed, the rig would make a sturdy structure around which we could gather and work out our survival plan. I hurried to help.

We worked fast, for the *Houston* threatened to capsize at any moment. The heavy float was manhandled out of the hangar while I worked feverishly to take down the starboard lifelines so it could be heaved over the side. I had uncoupled one and was about to break loose the second when, suddenly, the quarterdeck jumped and buckled underfoot. A tremendous geyser of oil and salt water leaped high overhead and pounded back down upon us. The torpedo struck directly below where I was standing, yet I heard no noise. There was no time to reason why.

Until that moment, I had been much too fascinated with the unreality of the nightmare I was living to become frightened. But the torrent of fuel oil and water was for real. It was happening to me, and all I could think of was fire. I had not entertained the thought of being killed or wounded, but this—this was something different. I visualized blazing fuel oil on my body and covering the surface of the sea. I was frantic with the thought that I might not be able to swim through such an inferno. Spontaneously, most of us raced from the starboard side into the dubious shelter of the port hangar. Just as we cleared the quarterdeck, a salvo of shells plowed through it and exploded deep inside the ship.

The fuel oil failed to ignite, but the *Houston* was listing well over to starboard. With shells slamming into her from all sides, there was only one thing left to do—get the hell off the ship, and the faster the better. I climbed down a cargo net draped over the port side, and dropped into the warm Java Sea. In the dark, with the sounds of combat ringing in my ears, I found myself surrounded by faceless men swimming for their lives. I was sick at heart to hear the anguished cries for help from drowning shipmates, cries to which few, if any, of us could respond. All at once the sea had become an oily battleground where individual men were pitted against death. I thought of the powerful suction created by a sinking ship and swam as hard as I could away from the *Houston*.

A hundred or more yards astern of my mortally wounded ship, I turned, exhausted and gasping for breath, to witness her last moments. Destroyer searchlights illuminated *Houston* from bow to stern. She was heeling to starboard, and enemy shells continued to pound into her. I prayed no one on board was still alive. Several heavy shells burst in the water among groups of swimming men. As far removed as I was, the underwater shock waves slammed into my guts like giants fists, making me wince. I shuddered to think of the havoc they inflicted on the poor souls closer to them.

Dazed, unable to believe the macabre scene was real, I floated alone and watched bewitched. The sinking *Houston* listed further and further to starboard until her yardarms barely dipped into the sea. Even so, the enemy was not yet finished with her. A torpedo, fired by the vindictive foe, exploded amidships on her port side. After having been subjected to so much punishment, the ship should have capsized instantly. Instead, the *Houston* tediously rolled back on an even keel. With decks awash, the proud ship paused majestically, while a sudden breeze picked up the Stars and Stripes, still firmly two-blocked on her mainmast, and waved them in one last defiant gesture. Then, with a tired shudder, the magnificent *Houston* vanished beneath the Java Sea.

# 20

# THE CRUEL FATE OF THE DESTROYER USS *POPE* (DD-225)

One of the blackest days in the history of Destroyer Squadron 29 was 1 March 1942, when four of its ships were lost to enemy action. The *Pope* (DD-225) was one of them. Commanded by Lieutenant Commander Welford C. Blinn, she had acquitted herself admirably in the night battles off Balikpapan and the southeastern coast of Bali. Due to engineering problems, however, she was forced to remain in the Surabaja Navy Yard for repairs, and unable to participate in the Battle of the Java Sea.

The *Pope* was ready to put to sea in the late afternoon of 27 February 1942, and was ordered to assist the destroyer *Encounter* in escorting the crippled heavy cruiser *Exeter* back to Surabaja from the Java Sea battle. These ships were joined in port several hours later by the four American destroyers *John D. Ford, John D. Edwards, Alden,* and *Paul Jones,* which returned from the battle out of torpedoes and critically low on fuel.

The next morning, 28 February 1942, news of the calamitous defeat of the Allied fleet in the Battle of the Java Sea made it painfully apparent that the Netherlands East Indies were doomed and that to avoid complete disaster the ships at Surabaja must dash for safer ports south of the Malay barrier.

Numerous Japanese warships and troop-laden transports were reported in all quadrants of the Java Sea. The handful of Allied ships was all but trapped. There were only two possible escape routes into the Indian Ocean. The one through Bali Strait, between Java and Bali, was the closest; but the best way to it, through the passage east of Surabaja, was considered too shallow for the *Exeter*. In addition, with enemy forces already occupying the island of Bali, the strait was believed to be heavily guarded. The other route, through Sunda Strait, lay between Java and Sumatra, more than 400 miles to the west. It too would be heavily guarded, and the sea lanes along the way crawling with enemy men-of-war. Neither passage left room for optimism.

That afternoon the *Exeter* reported emergency repairs had been made to permit a speed of 16 knots on three boilers. Rear Admiral Arthur F. E. Palliser, then chief of staff to Vice Admiral Helfrich, ordered the *Exeter*, accompanied by the *Encounter* and the *Pope*, to proceed west through the Java Sea to transit Sunda Strait and head for Ceylon. The destroyers *John D. Edwards*, *Paul Jones*, *Alden*, and *John D. Ford* were directed to take the shortcut through Bali Strait.

Under cover of darkness, the Allied ships moved out of Surabaja harbor. The *Exeter*, *Encounter*, and *Pope* took the north channel and cleared the minefields to head on a westerly course. The four American destroyers, lacking their main armament—torpedoes—departed through the eastern passage and hit Bali Strait at full speed. As luck would have it, there were only two or three Japanese destroyers stationed in the strait. Before the Nipponese were alerted, the American "cans" went racing past them. For about ten minutes there was a furious exchange of gunfire, but when it was over, the intrepid destroyermen, led by Commander Henry E. Eccles in the *John D. Edwards*, had escaped unscathed into the Indian Ocean. The three ships heading for Sunda Strait were not that fortunate.

The *Exeter*, commanded by Captain O. L. Gordon, was proceeding west, with the *Pope* and *Encounter* keeping station on either bow, when, at 0700 on 1 March 1942, the *Exeter*'s foretop lookout reported an enemy destroyer and two cruisers. Course was quickly changed to avoid them, but as these ships passed from view a new threat appeared in the form of a single-engine seaplane. It flew from over the horizon to hover, out of gun range, over the Allied ships. No one doubted that it was radioing their position at least to the cruiser from which it had been launched.

At 0900 the *Encounter*, on the *Exeter*'s port bow, sighted a destroyer steaming across their course from the south, and immediately increased speed to close her. The *Exeter* and *Encounter* opened fire at extreme range, whereupon the enemy ship discretely turned tail and ran over the horizon. Minutes later, however, she returned accompanied by three more destroyers and two heavy cruisers, all racing bone-in-teeth to do battle.

As the range closed, the *Pope* and *Encounter* opened fire on the destroyers while the *Exeter* engaged the cruisers. The *Pope*'s guns scored a hit on the stern of one of the destroyers, which retired on fire and trailing dark brown smoke. By this time, the *Exeter* was having serious problems. Salvos of heavy shells were falling dangerously close, and it appeared that at any moment she might suffer a fatal hit. Lieutenant Commander Blinn immediately ordered the *Pope* to make smoke, and raced his ship to screen the outgunned British cruiser from enemy view. Simultaneously, the *Exeter* and *Encounter* commenced making smoke. This gambit so hindered the Japanese spotters that their onrushing ships were forced to cease firing temporarily while closing to within range of Allied torpedoes.

Under cover of smoke, the *Exeter* changed course to the south and then to the east in a desperate but futile effort to escape. Although the three Allied ships had been heavily fired upon, they were holding their own when, at 1100, their doom was sealed. Two more heavy cruisers of the Ashigara type, accompanied by three destroyers, joined the battle. Two of the enemy destroyers, their guns blazing, closed on the *Pope*, whose own guns fired back at the leader. The *Encounter* engaged the second. At the same time, the *Exeter* was under fire from almost every direction, and the sea around her churned with the splashes of 8-inch shells. But the valiant British cruiser, handicapped by lack of speed, kept zigzagging and fighting back. Added to her woes, the *Exeter*'s fire control gear was malfunctioning, seriously reducing the effectiveness of her main battery.

At 1105, the *Exeter* launched torpedoes at the cruisers on her port quarter. Minutes later, the *Pope* fired four torpedoes at the same targets, which had closed to within 6,000 yards. In an effort to take pressure off the *Exeter*, Blinn maneuvered the *Pope* ahead and, while making dense black smoke, fired his remaining five torpedoes at cruisers to starboard. During this time, an explosion racked one of the Japanese destroyers to port. On fire, it retreated from the battle. Immediately thereafter, another violent explosion occurred on the bow of a cruiser also to port. The "tin fish" had drawn enemy blood. Whether the *Exeter* or the *Pope* had scored the hit was not known, but nobody gave a damn.

Determined to finish off the Allied ships, the Japanese relentlessly pressed home their attacks. Hopelessly outgunned, the *Exeter*, *Encounter*, and *Pope* were running out of time. At about 1130, the *Exeter* was seriously hit. Swept by flames, the famous fighting ship lay dead in the water spewing clouds of heavy smoke and steam. Her guns, forlornly pointing in all directions, were silenced forever as more and more shells ripped her from stem to stern.*

*Of no historical importance but adding whimsy to disaster is the fact that several ducks, kept on the *Exeter*'s main deck aft to provide fresh eggs for the captain's mess, had been freed at the last moment. Survivors, swimming for their lives, were strangely amused to see the ducks flop over the side and, quacking merrily, swim briskly north-ward, apparently headed for the Borneo coast.

The heavy cruiser HMS *Exeter*, sunk in the Java Sea on 1 March 1942 by Japanese naval and air forces. Imperial War Museum

Lieutenant Commander E. V. St. J. Morgan, commanding the *Encounter*, knew he was trapped, for his ship did not have speed enough to outrun the enemy. He could see the *Pope* was trying to clear out of the area and, to help her escape, he took the *Encounter* between the American destroyer and the Japanese to draw their fire and delay pursuit. The *Encounter* had endured more than two hours of hellish shelling. Shells, screaming overhead and exploding damnably close, had been the order of the day, but up to this point she had not been hit. The *Encounter* was maneuvering fast to outwit the Japanese gunners, when suddenly both suction lines to the fuel pumps broke and her overworked engines groaned to a stop. Now she was in desperate trouble. With enemy shells pounding his striken ship, Morgan had no alternative but to order the *Encounter* scuttled and abandoned.

Powerless to aid survivors of the British ships, Blinn was determined to save his own ship and crew. He pushed the *Pope* as fast as her ancient engines would allow toward a small rain squall several miles away. Its timely appearance offered a glimmer of hope that, blanketed in the downpour, they might yet escape. Shells from the cruisers were kicking up nasty geysers just off her fantail when the *Pope* vanished from view into the heart of the squall. And none too soon, for at that precise moment, the brick walls of number 3 boiler crumbled and fell inside. The boiler was secured immediately, but as a result the *Pope* lost considerable speed.

Temporarily safe in the driving rain, Blinn took advantage of the reprieve to assess the situation. They had fired 345 main battery shells and the forward magazines were almost empty. Additional shells were brought up from the after magazine. The only battle damage was to the main radio antenna, which had been partially shot away. Blinn knew that the *Pope*'s chances of escaping to Australia were beyond betting range, but he had a plan. He would attempt to elude the Japanese by skirting the southern coast of Borneo and, under cover of night, make a dash for it through Lombok Strait into the Indian Ocean. Even there he would not be safe from enemy sea and air forces, but he would have more maneuvering room.

The rain cover lasted for about ten minutes, then the *Pope* was bathed in dazzling sunshine. Fortunately, the squall line masked her from the enemy until the *Pope* was able to slice into another small shower. In a matter of minutes, however, this too ended, leaving the *Pope* exposed in an unfriendly sea with not a cloud in sight. Five minutes later, at 1215, an enemy single-engine seaplane located and began shadowing the *Pope*. It was soon joined by another. Apprehensively, all eyes focused on these unwelcome metal birds, for everyone knew the *Pope*'s movements were being relayed to big brothers that were bound to follow. Darkness, their only hope, was seven long hours away.

Fifteen minutes later, six more cruiser planes appeared and all eight then began making individual bombing runs on the *Pope*. To fight them off, the *Pope* had only two .50-caliber and two .30-caliber machine guns. Nevertheless, the gunners met each attack with all the fury their guns could muster.

In rapid succession the planes dove, and on each pass released two bombs. On the third attack, a bomb exploded close aboard off the port bow. Fragments tore a 4-inch hole through the range finder and wounded two men on number 1 gun. On the eleventh attack, a bomb barely missed the ship and exploded abreast number 4 torpedo tube, ripping a gaping hole aft below the waterline and springing hull plates for a considerable length. The force of the blast knocked the port propeller shaft out of line, causing such violent vibration that the forward engine had to be shut down.

Just as the cruiser planes dropped the last of their bombs and were no longer a threat, six twin-engine Mitsubishi bombers appeared. Machine guns that had fired effectively enough to disconcert the previous attackers now did not have a chance. These were bigger and faster planes, armed with numerous machine guns, cannon, and heavier bombs. Fearful yet determined to do their best, men of the *Pope* watched the bombers circle in the distance preparing for their first attack.

Lieutenant Commander Blinn knew the *Pope* was grievously damaged. As he prepared to meet this new threat, serious flooding in the after engine room began to spread rapidly into the living compartments. Damage control parties worked feverishly to plug the hole in the hull but, with water cascading into her guts, the *Pope* was growing increasingly sluggish to the helm. With only one propeller shaft operable, maneuvering successfully to evade bombs was going to be difficult, if not impossible.

The crew of the *Pope* watched the approaching bombers, and prayed their luck would hold. Unflinching, Blinn studied their approach pattern. At the bomb release point, he turned the *Pope* as hard as he dared away from the base course. It was barely enough, but the bombs missed and exploded close aboard, causing no damage.

The *Pope* was now dangerously waterlogged, and damage control reported the flooding could not be checked. Blinn cast a quick, anguished look aft. His ship was settling by the stern. This was the end. The *Pope* was finished.

After a hurried conference with his damage control officer, Lieutenant R. H. Antrim, who assured him that nothing more could be done to keep the ship afloat, Blinn decided he must act fast to save as many of his crew as possible. He ordered the ship's company to stand by to abandon ship. Hurried preparations were made to scuttle the *Pope*, while the crew continued to man gun stations and maneuver the ship as best they could to confuse the bombers.

They destroyed all classified material, jettisoned depth charges, opened watertight doors, and set a large demolition charge in the forward engine room. The wounded were loaded into the ship's only motor whaleboat, and all rafts were readied to go over the side. There was no fear or panic; like the seasoned professionals they were, the crew worked quickly and efficiently. This was not strange. In battle men seldom fear death when finally they meet it face to face. It is the long hours striving to avoid such a confrontation that drives the terror into men's hearts.

Everything was ready, but again the bombers moved in. The *Pope* could manage only a labored, slow turn, but it was enough. By the grace of God, these bombs also missed. Following the bomb bursts, Blinn ordered all engines stopped. The weather deck aft was awash when he gave the order, "Abandon ship."

Last to leave were those charged with insuring that the *Pope* would never fall into enemy hands. Among them was Lieutenant Commander Blinn, who made a hurried inspection trip below decks to assure himself that sea cocks were open, magazines were flooding, and no wounded remained on board. The gunnery officer recommended that the captain leave the ship before the demolition charge was detonated, and Blinn went over the side to be picked up by the motor whaleboat.

Minutes later the demolition charge, 10 pounds of TNT, went off with a roar, ripping hell out of the forward engine room. With this, men of the demolition gang, who had waited topside well aft of the blast area, dove into the sea and swam as though possessed away from the dangerous suction.

Men were still scrambling on board life rafts or swimming to reach them when violent explosions suddenly shattered the sea around the *Pope*. Aghast, the survivors looked up to discover that two Japanese cruisers had moved in unnoticed to fire on the sinking ship. The *Pope* had been abandoned with no time to spare, for the sixth salvo literally tore her apart. Within seconds, the little grey four-stack destroyer vanished, leaving behind a heavy cloud of smoke and steam.

The two cruisers charged toward the survivors, who watched grimly, assuming they would soon be either killed or captured. But when the cruisers closed to within 4,000 yards, a strange thing happened. All at once, great geysers of water erupted around the cruisers. No planes

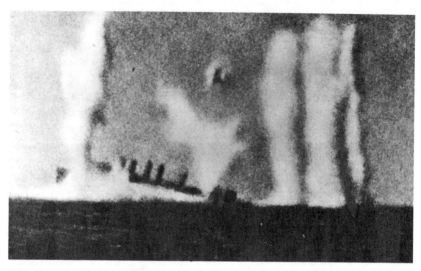

The USS *Pope* (DD-225) sinking in the Java Sea on 1 March 1942 (captured Japanese photograph). National Archives, 80–G–178997

were visible, but it was obvious that the Japanese ships were under attack from the air. With this wild turn of events, men of the *Pope* were spared whatever immediate fate might have befallen them, for the cruisers abruptly wheeled and high-tailed it out of sight.

There is no evidence to suggest that any Allied planes were left in Java to mount such an attack. Most likely, Japanese Army bombers mistook their own cruisers for the enemy. Nevertheless, the *Pope*'s survivors were given a new lease on life. The bombing, by what they believed were Allied planes, coupled with the fact that they had sent out numerous distress calls before the ship sank, gave all hands cause to think that at any moment an American submarine might surface to rescue them.

Blinn circled the area in the crowded motor whaleboat, rounding up swimmers and placing them with the life rafts. There were only three rafts, two small and one large. One other large raft had been destroyed by the near miss on the port side. They found the ship's wherry, badly damaged but still afloat, lashed it to the side of the motor whaleboat, and crammed it with survivors. While this was in progress, Japanese cruiser planes made several strafing runs on the hapless men before flying away. Fortunately, their aim was poor. Only one man was hit, and he suffered only a slight flesh wound.

With the three rafts tied behind the whaleboat, muster was held. Except for one man killed on board ship, all 151 personnel were present. It was hard to believe that during the entire battle, against vastly superior forces, only one man had been killed and a handful wounded.

Since they had only a meager supply of water and food, it was decided to remain near the spot where the *Pope* had gone down in the hope that a submarine would rescue them. As time wore on, men clinging to the overcrowded rafts grew tired. To give each one a spell out of the water, all able-bodied officers and men were divided into six watches, one of which would ride atop a raft every thirty minutes.

At 2200, Blinn ordered a red flare fired. It brilliantly shattered the darkness, illuminating the lonely sea around them. If a submarine was searching for survivors, it would probably be on the surface at that hour. All hands watched the flare slowly burn out and die, leaving them again in darkness. Silently, men prayed that friendly eyes, not those of the enemy, had seen their distress signal.

Long, uneventful hours passed until the next afternoon, 2 March, when a lone enemy seaplane briefly circled the survivors and flew away. With the passing of time, the men were becoming restless. To help keep up morale Blinn ordered the whaleboat engine started. At a slow, agonizing pace it began to tow the raft toward the Java coast, over 100 miles away. By this time the wherry had been repaired and was used to pick up men who either had fallen asleep and drifted away from the rafts or had become too weak to hang on any longer.

At about 0100, as moonbeams streaked across the somber Java Sea, the startled men saw the ominous silhouettes of two enemy destroyers moving across their path several miles ahead. Blinn quickly ordered the engine shut down and all hands remained silent until, without noticing them, the ships passed on into the night.

Gasoline ran out about 1200 on the third day, but the forlorn survivors, seared by the tropic sun and desperate for water, refused to quit. With a blanket they rigged a sail at the bow to keep the whaleboat pointed in a southerly direction and the strongest among them rowed in relays, using oars or pieces of driftwood.

That afternoon a low-flying seaplane circled the survivors. Many feared they might be strafed, but the Japanese pilot seemed more interested in looking them over than in killing them. The plane remained over them for several minutes, then flew off to the west. There was some solace in knowing that at the Japanese were aware of their plight, for, with a speed calculated at no better than 2 miles an hour and without food or water, they would never make it to the Java coast, still many miles away. Now, rather than dying at sea, they might be captured by the enemy. This hitherto unthinkable possibility suddenly became a yearned-for lesser of two evils.

Nightfall found most of the survivors completely exhausted. All had ceased paddling hours before. Those no longer able to hang onto the rafts were jammed on top of them or placed in the vastly overcrowded whaleboat. Fortunately the seas remained calm, for with her gunnals nearly awash, the boat was dangerously close to capsizing. Occasionally, men drained of all strength drifted away from the rafts, but their shipmates refused to let them die. Men who somehow summoned enough strength to swim after and tow them back made many an unsung rescue.

Near midnight the survivors became aware of a black, sinister shape bearing down on them. As it approached, looming ever larger against the star-flecked sky, the men saw it was a Japanese destroyer. With mixed fear and hope, the survivors silently waited. Fifty yards away the ship hove to and focused a powerful searchlight on the pathetic little sea train.

Numbly, all hands waited and wondered if death would be their reward, for they could see the outlines of big guns menacingly trained on them. In a matter of minutes a small boat, manned by heavily armed sailors, approached. A harsh, guttural voice shouted at them in Japanese. Lieutenant William R. "Bill" Wilson, who had been attached to the American Embassy in Tokyo prior to the war and spoke fluent Japanese, answered the hail and established that the Japanese would rescue them. But, he cautioned, if anyone attempted to resist, they all would be killed.

The 151 bedraggled officers and men of the *Pope* were hauled from the Java Sea and treated well on board ship, an act of compassion for which they would be ever grateful to the Japanese Navy. But, as prisoners of war, they were to suffer many hellish ordeals. With the fall of Japan three and one-half years later, the survivors were liberated, but twenty-seven of their shipmates had succumbed to malnutrition and disease. One hundred twenty-four officers and men, including their highly respected commanding officer, Lieutenant Commander Welford C. Blinn, finally were repatriated, clearing up the mystery about the fate of the little four-stack destroyer USS *Pope*.

Soon after the *Exeter* and *Encounter* were sunk, enemy warships moved in close to the survivors and, after observing them for a little while, steamed off leaving them to their fate in the sea. The next day, however, evincing an apparent change of heart, the Japanese returned to rescue them.

# 21

# ABANDON SHIP

It is ironic to think that, although the United States Navy's first aircraft carrier, the *Langley*, was sunk at sea with fighter planes on her flight deck, the historic old ship was no longer an operational aircraft carrier, and the planes on board belonged to the U.S. Army Air Corps.

The ship, originally the fleet collier *Jupiter*, was commissioned and put to sea in 1912. Eight years later, she was converted to an aircraft carrier, and renamed in honor of Professor Samuel Pierpoint Langley. By 1937, larger and faster ships, especially configured to accommodate a new generation of combat aircraft, had joined the fleet to make the *Langley* obsolete. But the old gal was not finished yet. With the forward third of her flight deck cut away, making it impossible to launch or retrieve aircraft, the *Langley*, once the pride of the navy, was retained on duty in the unromantic role of seaplane tender. It was in this capacity that she was serving with Patrol Wing 10 of the Asiatic Fleet when World War II began.

The beginning of the end came for the *Langley* when she and the cargo vessel *Sea Witch* steamed out of Fremantle Harbor, Australia, on 22 February 1942, bound for Tjilatjap, Java. Initially, they were with three merchant ships loaded with U.S. Army personnel, including pilots and ground support crews, ten P-40 aircraft, numerous motor vehicles, and escorted by the cruiser *Phoenix*. This convoy, on a north-westerly course en route to Burma, would pass well south of Java, and far removed from the waters between the Netherlands East Indies and northern Australia, where Japanese bombers and men-of-war were relentlessly hunting down Allied ships. Rather than send the *Langley* and *Sea Witch* on a direct line through the dangerous area, it was planned for them to remain under the protective guns of the *Phoenix* until southwest of Tjilatjap before proceeding independently. This, it was believed, would bring them safely through the back door.

Both ships carried precious cargo in the form of fighter planes, which were in short supply and desperately needed on all war fronts. On board the *Langley* were thirty-three U.S. Army Air Forces pilots and twelve ground crewmen. Their thirty-two P-40 fighter planes were closely dogged down on the one-time flight deck, and on all weather deck space capable of accommodating them. The *Sea Witch* carried no pilots or ground crewmen, and her twenty-seven P-40 aircraft were disassembled in crates.

In the evening of the first day at sea, Commander Robert P. McConnell, in command of the *Langley*, received orders from Vice Admiral Conrad E. L. Helfrich, the Dutch commander of Allied naval forces in the Netherlands East Indies, immediately to detach his ship from the convoy and proceed independently to Tjilatjap. The *Langley* was to arrive there at 0930 on 27 February. The *Sea Witch* received somewhat similar orders, but she was not to leave the convoy until several hours later.

The strange thing about Admiral Helfrich issuing orders for the ships to detach themselves earlier than planned was that he had no firm jurisdiction over them.* The concurrence of U.S. Commander, Southwest Pacific, Vice Admiral William A. Glassford, Jr., was not solicited initially. When Helfrich apprised Glassford of his action, the latter raised no objection. Glassford later stated in his report, "I did in fact share completely his [Helfrich's] views as to the necessity for taking the risk and suscribed fully to his decision."

Helfrich's orders to the *Langley* and the *Sea Witch* were born of desperation. Overwhelming numbers of Japanese invasion forces were closing in on Java, and their bombers were devastating the country. There were no more than fifteen fighter planes in all of Java and, if the island was to be saved, the ABDA command had to have fighters. Helfrich was so frantic, he failed to comprehend the futility of his actions. Dismissing the fact that Tjilatjap had no airdrome, he directed the use of an open field on the outskirts of town. It is doubtful that the "hot" P-40s could have taken off from such a rough field, but even if they had, they would have been forced to operate out of airdromes at

*Vice Admiral Helfrich, RNN, had replaced Admiral Thomas C. Hart, USN, as commander of ABDA naval forces on 14 February 1942. At that time, Vice Admiral William A. Glassford, Jr., USN (newly promoted), remained on the ABDA staff and, as commander, Southwest Pacific, was responsible for the movement of all U.S. naval vessels in the area.

Batavia and Surabaja, which already were being subjected to punishing air attacks. Unloading the assembled aircraft from the *Langley* to the dock was one thing, but hauling them through the streets of Tjilatjap would necessitate knocking down buildings, trees, and other obstacles. To complicate the problem further, most native laborers had taken to the hills for fear of bombing attacks.

Directing the *Sea Witch* to Tjilatjap was an exercise in absolute folly, for once the crated aircraft were unloaded, there were neither mechanics nor equipment available to assemble them.* But time was running out, and Helfrich was not about to be bothered with details. He needed fighter planes, and the crates contained fighters. Amen.

When McConnell turned the *Langley* out of the convoy and headed for Tjilatjap, he was aware of the dangers ahead. Japanese cruisers and aircraft carriers were reported operating in areas of the Indian Ocean through which his ship would have to pass and, as he approached Java, land-based bombers would have to be reckoned with. He was justifiably concerned that with his ship's top speed not much more than 13 knots, and armed with a few ineffectual 3-inch antiaircraft guns and four ancient 5-inch deck guns, the *Langley* could only get *into* trouble, not out of it.

At 1500 on 26 February 1942, lookouts reported two unidentified aircraft approaching. These turned out to be Dutch PBY seaplanes, which signalled the *Langley* had an escort 20 miles to the west. At this welcome news, McConnell altered course to rendezvous with the vessel. Unfortunately, the so-called escort was no more than a small Dutch minelayer, the *William Van der Zaan*. What dubious protection such a ship might provide was lost in the fact that she was experiencing boiler trouble and could make no more than 10 knots. At such a slow speed it would be impossible for the *Langley* to make Tjilatjap by 0930, as ordered. McConnell, therefore, took leave of the minelayer and continued on.

That evening, the *Langley* received a message from Glassford directing her to proceed to Tjilatjap escorted by the *William Van der Zaan* and two PBY aircraft. Complying with these strange orders, McConnell reversed course to rejoin the *Van der Zaan*. Several hours later, with the minelayer in sight, new orders from Glassford directed the *Langley* to rendezvous the following morning with the destroyers *Edsall* and *Whipple*, about 200 miles south of Tjilatjap. Once again McConnell altered course and headed the *Langley* north for the rendezvous. Thanks to

*The *Sea Witch* reached Tjilatjap, Java, and unloaded her cargo of trucks and crated P-40 aircraft, which were soon captured by the Japanese. She escaped from the harbor on the night of 1 March 1942, and, escorted by the *Isabel*, arrived safely at Fremantle, Australia.

these confusing orders, her time of arrival at Tjilatjap would be delayed until 1700 the next day.

About midnight, those on board the *Langley* observed with concern two series of brilliant white flashes some distance off the port bow. Believing they were being fired upon, McConnell immediately ordered general quarters, emergency full speed, and a change in course 90 degrees to starboard. Tensions diminished somewhat when the ship became blanketed in a series of heavy line squalls. McConnell held this course until he was reasonably certain they had lost contact with the ship, then again headed toward the rendezvous point.

At 0720 on 27 February 1942, the destroyers *Whipple* and *Edsall* were sighted on the horizon, with two Dutch PBYs circling over them. The *Whipple* signalled that the *Edsall* was standing by a submarine contact and that the *Langley* should remain out of the area. McConnell ordered a course change to clear a 12-mile circle around the point of contact, and the *Whipple* moved to put herself between the aircraft tender and the submarine. When the *Edsall* lost contact with the submarine, she joined with the *Whipple* to form an antisubmarine screen on either bow of the *Langley*. Then, with their air escort, the ships headed for Tjilatjap.

The first indication of trouble occurred at 0900, when an unidentified plane was sighted flying at high altitude. Since the two Dutch PBYs could not provide adequate protection against air attack, McConnell sent an emergency message to Glassford reporting the contact and requesting fighter escort. He stated that it was obvious his ship's location, course, and destination were known to the enemy, and that attacks could be expected in about two hours from land-based bombers, or sooner if an enemy carrier was in the area.

McConnell's plea was but a cry in the dark. Fighters could not be provided, because there were less than a dozen flyable planes left in all of Java, and these were scattered throughout the island to operate independently as best they could. There was no possible way that fighters could be assembled and sent to cover a ship 130 miles at sea.

Japanese bombers came as predicted. At 1140, the *Edsall* signalled "Aircraft sighted." The *Langley* immediately went to general quarters as nine twin-engine bombers approached at an altitude of 15,000 feet. She was zigzagging on a base course of 357 degrees in an effort to confuse the enemy bombardiers, but at just over 13 knots she was hardly an elusive target. When the planes steadied on their approach course, the *Langley*'s antiaircraft guns commenced firing. The gun crews, with their old 3-inch weapons, did their best, but they could not reach the attackers, who came steadily on, cocky in the knowledge that they were out of range.

McConnell, conning his ship from the signal bridge through a voice tube to the navigation bridge directly below, kept his eyes riveted on the attackers. He knew that the bomb release point had to be at an angle of about 80 degrees above his ship. When he judged that the planes had reached that point, he immediately ordered full right rudder. The *Langley*, always sluggish in response to the helm, commenced a slow right turn just as the bombs were released. The deadly salvo missed off the port bow. Underwater explosions caused the old ship to tremble, and bomb fragments knifed through her steel plates forward on the port side, shattering windows on the bridge, but causing no casualties.

The battle was an uneven contest from the beginning, but the *Langley*'s crew fought the ship superbly. The antiaircraft gun crews fired furiously at the attackers, although they knew only too well there wasn't a snowball's chance in hell of downing one. They could only hope to force the planes to higher altitudes and thereby reduce bombing accuracy.

Trying desperately to elude the second Japanese attack, McConnell steered the slow, difficult-to-maneuver *Langley* on zigzag courses and turns, hoping that if he could hold out a little longer, fighter planes would appear to save his ship from certain destruction. Again his evasive actions were successful, and the enemy planes were forced to turn away without dropping their bombs.

The bombers made a wide circle and came back a third time. Cannily the enemy pilots followed the *Langley*'s last possible course change and dropped their bombs accordingly. In a matter of seconds violent explosions from five direct hits and three near misses racked the ship. Instantly, fires broke out throughout the ship. Motorboats and aircraft were ablaze on the main and flight decks. Men raced to extinguish the fires, but were hampered by ruptured water mains.

Near-misses tore gaping holes in the *Langley*'s sides below the water-line forward, and she was taking on water rapidly. There was serious flooding in the engine room, but the bilge pumps had been knocked out of commission and nothing could be done about it.

The gyro compass was destroyed, disrupting steering from the bridge until the secondary steering mechanism could be activated; and McConnell had difficulty communicating with various parts of the ship, for the telephone system and many of the voice tubes were wrecked.

In the midst of all this, six Japanese fighter planes appeared and attempted a low-level strafing attack. The *Langley*'s antiaircraft guns, whose crews stood in the rubble of blasted aircraft and savagely fought back, forced all but one of attackers to turn away. Projectiles from that fighter's cannon caused considerably more damage to the P-40s on the flight deck. Fortunately, only one attack was pressed home. Then, to everyone's relief, all enemy aircraft withdrew to the east.

To help his men fight the fires, McConnell maneuvered for a zero wind condition. The ship was listing 10 degrees to port, and the listing persisted even after the crew jettisoned five shattered P-40s from the flight deck and resorted to counterflooding starboard compartments. The engineering officer reported conditions below decks were not improving. Fire room bilges were awash, and water was 4 feet deep in the motor pits.

McConnell realized he could never bring the *Langley* into port, for she was drawing too much water to negotiate the channel at Tjilatjap, and the nearest harbors of refuge were hundreds of miles away in Australia. Although he doubted the *Langley* could make it, McConnell decided to try to take her close to the Java coast, 130 miles to the north, where his crew might have a better chance of surviving. He had no other choice.

As the *Langley* labored on, McConnell ordered boats and life rafts made ready for lowering in case it became necessary to abandon ship. Some men misunderstood this order and jumped over the side. The destroyer *Edsall*, which was trailing the *Langley*, plucked them from the sea as she had rescued others who had jumped to escape fires, or were blown over the side by the force of exploding bombs.

While all hell was breaking loose topside, Chief Radioman Leland E. Leonard relieved Radioman First Class Claud J. Hinds, Jr., who had worked the transmitter for the first twenty-five minutes of the attack.* Leonard continued to send out messages until ordered to abandon ship. The following are excerpts from the radio log, recorded in Greenwich mean time:

> 0358  Got off warning of attack to Nerk
> 0400  Air raid raid raid
> 0405  Air raid raid raid / We ok
> 0412  *Langley* being attacked by sixteen aircraft
> 0414  Got hit on forecastle that put us out for a few minutes. . . . Lost local control. . . . Transmitter is now out but I plugged in rak ral batteries an am back now
> 0422  Mr Snay went to bridge as they do not answer us. Gave command to Leonard CRM
> 0425  Tried nr one generator and it was ok. . . . Back to ships power to save batteries

---

*Chief Radioman Leland E. Leonard survived the *Langley*'s sinking, but lost his life when the *Pecos* was sunk.

0431  Japs working close to our freq
0432  We all ok so far
0435  Mama said there would be days like this. She must have
      known. Warnes came in said hit on flight deck on planes and
      one on well deck one on foscle. . . .
0437  Someone tuning now
0440  Sez planes at about 30,000 feet, too high for our guns
0442  Still tuning from somewhere. A decided list
0515  Power off on ships ac. . . . Back to batteries
0520  Jap jamming us as much as possible
0529  We are securing as ship is listing. . . . Shot to hell
0530  Signing off per LEL CRM. . . .

McConnell, on the bridge of his stricken ship, was notified that all engines had stopped due to water in the electric motor pits,* and that the fire room would soon be completely flooded because the drainage system was inoperative. The *Langley* coasted to a dead stop, her list now increased to a frightening 17 degrees. With 104 tons of aircraft riding high on her flight deck, the ship could capsize at any moment. Grimly accepting the fact that the *Langley* was finished, McConnell ordered abandon ship.

Life rafts were lowered over the side, and boats from the destroyers *Whipple* and *Edsall* stood by to pick up swimming survivors. Unfortunately, as one motor whaleboat loaded with wounded was being lowered, a jagged metal splinter severed the after falls, dropping the stern and dumping all hands into the sea. Shipmates quickly swam to the rescue, and all of the wounded men were saved.

The order to abandon ship had been given at approximately 1345 Pacific time. About fifteen minutes later the executive officer, Commander Lawrence E. Divoll, came to the bridge to inform the captain that all survivors were clear of the ship. Then the two men made one last check to make sure that classified publications and the top secret coding machine had been properly destroyed.

Heartsick over the impending loss of his ship, McConnell was determined to go down with her and ordered Divoll to leave before it was too late. As his intentions became clear to his men, they began to shout, imploring him to leave the ship. McConnell was deeply touched by his crew's concern for his life. Realizing that his action was holding up rescue operations and unnecessarily detaining the two destroyers in an area where they were exposed to possible air or surface attack, he relented.

---

*The *Langley* was the first U.S. Navy ship to have an electric drive propulsion system.

The seaplane tender USS *Langley* (AV-3), shown here in 1937, was sunk in the Indian Ocean south of Java on 27 February 1942 by Japanese aircraft. Naval History, NH 63547

With all survivors accounted for, it was imperative that the destroyers clear the area quickly before the enemy reappeared. But the *Langley* was still afloat and, although obviously sinking, she was taking the devil's own time in doing so. To speed the process, McConnell requested the *Whipple* to finish her off with torpedoes. The first torpedo hit aft of the starboard jib crane in the magazine area, but the magazine failed to explode. Instead, to everyone's amazement, the *Langley* slowly rolled back to an almost even keel. A second torpedo, fired into the port side amidships, set off a wild fire at the break of the poop deck. Then nine 5-inch shells were fired into her at the waterline. Still she remained afloat.

As torpedoes were in very short supply, it was deemed unwarranted to expend more to accelerate the sinking. The plan now was to clear out of the area and return after dark. If the *Langley* was still afloat, additional torpedoes would be used to finish her. As the destroyers moved off on a westerly course, the *Langley* was burning furiously, very low in the water, and settling on an even keel. It was obvious that the historic ship would soon be lost forever beneath the Indian Ocean.

About 484 officers and men had been on board the *Langley* when she was attacked, including 33 pilots and 12 crew chiefs of the U.S. Army Air Corps, yet casualties were miraculously low. In all, 2 naval officers and 6 seamen were killed, 5 seamen were listed as missing, and 11 were wounded. Two of the Army Air Forces pilots, Second Lieutenants Gerald Dix and William Ackerman, were wounded. The major factor in saving so many lives was superb shiphandling by the captains of the *Edsall* and *Whipple*.

McConnell sent a dispatch from the *Whipple* to Commander, Southwest Pacific Glassford, stating that the *Langley* was sinking and that survivors were on board the two destroyers, which were steaming westward. He requested that air reconnaissance verify the sinking to eliminate the need for returning to the area.

Glassford immediately ordered the gunboat *Tulsa* and the minelayer *Whippoorwill* to search the area for possible *Langley* survivors. Later that evening, after a Dutch PBY reported seeing the *Langley* sink, he ordered the *Whipple* and *Edsall* to rendezvous with the tanker *Pecos* in the lee of Christmas Island at 1030 the next day. The *Langley* personnel and the two wounded pilots were to board the *Pecos* for transportation to Australia. The Army Air Corps men were to be taken by the *Edsall* to Tjilatjap where, according to Glassford, they were needed to man the aircraft yet to be unloaded from the *Sea Witch* and assembled.

At 0930 on 28 February 1942, the day after the Allied defeat in the Battle of the Java Sea, the three ships met off Christmas Island.

Preparations to transfer the survivors were suddenly disrupted by an air raid alarm. Three twin-engine bombers appeared overhead and the ships raced for the protection of a nearby rain squall. The planes flew directly overhead, but ignored the ships to drop bombs on shore installations. Although the planes made what appeared to be several determined bombing runs on the *Whipple*, which took high-speed evasive action, they dropped no bombs and soon winged away to the north.

During the bombing attack, a new menace appeared in the rendezvous area—the white plume of a periscope wake. When Vice Admiral Glassford received this information, he was preparing to escape from doomed Java to Australia. Although well aware that Japanese landings on Java were occurring unopposed, Glassford said nothing to prevent the Army Air Corps men from attempting to land at Tjilatjap. Instead, he ordered the ships to proceed westward to an area more likely to be safe from air or submarine attack before transferring the personnel.

The ships steamed west until dawn the following day, 1 March 1942, when the transfer of survivors was safely conducted. The three vessels then separated to carry out their respective orders.

The tanker *Pecos*, with survivors of the *Langley* on board, headed for southern Australia on a course calculated to skirt 600 miles from the Den Pesar airfield on Bali, the nearest Japanese bomber base. But in the Indian Ocean there were Japanese aircraft carriers whose whereabouts were unknown, and at 1000 a scouting plane from one of them spotted the *Pecos*. The single-engine plane circled the *Pecos* twice, then flew off to the northeast. This was bad news for a lone ship armed only with two 3-inch antiaircraft guns and two .50-caliber and four .30-caliber machine guns, for there was no doubt in anyone's mind that visitors of the most unwelcome kind would soon be calling. Although no help could be expected, the *Pecos* immediately sent out a contact report.

At 1145 the bone-chilling whine of dive bombers suddenly broke the stillness. Before lookouts could spot them, three planes dove out of the sun, and each unloaded a high-explosive bomb. All three missed, but winging close behind them came three more. This time one bomb exploded near the forecastle, killing and wounding several sailors manning number 1 antiaircraft gun.

For the next four hours dive bombers attacked the practically defenseless ship. In all, fifty bombs were dropped, five of them direct hits and six damaging near misses. Although this poor percentage reflected little credit upon the Japanese pilots, the officers and men crowded on board the *Pecos* found little solace in the statistics.

By 1530, when her captain, Lieutenant Commander E. P. Aber-nethy, ordered abandon ship, the *Pecos* was a bomb-shattered hulk with dead and wounded sprawled grotesquely over her bloody decks. Soon afterwards, survivors in the water watched spellbound as the *Pecos*'s bow gradually disappeared from view, leaving her stern poised momentarily in the air before it too was gobbled up by the sea.

Heavy oil, covering the surface of the sea, coated the swimming men with thick black scum. It burned their eyes and, when swallowed accidentally, caused severe spasms of vomiting. Floundering alone in a vast expanse of unfriendly ocean, the survivors appeared doomed to certain death. Without food or water, even those fortunate enough to be in or clinging to overloaded life rafts could not live for long. To add to their plight, Japanese planes made several strafing runs on them before departing.

The survivors had been in the water for almost four hours. Some had given up in despair and drowned, and most of the others had all but given up hope of rescue, for the sun was hull down in the west. All at once, the most beautiful ship any of them had ever seen came racing, bone-in-teeth, over the horizon. The little four-stack destroyer *Whipple* had intercepted the *Pecos*'s frantic radio calls for help and come to the rescue.

By the time the *Whipple* arrived on the scene, it was 1930 and almost dark. In the gathering dusk, it became increasingly difficult to locate men in the water and load them into the ship's small motor launch. When informed that many survivors were stranded in the midst of a large oil slick off the starboard bow, the *Whipple*'s commanding officer, Lieutenant Commander Eugene S. Karpe, carefully maneuvered among them. Several seamen on the *Whipple* tied lines around them-selves and jumped into the oily water to rescue those unable to make it on their own.

For over two hours, desperate attempts to locate and save the be-draggled survivors continued without letup. Then, at 2141, those manning the underwater detection gear reported the ominous beat of submarine propellers. Rescue work had to be suspended and the *Whipple* headed full speed toward the contact. She dropped depth charges, with undetermined results, and lost the contact.

Fifteen minutes later, with the submarine temporarily silenced, the *Whipple*'s crew renewed the search for survivors. But it was now com-pletely dark and time to make a difficult and painful decision. Should the *Whipple* continue to search and risk being torpedoed, with the consequent loss of ship, crew, and survivors, or clear out and run for safety? Commander E. M. Crouch, commander of Destroyer Division

57, on board the *Whipple*, concluded it would be foolhardy to take the risk. This decision was concurred in by the commanding officers of the *Langley*, *Pecos*, and *Whipple*. Accordingly, at 2207, the ship steamed out of the area.

Of the 666 officers and men who had been on board the *Pecos*, the *Whipple* had been able to rescue only 220, including the two wounded Army Air Corps pilots. Many had been killed during the bombing and strafing attacks; others had perished in the water. Only 146 of the *Langley*'s original ship's company of about 439 officers and men, including Commander McConnell, had survived the two sinkings.

Many wondered why the destroyer *Edsall* did not come to the rescue, but that little ship was having troubles of her own. Following the transfer of personnel, the *Edsall* steamed off for Tjilatjap to vanish without a trace. Not until the war ended did anyone know what had happened to her. Captured Japanese films showed the hapless four piper being blasted out of existence by enemy cruisers. Not one of the *Edsall*'s crew, nor any of her army passengers were seen again.

The destroyer *Whipple*, her decks jammed with forlorn survivors, reached safety in Fremantle, Australia, on 4 March 1942. Commander McConnell immediately wrote his report concerning the sinking of the *Langley* and submitted it to commander, U.S. Naval Forces Southwest Pacific—Vice Admiral Glassford, who had escaped the Japanese by flying out of Tjilatjap on 1 March 1942.

Glassford forwarded McConnell's report to Commander in Chief, United States Fleet, Admiral Ernest J. King, stating:

1. "Forwarded. An examination of this report makes it doubtful that every effort was made to save the USS *Langley* and that her abandonment and subsequent endeavors to assure her sinking failed to uphold the best traditions of the naval service.

2. "This opinion was communicated to the Commander-in-Chief, United States Fleet, by dispatch, with a recommendation that these matters be the subject of further investigation."

McConnell was aghast. Such an accusation, if upheld, could ruin his name and his future in the naval service. In his own mind, he was innocent of wrongdoing. He had fought the *Langley* to the best of his ability, abandoning her only when it became apparent that such action was the only solution to a desperate and hopeless situation.

For almost three months McConnell worried and waited. Finally, Admiral King's answer came, in the form of a copy of his letter to the secretary of the navy. It read in part, "The Commander-in-Chief does not agree with the then Commander U.S. Naval Forces, Southwest Pacific—that there is a question as to whether or not the best traditions of the naval service were upheld. He recommends that this matter be considered closed, without prejudice in any form whatsoever to the record of Commander McConnell."

The case of America's first aircraft carrier, the *Langley*, was closed, but Commander Robert P. McConnell continued his naval career to attain the rank of rear admiral before retiring from the naval service.

# 22

# LOSS OF THE USS *PERCH* (SS-176)

The fleet-type submarine *Perch* was first hexed by the Japanese while making a night surface attack on a large, unescorted merchant ship off the southeastern reaches of Celebes Island on 25 February 1942. To insure a kill, the submarine was closing to point-blank range. Just as Lieutenant Commander David A. Hurt, the commanding officer, gave the order, "Stand by to fire," the merchantman opened up with a well-concealed deck gun. The first round fell short, but the second, a direct hit, ripped through the conning tower fairwater to rupture the main antenna trunk, sever some electrical leads, and wreck the gyro compass. Instantly, Hurt pulled the plug and dove to safety, unable to fire torpedoes.

The men of the *Perch* were maddened at losing such a fat target, but thankful the shell had not punctured the pressure hull. There were other fish to be taken, scores of them. Japanese invasion fleets were reported poised for an imminent assault on Java. Exactly where landings would occur was not yet determined, and the *Perch* was ordered to take station in the Java Sea south of Bawean Island to await developments.

Although no targets of opportunity ventured into the *Perch*'s area, not many miles away, on 27 February 1942, a small Allied fleet of American, British, Dutch, and Australian fighting ships, in a suicidal gamble to prevent the fall of Java, engaged a superior Japanese force, and lost disastrously. News of the Allied defeat in the Battle of the Java Sea did not reach Lieutenant Commander Hurt until the *Perch* surfaced on the night of 28 February.

Coupled with the destruction of Allied air forces in the Netherlands East Indies, the loss of all major warships in Asian waters permitted the Japanese to land unopposed wherever they chose. With the island of Java now doomed, members of the Allied (ABDA) high command scrambled frantically to get out of Java. Coincident with the pandemonium ashore, communications went into a flat spin. The last radio contact the *Perch* had with Allied headquarters occurred on the night of 28 February, when the submarine was ordered to attack transports at a landing point a few miles east of Surabaja. This irrational directive was probably tossed out by some distraught officer about to run for his life, for that portion of the Java Sea was much too shallow to permit effective submarine operations. Though keenly aware of the dangers ahead, Hurt kept his fears to himself and grimly headed the *Perch* for the enemy.

Twenty miles north of Surabaja, on 1 March 1942, the *Perch* surfaced at dusk to recharge batteries and move into attack position. Ninety minutes later, two Japanese destroyers came into view. Although a dim moon was positioned in the *Perch*'s favor, the enemy tin cans somehow got wind of her and changed course to attack. Flabbergasted at having been sighted, Hurt quickly dove the boat to periscope depth and watched as the destroyers passed well astern. They continued on, then, just as it seemed a dangerous situation had been averted, one of them abruptly reversed course. If the destroyer held that course, she would pass about 600 yards astern, and Hurt decided to fight. He would sink the "can" with stern tube torpedoes. The range closed rapidly. On board the submarine all was in readiness. The order to fire was only moments away when the destroyer suddenly turned and, instead of presenting a broadside target, knifed head-on toward the *Perch*.

Charts of the area indicated a depth of 200 feet, and Hurt immediately ordered a dive to 180. At 100 feet the ominous pounding of propellers reverberated overhead. Seconds later six awesome explosions were felt. Fortunately, they were well off target and did no damage. But in reaching for the safety of deeper water, the *Perch* slammed into the muddy bottom of the Java Sea at 140 feet, and abruptly stopped. Desperate to break free, Hurt backed down full, but the mud would not release its grip.

Quick on the heels of the first attack came the second. This time the stranded boat was not so lucky. Depth charges exploding almost on top of the boat sent giant shock waves coursing throughout its length. The lights dimmed weirdly, and glass could be heard shattering everywhere on the deck. When the fury of the explosions subsided, damage was assessed. Ninety per cent of the engine room gauges were jammed or broken beyond repair. Only the auxiliary gauges on the thwartship boards were intact and working. The hull ventilation supply stop was frozen closed. High-pressure air banks in the after battery tank were leaking badly. Both batteries showed a full ground. The hull in the after battery compartment on the starboard side had been pushed in more than 2 inches over an area 6 feet long by 1 foot wide. The crew's toilet bowl was shattered.

Unable to take evasive action, Hurt stopped all engines in the hope of fooling the Japanese into believing the *Perch* had been done in. But the persistent enemy dropped another string of punishing depth charges for good measure. This time most of the damage and shock occurred amidships. In the control room the hull exhaust duct section flooded, soaking the fire control panel. All depth gauges except that of the bow planeman and the one in the commanding officer's stateroom were ruptured. The conning tower was dangerously compressed above the chart desk to a depth of 2 inches over an area about 3 feet by 1 foot, and all dials in the conning tower were shattered. Number 2 periscope was frozen. Number 1 could be raised, but required four men to turn it. The engine room hatch, conning tower hatch, and conning tower door gaskets were crimped and leaking steadily. More water was pouring into the boat where the air compressor water cooling supply flanges had cracked at the weld. Without air-conditioning, the boat became hotter than the hinges of hell, and the stench from sweating bodies made each breath an ugly experience.

When they heard no sounds from the ocean depths, the Japanese apparently concluded they had sunk the submarine and steamed away. When he was absolutely certain it was safe, Hurt started the motors. After several vigorous attempts, the *Perch* broke free of the mud to surface at 0300 on 2 March.

Crewmen came out on deck in the fresh predawn air to find it littered with depth-charge strips. They cursed to discover the damage topside. The antenna was down, and the blinker light smashed flat. That, however, was the least of their troubles. Number 1 main engine ran away on starting and had to be shut down. Number 2 started, and was immediately put to charging batteries. With only number 3 main engine available for propulsion, Hurt headed his crippled boat north to find quiet, shallow water where the submarine could safely rest on the bottom while interior damage was repaired.

The *Perch* had been on the surface only a few minutes when lookouts shouted the alarming news—two Japanese destroyers were heading their way. Hurt immediately dove the *Perch* for the bottom, figuring their only chance to elude the enemy was by lying still with all machinery stopped. But the Japanese had sighted the *Perch* just before she dove.

Like foxhounds, the destroyers dashed to the spot where the submarine went down. The first string of six depth charges exploded off target and did no damage to the *Perch*, resting on the bottom at 200 feet. The second attack with five ash cans was murderous. One after another, violent explosions pounded the *Perch*. Main ballast tanks 1 and 3 ruptured and lost their air. Leaks they had repaired in the air compressor opened again. A nasty leak in the antenna trunk rendered the transmitter inoperative. Throughout the boat high pressure air and water lines were leaking. The submarine was taking a terrible beating, but like a punch-drunk fighter she refused to go down for the count. Everyone wondered just how much more she could withstand.

Further attacks ceased with the second round of depth charges, although the destroyers still circled overhead. Convinced they were biding their time until sunup to make certain their efforts had succeeded, Hurt decided to try sneaking out of the area. To his dismay, the *Perch* would not move. Once again the mucky sea bottom, like a fist clenched in death, held the submarine fast. Not daring to make full-power efforts to break free and probably alert the enemy, Hurt ordered the motors shut down.

Soon after the hour of sunrise, the destroyers were heard moving to attack again. With the *Perch* lying helpless in the mud, all hands waited and prayed their battered boat would stand up under all the enemy had to offer. The first string of five depth charges, laid along the length of the *Perch*, exploded close aboard with such murderous force that torpedoes in tubes 1 and 2 made hot runs. Fearful that the heat might detonate the warheads in the tubes, the trapped men sweated it out until the propulsion units ran their course. This time the bow planes, set on a 20 degree rise, were so violently rigged in by the shock waves that the bow plane rigging panel was burned up. The JK sonar sound head and receiver were knocked out, and more leaks opened up in all compartments.

Quick on the heels of the first series, the enemy laid a string of four more depth charges parallel to the *Perch*. These caused the support studs on the bow plane tilting motor to elongate, and a coupling shin to fall out. From then on, bow planes would have to be operated by hand. The remaining toilet bowls shattered, and it seemed as though only the steel shell of the submarine itself was left to be damaged beyond repair.

At 0830, the fifth and worst attack of all occurred. Only three depth charges were dropped, but each had a terrifying personality all its own. The rugged submariners on board the *Perch* had endured long, torturous hours of punishment without going mad, but these horrendous explosions practically on top of the boat sounded as though the end of the world had come. Shock waves of monstrous intensity caused the *Perch* to jerk and vibrate violently. Men were slammed into machinery and against bulkheads. Along the length of the submarine, steel plates twisted and groaned, threatening to rip asunder at the seams. The lights went out briefly, and blue flames snapping from short circuits spooked the darkness like torches of the devil.

One gigantic blast caused the depth gauge to jump suddenly from 200 feet to 230 feet, and generated the haunting fear that they had been entombed on the mucky bottom of the Java Sea. Water was now streaming in from warped hatches. Fuel and lube tanks ruptured. Most gauge lines for temperature, pressure, oil, and water were broken. Electric alarm systems and all telephone circuits were dead, their cables cut by instruments torn from bulkheads.

On the engine room deck the supporting stanchions between the overhead and the deck were fractured at the hull weld. Dents everywhere attested to how perilously close the hull had come to being crushed. One in the overhead of an officer's stateroom bulged inward over a 2-foot by 5-foot area. High bilge water flooded from number 2 generator, and numerous battery cells were cracked. The proud *Perch*, like her courageous crew, was close to the end of the line. With one more such attack, they would all be dead.

Praise the Lord, the attacks ceased. Either the destroyers were out of depth charges, or the oil and air bubbling to the surface convinced the enemy that one Yankee submarine had been silenced forever. When it became obvious the enemy cans had gone, tensions eased somewhat, but there was extensive damage to be repaired before trying to take the *Perch* to the surface. Water pouring into the boat made constant pump-

The USS *Perch* (SS-176). Seriously damaged and unable to submerge, she was scuttled in the Java Sea on 3 March 1942 to prevent capture by the enemy. James C. Fahey Collection, U.S. Naval Institute

ing necessary to keep the motors from flooding. One monumental question haunted all hands—could the *Perch* break free of the mud? But that question could not be answered until after dark, for she dared not surface in daylight.

For the next thirteen hellishly long hours the crew worked to ready the boat. It was rough, hard work made infinitely more difficult by the feverish, humid air that grew more foul with every breath. What little compressed air remained had to be used sparingly.

Finally, at 2000, damaged electric motors had been jury-rigged to provide power to both shafts, and the fateful try to surface commenced. A tomb-like stillness shrouded the submarine as Lieutenant Commander Hurt gave the order for maximum power on both shafts ahead. The *Perch* trembled as she strained to break free, the heavy churning of propellers echoing throughout the boat. She would not budge. Full astern produced the same result. Grim-faced, exhausted men stood by in silence while the propellers pounded first full ahead, then full astern. After almost an hour of anguished trying, with no noticeable results and with battery power waning, the hope of living to see another day also began to fade. Suddenly, there was a slight movement forward. Slowly, painfully the *Perch* inched ahead, then picked up speed. Smiles of hope spread over haggard faces.

Somehow, the *Perch* managed to rise from the depths to surface at 2100 on 2 March 1942. As hatches opened and cool, refreshing air flowed into the boat, rugged submariners, well aware of the tremendous odds they had overcome, readily conceded that their lives had been spared by nothing short of a miracle.

But serious problems lay ahead. The *Perch* had suffered so much damage that she was useless in offensive action and would be hard-pressed to defend herself. Only one of her four main engines could be started and, with this, she could make no more than 5 knots on the surface. The steering gear was so damaged that, with port rudder angle on, it could be shifted amidships only with great difficulty. Then, upon reaching the amidships position, it would jump to extreme starboard. Hull leaks were so bad that both trim and drain pumps had to be kept running at full capacity to prevent the bilges from flooding. Torpedoes could not be fired as all outer doors were frozen shut. This, coupled with the jamming of the deck gun training mechanism, rendered the *Perch* utterly defenseless.

All Hurt could do now was to head his submarine for the nearest exit from the Java Sea into the Indian Ocean and pray they could make Australia, 1,700 miles away. This would require another miracle, for the *Perch* could not survive another depth charge attack and would have to remain submerged during daylight. But the *Perch* was in no condition to submerge. With quarter-inch-square strips gouged out of gaskets in the forward escape trunk and conning tower doors, and gaskets on all hatches badly crimped and leaking, to dive could prove disastrous. In the four hours until dawn, exhausted crewmen strove to plug leaks and repair damage, hoping to make the boat capable at least of shallow dives during daylight. With enemy forces swarming over the Java Sea, this was a must for survival.

An hour before sunrise on 3 March 1942, Hurt decided to make a test dive to assess the submarine's watertight condition. Sufficient water was pumped out of trim tanks to make her definitely light and, at one-third speed, Hurt slowly took the boat down by flooding the main ballast. As the *Perch* went under, sea water gushed in through the engine room and the conning tower hatches, which failed to seat. Nevertheless, Hurt continued the slow dive in the belief that the increased pressure would seal the hatches. It didn't work. Flooded with water, the *Perch* grew sluggish and suddenly took a dangerous down angle. At once, the diving officer commenced blowing ballast tanks. Before the dive could be stopped, they were at periscope depth with the sea pouring into the engine room at a fearful rate. By the time the *Perch* clawed her way back to the surface, water in the engine room bilges was up to the generators. A few minutes more, and all would have been lost.

Because of heavy flooding in the after compartments, only the forward half of the deck floated free of the waves, and every available pump was kept running at maximum capacity to prevent the *Perch* from foundering. With no thought of quitting, determined men again worked to reseat the conning tower hatch and plug other leaks so they could submerge by dawn.

At dawn, the *Perch* was still on the surface unable to dive. As the sun loomed over the horizon, so did three Japanese destroyers, followed by two cruisers. The nearest destroyer opened fire with one gun, and the shell fell short by 300 yards. The second and third shells were also short, but in deflection and falling closer. Helpless to fight back and with the odds on their being blown to hell narrowing with every second, Hurt ordered the *Perch* scuttled and abandoned. Swiftly, the *Perch*'s nine officers and fifty-three men carried out their orders. Classified material, heavily weighted down, was given the deep-six and, as flood valves were opened, everyone went over the side. From a safe distance, the crew sadly watched as great volumes of water surged into her guts, and their beloved *Perch* vanished beneath the Java Sea.

Within an hour's time, the destroyers had picked up the *Perch*'s entire crew and, for the next three and one-half years, these hapless men remained prisoners of the Japanese. Nine of the *Perch*'s crew died in Japanese prisoner-of-war camps from malnutrition and disease. The fifty-three others, including Lieutenant Commander David Hurt, who suffered incredible torture through his imprisonment, survived.*

*Final tragedy came when the courageous Captain Hurt was killed in a hunting accident two and one-half months after returning home.

# 23

# THE EXPENDABLE SHIP
# USS *ISABEL* (PY-10)

In all probability only a few old China hands will remember the *Isabel*. Yet, on that hideous "day of infamy," she was a unit of the U.S. Asiatic Fleet operating out of Manila Bay. Although *Isabel*'s fighting role in the futile attempt to halt the Japanese conquest of Southeast Asia never made headlines, those rugged souls who manned her did an outstanding job with what little they had and, like so many other heroes of the Asiatic Fleet, went unsung for their efforts.

As a fighting ship, the *Isabel* was somewhat of a navy bastard. Two hundred forty-five feet long with a 28-foot beam, she was designed more or less along destroyer lines, and was under construction as a private yacht when America became involved in World War I. The navy, hard pressed for ships to meet the challenge of German U-boats, purchased her in 1918, and christened her the USS *Isabel*. Outfitted with four 3-inch deck guns, torpedoes, and depth charges, the daughty little ship steamed forth to fight the war in the Atlantic.

Four years after the "war to end all wars," the *Isabel*, stripped of her torpedo tubes and depth-charge racks, was painted white and sent to the Asiatic Fleet to serve as flagship for commander, Yangtze Patrol. In 1928 the new river gunboats *Luzon* and *Mindanao* arrived to serve as flagships for commander, Yangtze Patrol, and commander, South China Patrol, respectively. From that time on, the *Isabel*, with most of her fighting teeth pulled, was relegated to the inglorious role of "relief" flagship for the commander in chief, Asiatic Fleet, whose flag would fly on a rotational basis from the cruisers *Pittsburgh*, *Rochester*, *Houston*, *Augusta*, and lastly the *Houston* again. Occasionally, she took visiting dignitaries on cruises throughout the Philippine archipelago or was ordered, for no particular reason other than to keep her engines from rusting, to patrol seaward of Corregidor. Thus, the *Isabel* became a ship without a mission and, for the most part, swung around the hook in Manila Bay.

On the morning of 3 December 1941, the *Isabel's* commanding officer, Lieutenant John Walker Payne, was unexpectedly summoned to the office of Admiral Thomas C. Hart, commander in chief of the Asiatic Fleet. Alone with the admiral, he was given some startling news. Wild rumors abounded on the Asiatic Station that war with Japan was imminent, and these were grimly confirmed when the admiral informed him that the situation was critical. He was then given strange and perplexing oral orders, which the admiral insisted he memorize and repeat until he had them letter perfect.

A large concentration of Japanese transports and warships had been sighted in Camranh Bay, Indochina. The *Isabel* was to proceed there and report on their movements. Admiral Hart gravely cautioned that the utmost secrecy was to be observed. No one, and he stressed *no one*, other than the two of them, was to know the *Isabel's* actual mission. Once at sea, only his executive officer Lieutenant (jg) Marion H. Buass, was to be taken into confidence. To give the *Isabel* some cover, a fake operational dispatch had been transmitted ordering her to search from Manila west to the Indochina coast for a lost PBY seaplane from Patrol Wing 10. It was hoped that this would be intercepted by the Japanese and provide a reason for the ship's activities.

The *Isabel* was to remain painted white. At night, running lights were to be dimmed to give the appearance of a fishing boat, and the Indochina coast was to be approached only under cover of darkness. Reports of all Japanese ship movements would be made two hours after sighting to help allay suspicion as to their real mission. To make these reports, Payne was given a small notebook containing a secret cipher. Its only counterpart, he was told, the admiral would retain.

Payne was further directed to proceed immediately to the Cavite Navy Yard to provision ship and top off with fuel and water. All topside weights, including the motorboat and gangways, were to be removed and all confidential material transferred to the district communications officer for safekeeping. That done, the *Isabel* was to get under way without delay. The ship was to be steamed at its most economical speed and, as the situation developed, either return to Manila for fuel or put into a friendly port in Borneo.

As the admiral spoke, Payne's mind churned with disturbing thoughts. Could it be that the *Isabel* was being set up to start a war everyone seemed to agree was inevitable? His worsening suspicions took a turn for the worst when the admiral cautioned that he was to fight his ship as necessary, and destroy her rather than let her fall into enemy hands. He winced inwardly at the admiral's use of the word *enemy*, for he suddenly envisioned the little *Isabel*, with four ancient 4-inch guns and four .30-caliber machine guns, taking on the entire Japanese Navy.

Before departing, Payne repeated his orders to the admiral's satisfaction, and the meeting concluded with the admiral vigorously shaking his hand and wishing him the very best of luck. As Payne headed for the door, Admiral Hart said with conviction that he wished he were going along as it entailed much more fun than what he would be doing in Manila. The lieutenant departed absolutely convinced that the gutsy "Old Man" was dead serious about going along, but with strong reservations about how much fun it was going to be.

What Payne did not know was that Admiral Hart was not acting on his own initiative. He had received a priority dispatch from the chief of naval operations, Admiral Harold R. Stark, which he later wrote was ". . . a definite and flat order, so worded as to bear highest priority. We received it with consternation." The top secret message, dated 1 December 1941, read

> President directs that the following be done as soon as possible and within two days if possible after receipt this dispatch. Charter three small vessels to form a quote defensive information patrol unquote. Minimum requirements to establish identity as a United States man of war are command by a naval officer and to mount a small gun and one machine gun would suffice. Filipino crews may be employed with minimum number naval ratings to accomplish purpose which is to observe and report by radio Japanese movements in West China Sea and Gulf of Siam. One vessel to be stationed between Hainan and Hue one vessel off the Indo-China coast between Camranh Bay and Cape St. Jaques and one vessel off Pointe de Camau. Use of Isabel authorized by president as one of these three but not other naval vessels. Report measures taken to carry out president's views. At same time inform me as to what reconnaissance measures are being regularly performed at sea by both army and navy whether by air surface vessels or submarines and your opinion as to the effectiveness of these latter measures.

Admiral Hart already had these areas under surveillance by air. This he deemed a more effective and less provocative method than stationing picket ships, which ran counter to his other directives that our forces make no menacing moves. What astounded him the most, however, was the fact that the president himself had directed what on the surface appeared to be a very minor tactical operation. "We on the spot," he recorded, "could not understand it."

The only ship immediately available for what had all the earmarks of a one-way mission was the *Isabel*. The recently purchased yacht *Lanikai* was outfitting and scheduled to depart on 8 December 1941. The other vessel involved was the schooner *Molly Moore*. She was a recent navy purchase, but time would run out before she could be put into commission. Eventually the good ship *Molly Moore* was burned in the Pasig River to avoid her being captured by the Japanese. In the end, only the *Isabel* would venture forth on this perplexing and dangerous mission.

The *Isabel* cleared the minefields guarding the entrance to Manila Bay that evening and, in the throes of a northeast monsoon, set course for the Indochina coast. The following morning, with tarpaulins masking her deck guns in an attempt to make her look as much as possible like a merchant ship, the *Isabel* wallowed on through an angry sea, shrouded by low scudding clouds and drenched intermittently by torrential rains. Skies had lifted somewhat when at 1315 a large, clipper-bowed ship, painted gray, was sighted well ahead, crossing the *Isabel*'s bow from starboard to port. The ship flew no colors and appeared to increase speed. From her course, she was presumed to be steaming for Palawan Passage in the Philippine archipelago. As shipping lanes were nonexistent in this section of the China Sea, the vessel's unexpected presence caused Payne to have an uneasy hunch that she was a Japanese tender, perhaps heading for Davao. For fear of giving away his real mission, he made no attempt to close the range and, according to instructions, two hours later radioed the contact report to Admiral Hart.

As the day progressed, the *Isabel*'s crew became increasingly suspicious of their announced orders to search for a downed PBY. For the most part, they were seasoned China hands and much too worldly to be easily duped. Intuitively, they sensed their mission was something other than what they had been told. Many attempted to pry from their officers, who knew no more than they did, the real nature of the mission. Failure to get satisfaction spawned numerous rumors. Some asserted that the *Isabel* was going to Shanghai to evacuate high officials, but they could not explain the course. The most ominous scuttlebutt suggested that they were out to tease the Japanese into creating another *Panay* incident to set off a full-blown war. These men, perhaps, were closer to the truth than they knew, but no one on board showed any fear of such an eventuality.

At 0830 on 5 December 1941, a strange plane was sighted approaching from the west. Excitement ran high when general quarters was sounded and all hands were ordered to remain below decks or out of sight, but ready to man guns on the double if necessary. The *Isabel* was now not more than 170 miles from the Indochina coast in an area where, Payne knew only too well, anything could happen. Apprehensively, he watched the approaching plane, which turned out to be a single-engine, low-wing monoplane with twin floats and twin tails. Painted beneath the wings and on each side of the fuselage were solid red circles. These "meatballs" unmistakably identified the aircraft as Japanese.

The seaplane circled the *Isabel* while the Nipponese crewman in the rear seat could be seen taking pictures and eyeballing the *Isabel* through binoculars. Not to be outdone, Payne did the same. The bothersome bird circled for about half an hour before winging away, but it returned twice more during the afternoon to hover over the ship like a mechanical vulture.

During the day, when the plane was not around, Payne ordered the crew exercised in general quarters and demolition drills. All of this, coupled with news that an emergency radio was being readied for the motor launch, made the men more certain than ever that the *Isabel*'s stated mission was phony.

In the late afternoon, a large ship was sighted on the far horizon hightailing toward the northwest. It vanished from sight before identification could be made.

The sun was a giant, blood-red sphere hanging low in the western sky when the Indochina coast, dark and foreboding, was sighted a mere 22 miles distant. The Japanese were well aware of the *Isabel*'s presence in the area and, as Payne ordered the course changed to a more southerly one to bring them closer to Camranh Bay, he grimly pondered what they would do about it.

Coincident with the course change, a cryptic priority message was received from commander in chief, Asiatic Fleet (CinCAF), ordering the *Isabel*'s immediate return to Manila. To Payne and his executive officer, Buass, this sudden but welcome change in orders had an ominous ring, like the death knell of a ponderous bell. War was in the wind, and the sooner they reached Manila Bay, the better.

Throughout the night, as the *Isabel* plied her way home, she was bedeviled by foul weather. Bucking heavy seas and furious rain squalls, she had to reduce speed to 11 knots. Nothing was sighted until 1157 on 6 December, when a low-flying twin-engine Japanese bomber dropped out of the clouds on the port quarter. It circled the *Isabel* several times and then flew away. It briefly appeared again that afternoon. No doubt about it, the Japanese were keeping a close watch on the *Isabel*, and by now all hands were convinced that their ship was but a sacrificial pawn in the deadly game of war.

The island fortress of Corregidor, guarding the entrance to Manila Bay, was in sight when at 0326 on 8 December 1941 (in another time zone, it was 7 December in Honolulu) they received a CinCAF message of shocking proportions. It read: "Japan has started hostilities, govern yourself accordingly, execute War Plan 46 against Japan."

Payne immediately assembled the crew and read the message. The news did not seem to disturb the men unduly, for they had anticipated it, but all hands wished to hell they had something more awesome with which to fight a war than the *Isabel*. They were also thankful that they were no longer within spitting distance of the Indochina coast.

Payne and Buass were puzzling over the directive to execute War Plan 46, which neither of them had ever heard of before, when another dispatch arrived telling them to be prepared for an air raid at dawn. The question immediately arose, prepare with what? Against aircraft their four ancient 3-inch deck guns and four .30-caliber machine guns were as useless as tits on a boar.

The *Isabel* dropped the hook in Manila Bay at 0822 and Lieutenant Payne went ashore to report to the admiral for orders. Upon entering the "Old Man's" office, he was somewhat shaken when the admiral looked him straight in the eye and remarked seriously, "Well, I never thought I'd see you again." This stark comment bugged Payne, who could not figure out whether Admiral Hart feared the *Isabel* would be sunk off the Indochina coast or while returning following the commencement of hostilities. He was, however, inclined to favor the former eventuality. Payne's orders from the admiral were brief. He was to refuel the *Isabel* and stand by until dark to lead submarines through the Corregidor minefields.

It was 1230. Refueling had just been completed when the doleful wail of sirens heralded the presence of Japanese aircraft. No aircraft were seen, but the rolling thunder of exploding bombs, accompanied by huge volumes of oily black smoke to the north of Manila indicated that Clark Field, the main U.S. Army Air Forces base in the Philippines, was taking a fearful beating. Suddenly, men on board the *Isabel* soberly realized that the war was for real, and not far away men were being killed. The attack lasted less than an hour, but when it was over, more than half of General MacArthur's irreplaceable Far East Air Force lay in ruins.

After dark, the *Isabel* got under way for the entrance to Manila Bay, closely followed by two submarines. This activity alerted the commander, Inshore Patrol, who immediately demanded to know what was going on. Not having been notified of any ship movements, he ordered the *Isabel* to heave to until he was properly informed. When Payne refused to comply, he threatened to open fire. Payne told him to go to hell, and continued on course. The incident ended there, but that was to be the least of Payne's worries that night.

Under normal conditions, traversing the minefields at night was a hairy operation, for a ship's small deviation from the channel could bring much anguish to the next of kin. Now, it was even more hazardous. Because of the possible presence of enemy bombers, all minefield navigation lights were turned off. To make matters worse, the *Isabel's* magnetic compass was acting erratically. With practically everybody but the ship's cat acting as lookouts, Payne cautiously nosed his ship into the minefield channel. By now, all hands were convinced that in the eyes of CinCAF, the *Isabel* was expendable. Better for her to be blown up by a mine than to lose a submarine.

Using only the black, practically indistinguishable silhouettes of reference points on the Bataan Peninsula to starboard and Corregidor Island to port, Payne successfully navigated the *Isabel* and her submarine charges through the danger area. Once the submarines were safely at sea, the *Isabel* returned through the minefields to Manila.

On 9 December there were more air raids, and enemy planes were observed bombing and strafing distant targets, but ships in the harbor were not attacked. At nightfall, the *Isabel* was once again assigned the task of escorting submarines through the darkened minefields.

The *Isabel* was seaward of Corregidor at 2200 when a large ship loomed out of the night heading at high speed for the entrance to Manila Bay, and into the center of the minefield. Payne directed the blinker light to commence flashing orders to stop. When the ship failed to respond, Payne took the *Isabel* at full speed to intercept the vessel before she became unglued on a mine. Five hundred yards short of the first row of lethal spheres the ship, a British freighter, was brought to a halt. The *Isabel* then closed out her "Good Samaritan" work for the night by leading her safely into Manila Bay.

Ten December 1941 was a graveyard-black day for men of the Asiatic Fleet, a day which would remain etched in the minds of those who saw and survived it, and would haunt them for the rest of their lives. Early that morning, Payne anchored the *Isabel* off the Cavite Navy Yard and went ashore, hoping to obtain .50-caliber machine guns to bolster his ship's pitiful antiaircraft defenses, and to have depth-charge racks installed to give the *Isabel* an attack capability against submarines. Unfortunately, heavy machine guns were not available, but the racks and depth charges were.

A few minutes past noon, a large floating crane carrying the depth-charge racks moored alongside the *Isabel*. The small yard tug *Santa Rita*, which towed it there, had backed off and lay waiting at anchor some 30 yards astern. Work was about to commence when at 1230 a priority CinCAF message was received, "Many enemy planes approaching from the north. ETA Manila 1255." Because of the crane moored alongside, Payne sent his crew to battle stations, but did not get under way. His ship, defenseless against submarines, urgently needed those depth-charge racks, which were still on board the crane. If only the Japanese would leave them alone, they could be installed in a few hours. He would wait to see where the bombs were destined to fall.

There were many ships in or anchored just off the navy yard, so work on board could be rushed to completion. The four piper destroyers *Peary* and *Pillsbury* were moored alongside Central Wharf. Nearby Machina Wharf was overloaded, with the fleet-type submarines *Seadragon* and *Sealion* and the minesweeper *Bittern* tied up side by side, and the submarine tender *Otus* moored at the head of the wharf. Not far away, several other vessels were anchored, including the minesweeper *Whippoorwill* and the submarine rescue vessel *Pigeon*. In the yard itself, several thousand navy and civilian employees were hard at work. To defend the yard against air attack, the marines had only nine old 3-inch antiaircraft guns and a handful of .50-caliber machine guns. The stage was set for disaster.

At 1255 the ugly drone of enemy aircraft engines filled the air, and fifty-four twin-engine bombers were sighted flying toward the yard. The few Army Air Corps fighters that somehow had survived the initial attacks valiantly took wing to intercept them but, hopelessly outnumbered by escorting Japanese fighters, they never had a chance.

Cavite Navy Yard following bombing by Japanese aircraft on 10 December 1941. National Archives, 80–G–46882

In the confusion that followed, at least one friendly P-40 was shot down by excited navy gunners.

In nine-plane "V" formations, the bombers methodically headed in for the kill. In vain, guns in the yard and on board every ship in the area opened fire. Flying at altitudes over 18,000 feet, the planes were well out of range. The first nine-plane salvo fell short of the yard in the water just off Machina Wharf. Exploding bombs completely bracketed the *Isabel*, throwing volumes of water over her decks, but causing no damage. The tug *Santa Rita*, however, anchored astern of the *Isabel*, took a direct hit amidships. Bodies and indefinable debris hurtled grotesquely through the air and, in an instant, the little vessel vanished.

With this sobering, narrow escape from destruction, Lieutenant Payne ordered the crane cut loose, then rang up full speed ahead to get his ship into Manila Bay where, if attacked, he at least would have some maneuvering room. As much as Payne yearned for the depth-charge racks still on board the floating crane, they would not be worth a damn if the *Isabel* was deep-sixed in the process.

From that time on, Japanese planes ignored the *Isabel*, but her crew could not escape witnessing the horrible destruction they inflicted upon the defenseless navy yard. Unchallenged, formation after formation flew overhead, leaving in their wakes violent explosions and rampaging fires that puked skyward volumes of oily black smoke. To imagine the fate of those pitiful souls caught in the midst of that grisly holocaust was heartrending.

Most ships in the yard were able to get under way to seek refuge in Manila Bay, but the submarine *Sealion* was sunk near Machina Wharf, and the destroyer *Peary*, lying cold iron alongside Central Wharf, took many casualties when she was hit and set on fire. The *Peary* was saved from complete destruction only by the heroic efforts of Lieutenant Charles A. Ferriter, commanding the minesweeper *Whippoorwill*, and his crew, who braved bombs and fierce fires to tow her to safety. In a similar, supremely courageous effort, the submarine rescue vessel *Pigeon*, commanded by Lieutenant Richard E. Hawes, saved the submarine *Seadragon*, which was wedged between the sunken *Sealion* and blazing Machina Wharf.

For almost two hellish hours the bombers terrorized the area, and during this time the *Isabel's* gunners fired 128 rounds of 3-inch antiaircraft shells without scoring a hit. When the all clear sounded, Payne returned to anchor as close to the yard as he dared, for the ammunition dumps, which had not been hit, lay in the midst of raging fires, and were feared ready to blow. Communications between Asiatic Fleet headquarters in Manila and Cavite were nonexistent because the signal searchlights and the communications building on top of which they had been located lay in cindered ruins. The *Isabel*, having visual communications with Manila and semaphore with the yard, became a relay station to give CinCAF an account of what was happening, and help direct rescue operations.

To assess the situation better and help with the wounded, Payne took a first aid party ashore in a pulling whaleboat, the *Isabel's* motor launch having been cut adrift by the initial bomb blasts. They found the yard completely destroyed and passage from one area to another blocked by sheets of flames and smoldering debris. Dead and wounded men were everywhere. The few doctors and corpsmen who had survived were overwhelmed, and the men from the *Isabel* pitched in to help wherever they could.

Payne and his men were recalled to the ship on orders from CinCAF to proceed to Manila, where he would paint the *Isabel* war color and be prepared to sail at 1800. Accordingly, paintbrushes were issued, and all hands turned to slopping grey and dark blue on everything that did not move.

Near sundown the *Isabel* got under way as a unit of Destroyer Division 59, then comprised of the destroyers *John D. Ford, Pope,* and *Paul Jones.* These ships were to operate as the screen for the destroyer tender *Holland* and the submarine tender *Otus,* which were ordered to safer ports in the Netherlands East Indies. As usual, the *Isabel* was accorded the dubious honor of leading the ships through the darkened minefields.

As the little force headed out on a southerly course for the Sulu Sea, far to port the pitch-black sky mirrored the yellow glare of fires still gutting the Cavite Navy Yard, and brought home to all hands the desolate truth that the U.S. Navy's only operating base in the Far East was no more.

Throughout the night the ship's company continued to paint the *Isabel* grey and blue. When dawn broke, she appeared so different that other ships in the force challenged her. Although the *Isabel* looked awful up close, some ships were quick to signal their compliments on a fine camouflage job.

Payne had not been informed of their destination, but he knew that at normal cruising speed the *Isabel* had fuel for no more than 900 miles. Throughout the day, however, jittery lookouts on various ships kept reporting submarine periscopes, and the *Isabel* always seemed to be the one ordered to investigate. No submarines were discovered, but these high-speed runs consumed oil at an alarming rate. Because fuel oil also ran the evaporators, fresh water was rationed and turned on for only half an hour three times a day. Payne reported these problems to the officer in tactical command, who simply acknowledged receipt of the message.

On 12 December the *Isabel*, with no submarine detection gear or depth charges, was ordered to occupy position number 1 ahead in the screen. At 1900 a large warship loomed up on the horizon. The *Isabel* challenged the stranger with her signal light. The situation was tense. Flashes from the big ship's bridge, however, were not from guns, but from a signal light replying correctly to the challenge. She was the heavy cruiser *Houston*, behind which steamed the formidable light cruiser *Boise*. It was reassuring to know that "big brothers" had come to help.

The next day at 0930, the *Isabel's* rudder jammed, forcing her to stop all engines and hoist the breakdown flag. It took twenty minutes to discover that a paintbrush somehow had become lodged in the pilot valve screw. By the time the problem was corrected, the *Isabel* had dropped behind the task force and was ordered to take position 8 miles astern to detect trailing submarines.

That night the task force made unpredictable course and speed changes which, due to thick weather, the *Isabel*, as "tail-end Charlie," was unable to detect. She lost contact, and dawn the next morning found the *Isabel* alone in the Celebes Sea not far off the Borneo coast. Two hours later she caught up with the others.

Plans to refuel at Tarakan were sidetracked when Japanese forces were reported nearby, and the ships proceeded to the oil port of Balikpapan, Borneo, 300 miles further south. The *Isabel*, practically bone dry of oil, managed to make port. Her condition, however, seemed of little concern to anyone, as ships were ordered to refuel according to seniority, which made her "low man on the totem pole."

At 2100 Admiral Glassford held a conference of all commanding officers to announce that because Japanese forces were reported moving toward Balikpapan, all refueled ships would get under way for Makasar, on the southeastern tip of Celebes Island, in two hours. Those not refueled would remain behind until they were ready.

Payne was on the spot. The *Isabel* was anchored in Balikpapan Bay, but between her and the refueling docks were treacherous reefs, difficult to navigate in daylight, but more so at night with all navigation lights blacked out. Not wishing to be left behind and possibly face the enemy, Payne decided to brave the reefs.

Following close behind the ship's pulling whaleboat, whose crew found the channel by using a lead line and a boat hook, the *Isabel* slowly groped her way. She reached the refueling dock about midnight, but it was deserted. Payne wandered through the darkened town searching for some kind of an official, but the place seemed to be deserted. Finally a native was found who spoke only fractured English. Fortunately, he was familiar with the refueling procedures, and was induced to give the ship's company a hand in activating the pumps.

The *Isabel* refueled and got under way at about 0200 on 15 December 1942. Once again, following close behind the whaleboat, she safely crossed the reefs into the bay. Payne was certain the task force had moved out, but was happily surprised to find the *Holland* still at anchor. The sortie had been delayed until dawn because Rear Admiral Glassford had second thoughts about attempting to navigate through the minefields at night.

By 0800 all ships had cleared Balikpapan and were heading south at 15 knots. Payne felt less concern now that his ship was topped off with fuel and water, even though the *Isabel* was again steaming 8 miles astern of the formation.

On the morning of the sixteenth, the *Houston* left the task force and headed southwest for Surabaja, Java. At the same time the *Isabel* was ordered to proceed independently to Makasar to bring back harbor pilots for the *Boise, Holland,* and *Otus.* Normally such an assignment would be considered routine, but Payne entertained no such illusions. Ships of the Asiatic Fleet possessed only old charts of the Netherlands East Indies, charts whose reliability was highly questionable. The approaches to Makasar were laced with treacherous reefs, and it was not known if these had been augmented by a minefield. At any rate, the expendable *Isabel* would be the first to test the charts' validity.

Ever so cautiously, Payne worked the *Isabel* safely into Makasar harbor, where the arrival of such a weirdly painted ship caused a near panic among the natives, who feared the Japanese were upon them. After assuring the populace that they were the "good guys" come to save the Indies, Payne was able to obtain three pilots and return with them to the task force.

On the seventeenth, the *Isabel,* comfortably moored next to the *Holland* at dockside, was ordered to move out to anchor in the harbor entrance as a submarine picket. Her sinking, if nothing else, would give warning to the others that a Japanese submarine was looking for trouble.

More sanctuary-seeking refugees from the Philippines arrived off Makasar the following morning. Escorted by ships of Destroyer Division 58 were the light cruiser *Marblehead,* the aircraft tender *Langley,* the transport *Gold Star,* and the tanker *Trinity.* It was, of course, the *Isabel* that took out the pilots to insure their safe passage through the tricky channel. Now, most of the Asiatic Fleet's major support ships were congregated in Makasar harbor. As no one seemed to know what to do with them, they anxiously sat there awaiting orders to deploy to safer ports.

With the departure of Rear Admiral Glassford in the *Houston*, Captain S. E. Robinson, commanding the *Boise*, assumed the duties of task force commander. He was somewhat distressed when on 20 December the lilting voice of Tokyo Rose, courtesy of Radio Tokyo, announced that the war eagles of Japan would soon bomb Makasar and sink the American ships harbored there. Flashing back to Pearl Harbor and Manila, Robinson was not inclined to take such a warning lightly, and immediately ordered all ships moved to anchorages in the outer harbor, where they could quickly put to sea at the first indication of trouble. The *Isabel*, however, was an exception. She was ordered to remain in the inner harbor to act as liaison between the task force and the Dutch signal station ashore.

On 22 December Payne was directed, in the event the ships were ordered to move during the night, to stand by to activate a darkened navigational light to the south of Makasar. This was a hell of a good idea for everyone but the *Isabel*, because the light was situated on top of a partially submerged reef and access to it presented a dangerous problem even in daylight. At 0020, however, orders to activate the light were cancelled, and Payne was ordered to go ashore to inform the Dutch naval authorities that the task force was sailing.

The blacked out streets of Makasar were deserted except for native troops who sharply challenged Payne at every turn. It wasn't easy, but he finally located the lone Dutch naval officer left in town, to whom he delivered the message. The man didn't seem to give a damn one way or another, and Payne returned at 0340 to the *Isabel*, where he learned that the other ships had already departed and he was expected to follow without delay.

The moonless night was inky black. Because of the threat of Japanese bombers, all navigation lights were extinguished, and reference points ashore were impossible to find. Locating the channel and moving the *Isabel* safely through the reefs posed a touchy problem, but Payne's orders were to join the task force—period. As they had done successfully at Balikpapan, Lieutenant (jg) Buass, equipped with a lead line, boat hook, and flashlight, preceded the ship in the pulling whaleboat. Jabbing away at the reefs, he located the channel, and directed the *Isabel*'s movements by flashlight until she was safe in deep water.

When the *Isabel* caught up with the task force two hours later, she was ordered to backtrack toward Makasar to look for the destroyer *Paul Jones*, which was mysteriously missing. At dawn the *Paul Jones* was sighted proceeding slowly on course. She signalled that in clearing the harbor she hit a reef, damaging a propeller so severely that progress could be made only on one engine. The ship was in no danger of sinking and would follow on to Surabaja for repairs.

The task force arrived at Surabaja late in the afternoon of 24 December and the *Isabel* was directed to moor at the head of Holland Pier. No sooner was the gangway in place than a working party of sailors came on board with orders to take the ship's only radio transmitter. Lieutenant Payne vehemently protested, but got nowhere. The transmitter was urgently needed ashore to set up Admiral Hart's headquarters, and the Dutch had none to spare. To add insult to injury, they also walked off with most of the *Isabel's* navigational charts, including all of those pertaining to Australia.

Whether the Isabel was forgotten or no one knew what to do with her is unknown, but she remained inactive in Surabaja until 15 January 1942. During that time, depth-charge racks were installed, but lack of underwater detection gear made her less than a threat to enemy submarines. Nevertheless, she was assigned to escorting merchant ships between the ports of Surabaja and Tandjungpriok, Java, and on occasion up dangerous "bomb alley" to Palembang, Sumatra. For the most part, the *Isabel* was alone escorting ships that blithely steamed along believing she afforded them some means of protection.

The *Isabel* was at Palembang on 23 January, when that city experienced its first bombing, and at Tandjungpriok on the twenty-eighth, when Japanese bombers initially worked over that port. On neither occasion did the ship suffer damage, but it was becoming increasingly clear to all hands that the Japanese were moving ever closer and all-out air attacks on the Netherlands East Indies could not be thwarted by the puny ABDA air force on hand to defend them.

Surabaja experienced its first major air raid at 1007 on 3 February 1942, and among those present was the *Isabel*. More than fifty twin-engine bombers, flying at 20,000 feet, dropped their deadly loads on the airdrome, a few thousand yards from the *Isabel*. Antiaircraft guns went into action, but the planes were well out of range. A hangar and several parked aircraft were demolished, and flames from other buildings in the complex shot high in the air. At the same time, fighter planes, sweeping in at masthead level, strafed anchored PBY seaplanes in the nearby seadrome, sinking several of them. The *Isabel's* gunners fired their .30-caliber machine guns at the fighters whenever they came close, but the bullets went for naught. Frustrated seamen cursed their inability to fight back. Even one .50-caliber machine gun could have been used to advantage, but the *Isabel* was destined to face up to an aggressive, well-armed enemy with not much more than her crew's clenched fists.

When the planes had done their grisly work and the all clear sounded, Lieutenant Payne received word to stand by to take Rear Admiral Glassford and party on a special mission. At 1240, ten English-speaking Dutch naval officers equipped with high-frequency voice radios reported on board as part of the admiral's party. Payne attempted to learn their destination and the nature of their mission, but the Dutchmen clammed up, saying such information was top secret.

By 1600 the admiral had yet to arrive, and Payne went ashore to telephone headquarters for information. This was fortunate, for someone had dropped the ball. A near-frantic senior staff officer said the admiral was not going, but the *Isabel* should have been under way for several hours en route to rendezvous with a task force in Bounder Roads, about 90 miles east of Surabaja.

The task force of American and Dutch ships had been hurriedly thrown together for action against the Japanese. With no common codes and faced with a language barrier, communication among ships was impossible. Payne was told in no uncertain terms that the entire operation depended upon his getting the bilingual officers and their equipment to the American warships by 2330. Excuses for failure would not be accepted.

Payne had the *Isabel* under way by 1700, but he was deeply concerned because to arrive in time he would have to steam most of the way at the highest possible speed. Even then he might not make it if they encountered adverse winds or tides. The shortest route to the rendezvous was the east passage from Surabaja into Madura Strait. Although it led through a minefield and shoal water he had never traversed before, Payne, bedeviled by the urgency and importance of his mission and the knowledge that he had only six and one-half hours grace, headed the *Isabel* into the channel at 21 knots.

An hour out of Surabaja, while she was in the midst of the minefield, a sudden squall lashed the *Isabel* with sheets of rain. Visibility fell to 100 yards, forcing Payne to slacken speed, but he pushed on, navigating entirely by dead reckoning. The haunting fear of slamming into a mine or reef was intensified by the fact that a considerable error had been discovered in the magnetic compass. Whether or not they were correctly compensating for this error was a serious question.

Following two and one-half anxious hours, the *Isabel* broke into the clear and a fix was quickly obtained from shore tangents. Thanks to some fine by guess and by God navigation and some luck of the Irish thrown in for good measure, the ship was safely through the danger area and in the strait. It was somberly noted, however, that in getting there, the *Isabel* had run through a corner of the minefield.

The *Isabel* arrived at the rendezvous at 2340. She was ten minutes late, but had accomplished a nearly impossible feat, for which she received neither a derisive nor a congratulatory message. Assembled there, under the command of Rear Admiral Karel Doorman, were the Dutch light cruisers *De Ruyter* and *Tromp*, the heavy cruiser *Houston*, the light cruiser *Marblehead*, and seven destroyers—three Dutch and four American. Following the transfer of the communications personnel, the *Isabel* headed back for Surabaja without a soul on board knowing that the ABDA force would soon sail to attack Japanese cruisers and transports loitering near Makasar Strait.

By 0830 the next day, the *Isabel* was back in Surabaja, moored to Holland Pier, but there would be no rest for the weary. At 0920, bombers again attacked the navy yard, and Payne moved his ship into the channel to get as far away from falling bombs as possible. He tried to maneuver the *Isabel* into position to fire on the attackers, but her guns, as usual, were useless. Coincident with the raid, frantic radio messages came from the task force calling for fighter protection, but the few available fighter planes in Java had their own problems, and the ships under air attack were left to fend for themselves.

In the late afternoon, when the enemy planes had gone and fires were under control, it was learned that en route to the objective the task force had been attacked by enemy bombers. The heavy cruiser *Houston* and the light cruiser *Marblehead* had suffered major damage, and the mission had been aborted. This gloomy news was difficult to believe, but it reinforced the conviction of Payne and his crew that the Indies were doomed, while leaving unanswered the question, "What did the fates have in store for the *Isabel?*"

On 5 February 1942, the air raid alarm sounded at 0933 and once again the *Isabel* moved away from the dock as Japanese planes launched their usual morning attack on the navy yard and airfield. PBY seaplanes in the seadrome were strafed by Zero fighters, one of which was shot down by an Allied fighter. Another Zero, pulling out of a dive, passed within 200 yards of the *Isabel* and her old .30-caliber Lewis guns burped into action. Hits were scored as tracers could be seen ripping into the enemy plane, and all hands eagerly waited for it to spin in. But it didn't. Instead, the Zero, trailing black smoke, flew away out of sight. Nevertheless, all hands on board the *Isabel* were elated to think that at long last their guns had struck home and, with a little luck, they'd scored a kill.

At dusk the *Isabel* was ordered to escort the *Lillian Luckenbach*, a large American freighter, westward along the north coast of Java. In so doing, the *Isabel* was to transit a new channel through the complex

Surabaja minefields, the legs of which were marked by screened, colored lights ashore. As no local pilots were available, the crew of the *Isabel* again faced another hazardous nocturnal challenge.

It was dark. The *Isabel*, making 10 knots with the *Lillian Luckenbach* trailing astern by a mere 1,000 yards, was midway through the first leg of the minefield. Obtaining good bearings on the marker beacons had been no problem and, according to the plotted tangents, the ships were steaming safely in the middle of the channel. Suddenly a Dutch motor torpedo boat (MTB) was sighted racing toward the *Isabel* and flashing light signals for her to stop immediately. She was standing into danger! Payne signalled the *Luckenbach* to stop and ordered the *Isabel* stopped to await the approaching MTB.

A brisk wind was blowing and, as the ships lay to, Payne was concerned that the *Isabel* might drift out of what he thought was the channel into the minefield. But another danger threatened the *Isabel*. Lookouts yelled the warning, and Payne shot a glance astern to see the huge black bow of the *Luckenbach* bearing down on them. He instantly ordered full speed ahead, averting by a scant few yards a collision of terrifying proportions.

After getting squared away again in what his charts indicated was the middle of the channel, and believing he finally had the *Luckenbach* stopped, Payne again ordered the *Isabel*'s engines stopped to await the approaching MTB. Someone on board the MTB was shouting they were in the middle of the minefield and if they did not clear out they would be blown to hell when Payne, acting on a premonition of impending doom, glanced over his shoulder. Good God, there it was again. The bow of the *Luckenbach*, looming monstrous in the gloom, was about to crash down upon the *Isabel*. The engine room gang responded magnificently to frantic signals from the bridge and the *Isabel*, with only seconds to spare, moved away from certain destruction.

By this time Payne was beside himself. He had to make a quick decision. His course so far led him to believe his chart was correct and that those on the MTB knew nothing about the new channel. Besides, it appeared that he had more to fear from the *Luckenbach* than the minefield, so he chose to continue as before. When the ships finally passed safely through the minefields, Payne and most of the others on board the *Isabel* felt that during the transit they had aged at least five years.

The *Isabel* was back off the entrance to Surabaja harbor at noon on 7 February. Japanese bombers were pounding the city, and Payne waited for the all clear to sound before venturing into the narrow channel. He was still waiting at 1314, when an operational priority message from commander, Southwest Pacific was received, directing him to proceed immediately to a position about 75 miles west to pick up survivors of a small Dutch steamer, the *Van Cloon*. She was on fire and sinking as a result of torpedo and gunfire attacks by a submarine. The *Isabel* was also directed to report her estimated time of arrival in the rescue area. Because the radio transmitter, removed weeks before, had never been replaced, a typed message replying to the dispatch was passed to a Dutch patrol boat off the harbor entrance to be relayed by radio to U.S. Navy headquarters in Surabaja. Once this was accomplished, the *Isabel* raced to the rescue.

Three hours later, a Royal Netherlands Navy PBY seaplane flew overhead and signalled the location of the survivors. Course was changed and in about fifteen minutes six small lifeboats under sail were sighted heading in a southerly direction. They were now in waters where an enemy submarine was known to be hunting and, because the *Isabel* lacked submarine detection gear, additional lookouts were posted. Payne knew full well that Japanese submarines often lurked near their victims to knock off ships attempting to rescue survivors, and he had no intention of falling into such a trap.

Before picking up survivors, Payne combed the area, seeking signs of the enemy submarine. When nothing was seen, he maneuvered the *Isabel* alongside the first lifeboat, and was about to take on survivors when an alert lookout sighted a torpedo wake 1,000 yards away moving to intercept the *Isabel*. Lines to the lifeboat were immediately cast free, and the occupants cautioned to remain put. Payne ordered all engines ahead full and, when clear of the lifeboat, called for full left rudder. At the same time a submarine periscope was seen off the port quarter.

As the *Isabel* heeled in a sharp left turn, the submarine's conning tower began to emerge from the sea like some monster of the deep surfacing to gloat over its prey. Instantly the *Isabel*'s forward, port 3-inch gun opened fire. The shell was a little off in deflection to the left, and over in range. A rapid second shot exploded in the water close to the conning tower. Before a third could be fired, the submarine's commander pulled the plug to seek safety in the deep. Meanwhile, the torpedo intended for the *Isabel* passed harmlessly to starboard.

The patrol plane, attracted by the gunfire, flew to the area and dropped depth charges within 50 yards of the submarine's last known position. Three minutes later the *Isabel* was in the same area steaming in a tight circle to release five depth charges set to detonate at 200 feet. When the last charge exploded it threw high in the air a spout of oily water, which left behind a lingering rainbow spray. Damage to the submarine could not be assessed, but oil bubbling to the surface suggested that considerable damage had been inflicted.*

Convinced that if they had not sunk it they had given the submarine a lesson it would not soon forget, Payne returned to pick up the survivors. When the operation was completed at 1815, a muster roll check showed that all of the 187 passengers and crew, which included 10 women and children, were on board and none had suffered serious injury.

According to the *Van Cloon*'s commanding officer, the submarine surfaced about 6,000 yards from his ship and ordered him to stop and abandon ship. He responded by radioing for help and turning away in a vain attempt to outrun the submarine at full speed, which for the little steamer was all of 10 knots. With this, the submarine's deck gun went into action. Accuracy of fire was poor, but with superior speed the sub soon closed the range. When a shell slammed through the unarmed merchantman's side, rupturing a boiler, the captain ordered abandon ship.

The submarine stopped firing long enough for crewmen of the *Van Cloon* to lower away half the lifeboats, but when the gun again commenced lobbing shells, those still on board didn't linger to observe the fall of shot. They went over the side with a rush. The few lifeboats were dangerously overcrowded, but fortunately the sea was calm, minimizing their chances of capsizing. Under sail, the survivors beat away from the doomed ship, which was quickly dispatched by a torpedo.

When the last bedraggled survivor had been hoisted on board, Payne headed full speed for Surabaja. To elude submarines, he took a zigzag course, but all turns had to be made with a very small rudder angle because, with fuel tanks almost empty and a heavy deck load of passengers, the top-heavy *Isabel* heeled dangerously in a turn. That night the ship transited the minefields, and at 0436 discharged survivors at Rotterdam Pier.

Having gone without sleep for over thirty-six hours, the *Isabel*'s crew was dog tired, but rest and relaxation were not theirs for the taking. At 0955, enemy bombers attacked the navy yard, forcing the *Isabel* to clear the dock area and into the stream. When the all clear sounded an hour and a half later, Payne again moored his ship at Rotterdam Pier to refuel.

The tempo of air attacks on Surabaja increased, and on 9 February 1942, bombers terrorized the city from 0824 until 2000. For the first time, the downtown area was attacked along with the docks and

*According to the U.S. Navy's official history of the *Isabel*, the Dutch navy credited her with sinking the submarine. The PBY seaplane, which hovered over the area after the *Isabel* departed, confirmed the kill.

airfield. Numerous fires, which scorched the night, were hardly under control when, at 0748, the bombers were back. They returned at 1000 and hit again at 1240, while the *Isabel* was escorting the merchant ships *Van Outhoorn* (Dutch) and *Giang Seng* (British) through the minefields en route to Tandjungpriok. But the *Isabel's* charmed life was not jeopardized. Although she and her charges could take no evasive action, the Japanese ignored them.

Soon after clearing the minefields, the *Gian Seng* turned back; because of bad coal she could not generate enough steam. The *Isabel* and her remaining charge arrived at Tandjungpriok on 12 February. Needing minor engine room work, which required shutting down her power plant, the *Isabel* was permitted to berth alongside the KLM pier. Although electricity and water were obtained from the pier, there was insufficient water to run the ice machines properly, and the sultry equatorial heat soon found its way into the cold food lockers. In two days' time 1,000 pounds of beef, 200 pounds of pork, 100 pounds of chickens, and many other perishables which could not be replaced in that port city spoiled. This forced the entire crew to go on a diet of rice and canned corned beef.

Fifteen February 1942 was a disheartening day for the *Isabel's* crew. News of the appalling British defeat at Singapore was shocking enough, but also on that day Admiral Thomas C. Hart, commander in chief of the Asiatic Fleet and commanding the ABDA naval forces, was relieved of command and ordered home. Throughout the Asiatic Fleet, Admiral Hart was considered a brilliant naval officer, and was highly esteemed. This assessment of the admiral was in sharp contrast with that of the British and Dutch, who snidely suggested he was an "old fogy" and lacked war experience. It was, in fact, the British and Dutch who conspired behind his back to have him recalled. Three days later, as the cruiser *Durban*, carrying Admiral Hart out of the Netherlands East Indies, passed the *Isabel* close aboard, the admiral waved and sent a message to all hands, "May God bless you and keep you during the difficult days to come."

By 17 February, Tandjungpriok harbor was crammed with merchant ships awaiting sailing orders. The port area and the nearby city of Batavia were overrun with pitiful, confused refugees from Singapore and other areas of Southeast Asia, all hoping, for the most part in vain, to escape the onrushing armies of Japan.

That morning Lieutenant Payne visited Dutch naval headquarters in Batavia and was shocked to learn that the Japanese had landed on the island of Bali, less than 200 miles east of Surabaja. In addition, three large enemy invasion fleets were poised to strike at Java; one was coming down Banka Strait from Singapore, another from Bandjarmasin in southern Borneo, and the third from Makasar. This unnerving intelligence strongly indicated to Payne that it was high time his one-ship task force, along with the merchant ships in the harbor, hotfooted it through Sunda Strait to safer ports before the door slammed shut. In spite of the gravity of the situation, Payne, whose last vague directive from commander, Southwest Pacific (ComSoWesPac) was to take his instructions from Dutch headquarters in Batavia, was ordered to escort a British merchantman, the *Deucalion*, back to Surabaja.

It was almost midnight 18 February when, during a driving rain-storm, the two ships cautiously worked their way through the Surabaja minefield channel into the inner harbor. At dawn, Payne moored the *Isabel* alongside Holland Pier, which had been bombed the previous day but was still serviceable, and immediately went to U.S. Navy head-quarters for instructions. He was confounded to find the place de-serted and to learn that ComSoWesPac had been gone for several days. Most of the staff had moved to the port city of Tjilatjap on the south coast of Java, and the admiral to ABDA naval command headquar-ters—an elaborate, bombproof underground layout at Bandung in the mountains of central Java.

Payne then decided to check Dutch naval headquarters to find out what orders, if any, were there for the *Isabel*. En route he happened to meet a commander in the Royal Navy, the ex-shipping advisor in Singapore, who had learned on good authority that the Japanese had blocked Bali Strait. The only other escape route into the Indian Ocean lay through Sunda Strait, but a large enemy task force had been detected moving in that direction. This meant that the *Isabel* and all Allied ships in the Java Sea would soon be trapped. The Britisher, who was scheduled for air transportation to safer climes, concluded his gloomy report with a, "Cheerio, old chap—the best of luck." His parting remarks, however, did little to instill in Payne that "good all over" feeling.

At Dutch navy headquarters Payne met Commander Thomas H. Binford, commanding Destroyer Division 58, who had just arrived with the four pipers *Stewart*, *John D. Edwards*, *Parrott*, and *Pillsbury*. That night they, along with other Allied ships, were going to attack Japanese ships reported to be in Bandung Strait reinforcing their troops ashore on Bali. He suggested that if Payne wished to take the risk, the *Isabel* was welcome to tag along and hope to get through the strait during the melee. This invitation, quickly accepted by Payne, went up in smoke, however, when Dutch navy officials refused to permit it and insisted that the *Isabel* would escort a small convoy to Borneo.

Payne was beside himself, for in directing such an operation the Dutch showed a complete disregard for the plain facts of life. With the

Japanese controlling practically all of Borneo, and especially the air and seas surrounding it, this mission was doomed before it started. To verify that he must obey such unrealistic orders, Payne attempted to contact U.S. Navy headquarters in Tjilatjap. Failing that, he managed to phone Allied headquarters at Bandung, where he learned that the situation was normal, "All fouled up." The *Isabel*, it seems, was supposed to have been in Tjilatjap several days before, but someone at headquarters mislaid the message. They were sorry about that.

Payne was told to forget the Borneo caper and convoy the 10-knot American freighter *Collingsworth* west along the north coast of Java and attempt to pass through Sunda Strait into the Indian Ocean. If all went well, the ships would continue southwest toward Cocos Island. Further orders would be sent by radio. For such a voyage, the *Isabel* would have to refuel from the *Collingsworth* and, to do so, Payne was told to confiscate a hose if one could not be purchased.

While Payne was away from the ship there had been two air raids, in spite of which his executive officer, Lieutenant Buass, had managed to complete refueling the ship and to stock up on meat and fresh vegetables. All hands, having subsisted for more than four days on corned beef and rice, were especially happy about the latter.

Prior to getting under way, Payne and the *Collingsworth*'s captain met to discuss various aspects of their hazardous journey. The most pressing problem was that of communications. The *Isabel*'s radio transmitter had never been replaced and, ever since arriving in Java, the ship had been unable to communicate with anyone. It was, therefore, arranged that the *Isabel*'s messages for naval headquarters would be passed to the *Collingsworth* for transmittal. But there were complications. Although the merchantman could set up to transmit on the special navy frequency, she lacked a frequency meter to determine if the transmitter was putting out correctly. Besides, the navy frequency was beyond the range of the ship's receiver. To overcome these deficiences it was decided that the *Isabel* would listen in on her receiver and coach the *Collingsworth* on frequency by signal flags—HYPO for high and LOVE for low.

The two ships cleared the minefields at 2115, and set a course for Sunda Strait with the *Collingsworth* keeping station 500 yards astern of the *Isabel*. From the bridge, Payne, looking down on the forecastle, could see the black, snake-like outline of a great length of hose for which no money had changed hands. He would ask no questions as to how or where it was acquired, for that was the private business of a very enterprising crew.

On the afternoon of 20 February a burning ship was sighted about 10 miles to the north, but Payne did not desert the *Collingsworth* to investigate because his first responsibility was for his convoy's safety.

Earlier they had passed through the grim flotsam of a sunken ship which reaffirmed the unhappy truth that enemy submarines haunted the Java Sea. For all Payne knew, one could be lurking near the flaming hulk to claim another victim. It was a hard decision to make, but Payne continued on.

At 1330 on 21 February, the ships put into Bantam Bay on the northwest coast of Java to hide until dark before attempting the transit of Sunda Strait, a mere 30 miles away. The *Isabel* went alongside the *Collingsworth* to refuel using the confiscated hose, which was heavy and not very flexible. It worked fairly well in the sheltered bay, but there were serious reservations concerning its use in the open sea. This could pose a difficult problem if the *Isabel* were ordered to escort the *Collingsworth* further west, provided the ships made it safely into the Indian Ocean.

With sundown the moment of truth arrived, and the ships got under way for Sunda Strait. Japanese forces were rumored to have already landed on the Sumatra side, and it was likely that their submarines would be skulking in the strait to sink ships attempting to escape from the Java Sea. On board the *Isabel* battle stations were manned and tensions ran high as all available personnel kept a sharp lookout for signs of trouble. The plan was to hug the Java side, where against the blackness of the mountains the darkened ships would be less likely to be seen by enemy eyes.

Seldom more than 500 yards off shore, and at times passing between naked rocks and the beach, the ships pressed on at the agonizing speed of 10 knots—the *Collingsworth*'s best. Heavy clouds blanketing the sky were a godsend, but at 2305, with the ships only a third of the way through, the clouds vanished and a brilliant moon blew their cover. On they steamed, occasionally to see a Dutch patrol boat silently waiting in a cove along the route. It was reassuring to know they were not alone.

By 1115 the next day, the *Isabel* and her convoy were safely through Sunda Strait and steaming on a southwesterly course. ComSoWesPac had not been heard on the air for several days, which caused Payne to wonder if navy headquarters was still in Tjilatjap. The *Collingsworth* had received orders to proceed to Ceylon, but none had come for the *Isabel*. Payne was faced with a problem. Should he continue on with the *Collingsworth* or break radio silence to contact headquarters? The latter action was decided upon and, by using a line-throwing gun with a tin can attached to the line's bitter end, a coded message requesting instructions was passed to the *Collingsworth* for transmission to ComSoWesPac.

Calibrating the merchant ship's transmitter proved a frustrating operation, one which under other circumstances could have been funny. The *Isabel* monitored the transmissions, and by semaphore signalled the *Collingsworth* to come up or down on frequency. The *Collingsworth*'s captain was the only person on board who understood semaphore, so he would receive the directions and then go tell his radio operator. After making adjustments, they would try again. This jury-rig procedure continued for nearly four hours until, at last, the transmitter was correctly tuned.

Call after call went out to ComSoWesPac, who failed to answer. Fortunately the tanker *Pecos* in Tjilatjap harbor took the message to pass on by hand to ComSoWesPac, whose radio was inoperative. Late that afternoon the *Isabel* received orders to leave the *Collingsworth* and proceed to Tjilatjap. This was followed by another, more sobering message from ComSoWesPac: "Situation is critical, ABDAFLOAT wishes to inform and impress all hands with the necessity for exerting every effort to prevent enemy landing on Java. At every opportunity the offensive must be taken and sacrifices made in accomplishing this."

The *Isabel* entered Tjilatjap harbor to moor alongside the tanker *Pecos* on the afternoon of 23 February. The harbor, reached by a long, narrow channel, was jammed with more than fifty merchant ships, apparently waiting for sailing orders. Payne was concerned that enemy bombers might sink a ship or two in the channel and lock the remainder in for the duration. He found it impossible to rationalize why these ships were retained in such a vulnerable position.

For the next three days more ships—including the destroyers *Whipple*, *Bulmer*, *Pillsbury*, and *Parrott*; the minesweepers *Whippoorwill* and *Lark*; and the gunboat *Asheville*—continued to arrive in the already overcrowded harbor of Tjilatjap. Several times each day air raid alarms sent everyone racing to battle stations, but, praise the Lord, the enemy bombers failed to materialize.

On 27 February, two Japanese submarines were reported to have been seen on the surface outside the minefield, and it became painfully obvious that the noose was being tightened on the ships at Tjilatjap. Following an air raid alert that morning, the tanker *Pecos*, escorted by the destroyers *Whipple* and *Edsall*, got under way and moved safely out to sea. Immediately after them, as fast as they could file through the narrow channel, went more than forty unescorted merchant ships to seek safer ports far away from the Netherlands East Indies. Many would never make it.

Although Payne had been told to stand by to proceed south, he was ordered at dawn of the twenty-eighth to move the *Isabel* up the Kali Donan River, which empties into the harbor, moor alongside the east bank, and cover the entire ship with palms. Camouflaged as an innocent extension of the jungle, she might be able to escape any bombing that occurred. This led Payne to believe they might remain in Tjilatjap longer than expected and, while his crew diligently chopped down palm trees, he went ashore to be briefed on the situation.

At navy headquarters he was informed that plans had changed. The destroyer *Pillsbury*, originally scheduled to remain until the impending end to evacuate naval personnel, was departing that afternoon for Australia. Now to the *Isabel* would fall the dubious honor of being the last U.S. Navy ship to leave Tjilatjap. The decision had been predicated on the assumption that the *Isabel* was of no particular military value, and her loss would make little difference in the war against Japan.

Payne returned to his ship to find the crew fighting swarms of savage mosquitoes, and eating copious amounts of quinine to stave off malaria. To top this, Lieutenant Buass told him that while they were covering the ship with palm fronds, one of the Chinese mess boys, somewhat bewildered by the proceedings, asked if they were going to have a ship's party. Party!

Late the following morning, 1 March 1942, Payne visited headquarters to find it cloaked in gloom and abounding with the most depressing news. The Allied fleet had lost a disastrous battle in the Java Sea, and the fate of most ships was uncertain. Their prolonged and mysterious silence, however, forebode the worst. The fleet tanker *Pecos*, loaded with survivors from the aircraft tender *Langley*, which had been bombed and sunk on 27 February, radioed that morning that she was under attack by dive bombers. Nothing had been heard from her since, raising grave fears that she too had fallen prey to the Japanese.

To envelop gloom in gloom, Japanese forces were landing on the north coast of Java, and at least two enemy aircraft carriers, several cruisers, and an unknown number of submarines were roaming the Indian Ocean to intercept ships attempting to escape to Australia. Their presence was attested to by numerous frantic radio calls for help from merchant ships which had departed Tjilatjap during the last few days. It was obvious to Payne that the *Isabel*'s chances of avoiding a Japanese-induced rendezvous with Davy Jones were growing slimmer by the hour.

There was, however, one shred of good news. The *Isabel* would sail that night. Vice Admiral Glassford and staff would arrive later in the day from Bandung to embark in the *Isabel*, and Payne was directed to commence refueling at 1600, then stand by to get under way soon after dark.

The *Isabel* was at the refueling pier that afternoon when twenty-one officers and enlisted men reported on board for transportation. Other than Admiral Glassford and several of his senior officers, who would now depart Tjilatjap via a navy PBY seaplane, these were the last of the

U.S. Navy staff in Java. Payne was informed that Admiral Glassford, temporarily headquartered in the city's only hotel, wished to see him at once.

Although Payne was happy to show the *Isabel*'s heels to Java, it would be an understatement to say that he was less than enthusiastic with the admiral's orders, which had all the earmarks of a dangerous mission. The newly designated commanding officer of the submarine *Spearfish*, Lieutenant Commander James C. Dempsey, would sail with the *Isabel*. Seaward of the minefields, the *Isabel* would rendezvous with the *Spearfish* and put him on board. Following that, Payne was free to proceed to Exmouth Gulf, Australia, where fuel was available. Now Payne was aware that three submarines were known to be lying off the harbor entrance, two Japanese and one American. Without underwater detection gear, his ship, in the dark of night, was somehow supposed to locate the friendly submarine and transfer the officer. The thought pinged sharply through Payne's head that such an operation could result in the loss of the *Isabel* as well as the *Spearfish*. There was one other thing the admiral ordered Payne to do. The *Sea Witch*, a new C-3–type American merchantman, was in port, and he was made personally responsible that, no matter what, she sailed that night under escort by the *Isabel* to safe waters.

From headquarters Payne visited the harbor master to request a pilot for the *Sea Witch*. Here he met unexpected difficulty. The harbor master adamantly refused to permit the ship to sail until her cargo of P-40 fighter planes and trucks was completely unloaded, a task which would carry over well into the following day. Payne was flabbergasted. In view of the fact that Java was about to be overrun by the Japanese, and everyone who could was fleeing to safer lands, he tried to convince the man that it would only be a matter of a few days before the entire cargo would fall into enemy hands. The Dutchman, however, held fast, insisting that there would be no pilot until he gave the word.

Not to be outdone, Payne enlisted the services of a native cab driver who helped him find one of the harbor pilots. With the promise of three times the normal fee, he agreed to take the ship out that night. Payne then took the pilot to the *Sea Witch*, where he found the captain more than anxious to escape from Java. The harbor pilot agreed to meet the *Isabel* off the minefield entrance at midnight, regardless of any attempts of the harbor master to prevent the ship's sailing.

The *Isabel* got under way under the unwelcome glare of a full moon at 2110, and an hour later cleared the minefield to begin the dangerous search for the *Spearfish*. At 2325 the sea near the *Isabel* erupted, and the large black hull of a submarine hove into view. The *Isabel*'s guns quickly trained on the submarine and all hands remained tense until she was challenged and identified herself as the *Spearfish*. Without wasting time, Lieutenant Commander Dempsey was transferred, and the submarine slipped silently back into the depths of the Indian Ocean, leaving the *Isabel* alone to await the arrival of her convoy.

Midnight passed with no sign of the *Sea Witch*, and Payne feared something had happened to prevent her sailing. While he waited, Payne kept the *Isabel* steaming on various zigzag courses to counter possible moves by enemy submarines. The brilliant moonlight was cause for great concern, for there was no place the ship could hide, and at 0300 Payne's worst fears were realized. The frantic shouts of lookouts alerted Payne to a torpedo wake to port heading toward them. It was too late to take evasive action. Terrified, all hands watched the lethal tin fish speeding to intercept the *Isabel*. The ship was doomed. But a miracle occurred. The torpedo passed directly beneath the bridge without exploding and raced away into the night. Lacking means to locate the attacker, Payne rapidly changed direction and at full speed headed away from the danger area.

This narrow escape from oblivion was excuse enough for Payne to abandon the *Sea Witch*, but he decided to wait longer. One hour later, at 0130 on 2 March 1942, the *Sea Witch* stood out and joined up. As she did, the weather turned squally. With thick clouds blocking out the moon and shrouded in torrents of rain, the two ships headed south with the *Sea Witch* maintaining station 500 yards astern of the *Isabel*.

Payne's orders were to head for Exmouth Gulf, Australia, but the admiral's last words were to escort the *Sea Witch* to safe waters. At the time, however, there appeared to be no such thing as safe waters. To the east, Japanese forces were known to be sinking ships attempting to go directly to Australia, and Payne determined that his best bet was to steam due south before heading for Australia. He calculated that by the most economical use of fuel the *Isabel* could make Fremantle in southwestern Australia.

By noon of 2 March the storm clouds had lifted, and at 1235 a twin-engine Japanese bomber sighted the ships. On board the unarmed merchantman and the underarmed *Isabel*, men fearfully watched as the plane dropped lower and circled out of gun range. It remained in their vicinity for twenty minutes before flying away. Apparently it was on a reconnaissance mission and without bombs, otherwise it surely would have attacked the *Sea Witch*, a prime 10,000-ton target.

Fears did not diminish with the plane's departure, for, with their location now no secret, they could be attacked at any time by aircraft, warships, or both. But fortune smiled once again. The ships steamed on throughout the long afternoon until rain and darkness once again became their allies.

On 3 March the weather turned mean. Southwest winds of force five whipped up heavy seas, which pounded the *Isabel* unmercifully. Spray, blown high over the ship, condensed on the stacks, leaving them crusted with thick layers of salt. At 0900 the tops of a strange warship were sighted approaching at high speed bearing 227 degrees true. Earlier a frantic distress call of only two words, "Raider, raider," had been heard from the gunboat *Asheville*. Her silence from then on boded disaster, and the nature of this ship was of great concern. The seas were too rough to make a run for it. Besides, the *Sea Witch* was making her best speed, 14 knots. Nothing could be done but wait and pray.

The long minutes of waiting, while the ship loomed ever larger, were filled with unmasked tensions, especially when it was determined she was a cruiser. Suddenly, the stranger's signal light flashed a challenge. The *Isabel* replied. All hands were grimly silent as more light signals were exchanged, and then, the word was passed. She was the heavy cruiser *Phoenix*. Instantly, wild, delirious shouts went up from the *Isabel*'s crew. To know they were not alone in an ocean where the enemy roamed at will was cause for rejoicing. Although the *Phoenix* soon disappeared to the east, the cruel pressures of vulnerability, which for many days had plagued the *Isabel*'s crew, all at once vanished, replaced by a heartwarming aura of optimism.

Winds and seas abated during the early hours of 4 March and speed, which had been reduced to 12 knots, was increased to 14. This day was uneventful other than the receipt of a dispatch to all Allied ships warning of two enemy aircraft carriers launching planes. The position given was 400 miles to the northeast, too far away to cause trouble.

The two ships were again pounded by gale force winds and heavy seas on the fifth. Time after time, green water surged over the *Isabel*'s bridge, and the little ship, with her decks constantly awash, pitched and rolled and shuddered. Huge waves tore away the forward ammunition locker, and at times it seemed as though the ship itself would break in two. Steam pressure suddenly dropped off at 1045, and the *Isabel* lost headway. Sea water, sloshing down fuel tank vents, which were often underwater, had contaminated the oil. With a prayer that not all fuel tanks were contaminated, the chief engineer shifted to another. It worked, and within fifteen minutes pressure and speed were regained.

All hands cheered to see land that afternoon off the port quarter. It was far away, but the wild, unpopulated southwest coast of Australia was to them the promised land. They were now less than 400 miles

The USS *Isabel* (PY-10), "relief" flagship for commander in chief, U.S. Asiatic Fleet. Naval Institute Collection

from Fremantle, and if the oil held out and the *Isabel* did not come apart at the seams, they would make it. Both, however, posed serious problems. Their fuel, even without the contamination, was seriously low, and the seas, with the setting sun, were growing increasingly rough. They had been unable to prepare normal meals for more than two days. A few sandwiches and canned food had been the order of the day. There was a foot of water in the wardroom, and no place for passengers or crew to sleep except in a few sloppy-wet places topside. With the belief that the *Isabel* might founder, no one even attempted to sleep below decks. Existence for those on board the *Isabel* was miserable.

The weather calmed down somewhat by the next morning, and although the ship continued to experience trouble with contaminated fuel, speed was maintained at 13 knots throughout the day. Two empty fuel tanks were filled with water for ballast, and with the two remaining almost empty but fouled with sea water, the *Isabel*'s capability of making port was marginal.

Rottnest Island Light, marking the entrance to Fremantle harbor, was sighted at 0100 on 7 March 1942. Words cannot express the exhilaration which surged through the hearts of those on board the *Isabel*. A dreadfully long nightmare was about to be happily concluded. With only four hours' fuel remaining, the *Isabel* dropped the hook in Fremantle harbor, and the gutsy little ship and her courageous crew were safe at last.

In concluding the saga of the *Isabel*, it might be well to point out that the destroyer *Pillsbury*, which left Tjilatjap harbor in the *Isabel*'s place, vanished without a trace. The same fate was met by the gunboat *Asheville* and numerous merchant ships attempting to reach Australia. Thus, it is apparent that Lieutenant Payne's decision initially to sail on a southerly course was fortuitous. To confirm that, a PBY pilot reported that on the day after the *Isabel* left Tjilatjap, he sighted a Japanese cruiser and two destroyers a mere 40 miles east of her.

In summary, the *Isabel*, considered expendable even before the war began, superbly performed every dangerous assignment, and somehow managed to come through unscathed. Stripped of her radio transmitter and unable to communicate with headquarters or other units of the fleet, she was in a precarious position in wartime. Because of obsolete armament and lack of underwater detection gear, she was seriously disadvantaged in the face of enemy opposition. Scoffed at as a fighting ship and on occasion completely forgotten, the *Isabel*, manned by a derring-do crew, safely led elements of the fleet through dangerous minefields and treacherous reef-strewn waters, escorted numerous vessels through areas dominated by the enemy, probably shot down an attacking plane, sank a Japanese submarine, and rescued 187 survivors from a sunken ship.

The *Isabel* was there and narrowly escaped disaster in the bombing of the Cavite Navy Yard. Strangely enough, she happened to be in the harbors of Tandjungpriok and Surabaja, Java, and Palembang, Sumatra, when each of these cities suffered their initial bombing attacks. Because she was expendable, the *Isabel* was assigned the dubious distinction of being the last Allied naval vessel to leave port in Java, and upon her miraculous arrival in Australia, the *Isabel's* mail was found in the "Sunken Ships" file.

Ironically, the heroic achievements of the *Isabel's* crew went unnoticed, and not a single officer or enlisted man received a commendation of any kind. A grateful navy, however, did award the *Isabel* one battle star on the Asiatic-Pacific Service Medal for participation in Philippine Island operations from 8 December 1941 to 2 March 1942, a medal awarded to everyone else in the Asiatic Fleet, no matter what they did.

# 24

# A REFUSAL TO SURRENDER

Five May 1942 was doomsday minus one for Corregidor, the massive island fortress guarding the main channel entrance to Manila Bay. For four torturous months its valiant defenders had been subjected to merciless poundings by unopposed Japanese bombers and, with the fall of Bataan on 9 April, a new kill factor had been introduced— artillery fire. Standing hub to hub in the hills of Bataan, upwards of 200 heavy cannon had systematically pulverized the batteries and defense positions of the "rock," America's last bastion in all of Southeast Asia. Three smaller island forts—Hughes, Drum, and Frank, supporting Corregidor across the bay's southern reaches—had shared the same fate. Most of their big guns too lay silent among the rubble of demolished casemates.

That the end was near was no secret to the defenders of Corregidor and its satellite forts, who numbered about 9,145 Americans (nearly half of whom were navy men and marines), and their comrades-in-arms, 3,516 men of the Philippine scouts, army, and navy. Surrounded by the enemy and with no chance of outside help, these half-starved, battle-fatigued men doggedly fought on, obsessed with the foreknowledge that the impending end could bring only death or capture.

Anchored in Corregidor's south harbor was the minesweeper *Quail* (AM-15), the last of six such ships assigned to the Asiatic Fleet. Two had gone to the Netherlands East Indies in early December; Japanese bombs had sunk three more in Manila Bay. The *Quail*, however, was not without her problems. Most of the bridge had been torn away by 6-inch shells, which also smashed the upper portion of her stem section. She was leaking from minor underwater damage to her hull, and two-thirds of her crew had been ordered ashore to help man beach defenses on Corregidor. Despite these handicaps, the *Quail*, in the face of enemy shelling, had that day daringly swept a 600-foot channel through Corredigor's minefield to permit evacuation by launch of army and navy personnel to the submarine *Spearfish*, lying in wait offshore.

Four officers, including the commanding officer, Lieutenant Commander John H. Morrill, and twenty-two enlisted men were on board the *Quail* that night when, at 2030, Japanese artillery opened fire on Corregidor with a thunderous barrage. The continuous mass of exploding shells made the entire island appear like one vast sheet of flames. It was difficult to believe that any mortal could possibly survive that hell on earth. The crew of the *Quail* watched aghast as huge sections of the rock were gouged out, causing landslides which obliterated sections of the beach defenses. Soon Corregidor lay shrouded in a heavy cloud of dust and smoke. Defense searchlights were useless, their powerful beams appearing as vague yellow spots in a heavy fog. This grisly spectacle meant only one thing—the long-dreaded assault on Corregidor had commenced.

For three hours the devastating barrage continued. Then, with the bursting of a green flare over the fortress, the cannonading suddenly ceased. Those on board the *Quail* found the silence ominous, disquieting. It probably meant Japanese troops were storming the rock. Heavy machine-gun fire on the eastern end of the island confirmed this belief. Two and a half hours later, at 0200 on 6 May, the enemy fired a white rocket, and once again pounded Corregidor with heavy artillery. A half-hour later, two green rockets burst and the shelling stopped. Again the sounds of machine-gun and rifle fire rang out along the eastern reaches of the island.

Lieutenant Commander Morrill and his men had no way of learning what was happening on the rock. Hoping for the best, they feared the worst. Finally, at 0430, a message was received from navy headquarters on Corregidor, ordering those on board the *Quail* to help in the defense of Fort Hughes on Caballo Island, 3 miles south of Corregidor. All hands proceeded to the fort in the ship's motor launch, leaving the *Quail* anchored midway between Fort Hughes and Corregidor.

When they arrived at Fort Hughes, Morrill and his men were appalled to find it a mass of rubble and in the final stages of collapse. Mortar pit walls, tunnels, and shelter areas were torn and crumbling. Casualties had been heavy. Enemy shells, exploding in the gun pits, had killed and wounded men in the shelter areas. Shell fragments had even smashed through the heavily protected hospital section, taking a heavy toll of the wounded and hospital personnel. All but one of the fort's seventeen big guns had been destroyed, and that one, a 12-inch mortar, valiantly continued to fire on enemy positions.

At daylight, Japanese bombers attacked Fort Hughes, but could do little to add to the carnage already inflicted, or to knock out the remaining mortar. Only cease-fire orders from Corregidor, received at 0900 on 6 May 1942, silenced the gun forever.

Information concerning what was happening on Corregidor was unobtainable. Rumors of surrender abounded. The men of Fort Hughes, dazed from weeks of punishing bombardment, were confused as they apprehensively awaited the inevitable word to surrender.

At 1100, Morrill received orders from the commandant of the Sixteenth Naval District, headquartered on Corregidor, to scuttle the *Quail*. Immediately following that, all communications with Corregidor were lost. While Morrill assembled the scuttling party, consisting of himself, his gunnery officer, and four enlisted men of the engineering department, white flags were observed flying over Corregidor, Fort Drum, and Fort Frank. The colonel commanding Fort Hughes, having received no orders to surrender and thoroughly detesting the idea, did not immediately follow suit. This delay permitted Morrill to carry out his orders.

Arriving at the dock, the navy men were disgusted to discover their motor launch, holed by shells, resting on the bottom. Another motor launch, however, rode at anchor 200 yards away. Without hesitation, all six men, determined to keep their ship from ever flying a Japanese flag, dove into the water and swam to it. This launch was in good condition, and the engine started with no difficulty. En route to the *Quail*, they were strafed by Japanese aircraft and subjected to machine-gun fire from enemy positions on Corregidor. Although bullets churned the water close by, no hits were scored. Once on board the *Quail*, they quickly opened the seacocks, and in a matter of minutes the last navy minesweeper in Manila Bay headed for her watery grave.

During the return trip, a white flag was run up over Fort Hughes. Rather than go there to be captured, Morrill and his men took refuge in the *Ranger*, an abandoned army tug anchored off the south shore of Fort Hughes. Here they formulated a daring plan of escape to the island of Mindanao, where they could join U.S. Army forces fighting there.

Throughout the afternoon the Japanese continued to bomb and shell the hapless forts. Time and again the white flags were shot away but, in compliance with General Wainwright's orders, they were always replaced. This bombardment was a source of terrifying confusion to the defenders, who had been ordered to destroy all remaining big guns and to throw their small arms into the sea. What they did not know was that although General Wainwright had directed the surrender of Corregidor and the island forts to stop the wanton slaughter of his troops, it was not enough to satisfy Lieutenant General Masaharu Homma, commanding the Japanese forces. He refused to accept the surrender unless fighting everywhere in the Philippines ceased.

Wainwright argued that his authority did not permit issuing such orders. However, when Homma cold-bloodedly said that if he did not surrender the forces as demanded, all prisoners in Japanese hands would be put to death, General Wainwright had no alternative but to broadcast orders to end all resistance throughout the Philippines.

Fortunately, the tug *Ranger* was well stocked with firearms, ammunition, food, clothing, tools, a few charts, and other items useful for the long voyage through unfriendly seas to the island of Mindanao. These were carefully stowed in the 36-foot motor launch. It had been doctrine to keep drums of reserve diesel oil in all ship's boats and, from several of them anchored in the area, 450 gallons were obtained and loaded on board. All was in readiness. Their only fears were that a Japanese shell might blow the *Ranger* out of the water, or the enemy would land on Fort Hughes before they could return, under cover of darkness, to pick up their shipmates. It was impossible to contact the rest of the crew on Corregidor.

At nightfall, Morrill and his men landed at Fort Hughes, where they hurriedly assembled members of the *Quail*'s crew. After outlining the plan, Morrill stressed the hazards of such an undertaking, including the fact that Manila Bay was completely surrounded by Japanese picket boats and warships. Chances of getting through were slim. If caught, they would probably be killed. This, he assured all hands, was strictly a voluntary undertaking. Two officers and six enlisted men who indicated a willingness to go appeared so mentally upset and physically exhausted that Morrill considered it unwise to take them along. The others enthusiastically volunteered to attempt the trip.

Lieutenant Commander Morrill, Warrant Gunner Donald C. Taylor, and sixteen navy enlisted men of the *Quail* boarded their 36-foot motor launch at 2215 on 6 May 1942 and commenced the voyage into the unknown. Their departure came none too soon. Fifteen minutes later, Japanese artillery all at once opened up on Fort Hughes with a barrage similar to the one experienced by Corregidor the night before. A green rocket was fired at 2330, and the barrage lifted. This was followed by the sound of many motors, indicating the Japanese were about to land on the fort.

Morrill headed for the Luzon coast, seeking to remain as inconspicuous as possible in its shadows. Hugging the shoreline, he headed the launch out of Manila Bay on a southerly course. Two and a half hours after leaving the fort, a brilliant moon came out and, to their consternation, disclosed two Japanese destroyers, about 1 mile away, patrolling to seaward on a north-south course between Fortune Island and Olongapo. Worse than that, another destroyer and a patrol boat blocked their escape route to the south. Because of her overloaded condition, the motor launch could make no more than 3 or 4 knots, and Morrill decided to seek refuge in Hamilo Cove, a scant 10 miles from where they started.

They ran the launch up on a sandy beach and hurriedly camouflaged it with green branches cut from palm and other trees. When that was done, the men, physically exhausted from the long siege of Corregidor, lay down on jagged rocks in a small ravine and fell sound asleep.

At dawn, while attempting to improve on the boat's disguise, all hands were startled to hear low-flying aircraft rapidly approaching. Instantly, everyone dove for cover as two single-engine seaplanes flew overhead at treetop level. Fearing they might have been sighted, the men clung to the ground, not daring to move. When the planes failed to return for a closer look, life once again became beautiful. Their camouflage job had passed the first test.

All day long the little band of men remained concealed in the thick brush watching with concern Japanese destroyers and patrol boats moving back and forth a mere half-mile off the entrance to their hiding place. Once during the morning, the rolling thunder of artillery could be heard as, for some unknown reason, the Japanese seemed to be pounding Corregidor. If such were the case, this cruel shelling, they knew, was unnecessary, for the defenders of the defenseless forts were finished. They thanked God to be away from it all.

Plans to shove off that night were shattered when, at dusk, a Japanese destroyer steamed slowly into Hamilo Cove and anchored a few hundred yards from their hiding place. They knew that from a not-too-distant vantage point the boat's outline was clearly discernible, but it was now too late to do anything about it. Fearing a Japanese landing party might investigate, they lay hidden with rifles and automatic weapons at the ready. Darkness came to hide the boat from prying eyes, but later, when the moon came out, their fears were renewed. Fortunately, Japanese lookouts failed to detect the boat, and at dawn the destroyer got under way, leaving behind eighteen very tired, but happily relieved navy men.

Throughout the day, 8 May 1942, enemy warships continued to patrol just beyond the cove's entrance. Obviously the waters off Luzon were alive with Japanese ships. To pass undetected through them was bound to be difficult. In spite of the inherent dangers, Morrill and his men were anxious to get going. The last thing any of them wanted to delay their movements was another destroyer anchored near them overnight. Near sundown, however, a Japanese destroyer slowly headed for the cove. With that, the atmosphere turned indigo with curses, the likes of which only furious sailors of the old China Station could conjure. At the last moment, though, the tin can veered off to enter Looc Cove, a mile to the south.

When it was dark and the area was considered clear of enemy ships, they stripped the camouflage from the motor launch and got under way. Their plan was to move south cautiously, hugging the Luzon coastline, and anchor before sunrise in another cove east of the shipping lanes. Although all eyes searched for the enemy, lookouts were specifically posted to insure coverage in all quadrants. Stealthily they passed Looc Cove. In the darkness, the enemy destroyer anchored there was not visible, but uncomfortably close to seaward lookouts reported four enemy destroyers steaming in formation on a southerly course. These ships passed on without incident. A half-hour later, another destroyer was sighted entering a cove dead ahead. To prevent discovery, they were forced to detour to the west and away from the Luzon coast.

No sooner had they disposed of this danger than numerous patrol boats appeared ahead. Three of them were patrolling directly across their route between Fortune Island and the town of Nasugb on Luzon. There was no alternative but to change course to pass seaward of Fortune Island and hope to circumvent the enemy line. They rounded the island without incident and set a southerly course only to discover three high-speed patrol boats roaming back and forth between the western shore of Fortune Island and the Luband group of islands farther west. The situation now was desperate, for they had to get past these boats and back close to the Luzon coast before daylight, or all was lost.

Morrill maneuvered the launch as close as he dared into the dark shadows of the island. Here they waited and intently studied the intervals between patrol boats. With luck, they just might slip between them, but split-second timing was a must if they were to escape discovery. Finally Morrill was ready to make his move. When the innermost patrol boat completed its turn and headed away from the island, he immediately ordered full speed ahead, which was all of 3 knots. The timing was perfect, and they inched through the picket line undetected.

At daybreak they were some 20 miles down the west coast of Luzon. A treacherous reef prevented them from finding a hidden anchorage close to shore, and forced them to anchor in the open. Now it was imperative they disguise the boat. To make it look more like a nondescript native craft, the taffrail was removed and, with paint courtesy of the tug *Ranger*, the launch's GI issue battleship grey gave way to black. Although they were a considerable distance from the shipping lanes, the exposed position was cause for great concern throughout the day. But their luck held, and the only signs of the enemy were the masts of ships hull down over the horizon and several bombers, which passed on high overhead.

At nightfall, they cranked up the engine and headed south, then turned east through Verde Passage. In transiting the passage, Morrill had planned to take the shortcut north of Malacaban Island, but numerous suspicious-looking objects in the area forced a change of course to the south of it, to pass midway between Malacaban and Mindoro Islands.

They were not long on this course when a line of anchored picket boats was spotted strung between the southwestern end of Malacaban Island and Mindoro. Thanks to heavy clouds, which blotted out the moon, and the fact that the Japanese were smugly content in the knowledge that they controlled all the waters in Southeast Asia, they eased gingerly through the line of boats.

The joys of this successful maneuver were short-lived, for several miles farther along, a second line of picket boats confronted them. Moving ahead as before, they were midway through this line when the launch became locked in a strong current which stopped all forward movement. For three terrifying hours the launch remained hung in the same position, while the engineers worked feverishly to squeeze a few more turns out of the engine. Just as success seemed to crown their efforts and the launch began to move ever so slowly but surely ahead, the overtaxed engine conked out, and they drifted back through the line of pickets.

After much frantic tinkering by flashlight underneath a canvas hood, they got the engine to kick over once again, and the motor launch recrossed the picket line, unobserved.

Through all of this, the little boat, and her go-for-broke crew, had been surrounded by the enemy, who for some blessed reason failed to perceive it. Off the southwestern end of Malacaban Island a tanker and a large auxiliary, both lying at anchor, had been clearly identified. A little to the east lurked two destroyers and, at the eastern end of the island, they had somberly noted the black silhouettes of two very large submarines. Continuing on, they passed Verde Island, at the southwestern end of which a destroyer lay at anchor. Looking astern to the north of the island, they could see numerous other vessels. It was nerve-chilling and at the same time heartwarming to think that somehow they had passed safely through that deadly maze.

No ships could be seen ahead as they moved between Verde Island and the Luzon coast. With every reason to believe the worst was behind them, all hands breathed easier. But they were in for a shocker. The darkness masking them was suddenly shattered when two powerful searchlights, one on Verde Island and the other on Luzon, flashed on, centering the little craft in their beams. Attempting to look as innocent as possible, all but the helmsman ducked below the gunnels. Caught in the blinding lights and powerless to do anything about it, the eighteen men awaited some terrible end to their cherished dreams of escape. At an agonizing 4 knots, the launch kept chugging along on course with the cursed lights following its progress. It seemed an eternity until they passed around a point of land, and out of range of the prying fingers of light, once more to be blanketed in beautiful darkness.

At daylight on 10 May they put into the small barrio of Digas on Luzon and were delighted to find the natives friendly. No Japanese had ever been in Digas, but small garrisons of six to ten men were reported stationed in nearby towns. The men purchased rice and fresh fruits and were able to enjoy a much-needed rest after their harrowing night.

The launch departed Digas at dark and arrived the next morning near the barrio of Bondoc on the Bondoc Peninsula. Here the natives were also friendly, perhaps more so because all of the pro-Japanese had been eliminated by patriotic Filipinos. The Japanese had yet to visit Bondoc, but small garrisons were known to be stationed in towns to the north.

Because the boat's engine had been acting erratically and the men felt relatively safe in this area, they decided to overhaul the engine there before attempting the next leg of their perilous journey. Besides, with four automatic rifles, six standard rifles, eleven pistols, and plenty of ammunition, the navy men were determined to make life miserable for anyone trying to stop them.

During the two days it took to overhaul the engine, a trading banca arrived with a copy of the Japanese-controlled Manila newspaper. From this they learned the terms under which General Wainwright had been forced to surrender. Not only had he surrendered Corregidor, but all Filipino and American forces throughout the Philippines had been ordered to cease fighting. This was a foul blow to Morrill and his men. Their plans to join American forces fighting on Mindanao were all at once knocked in the head. There remained only one way to escape the Japanese. Sail to Australia, a distance of almost 2,000 miles through Japanese-controlled waters, without adequate charts or other navigational aids. This would be a wild and dangerous undertaking, but not a man dissented. All hands were eager to "give it a go." Because diesel oil might be difficult to obtain en route to Australia, the natives made them a bamboo mast and boom and supplied them with cordage to rig a sail.

The night of 13 May, Morrill and his men bid goodbye to friends at Bondoc and, with their overhauled engine working perfectly, headed southward through the Sibuyan Sea. Continuing on through 14 May, they passed around the southwestern end of Masbate Island, and on the morning of the fifteenth found themselves off the northern coast of Cebu Island. Although they had experienced grave misgivings, not an enemy ship or plane had been sighted since traversing Verde Passage. But now, as they headed on an eastward course from Cebu, they were alarmed to see a large Japanese tanker bearing down on them. She was on a southerly course between Cebu and Leyte.

Everyone but the helmsman hid as best he could on the bottom of the boat. Clutching their weapons, the cool, battle-hardened men waited to sell themselves dearly should the worst happen. As the tanker passed within 1,000 yards of the launch, Japanese sailors lined the rails to look it over. Seeing only the helmsman, dressed in a native straw hat and old civilian clothing, his face, hands, and bare feet darkly sun-tanned, the Japanese evidently considered the launch a harmless inter-island trader and passed on.

Early that afternoon they put into the town of Tabango on the northwest coast of Leyte. Here again, they were glad to encounter friendly natives. A Chinese merchant sold them canned goods, and from Filipino sources they were able to purchase a drum of diesel oil and 10 gallons of urgently needed lubricating oil. They learned that several detachments of Japanese troops were billeted on the north coast of Cebu, and a rather large one was at Tacloban, a city on Leyte's northeastern coast. The enemy was also known to be at Catabalogan on the nearby island of Samar. In both Tacloban and Catabalogan, Philippine and American troops were said to be surrendering in compliance with General Wainwright's orders. The governor of Cebu, however, had refused to surrender and was leading guerrilla forces based in remote provinces.

Obviously Morrill and his men were in an extremely dangerous section of the Philippines. Loyal Filipinos warned that defectors prob-ably had already spread the word of their arrival and affirmed that Japanese troops could be expected at any time. Even so, it was suicidal to set out during daylight. To mask their true intentions from possible informers, the Americans acted as though they were preparing to spend the night. When darkness came, however, they made a hurried

Lieutenant Commander John Morrill, standing in the stern sheets by the tiller, and his seventeen crewmen on board their camouflaged 36-foot motor launch. Courtesy Rear Admiral John Morrill

departure. They had left none too soon, for as the launch slowly worked its way out of Tabango Bay, hugging its dark shoreline, a fast, unidentified powerboat entered. In all probability it was manned by Japanese troops looking for them.

All that night and the following day, the launch moved southward through the Camotes Sea, heading for Surigao Strait. Under cover of darkness, they entered the strait using the passage south of Binegat Island. By hugging the east coast of Mindanao they hoped to remain clear of Japanese patrol boats and areas in the straits which might have been mined. If they did happen upon a minefield, the men trusted that their shallow-draft, wooden-hulled craft would see them through unharmed. By dawn of the seventeenth they had traversed Surigao Strait without so much as seeing anything that smacked of Japanese.

Early that morning, well down the east coast of Mindanao, they put into a small unnamed cove in the vicinity of Tandag. Natives in a nondescript barrio provided them with fresh water and a few provisions, mainly fresh fruits. When they learned that no Japanese forces were known to be near the area, the men, exhausted from their nerve-racking all-night vigil, rested until dark.

Leaving the sanctuary of the cove that night, they were soon faced with a serious problem of natural origin—heavy weather. Sailing down the east coast of Mindanao in the vast Philippine Sea, they were suddenly drenched by furious rain squalls. The little craft pitched and wallowed in the angry waves, which at times broke over the boat and threatened to capsize it. When daylight came on the eighteenth, they hastily sought refuge at Port Lamon on Mindanao.

The docks and the lumber camp of this small town had been demolished only the month before by a furious typhoon. Although Port Lamon boasted a radio receiving and transmitting station, it too had been knocked out by the storm. The residents, short of food, readily shared whatever they had with Morrill and his men. They also provided lumber to deck over the forward section of the launch to make it more seaworthy. These Filipinos assured Morrill that no Japanese had ever come to Port Lamon, but many of their troops were known to be in the city of Surigao—a place Morrill had fortunately chosen to bypass two nights before.

The navy men planned to remain in Port Lamon another day to rest, but at about 2200 a Filipino came racing to the boat shouting that the Japs were heading toward the harbor in power launches, and everyone in town was taking to the hills. No sooner was this message delivered than the ominous rumbling of motors became clearly audible. Quickly, the men picked up their weapons and took stations along the beach. Grimly, they waited as six large patrol boats nosed into the harbor. This could blast all their dreams of escape, for if such a large force discovered them, their only recourse would be to make a run for the hills.

The Japanese patrol boats, slowly feeling their way, came ever closer, the noise of their engines shattering the stillness of the night. Midway into the harbor, the boats abruptly reversed course and departed, heading south along the coast. This had been too close for comfort, and the navy men decided to get under way immediately.

The launch had gone only a short distance when men shouting in the water attracted their attention. Concerned that more disquieting news was in store for them, Morrill backed the launch down to find out. The Americans were happily surprised to find several Filipinos swimming toward them pushing a drum of diesel oil, which they previously had promised to provide. These brave, nameless men had done this in spite of their fear of the Japanese, and the fact that their own oil was in very short supply. After hoisting the drum on board and profusely thanking the Filipinos for their kindness, Morrill and company once again headed out to sea. To avoid enemy sea and air patrols, they sailed due east to put at least 100 miles of open Philippine Sea between them and the enemy-infested coast of Mindanao.

Late on 19 May, they set a southerly course for the island of Morotai in the Halmahera group. Taking care to cross the possible air lane between Mindanao and Pelelieu at night, they sailed on through a desolate sea to arrive off the northeastern tip of Morotai on the morning of 22 May. Here they planned to land at the village of Berebere, but as they approached the beach, a large motor launch flying the Japanese flag was spotted lying at anchor. Immediately they changed course and continued southward until the next morning, when they put into the tiny island of Sajafi in the Netherlands East Indies.

The natives on Sajafi spoke no English, but by using deftly contrived sign language the men were able to barter articles of clothing or other odds and ends for needed fresh water and provisions. The inhabitants of Sajafi were not overly friendly, nor were they openly hostile. They seemed indifferent to the war and apparently favored neither side. They made it quite evident, however, that the Americans' presence bothered them, and they wanted them to get the hell out of town as of yesterday.

The navy men left Sajafi that night and headed southeast to pass north of Gag Island, then headed south through the islands of the Jeff Family group. The next morning, just after sunup, lookouts shouted the alarm—two power-driven launches flying no flags were some distance to the east. All but the coxswain quickly vanished below the gunnels and unlimbered their guns. Fortunately, the launches held their course and were soon out of sight. This close call prompted

Morrill to put into a small, uninhabited island in the Jeff Family group, where they could remain out of sight for the remainder of the day.

That night, they moved out on a southeasterly course to pass Pisang Island, and then head due south. During the afternoon of the next day, 25 May, in order to relax for a few hours ashore, they put into an uninhabited island just to the north of Tioor Island. When they decided to leave, they were beset with serious trouble. The starter battery was too weak to turn the engine over. When numerous exhausting attempts to start the engine by hand cranking failed, it became apparent that they would now be forced to continue on, as best they could, under sail. Such a prospect was most discouraging, for with no centerboard the heavy motor launch was an exceedingly poor sailboat. Adding to their problems was the fact that the prevailing winds roamed from south to southeast, which would permit them to make no better than Portuguese Timor, far west of their intended course. Having come so far through so many dangers, it was frustrating to think that they just might not make those last tantalizing miles to freedom.

They were obliged to remain in their rather exposed anchorage overnight. There, with the boat rolling and pitching in the rough seas, they prepared to rig sails in the morning. By sunrise, however, several ingenious sailors had devised a tackle-leverage system which permitted the engine to be cranked and started by using the propeller shaft. At the sound of the engine revving up, the spirits of all hands moved into high gear, and course was set for the island of Tioor.

They reached Tioor by mid-morning on 27 May. Through a native who could speak Pidgin English the men were able to barter for water and provisions. Bartering was the only way of conducting business with the natives of the Netherlands East Indies, who had been thoroughly brainwashed by the Japanese and would not accept American or Philippine currency. Through this native linguist it was learned that for about six weeks no Japanese ships or aircraft had been seen in the area. Encouraged by this information, Morrill and his men put to sea just before sundown.

During the night, seas became increasingly wild, forcing the men to take refuge in the lee of Kur Island on the morning of 28 May. As they approached a native village, the men were perplexed to see a white flag hastily run up a pole. As the launch moved deeper into the harbor, a 50-foot native lugger was spotted alongside a rickety dock; it too ran up a white flag. Then the flag of surrender was suddenly lowered and a Japanese flag raised in its place. The navy men, their loaded guns at the ready, cautiously approached. When the launch closed within 10 yards of the lugger, its crew, noting they were white men, hauled down the

Japanese flag. Boarding the vessel, Morrill's men found only a handful of very frightened natives.

An English-speaking school teacher at Kur told the Americans that only two weeks before he had heard on the radio that Japanese forces occupied the entire island of New Guinea, as well as the islands of New Zealand and Tasmania. This, of course, was a Japanese pipe dream, but Morrill and his men, with no radio of their own to verify this information, were concerned about their chances of escaping the ever-victorious Japanese.

Departing Kur that afternoon, they proceeded on a southerly course, but heavy weather forced them to take refuge at a village on the island of Fado. Here the natives were a bit more friendly than in the previous East Indies Islands, and readily provided water and coconuts. They too indicated that during the preceding six weeks no Japanese ships or planes had been sighted.

At this juncture, the launch's stern tube bearing, which had become badly worn, needed to be replaced before serious damage was done. There was no place at Fado where the boat could be beached, so on the morning of 29 May it was moved a short distance away to the island of Taam and beached. Now a stern tube bearing for a U.S. Navy 36-foot motor launch is not something easily come by, especially in the remote little islands of the Netherlands East Indies, but without a replacement further use of the motor would be impossible. As so often is the case in dire emergencies, the ingenuity of American sailors surfaced to solve the problem. From a piece of hard driftwood, the engineer had pain-stakingly whittled a new bearing, which was inserted to replace the defective one made of lignum vitae.

The natives at Taam were quite antagonistic, and obnoxious in many petty ways. They vehemently expressed their desire to have the Americans leave. Morrill believed this was not so much because of the war, but rather that Taam was a center of Mohammedanism. Christians in their midst were not acceptable. The eighteen rugged navy men had been tolerated while they worked on their boat only because they were armed to the teeth.

With the makeshift bearing working perfectly, the Americans, with no desire to remain any longer than necessary among the surly natives, put out to sea at sunrise on 30 May. Heavy weather once again forced Morrill and his men to seek refuge, this time on a small island off the leeward side of Molu Island. Here the natives appeared to be of a different race than those encountered on other islands of the Nether-lands East Indies. They were lighter skinned, seemed more nearly like Filipinos, and were very friendly. No Japanese had ever visited their island, although some had camped on nearby Molu Island, but were no longer there. The navy men made no mention of the fact that they were Americans, yet the natives seemed to know and indicated that they were well-disposed toward the Allied cause. One of the natives confided that he intended to go to Darwin, Australia, soon on a trading vessel, but fearing he was attempting to draw them out, no one gave him so much as a clue to their destination.

The heavy weather modified somewhat by 2 June, and the navy men, prodded by the knowledge that only a few hundred miles of open Arafura Sea separated them from their cherished goal, eagerly got under way. This leg of the journey, if they could complete it, would take them to Melville Island, less than 100 miles north of Darwin. But this portion of their journey was not destined to be easy. The weather turned grim. Shrieking rain squalls and rough, pounding seas plagued the little craft. She pitched and rolled like a thing possessed, making life for the eighteen men on board anything but comfortable. Nevertheless, they took the pounding stoically, for they knew that every determined chug of the engine and the passing of each tedious hour brought them ever closer to friendly territory.

About midday of 4 June, surrounded by calmer seas, all hands strained to catch the first glimpse of the fabled "land down under," which was almost within reach. Long minutes of searching dragged on into agonizing hours. Then, suddenly, there it was—the landfall they sought. There, lying low on the horizon, barely discernible from the cresting waves, was the north coast of Melville Island. It was difficult to believe this was sanctuary at last, that their long ordeal was almost over and from then on it was going to be all downhill. Only those who have experienced the fearsome moments of such an adventure can know the pure, unbridled elation these navy man shared together on that occasion.

Moving through the Straits of Apali, they went ashore to a Catholic mission on Melville Island, where they were welcomed with open arms. Exhausted from battling angry seas, Morrill and his men basked in the generous hospitality thrust upon them at the mission and, to regain strength, rested during the daylight hours of 5 June. But eager to reach Darwin, they set out that night on the last leg of their journey.

The little motor launch, with its jubilant crew, arrived off Darwin harbor at 0900 on 6 June 1942, to find the harbor's entrance blocked by an antisubmarine net. Anxiously they waited for a challenge and instructions from harbor craft, but there were none. Undaunted, they searched until a gap was found between the net and shoal water through which the launch was able to pass and slowly chug into the harbor.

No brass band or cheering throng was on hand to greet these courageous adventurers. In fact, no one even challenged or acknowledged the presence of the weather-beaten motor launch until it pulled alongside the inner harbor control station dock, and Morrill shouted for instructions.

Deliriously happy to be safe at last among friends, the sun-bronzed, bewhiskered navy men, who, in their ragged, nondescript clothing, could easily be taken for Sulu Sea pirates, were in for a rude surprise. Having destroyed all means of identification in the event they fell afoul of the Japanese, they were unable to convince Australian authorities they were actually American escapees from Corregidor. Everyone on Corregidor was believed to have been either killed or captured, and the distance alleged to have been traveled in such a small boat seemed impossible. So Morrill and his men, suspected of being German spies, were tossed in jail to await positive identification.

Before long, Lieutenant Colonel Wurtsmith of the U.S. Army Air Force came to interrogate the strangers and try to determine if they indeed were Americans. Although the motley group answered his questions about life in the United States correctly, he was not absolutely certain until he suddenly looked Morrill straight in the eye and asked who won the previous year's (1941) Army-Navy game. Morrill, a Naval Academy graduate, promptly replied that Navy beat the hell out of Army, and gave the score. That did it. The colonel right away gave them his stamp of approval, and the Australians released them to a rousing welcome.

Thus, the eighteen navy men happily concluded their incredible 2,000-mile odyssey. They had managed safely to traverse enemy-infested, unfamiliar seas in their little 36-foot motor launch at an average speed of 5 knots, using a jury-rigged sextant to plot their way on inadequate navigational charts. This daring, seemingly impossible escape from Corregidor to Darwin, Australia, by Lieutenant Commander John H. Morrill and his men must surely stand tall among the all-time great achievements attributed to men of the United States Navy.

*The Officers*
Lieutenant Commander John H. Morrill
Warrant Gunner Donald C. Taylor

*The Enlisted Men*
Lyle Joseph Bercier
Philip Martin Binkley
Ralph William Clark
Nicholas George Cucinello
Harold Haley
George William Head

Jack Forest Meeker, Jr.
Ralph Waldo Newquist
Raid Ortumas Rankin
Bruce Roland Richardson
James Howard Steel
John Samuel Stringer
Glen Arthur Swisher
Earl Belvin Watkins
Charles Ernest Weinmann
Edward Stanley Woslegel

# EPILOGUE

Those early days of World War II evolved as a bleak and perilous period in our nation's history. A militarily unprepared United States, suddenly faced with war on several fronts, with a Pacific Fleet all but rendered useless and European Allies coursing toward disaster, had no choice at the outset but to stall for time in Southeast Asia, waging war as best she could with whatever forces were already there.

While major land fighting raged from the Philippines to Singapore, little attention was given to the beleaguered Asiatic Fleet, whose few battle reports, in the main, could impart only gloom to an already hapless situation. Thus, within a matter of three months' time, the little fleet, manned by courageous Americans short of everything but guts, a fleet whose victories were few but its unsung heroes many, passed without notice into the shadowy recesses of time.

It is my sincere hope that *The Fleet the Gods Forgot* will contribute an historical atmosphere conducive to a better understanding of the United States Asiatic Fleet in World War II—a proud little fleet that met a vastly superior enemy head on, and literally fought to the bitter end.

# U.S. ASIATIC FLEET DECEMBER 1941

Commander in Chief     Admiral Thomas C. Hart
Commander, Task Force 5     Rear Admiral William A. Glassford, Jr.

## Cruisers

*Houston* (CA-30), F
  Captain A. H. Rooks
*Marblehead* (CL-12)
  Captain A. G. Robinson
*Boise* (CL-47)
  Captain S. E. Robinson

## Submarine Squadron 20

Commander John Wilkes
*Holland* (AS-3), T
  Captain J. W. Gregory
*Canopus* (AS-9), T
  Commander E. L. Sackett
*Otus* (AS-20), T
  Commander J. Newsom
*Pigeon* (ASR-6)
  Lieutenant R. E. Hawes

\* Ships lost
F Unit flagship
T Unit tender

## SUBMARINE DIVISION 201

Lieutenant Commander R. B. Vanzant

*S-36
  Lieutenant J. R. McKnight, Jr.
S-37
  Lieutenant J. C. Dempsey
S-38
  Lieutenant W. G. Chapple
S-39
  Lieutenant J. W. Coe
S-40
  Lieutenant N. Lucker
S-41
  Lieutenant G. M. Holley


## SUBMARINE DIVISION 202

Commander W. E. Percifield

Seadragon (SS-194)
  Lieutenant Commander W. E. Ferrall
*Sealion (SS-195)
  Lieutenant Commander R. G. Voge
Searaven (SS-196)
  Lieutenant Commander T. C. Aylward
Seawolf (SS-197)
  Lieutenant Commander F. B. Warder


## SUBMARINE DIVISION 22

Commander J. A. Connelly

Snapper (SS-185)
  Lieutenant Commander H. L. Stone
Stingray (SS-186)
  Lieutenant Commander R. S. Lamb
Sturgeon (SS-187)
  Lieutenant Commander W. L. Wright
Sculpin (SS-191)
  Lieutenant Commander L. H. Chappell
Sailfish (SS-192)
  Lieutenant Commander M. C. Mumma, Jr.
Swordfish (SS-193)
  Lieutenant Commander C. C. Smith

## SUBMARINE DIVISION 203

Commander E. H. Bryant

*Porpoise* (SS-172)
   Lieutenant Commander J. A. Callaghan
*Pike* (SS-173)
   Lieutenant Commander W. A. New
*Shark* (SS-174)
   Lieutenant Commander L. Shane, Jr.
*Tarpon* (SS-175)
   Lieutenant Commander L. Wallace
*Perch* (SS-176)
   Lieutenant Commander D. A. Hurt
*Pickerel* (SS-177)
   Lieutenant Commander B. E. Bacon
*Permit* (SS-178)
   Lieutenant Commander A. M. Hurst

## SUBMARINE DIVISION 21

Commander S. S. Murray

*Salmon* (SS-182)
   Lieutenant Commander E. B. McKinney
*Seal* (SS-183)
   Lieutenant Commander K. C. Hurd
*Skipjack* (SS-184)
   Lieutenant Commander C. L. Freeman
*Sargo* (SS-188)
   Lieutenant Commander T. D. Jacobs
*Saury* (SS-189)
   Lieutenant Commander J. L. Burnside
*Spearfish* (SS-190)
   Lieutenant Commander R. F. Pryce

### Destroyer Squadron 29

Captain H. V. Wiley

*Paul Jones* (DD-230), F
   Lieutenant Commander J. J. Hourihan
*Black Hawk* (AD-9), T
   Commander G. L. Harris

Note: *Paul Jones* generally operated as a unit of Destroyer Division 59 without Captain Wiley embarked.

## DESTROYER DIVISION 57

Commander E. M. Crouch

*John D. Edwards* (DD-216), F
   Lieutenant Commander H. E. Eccles
*Alden* (DD-211)
   Lieutenant Commander L. E. Coley
*Whipple* (DD-217)
   Lieutenant Commander E. S. Karpe
*\*Edsall* (DD-219)
   Lieutenant Commander J. J. Nix

## DESTROYER DIVISION 58

Commander T. H. Binford

*\*Stewart* (DD-224), F
   Lieutenant Commander H. P. Smith
*Barker* (DD-213)
   Lieutenant Commander L. G. McGlone
*Parrott* (DD-218)
   Lieutenant Commander E. N. Parker
*Bulmer* (DD-222)
   Lieutenant Commander L. J. Manees

## DESTROYER DIVISION 59

Commander P. H. Talbot

*John D. Ford* (DD-228), F
   Lieutenant Commander J. E. Cooper
*\*Pope* (DD-225)
   Lieutenant Commander W. C. Blinn
*\*Peary* (DD-226)
   Lieutenant Commander H. H. Keith
*\*Pillsbury* (DD-227)
   Lieutenant Commander H. C. Pound


**Patrol Wing 10**

Captain F. D. Wagner
Patrol Squadron 101
   Lieutenant Commander J. V. Peterson
      (18 PBY Seaplanes)
Patrol Squadron 102
   Lieutenant Commander E. T. Neal
      (18 PBY Seaplanes)

Utility Unit
  Lieutenant J. C. Renard
    (4 J2F Amphibian Aircraft, 5 OS2U Seaplanes, 1 SOC Seaplane)
*Langley (AV-3), T
  Commander R. P. McConnell
Childs (AVD-1), T
  Lieutenant Commander J. L. Pratt
William B. Preston (AVD-7), T
  Lieutenant Commander E. Grant
Heron (AVP-2), T
  Lieutenant W. L. Kabler

## Motor Torpedo Boat Squadron 3
Lieutenant J. D. Bulkeley
* (6 Motor Torpedo Boats)

## Coastal Gunboats
*Asheville (PG-21)
  Lieutenant J. W. Britt
Tulsa (PG-22)
  Lieutenant Commander T. S. Daniel

## Inshore Patrol
Captain K. M. Hoeffel
*Oahu (PR-6)
  Lieutenant Commander D. E. Smith
*Luzon (PR-7)
  Lieutenant Commander G. M. Brooke
*Mindanao (PR-8)
  Lieutenant Commander A. R. McCracken
*Napa (AT-32)
  Lieutenant N. M. Dial
Lanikai (Yacht)
  Lieutenant K. Tolley

## Tankers
*Pecos (AO-6)
  Lieutenant Commander E. P. Abernethy
Trinity (AO-13)
  Commander W. Hibbs

**Minecraft**

MINE DIVISION 8
  Lieutenant T. W. Davison
*Finch* (AM-9)
  Lieutenant T. W. Davison
*Bittern* (AM-36)
  Lieutenant T. G. Warfield

MINE DIVISION 9
  Lieutenant Commander J. H. Morrill
*Tanager* (AM-5)
  Lieutenant E. A. Roth
*Quail* (AM-15)
  Lieutenant Commander J. H. Morrill
*Lark* (AM-21)
  Lieutenant Commander H. P. Thomson
*Whippoorwill* (AM-35)
  Lieutenant Commander C. A. Ferriter

RELIEF FLAGSHIP (Asiatic Fleet)
*Isabel* (PY-10)
  Lieutenant J. W. Payne

# NOTES

This book concerning the operations of the U.S. Asiatic Fleet in World War II was written principally from official reports contained in the Operational Archives of the U.S. Navy. These were augmented by action reports, pertaining to the battles of the Java Sea and Sunda Strait, which were generously provided by the Royal Navy and the Royal Australian Navy. Three books published by the Naval Institute Press were extremely important in double-checking the accuracy of various segments of this work: *United States Destroyer Operations in World War II* and *United States Submarine Operations in World War II*, both by Theodore Roscoe; and Rear Admiral Kemp Tolley's *Cruise of the Lanikai: Incitement to War.*

Material researched for my book *Ghost of the Java Coast—Saga of the Heavy Cruiser USS* Houston, which includes notes from interviews with American, British, Australian, and Dutch naval officers during my three and one-half years as a Japanese prisoner of war, also lent their firsthand ink to the historical pen.

It is noteworthy that the former officers of the wartime Asiatic Fleet whose names are cited in my Acknowledgements generously contributed to the accuracy of this work by making constructive comments about the matters on which they are particularly knowledgeable. In addition, as an officer on board the Asiatic Fleet's flagship during all of her wartime operations, I gained an intimate understanding of and appreciation for the manifold problems that beset the beleaguered fleet.

Most of the main outlines and detailed accounts contained in this book are readily available to the researcher in the Operational Archives Branch of the U.S. Naval Historical Center, Washington Navy Yard, Washington, D.C. Because many of the sources have been used at various points throughout this book, substantiating reference material is presented in a discursive manner rather than in the standard format. For the sake of convenience and clarity, full citations for both primary and secondary sources have been confined to the bibliography.

## I. OPERATIONS

### 1. PROFILE OF A FLEET

Most of the material upon which this chapter is based is derived from two official reports: Admiral Hart's "Narrative of Events for the Asiatic Fleet Leading to War, and for 8 December 1941 to 15 February 1942" and his "Supplement of Narrative of Events for the United States Asiatic Fleet, 8 December 1941 to 15 February 1942." Other official reports associated with this chapter are: Rear Admiral Francis W. Rockwell's "Narrative of Events for 1 December 1941 through March 1942" and "Supplement of Narrative for 1 December 1941 through March 1942," and Captain Frank B. Wagner's "Patrol Wing Ten War Diary from 8 December 1941 to 19 March 1942" and "Log and Status of Aircraft, Asiatic Fleet, from 8 December 1941 to 19 March 1942." The official publication *U.S. Army in World War II: The War in the Pacific—The Fall of the Philippines*, written by Louis Morton for the chief of military history, augmented Hart's reports by providing information concerning the status of U.S. Army forces in the Philippines at the beginning of hostilities and the destruction of the U.S. Army Air Corps. Additional source material was found in: Lewis H. Brereton, *The Brereton Diaries*; Thomas C. Hart, *History of the Second World War*; Theodore Roscoe, *United States Destroyer Operations in World War II* and *United States Submarine Operations in World War II*; and Kemp Tolley, *Cruise of the* Lanikai and *Yangtze Patrol*.

An accurate accounting for Japanese ships damaged or sunk is impossible to obtain. Officers throughout the Asiatic Fleet firmly believed that many more Japanese ships were seriously damaged and sunk, during the early months of the war, than the enemy admitted. While searching for the facts, the author found, in the official publication Japanese Major Warship Losses, written in 1946 by the U.S. Technical Mission to Japan, a clue as to why these contentions can never be verified. The introduction to this report states: "The Japanese Naval Ministry probably kept the most meager and inaccurate records of any major Navy Department in the world. The majority of what records were compiled during the war were burned either when the Naval Ministry was destroyed by fire in the spring of 1945, or by order during the period 15–17 August 1945, during which the Japanese Government was reaching the decision to surrender."

### 2. CRUISERS

Here again considerable information was obtained from Hart's "Narrative of Events for the Asiatic Fleet Leading to War," as well as his "Supplement of Narrative of Events." Other official reports important to this chapter are: Eccles, "Java Sea Battle, 27 February 1942, and Transcript of Ship's Log for Period of the Battle"; Glassford, "Narrative of Events in Southwest Pacific, 14

February 1942 to 5 April 1942 to 5 April 1942"; Maher (senior survivor and gunnery officer, USS *Houston*), "Postwar Reports," numbers 1 through 5; Parker, "Action between ABDA and Japanese Forces on 27 February 1942"; Robinson, "Engagement of 4 February 1942 with Japanese Aircraft"; Talbot, "Action 23–24 January 1942 against Japanese Forces in Makasar Strait by U.S. Destroyers." Of particular value, insofar as the battles of the Java Sea and Sunda Strait are concerned, were the following reports provided the author courtesy of the Royal Navy and the Royal Australian Navy: Gordon, "The Battle of the Java Sea," dated 1 October 1945; Harper, "Final Action and Loss of HMAS *Perth*," dated 1 October 1945; Lowe, "Last Action of His Majesty's Australian Ship *Perth*," dated 5 September 1945; and Waller's rough report submitted to the commodore commanding the China force at Batavia, Java, concerning the Java Sea battle, 28 February 1942.

## 3. SUBMARINES

Admiral Hart's "Narrative of Events for the Asiatic Fleet Leading to War" and his "Supplement" were most important in delineating the command structure of Asiatic Fleet submarines, and in detailing the many problems encountered in their wartime operations. Admiral Hart's assessment of damage inflicted upon Japanese ships resulted from reports by submarine commanders who had every reason to believe they were right. These reports do not appear to be completely accurate in the face of postwar findings which do not verify all of them. To provide the best possible assessment of submariners' claims and to augment Admiral Hart's reports, I consulted the two most historically important books ever published on the subject: Roscoe, *United States Submarine Operations in World War II*, and Blair, *Silent Victory*. Official reports specifically relating to accounts contained in part II, but useful here to portray at first hand some of the difficult conditions under which Asiatic Fleet submarines were forced to operate are found in: Chapple, "War Patrol Report for Period 8 December 1941 to 27 December 1941"; Hurt, "Statement Concerning the Loss of the USS *Perch* on 3 March 1942"; and Schacht, "Loss of the USS *Perch* on 3 March 1942."

## 4. DESTROYERS

In addition to Admiral Hart's report "Narrative of Events for the Asiatic Fleet Leading to War" and his "Supplement of Narrative of Events," the following books contributed to this chapter: Roscoe, *United States Destroyer Operations in World War II*; and Tolley, *Cruise of the Lanikai*. Official reports used extensively in portions of part II, but important in confirming and augmenting information in this chapter derived from other sources are: Glassford, "Narrative of Events in Southwest Pacific, 14 February 1942 to 5 April 1942"; Bermingham, "Engagements with the Enemy" for 28 December 1941; Catlett, "Sinking of the USS *Peary*"; Talbot, "Action 23–24 January 1942 against Japanese Forces in Makasar Strait by U.S. Destroyers"; Coley, "Battle of the Java Sea on 27 February 1942"; Cooper, "Action of Allied Naval Forces with Japanese Forces off Surabaja, Java, on 27 February 1942"; Parker, "Action between ABDA and Japanese Forces on 27 February 1942" and "Engagement between U.S. Destroyers and Japanese Forces in Bali Strait on 1 March 1942"; Eccles, "Java Sea Battle, 27 February 1942, and Transcript of the Ship's Log for Period of the Battle"; Maher, "USS *Houston* in the Battle of the Java Sea, 27 February 1942"; Crouch, "Report Concerning the Sinking of the USS *Langley* and USS *Pecos*"; and Blinn, recorded narrative, "Sinking of the USS *Pope*." In the same category as the foregoing reports is that of Captain O. L. Gordon, RN, commanding the heavy cruiser HMS *Exeter*, "The Battle of the Java Sea," dated 1 October 1945, and interviews with him and Lieutenant Commander E. V. St. J. Morgan, RN, commanding the destroyer HMS *Encounter*, conducted while we were prisoners of war at Zentsuji, Japan, and recorded in my diary.

## 5. AIRCRAFT

Having been a member of Patrol Wing 10 prior to being transferred to the aviation unit on board the USS *Houston* in mid-August 1941, I knew everyone in the wing. On several occasions, during the war, I was able to visit with my former associates and learn first hand of their nerve-racking war experiences. I recorded what they related to me in my diary, which also contained my own day-by-day impressions of the war. On 18 February 1942 I gave this diary to an Australian naval officer in Darwin. As I requested, he sent it to my father in New York City. It has been most helpful in writing portions of this book, especially where Patrol Wing 10 is concerned, for no official, in-depth record of its activities exists.

Admiral Hart's official reports provided some background information, but the following documents were the most useful: Wagner, "Patrol Wing Ten War Diary from 8 December 1941 to 19 March 1942" and "Log and Status of Aircraft, Asiatic Fleet, from 8 December 1941 to 19 March 1942"; Pollock, "Partial List of Combat Patrol Reports for Period December 1941, and February 1942"; Renard (Asiatic Fleet Utility Squadron), "Summary of War Activities"; McConnell, "Operations, Action, and Sinking of the USS *Langley*, Period from 22 February to 5 March 1942"; Glassford, "Narrative of Events in Southwest Pacific, 14 February 1942 to 5 April 1942" and "Operations, Action, and Sinking of USS *Langley* (AV-3), Period 22 February to 5 March 1942."

## 6. GUNBOATS

The most complete information concerning the river and coastal gunboats of the U.S. Asiatic Fleet was found in the book by Tolley, *Yangtze Patrol and the U.S. Navy in China*. Additional information concerning the use and ultimate fate of these gunboats appears in Tolley's *Cruise of the* Lanikai: *Incitement to War* and in the following official reports: Hart, "Narrative of Events for the Asiatic Fleet Leading to War"; Rockwell, "Narrative of Events for 1 December 1941 through March 1942"; and, to a lesser degree, Glassford, "Narrative of Events in the Southwest Pacific, 14 February 1942 to 5 April 1942."

## 7. MINECRAFT

Because there are no official reports concerning the wartime operations and final disposition of Asiatic Fleet minecraft to be found in the Operational Archives Branch of the U.S. Naval Historical Center in Washington, this composite was made from fragmentary information contained in the following sources: Roscoe, *United States Destroyer Operations in World War II*; Karig and Kelly, *Battle Report—Pearl Harbor to Coral Sea*; Morison, *The Rising Sun in the Pacific*; and Tolley, *Cruise of the* Lanikai. In addition, the following official reports were useful: Bulkeley, "Summary of Operations from 7 December 1941 to 11 April 1942"; Glassford, "Narrative of Events in Southwest Pacific, 14 February 1942 to 5 April 1942"; Hart, "Narrative of Events for the Asiatic Fleet Leading to War, and for 8 December 1941 to 15 February 1942"; and Morrill, "Escape from Corregidor." Last but not least was the personal diary of Lieutenant (jg) Marion H. Buass, for the period from 29 November 1941 to 7 March 1942.

## 8. TORPEDO BOATS

This account of Motor Torpedo Boat Squadron 3 closely follows Lieutenant Bulkeley's two reports: "Summary of Operations from 7 December 1941 to 11 April 1942" and "Report to the Commander in Chief, U.S. Fleet." Considerable detailed information was obtained from Bulkeley's *At Close Quarters*. Some confirming information was obtained from two additional reports: Hart, "Narrative of Events for the Asiatic Fleet Leading to War, and for 8 December 1941 to 15 February 1942"; and Rockwell, "Narrative of Events for 1 December 1941 through March 1942." The former commander of Motor Torpedo Boat Squadron 3, Rear Admiral John D. Bulkeley, USN (Ret.), personally reviewed the entire account and made pertinent suggestions, which have been incorporated in the text.

## II. BATTLE REPORTS

## 9. THE DOOMED DESTROYER—USS *PEARY* (DD-226)

This account was written from information contained in the following official reports: Bermingham, "Engagements with the Enemy," and enclosures A through F, which cover the time frame 10 December to 21 December 1941; and Catlett, "Sinking of the USS *Peary*." Additional material about the ship's bombing in the Cavite Navy Yard was found in Roscoe, *United States Destroyer Operations in World War II*; and in Rockwell, "Narrative of Events for 1 December 1941 through March 1942."

## 10. THE OLD LADY—USS *CANOPUS* (AS-9)

The most important source was the privately published and distributed monograph by Commander Earl L. Sackett, USN, last commanding officer of the *Canopus*. Especially helpful was a postwar interview with Rear Admiral

Henry W. Goodall, USN (Ret.), who, as a lieutenant commander, was the ship's executive officer and in command of the "Mickey Mouse Navy." Additional information about the *Canopus* and the naval battalion on Bataan was extracted from the following reports: Bridget, "Action at Longoskawayan Point"; and Rockwell, "Narrative of Events for 1 December 1941 through March 1942." A wartime interview with fellow prisoner of war Lieutenant (jg) George Trudell, USNR, who was wounded during the fighting on Longoskawayan Point, was also useful. Two additional sources were: Roscoe, *United States Submarine Operations in World War II*; and Morton, *U.S. Army in World War II: The War in the Pacific—Fall of the Philippines*.

## 11. THE *S-38* IN LINGAYEN GULF

Written from information contained in the following: Chapple, "War Patrol Report for Period 8 December 1941 to 27 December 1941"; and Roscoe, *United States Submarine Operations in World War II*. Rear Admiral Wreford G. Chapple, USN (Ret.), who, as a lieutenant, commanded the *S-38* in this engagement, reviewed this account and made constructive suggestions.

## 12. DISASTER AT JOLO

This chapter is based upon the following official reports: Christman, "Dawn Bombing Attack on Jolo, P.I., on 27 December 1941"; Dawley, "Bombing Attack on Jolo, Sulu, on 27 December 1941"; Wagner, "Patrol Wing Ten War Diary from 8 December 1941 to 19 March 1942." My personal diary was a source for additional material. It contains notes taken by me during a visit with officers of Patrol Wing 10 on 28 January 1942 in Surabaja, Java. Among the naval aviators I talked with were four who survived the Jolo raid: Jack B. Dawley, E. L. Christman, W. V. Gough, and Ira W. Brown.

## 13. THE LITTLE GIANT-KILLER—USS *HERON* (AVP-2)

Chapter based upon the official report by Kabler, "Attack by Japanese Aircraft on 31 December 1941."

## 14. A FIRST FOR THE NAVY

Chapter based upon the official report by Ralston, "Aerial Combat, and Resulting Experiences."

## 15. THE BATTLE OF BALIKPAPAN

Chapter primarily based upon the official report by Talbot, "Action 23–24 January 1942 against Japanese Forces in Makasar Strait by U.S. Destroyers." Koscoe's *United States Destroyer Operations in World War II* was also useful. Admiral Hart's report, "Narrative of Events for the Asiatic Fleet Leading to War, and for 8 December 1941 to 15 February 1942," added nothing definitive.

## 16. THE MIRACULOUS SURVIVAL
## OF COMMANDER GOGGINS

The primary source of information for this chapter was the report by Commander Goggins, "Narrative of Events from 25 November 1941 to 13 March 1942." Important secondary sources were: Robinson, "Engagement of 4 February 1942 with Japanese Aircraft"; and Smellow's monograph on the wartime activities of the *Marblehead*.

## 17. DELAYED REPORT OF A "ROUTINE PATROL"

Chapter based upon the official report by Hargrave, "Aerial Combat and Resultant Experiences."

## 18. THROUGH HELL AND HIGH WATER

Chapter based upon the official report by Moorer, "Aerial Combat on 19 February 1942 and Resultant Experiences."

## 19. THE HEAVY CRUISER USS *HOUSTON* (CA-30)

In writing this chapter I have drawn on many sources, all of them related to research for my book, *Ghost of the Java Coast—Saga of the Heavy Cruiser USS Houston*. The most significant information was obtained from the following reports: Coley, "Battle of the Java Sea on 27 February 1942"; Eccles, "Java Sea Battle, 27 February 1942, and Transcript of Ship's Log for Period of the Battle"; Goggins, "Narrative of Events from 25 November 1941 to 13 March 1942"; Maher, "Postwar Reports," numbers 1 through 5; Parker, "Action between ABDA and Japanese Forces on 27 February 1942"; Robinson, "Engagement of 4 February 1942 with Japanese Aircraft"; Sholar, "RNNS *De Ruyter*'s Final Action"; Gordon, "The Battle of the Java Sea"; Harper, "Final Action and Loss of the HMAS *Perth*"; Lowe, "Last Action of His Majesty's Australian Ship *Perth*"; Waller, rough report concerning "The Java Sea Battle."

In addition to the foregoing were the discussions I had as a prisoner of war with Australian, British, American, and Dutch naval officers concerning the battles of the Java Sea and Sunda Strait. Important aspects of these battles were entered in my diary, which I kept hidden from the Japanese and took home with me after the war. My other diary, covering events in Southeast Asia from before the war to 12 February 1942, also provided pertinent information. My account of the *Houston* appeared in 1949 in the U.S. Naval Institute *Proceedings* and the following year in *Reader's Digest*.

## 20. THE CRUEL FATE OF THE DESTROYER USS *POPE* (DD-225)

Chapter based upon the official report by Blinn in the form of a recorded narrative, "Sinking of the USS *Pope*." Additional information was obtained while a prisoner of war from Lieutenant Commander Morgan, RN, commanding officer of the destroyer HMS *Encounter*. Rear Admiral Welford C. Blinn, USN (Ret.) reviewed this account and offered interesting suggestions, which have been incorporated.

## 21. ABANDON SHIP

The main report used in writing this chapter is that of McConnell, "Operations, Action, and Sinking of the USS *Langley*." Other significant reports are: Crouch, "Report Concerning the Sinking of the USS *Langley* and USS *Pecos*"; Glassford, "Narrative of Events in Southwest Pacific, 14 February 1942 to 5 April 1942" and "Operations, Action, and Sinking of USS *Langley* (AV-3), Period 12 February to 5 March 1942"; Karp, "The Sinking of the USS *Langley* (AV-3), and USS *Pecos* (AO-6)"; King, "Letter to Secretary of the Navy Concerning Operations, Action, and Sinking of USS *Langley*, Period 22 February to 5 March 1942."

## 22. LOSS OF THE USS *PERCH* (SS-176)

Chapter written from the following reports: Hurt, "Statement Concerning the Loss of the USS *Perch* on 3 March 1942"; Schacht, "Loss of the USS *Perch* on 3 March 1942"; and Crist, "Statement Concerning the Sinking of the USS *Perch*." Information contained in Roscoe, *United States Submarine Operations in World War II*, was quite helpful.

## 23. THE EXPENDABLE SHIP USS *ISABEL* (PY-10)

Two very interesting reports provided the information for this chapter. They were Buass, "Personal Diary, Period 29 November 1941 to 7 March 1942"; and Payne, "Activities of the USS *Isabel* from 3 December 1941 to 7 March 1942." Tolley's book *Cruise of the* Lanikai was especially enlightening in suggesting the reasons behind the *Isabel*'s strange orders to patrol off the Indochina coast a few days prior to the outbreak of war with Japan.

## 24. A REFUSAL TO SURRENDER

Chapter written principally from the report by Morrill, "Escape from Corregidor." Rear Admiral John Morrill reviewed the entire chapter and made some very helpful suggestions.

# BIBLIOGRAPHY

**PRIMARY SOURCES**

OFFICIAL U.S. NAVY REPORTS

From the Operational Archives Branch, U.S. Naval Historical Center, Washington Navy Yard, Washington, D.C.

Abernethy, Lieutenant Commander E. P., Commanding Officer, USS *Pecos* (AO-6). "Sinking of the USS *Pecos*."

Arnette, Fireman First Class E. H., USS *Perch* (SS-176). "Statement Concerning the Sinking of the USS *Perch*."

Bermingham, Lieutenant Commander J. M., Commanding Officer, USS *Peary* (DD-221). "Engagements with the Enemy," with enclosures:
  A. Executive Officer's Report
  B. List of Damage in Navy Yard, Cavite
  C. Navigator's Report
  D. Gunnery Officer's Report
  E. Assistant Gunnery Officer's Report
  F. Engineer Officer's Report

Blinn, Lieutenant Commander W. C. , Commanding Officer, USS *Pope* (DD-225). Recorded Narrative, "Sinking of the USS *Pope*."

Bridget, Commander Francis J., Commanding the Naval Battalion on Bataan. "Action at Longoskawayan Point."

Buass, Lieutenant Marion H., Executive Officer, USS *Isabel* (PY-10). "Personal Diary, Period 29 November 1941 to 7 March 1942."

Bulkeley, Lieutenant John D., Commanding Officer, Motor Torpedo Boat Squadron 3. "Summary of Operations from 7 December 1941 to 11 April 1942."

————. "Report to the Commander in Chief, U.S. Fleet."

Catlett, Lieutenant W. J., Senior Survivor, USS *Peary* (DD-226). "Sinking of the USS *Peary*."

Chapple, Lieutenant Wreford G., Commanding Officer, *S-38*. "War Patrol Report for Period 8 December 1941 to 27 December 1941."

Christman, Ensign E. L., Patrol Wing 10. "Dawn Bombing Attack on Jolo, P.I., on 27 December 1941."

Coley, Lieutenant Commander L. E., Commanding Officer, SS *Alden* (DD-211). "Battle of the Java Sea on 27 February 1942."

Cooper, Lieutenant Commander J. E., Commanding Officer, USS *John D. Ford* (DD-228). "Action of Allied Naval Forces with Japanese Forces off Surabaja, Java, on 27 February 1942."

Crist, Electrician's Mate Third Class Daniel, USS *Perch* (SS-176). "Statement Concerning the Sinking of the USS *Perch*."

Crouch, Commander E. M., Commander, Destroyer Division 57. "Report Concerning the Sinking of the USS *Langley* and USS *Pecos*."

Dawley, Ensign J. B., Patrol Wing 10. "Bombing Attack on Jolo, Sulu, on 27 December 1941."

Eccles, Commander Henry E., Commanding Officer, USS *John D. Edwards* (DD-216). "Java Sea Battle, 27 February 1942, and Transcript of Ship's Log for Period of the Battle."

Glassford, Vice Admiral William A., Commander, U.S. Naval Forces, Southwest Pacific. "Narrative of Events in Southwest Pacific, 14 February 1942 to 5 April 1942."

————. "Operations, Action, and Sinking of USS *Langley* (AV-3), Period 12 February to 5 March 1942."

Goggins, Commander William B., Executive Officer, USS *Marblehead* (CL-12). "Narrative of Events from 25 November 1941 to 13 March 1942."

Hargrave, Ensign William W., Patrol Wing 10. "Aerial Combat and Resultant Experiences."

Hart, Admiral Thomas C., Commander in Chief, U.S. Asiatic Fleet, and Commander, American, British, Dutch, and Australian (ABDA) Naval Forces. "Narrative of Events for the Asiatic Fleet Leading to War, and for 8 December 1941 to 15 February 1942."

————. "Supplement of Narrative of Events for the United States Asiatic Fleet, 8 December 1941 to 15 February 1942."

Hurt, Lieutenant Commander David A., Commanding Officer, USS *Perch* (SS-176). "Statement Concerning the Loss of the USS *Perch* on 3 March 1942."

Kabler, Lieutenant W. L., Commanding Officer, USS *Heron* (AVP-2). "Attack by Japanese Aircraft on 31 December 1941."

Karp, Lieutenant Commander Eugene S., Commanding Officer, USS *Whipple* (DD-217). "The Sinking of the USS *Langley* (AV-3), and USS *Pecos* (AO-6)."

King, Admiral Earnest J., Commander in Chief, U.S. Fleet, and Chief of Naval Operations. "Letter to Secretary of the Navy Concerning Operations, Action, and Sinking of USS *Langley*, Period 22 February to 5 March 1942."

Maher, Captain Arthur L., Senior Survivor and Gunnery Officer, USS *Houston* (CA-30). "Postwar Reports Compiled with the Assistance of Surviving Senior Officers:
1. USS *Houston* on 4 February 1942 against Enemy Aircraft
2. USS *Houston* in Defense of a Convoy off Darwin, Australia, on 16 February 1942
3. USS *Houston* on 25, 26, and 27 February 1942 against Aircraft
4. USS *Houston* in the Battle of the Java Sea, 27 February 1942
5. USS *Houston* in the Battle of Sunda Strait, 28 February 1942."
McConnell, Commander Robert P., Commanding Officer, USS *Langley* (AV-3). "Operations, Action, and Sinking of the USS *Langley*, Period from 22 February to 5 March 1942."
Moorer, Lieutenant Thomas H., Patrol Wing 10. "Aerial Combat on 19 February 1942 and Resultant Experiences."
Morrill, Lieutenant Commander John H., Commanding Officer, USS *Quail* (AM-15). "Escape from Corregidor."
Parker, Lieutenant Commander Edward N., Commander, Destroyer Division 59. "Action between ABDA and Japanese Forces on 27 February 1942."
———. "Engagement between U.S. Destroyers and Japanese Forces in Bali Strait on 1 March 1942."
Payne, Commander John Walker, Commanding Officer, USS *Isabel* (PY-10). "Activities of the USS *Isabel* from 3 December 1941 to 7 March 1942."
Pollock, Captain Thomas F., Patrol Wing 10. "Partial List of Combat Patrol Reports for Period December 1941, and February 1942."
Ralston, Lieutenant (jg) Frank M., Patrol Wing 10. "Aerial Combat, and Resulting Experiences."
Renard, Lieutenant Commander Jack C., Commanding Officer, Asiatic Fleet Utility Squadron. "Summary of War Activities."
Robinson, Captain Arthur C., Commanding Officer, USS *Marblehead* (CL-12). "Engagement of 4 February 1942 with Japanese Aircraft."
Rockwell, Rear Admiral Francis W., Commandant, Sixteenth Naval District. "Narrative of Events for 1 December 1941 through March 1942."
———. Supplement of Narrative for 1 December 1941 through March 1942."
Sackett, Captain Earl L., Commanding Officer, USS *Canopus* (AS-9). "The History of the USS *Canopus*."
Schacht, Lieutenant Kenneth G., Torpedo Officer, USS *Perch* (SS-176). "Loss of the USS *Perch* on 3 March 1942."
Sholar, Signalman First Class Marvin E., member of the USS *Houston*'s ship's company assigned to the RNNS *De Ruyter* as signalman assistant during Battle of the Java Sea. "RNNS *DeRuyter*'s Final Action."
Talbot, Commander Paul H., Commander, Destroyer Division 59. "Action 23–24 January 1942 against Japanese Forces in Makasar Strait by U.S. Destroyers." (Talbot was relieved as commander, Destroyer Division 59 by Lieutenant Commander E. N. Parker on 29 January 1942.)
Wagner, Captain Frank B., Commander, Aircraft, U.S. Asiatic Fleet. "Patrol Wing Ten War Diary from 8 December 1941 to 19 March 1942."

————. "Log and Status of Aircraft, Asiatic Fleet, from 8 December 1941 to 19 March 1942."

## OFFICIAL ROYAL NAVY AND
## ROYAL AUSTRALIAN NAVY REPORTS

Courtesy of the Royal Navy and the Royal Australian Navy.

Gordon, Captain O. L., RN, Commanding Officer, HMS *Exeter*. "The Battle of the Java Sea."

Harper, Lieutenant Commander L. A., RN, Navigator, HMAS *Perth*. "Final Action and Loss of HMAS *Perth*."

Lowe, Lieutenant Commander Ralph F. M., RAN, Paymaster, HMAS *Perth*. "Last Action of His Majesty's Australian Ship *Perth*."

Waller, Captain H.M.L., RAN, Commanding Officer, HMAS *Perth*. This was a rough report concerning "The Java Sea Battle," which Captain Waller submitted to the commodore commanding the China force while at Batavia, Java, on 28 February 1942, several hours before his death in the Battle of Sunda Strait.

## INTERVIEWS

While a Japanese prisoner of war, I was privileged to interview many Allied prisoners of war, and to record their experiences in my diary. Included were surviving officers of the *Houston*, *Perch*, *Pope*, Patrol Wing 10, and the following British and Australian naval officers:

Brougham, Lieutenant Patric, RN, Officer of the Deck, HMS *Exeter*, during the Battle of the Java Sea

Gay, Lieutenant William L., RAN, Assistant Gunnery Officer, HMAS *Perth*

Gordon, Captain O. L., RN, Commanding Officer, HMS *Exeter*

Harper, Lieutenant Commander John, RN, Navigator, HMAS *Perth*

Morgan, Lieutenant Commander E. V. St. J., RN, Commanding Officer, HMS *Encounter*.

## SECONDARY SOURCES

## BOOKS

Bergamini, David. *Japan's Imperial Conspiracy*. New York: William Morrow, 1972.

Blair, Jr., Clay. *Silent Victory*. Philadelphia: J. B. Lippincott, 1975.

Brereton, Major General Lewis H. *The Brereton Diaries*. New York: William Morrow, 1946.

Hara, Tameichi. *Japanese Destroyer Captain*. New York: Ballantine Books, 1961.

Hart, Liddel. *History of the Second World War*. New York: G. P. Putnam's Sons, 1971.

Karig, Commander Walter, USNR, and Kelly, Lieutenant Welbourn, USNR. *Battle Report—Pearl Harbor to Coral Sea*. New York: Rinehart, 1947.

Lockwood, Douglas. *Australia's Pearl Harbour—Darwin 1942.* Adelaide, Austra-
lia: Rigby, 1973.
McKie, Ronald. *The Survivors (HMAS* Perth). Indianapolis: Bobbs-Merrill,
1953.
Morison, Samuel Eliot. *The Rising Sun in the Pacific.* Boston: Little, Brown,
1950.
Payne, Alan. *HMAS* Perth—*The Story of the 6 Inch Cruiser.* Garden Island, NSW,
Australia: Naval Historical Society of Australia, 1978.
Perry, George Sessions, and Leighton, Isabel. *Where Away: A Modern Odyssey.*
New York: Whittlesey House, McGraw Hill, 1944.
Roscoe, Theodore. *United States Destroyer Operations in World War II.* Annapolis:
Naval Institute Press, 1953.
———. *United States Submarine Operations in World War II.* Annapolis: Naval
Institute Press, 1949.
Toland, John. *The Rising Sun.* New York: Random House, 1970.
Tolley, Rear Admiral Kemp. *Cruise of the* Lanikai: *Incitement to War.* Annapolis:
Naval Institute Press, 1973.
———. *Yangtze Patrol and the U.S. Navy in China.* Annapolis: Naval Institute
Press, 1971.
Wigmore, Lionel. *The Japanese Thrust.* Adelaide, Australia: Griffin Press, 1957.
Winslow, Walter G. *Ghost of the Java Coast—Saga of the Heavy Cruiser USS*
Houston. Winter Haven, Florida: Coral Reef Publications, 1973.

## MONOGRAPHS

Sackett, Commander Earl L., USN, Commanding Officer, USS *Canopus.*
Narrative Concerning the Wartime Activities of the Submarine Tender
USS *Canopus* (AS-9). Privately duplicated and distributed, 1942 (Sackett
retired with the rank of Rear Admiral).
Smellow, Rear Admiral Morris, Supply Corps, USN (Ret.), Supply Officer,
USS *Marblehead.* Wartime Activities of the USS *Marblehead* (CL-12) from 3
February 1942 to 4 May 1942. Privately duplicated and distributed follow-
ing retirement in 1954.

## OFFICIAL PUBLICATIONS AND REPORTS

Administrative Division, Second Demobilization Bureau. Japanese Naval Ves-
sels at the End of the War. Unpublished report, April 1947.
Bulkeley, Jr., Captain Robert J. *At Close Quarters: PT Boats in the United States
Navy.* Washington, D.C.: Naval History Division, Department of the Navy,
1962.
Joint Army-Navy Assessment Committee. *Japanese Naval and Merchant Shipping
Losses during World War II by All Causes.* Washington, D.C.: Government
Printing Office, February 1947.
Military History Section, General Headquarters, Far East Command. The
Imperial Japanese Navy in World War II: A Graphic Presentation of the
Japanese Naval Organization and List of Combatant and Non-Combatant
Vessels Lost or Damaged in the War. Unpublished report, February 1952.

Morton, Louis. *U.S. Army in World War II: The War in the Pacific—The Fall of the Philippines*. Washington, D.C.: Office of the Chief of Military History, Department of the Army, 1953.

Naval History Division. *Dictionary of American Naval Fighting Ships*, vols. 1, 2, 3. Washington, D.C.: Naval History Division, Department of the Navy, 1959, 1963, 1968.

Statistical Section, Division of Naval Intelligence. *Japanese Merchant Vessels Lost*. Washington, D.C.: Division of Naval Intelligence, Department of the Navy, January 1946.

U.S. Technical Mission to Japan. Japanese Major Warship Losses. Unpublished report, 1946.

# INDEX

If not otherwise identified, vessels are American.

ABDA Command, 12, 18, 196, 230; formation of, 10–11; dissolution of, 32, 50, 243

ABDAFLOAT: formation of, 11; commanders, 11, 41*n*, 200*n*; at Battle of Java Sea, 19, 20, 200–201, 242; at Makasar Strait, 40, 41, 265; at Balikpapan, 151; tries to prevent Java landing, 273

ABDAIR, 10

ABDARM, 10

Abernethy, E. P., 239, 303

Abubakar, Yusup, 129, 130

Ackerman, William, 237, 240

*Admiral Halstead* (freighter), 94

Air Force, Royal Australian, 182, 190, 192

Akers, Anthony B., 71, 74, 76, 82

*Alden* (DD-211), 38, 39, 220, 302; at Battle of Java Sea, 20, 41, 206, 219

Alpad, Arasid, 129

Amahai (Ceram), 177–78

Ambon (Amboina Island): ABDA seadrome base, 120, 121, 150; as haven, 141, 145; occupied by Japanese, 172, 173, 176, 180, 184

Antrim, R. H., 224

Arafura Sea, 179, 295

Army, Australian: soldiers escaping Ceram, 176–82

Army, Dutch, 164, 165, 199

Army, Japanese: Indochina landings, 3, 5, 6; Malaya landing, 8; Philippine landings, 10, 26

Army, Philippine, 133

Army, U.S.: Far East command, 7, 182; Air Force in Java, 166; Air Corps, 229, 230, 237, 238, 257–58. *See also* Far East Air Force

*Asagumo* (destroyer, Japanese), 20, 23

*Asami Maru* (transport, Japanese), 156

*Asashio* (destroyer, Japanese), 41

*Asheville* (PG-21), 52, 55, 56, 273, 303; disappears, 43, 55, 277, 279

*Ashigara* (heavy cruiser, Japanese), 44

*Ashihara* (heavy cruiser, Japanese), 43

Asiatic Fleet: historical overview, 3, 4, 7–8, 9, 11, 12, 298; composition, 8, 12, 24, 37, 299–304; compared to Japanese fleet, 8; individual histories mentioned throughout

Asiatic Station, 4

*Augusta* (CA-31), 250

Australia: received remnants of Asiatic Fleet, 11–12, 182–83, 295–96; convoyed troops to Timor, 18; attacked at Darwin, 19, 40, 93–95, 184, 194; naval facilities, 30. *See also* individual cities

Australian Army. *See* Army, Australian

Aylward, T. C., 300

Bacon, B. E., 301
Bali, 31, 269
Balikpapan (Borneo), 151, 152, 153, 260–61
Balikpapan, Battle of, 16, 40, 151–57
Bali Strait, 219–20
Banda Sea, 172
Bandung (Java), 10, 165, 270
Bandung Strait, Battle of, 40–41
*Bankert* (destroyer, Dutch), 197
Banquist, Joseph, 124, 130
Bantam Bay (Java), 272
Bantam Bay, Battle of, 212–18
*Barker* (DD-213), 15, 31, 38, 302; in battle of Flores Sea, 40, 197
Barron, E. J., 193
Bataan (Philippines), 6, 10, 27, 57, 72, 281; defended by "Navy Battalion," 101, 103–4, 107–8
Batavia (Java), 195, 196, 269
Bathurst Island, 189, 190
Battery Craighill, 57, 58
Battery Gillespie, 57
Battleship Row, 7
Batu Batu, 132–33
Bean (Aviation Machinist's Mate), 175
Bercier, Lyle Joseph, *290*, 296
Bermingham, John M., 88–92, 94–95
Billman, C. B., 132–33, 134
Binanga Bay, Battle of, 65–68
Binford, Thomas H., 41, 270, 302
Binkley, Philip Martin, *290*, 296
*Bittern* (AM-36), 35, 60, 304; bombed at Cavite Navy Yard, 61, 85, 87, 257
*Black Hawk* (AD-9), 31, 38, 39, 43, 299
Blair, Clay, Jr., 33*n*
Blessman, Edward M., 159, 162
Blinn, Welford C., 302; attempts escape from Java, 219, 221, 223, 224; scuttles ship, 44, 225; adrift in Java Sea, 226, 227; captured by Japanese, 228
*Boise* (CL-47), 5, 9, 13, 15, 299; after Cavite Navy Yard bombing, 260, 261; at Battle of Balikpapan, 16, 151, 152
Bondoc (Philippines), 288, 289
Borneo, 138–39, 153. *See also* individual cities
Bounder Roads, 264
Bounds, Dave W., 127, 130, 133, 136
Bratingham, Henry J., 82
Bridget, Francis J., 102–3, 104
Brilliantes, Fernando, 125–26, 129, 131, 132
Brisbane (Australia), 182
British Far East Fleet, 6
British Naval Liaison Office, 196
Britt, J. W., 303

Brooke, G. M., 303
Brown, Fred Lewis, 55, *56*
Brown, Ira, 127, 129, 133, 136
Buass, Marion H., 251, 254, 255, 262, 271, 274
Buck, Howard L., 118
"Buda," 215–16
Bulkeley, John D.: commander MTB Squadron 3, 63, 303; action in Manila Bay, 64, 68–69; action in Binanga Bay, 65–68; action in Subic Bay, 69, 71, 72; evacuates MacArthur, 73, 74, 76; evacuates President Quezon, 76–78; action in Cebu, 78–79, 81, 82
Bull, Richard, 172–75
*Bulmer* (DD-222), 38, 273, 302; in Battle of Flores Sea, 197; damaged, 31–32, 40
Burnside, J. L., 301
Buru Island, 172

Callaghan, J. A., 301
Campbell, Duncan A., 122
Camranh Bay, 251, 254
*Canopus* (AS-9), *109*, 299; on China Station, 96; in Manila Bay, 9, 10, 26, 85, 96–98; in Mariveles, 27, 29, 98–110; tender duties, 25, 28, 70, 100–102; scuttled, 29, 35, 110–11
Carpender, Arthur S., 12
Catabalogan (Samar), 289
Catlett, W. J., 95
Cavite Navy Yard (Philippines), 25, 251, 257; destroyed by Japanese, 8, 25, 85–87, 98 256–59
Cebu (Philippines), 289
Celebes Island, 152, 153, 158, 242
Celis, J., Jr., 133
Ceram (East Indies), 172, 176, 177–79
Chanco, Isaoani, 129, 130
Chandler, Barron W., 66, 68
Chappell, L. H., 300
Chapple, Wreford G. ("Moon"), 113–19, 300
Chiang Kai-Shek, 3
*Childs* (AVD-1), 30, 47, 49, 51, 303
China Patrol, South, 250
Christman, E. L., 122–26, 129
Christmas Island, 237
*City of Manchester* (merchantman, British), 61
Clark Field (Philippines), 97, 255
Clark, Francis E., 45
Clark, Ralph William, *290*, 296
Cleland, "Dad," 78
Coburn, C. H., 159, 168
Coe, J. W., 300

Coley, L. E., 302
Collingsworth (freighter), 271–73
Connelly, J. A., 300
Cooper, J. E., 302
Corregidor: retreat to, 10, 27, 110; supply of, 33, 187; battle of, 6, 56–57, 71, 99, 107–8; retreat from, 29, 72–74, 284–96; fall of, 12, 284
Corregidor (inter-island steamer, Philippines), 64
Cox, George E., Jr., 71, 76, 79, 82
Crouch, E. M., 239, 302
Cucinello, Nicholas George, 290, 296
Cusack (Radioman Third Class), 174–76, 177

Daniel, T. S., 303
Darwin (Australia): submarine base, 29–31; bombing of, 40, 50, 93–95, 184, 194; as refuge, 295–96
Davis, Frank A., 35–36
Davison, T. W., 304
Dawley, Jack B., 122, 126–28, 130–40 passim
Deede, Leroy C., 51, 121
DeLong, Edward G., 66, 67–68, 69, 70
DeLude, Joe, 162
Dempsey, James C., 25, 275, 276, 300
Den Pesar airfield, 238
Department of Navy. See Navy Department
Department of State. See State Department
Department of War. See War Department
De Ruyter (light cruiser, Dutch): in Flores Sea, 16, 197; in Java Sea, 19, 20, 21, 158, 200, 202, 204–6, 209, 265; at Bandung Strait, 41
DeSanty (Dutch controller), 149
Destroyer Division 57, 39, 302
Destroyer Division 58, 261, 302
Destroyer Division 59, 259, 302
Destroyer Squadron 29: 37–46, 301–2; at Balikpapan, 16, 151, 152, 219
Deucalion (merchantmen, British), 270
Dewey Floating Dry Dock, 108
Dial, N. M., 303
Dias (customs agent), 136–37
Digas (Luzon, Philippines), 288
Divoll, Lawrence E., 235
Dix, Gerald, 237, 240
Dobo (Aru Island), 179, 180
Dominador (Judge), 136
Don Isadore (steamer), 187–88
Doorman, Karel: in Flores Sea, 197; at Makasar Strait, 40, 159, 265; at Bandung Strait, 40; in Java Sea, 19, 21, 41, 200, 203–10 passim
Doyle, Walter E., 28
Dugasan, Idris, 130
Dugasan, Iman Lakibul, 130
Durban (cruiser), 269

Eccles, Henry E., 21, 220, 302
Edsall (DD-219), 38, 39, 302; sinks Japanese submarine, 40; in Java Sea, 231, 232; rescues Langley survivors, 43, 61, 234, 235, 237; destroyed, 43, 240
Electra (destroyer, British), 19, 20, 205, 206
Encounter (destroyer, British): in Java Sea, 19, 21, 205, 206; rescues Kortenaer survivors, 208; at Sunda Strait, 44, 219, 220–23; sunk, 223, 228
Exeter (heavy cruiser, British), 222; in Java Sea, 19, 20–21, 200, 201, 202–6; at Sunda Strait, 44, 219, 220–21; sunk, 228

Fado Island (East Indies), 294
Fairchild, A. P., 184–86, 191
Far East Air Force, 7, 8, 49, 97, 112. See also Army, U.S.
Ferrall, W. E., 300
Ferriter, Charles A., 39, 60, 86–87, 258, 304
Fife, James, 29, 30
Filipino Scouts, 105, 106
Finch (AM-9), 54, 55, 60, 61, 304
Fletcher, Robert C., 113
Florence D (merchant ship), 187–89
Flores, R. L., 133
Flores Sea, Battle of, 152, 159–63, 197
Follmer, F. E., 185–87, 191
Fort Drum, 281, 283
Fort Dundas, 187
Fort Frank, 281, 283
Fort Hughes, 57, 281, 282–83, 284
Fortune Island (Philippines), 285, 286
Fourth Marines, 4, 5–6
Fred Morris (merchantman), 28. See also Otus
Freeman, C. L., 301
Freemantle (Australia), 171, 240, 279
Fryman, G. A., 91

"Galloping Ghost of the Java Coast." See Houston
Gelarins (Dutch sailor), 168
Geser (Ceram), 177, 178, 179
Giang Seng (merchantman, British), 269

Glassford, William A., Jr.: heads Yangtze Patrol, 6, 52, 53–55; heads Task Force 5, 6, 10, 299; as ComSoWesPac, 11, 12, 264, 270, 272–73; relationship with ABDA Command, 230; in Sulu Sea, 15–16; at Balikpapan, 151–52, 260, 261, 262; in Java, 237, 238, 240; retreat from Java, 11–12, 30, 31, 32, 50, 240, 274–75
Goggins, William B., 159–71 *passim*
*Gold Star* (transport), 261
Goodall, Henry W. ("Hap"), 103, 105, 106
Goodhue, Arthur A., 168
Gordon, Oliver L., 203, 220
Gough, William V., 124, 129–30, 133
Grant, E., 303
Green, Billy E., 91
Gregory, J. W., 299
Gustafson, Arthur L., 88

*Haguro* (heavy cruiser, Japanese), 44
Haley, Harold, *290*, 296
Hall, Earl B., 126
Hamilo Cove (Philippines), 285–86
Hamlin, Harold S., Jr., 211
Harbin, E. C., 118
Hargrave, William, 173–83 *passim*
Harris, Andrew E., 53
Harris, David W., 80, 81
Harris, G. L., 301
Hart, Thomas C., 3–10, *9*, 299; secret conference, 6–7, 38–39; commands ABDAFLOAT, 10–11, 12; relieved of command, 12, 19, 41*n*, 269; in China, 3; in Manila Bay, 3–10, 26–29, 98, 251–52, 254, 255; at Battle of Balikpapan, 151, 152; in Java, 10, 164, 263; assesses Darwin, 31; on *Houston*, 19; on submarines, 10, 26, 32–33; on destroyers, 7, 37; directs PatWing 10, 48; directs gunboats, 52–53, 54; directs *Isabel*, 251–52, 254, 258–59, 263
*Harukaze* (destroyer, Japanese), 23
Hastings, Burden R., 120–21, 122
Hawes, Richard E., 35, 87, 258, 299
Head, George William, *290*, 296
Headhunters, 180–81
Helfrich, Conrad E. L.: appointed ABDAFLOAT commander, 11, 41*n*, 200*n*; policy on Java, 19, 21, 41, 200; responsibility for Bali operation, 41*n*; jurisdiction over U.S. Navy, 230
"Hello Joe," 126, 135
*Heron* (AVP-2), 47, 48, 49, 51, *143*, 303; battle in Molucca Sea, 141–45
Hibbs, W., 303
Hila (Amboina Island), 174, 175–76, 177

Hinds, Claud J., Jr., 234
Hoeffel, Kenneth M., 56–57, 303
*Holland* (AS-3), 25, 299; in Philippines, 28, 85; ordered to East Indies, 10, 26, 98, 259; sent to Darwin, 29–30; rerouted to Java, 31; in Makasar harbor, 261
Holley, G. M., 300
Homma, Masaharu, 284
Hopkins (American in Java), 168
*Horai Maru* (passenger-cargo ship, Japanese), 23
Horn Island (Australia), 182
Houlihan, John L., 77
*Houston* (CA-30), 6, 13, *14*, 15, 250, 299; in Flores Sea, 16, 40, 158–60, 163, 164, 197–99, 265; off Darwin, 18–19, 93; at Balikpapan, 151, 152, 260, 262; in Java, 19–21, 199–211, 261; at Sunda Strait, 22, 44, 195–97, 211–18
Hurd, K. C., 301
Hurst, A. M., 301
Hurt, David A., 35, 242–44, 247, 248–49, 301
Hyland, John J., 120–21

*I-24* (submarine, Japanese), 40
Imamura, Hitoshi, 22
Indangi, Namli, 127, 128
*Indomitable* (aircraft carrier, British), 5
*Isabel* (PY-10), 59, 250, 279–80, 304; in China, 250–51; in Philippines, 85, 251–59; ordered to Java, 259–74; retreat from Java, 43, 167, 231*n*, 274–79

Jackobson (Ensign), 51
Jacobs, T. D., 301
Jamdena Island (East Indies), 172
*Janssens* (inter-island vessel, Dutch), 168–71
Japal, Amirhamja, 134, 136
Japan, 3, 5, 6; invades Malaya, 8, 48; attacks Pearl Harbor, 7; takes Singapore, 11; attacks Philippines, 8, 9, 10, 26, 85–87, 97–99, 112; Bali landing, 31; Java landings, 11, 19, 20–21, 32, 43, 44, 50, 243
Japanese Army. *See* Army Japanese
Japanese Navy. *See* Navy, Japanese
Java: Dutch naval base, 8; ABDAFLOAT headquarters, 10, 158; invaded by Japanese, 11, 19, 32, 44, 269–70, 274; fall of, 12, 165–69, 178
*Java* (light cruiser, Dutch), 19, 20, 21, 41, 200, 202–6, 209
Java Sea, Battle of: breaks ABDAFLOAT Command, 11, 43, 219, 274; ABDA tactics, 19–20; events, 20–21,

41, 242; effect on Dobo, 179; role of *Houston*, 201–11
Jesus, Mr., 131
Jogjakarta (Java), 164, 166
*John D. Edwards* (DD-216), 302; ordered to Singapore, 39; in Flores Sea, 40, 197; in Java, 20, 21, 41, 45, 206; retreat from Java, 219, 220, 270
*John D. Ford* (DD-228), *154*, 302; in Manila, 38, 259; action at Balikpapan, 40, 152–56; in Java Sea, 20, 41, 206; retreat from Java, 219, 220
Jolo, 120–40
*Jupiter* (destroyer, British), 19, 205, 206, 208

Kabler, William L., 141, 303
Karpe, Eugene S., 239, 302
Keith, Harry H., 86, 88, 302
Kelly, Robert B., 68, 71, 74, 75, 79–82 *passim*
King, Ernest J., 240–41
*Kinu* (light cruiser, Japanese), 23
Koivisto, Martin M., 88
Kondo, Nobutake, 184
*Kortenaer* (destroyer, Dutch), 20, 204, 206, 208
*Kuretake Maru* (transport, Japanese), 156
Kur Island (East Indies), 293–94
Kurusu, Saburo, 6

Lamb, R. S., 300
Landers, Paul H., 123–24, 129, 130
*Langley* (AV-3), 47, 229, *236*, 303; ordered out of Manila, 10, 261; in Sulu Sea, 15; in Malay barrier islands, 49; in Java Sea, 50, 61, 229–37, 240; assisted by *Pecos* and *Edsall*, 43, 237, 274
Langley, Samuel Pierpoint, 229
*Lanikai* (yacht), 58, 253, 303
*Lark* (AM-21), 43, 55, 60–61, 273, 304
LeBaron, T. R., 185, 191
Leonard, Leland E., 234–35
Levitt, Herbert, 215
Light, James D., 77
*Lillian Luckenbach* (freighter), 265–66
Lingayen Gulf (Philippines), 112–19
Lombok Strait, 223
Looc Cove (Philippines), 286
Luband Islands (Philippines), 286
Lucker, N., 300
Lurvey, Don D., 124–26, 129
*Luzon* (PR-7), 6, 53–58 *passim*, *58*, 303

MacArthur, Douglas, 6–7, 26, 38; declares Manila open city, 10, 98; escapes from Corregidor, 72–76

McConnell, Robert P., 230, 231–37, 240–41, 303
McGlone, L. G., 302
Mack, William P., 156
McKinney, E. B., 301
McKnight, John R., Jr., 35, 300
McLawhorn, Evern C., 126, 127, 129, 133, 138
Maher, Arthur L., 13, 201, 206
Makasar, 261–62
Makasar Strait, 16, 151, 152, 153, 156, 197
Malacaban Island (Philippines), 287
Manado (Celebes Island), 92, 146, 147
Manees, L. J., 302
Mangoli Island, 149
Manila: as U.S. headquarters, 1, 4, 9; marines arrive, 4, 6; attacked by Japan, 10, 25, 26–27, 98; declared open city, 26, 98
Manila Bay, 10, 250–53 *passim*, 255–59, 281–84 *passim*
*Marblehead* (CL-12), 13, 15, *17*, 299; in Balikpapan, 16, 38, 151, 152, 153, 261; damaged in Flores Sea, 16, 40, 197, 198; in Java, 31, 158, 159–64, 265
Marine Corps, in Philippines, 6
Mariveles, 27, 29
Mariveles Bay, 98–99, 102–3, 107–8
Martino, John, 67, 80
*Mauna Loa* (transport), 18, 94
*Mayo Maru* (transport, Japanese), 114
Meeker, Jack Forest, Jr., *290*, 297
*Meigs* (transport), 18, 94, 194
Melbourne (Australia), 182, 183
*Melville*, HMAS (Australian naval base), 30
Melville Island (Australia), 187, 295
Merauke (New Guinea), 179, 182
*Michishio* (destroyer, Japanese), 41
*Mindanao* (PR-8), 53–58 *passim*, 287, 303
Mine Division 8, 60, 304
Mine Division 9, 60, 304
*Molly Moore* (schooner), 253
Molucca Sea, 141, 146, 147, 150
Moorer, Thomas H., 184–94
Morgan, E. V. St. J., 223
Moros, 125, 126–27, 128, 130–31, 133
Morotai Island (Philippines), 292
Morrill, John H., 282–96, *290*, 304
Mosley, W. H., 184–91
Motor Torpedo Boat Squadron 3, 63–82, 106, 303
Muller (Aviation Machinist's Mate Second Class), 174–76, 177
Mumma, M. C., Jr., 300
Mundos. *See* Moros
Murch, Douglas, 160, 162

*Myoko* (heavy cruiser, Japanese), 44

*Nachi* (heavy cruiser, Japanese), 44
*Nachi*-class heavy cruisers, 201
Nagumo, Chuichi, 55
*Naka* (light cruiser, Japanese), 156
*Napa* (AT-32), 58, 303
Nasugb (Philippines), 286
*Natsushio* (destroyer, Japanese), 25
Navy, Japanese: 5, 6, 8, 22, 157
Navy, Royal, 7, 8
Navy, U.S., headquarters, 182–83
Navy Department, 4, 5, 5–6, 11, 28, 29, 38
Neal, E. T., 302
Nelson (Radioman First Class), 174–83 *passim*
*Neptuna* (ammunition ship, British), 94
New, W. A., 301
New Guinea, 179–82
Newquist, Ralph Waldo, *290*, 297
Newsom, J., 299
Nichols Field (Philippines), 97
Nix, J. J., 302
Nomura, Kichisaburo, 6

*Oahu* (PR-6), 53–58 *passim*, 303
Oldendorf, Jesse B., 45–46
Oliver (Chief Aviation Machinist's Mate), 173, 175
Olongapo (Philippines), 72, 285
147th Field Artillery (U.S.), 18
148th Field Artillery (U.S.), 18
Opan Shipbuilding & Slipway Corporation, 78
*Oshio* (destroyer, Japanese), 41
Osmeña, Sergio, 33, 77
*Otus* (AS-20), 25, 28, 31, 299; bombed at Cavite Navy Yard, 257; ordered to East Indies, 10, 26, 98, 259, 261

Palembang (Sumatra), 263
Palliser, Arthur F. E., 11, 50, 220
*Panay* (gunboat), 3, 253
Parker, E. N., 302
*Parrott* (DD-218), 302; ordered to Tarakan, 38; action at Balikpapan, 40, 152, 155–56; in Java, 45, 270, 273; retreat from Java, 43
Patrol Squadron 22, 50
Patrol Squadron 101, 302
Patrol Squadron 102, 302
Patrol Wing 10, 47–48, 51, 302–3; served by *Langley*, 229; in Philippines, 4–5, 9, 48–49, 72; patrols Indochina, 59; at Jolo, 120–40; ordered to East Indies, 10, 26, 112; in Molucca Sea,

146–49; in Java, 49–50; from Saumlakki Bay, 172–83; evacuates Glassford, 12, 50
*Paul Jones* (DD-230), 37, *42*, 301; in Sulu Sea, 15; ordered to Tarakan, 38, 259; disabled at Makasar, 262–63; at Balikpapan, 40, 152, 155, 156; in Java Sea, 20, 41, 206; retreat from Java, 219, 220
Payne, John Walker, 251–79 *passim*, 304
Pearl Harbor, attack on, 7
*Peary* (DD-226), *93*, 302; damaged in collision, 38, 85; saved at Cavite Navy Yard, 39, 60, 85–88, 257, 258; ordered to Java, 88–92, 141; ordered to Darwin, 18, 92; sunk at Darwin, 40, 43, 93–95, 194
*Pecos* (AC-6), 10, 15, 273, 303; retreat from Java, 165, 237, 274; sunk, 234*n*, 238–39
Peirse, Richard E. C., 10
Peking, 4
*Perch* (SS-176), 35, 242–49, *246*, 301
Percifield, W. E., 300
*Permit* (SS-178), 72–76 *passim*, 152, 301
*Perth* (light cruiser, Australian), *213*; in Battle of Java Sea, 19, 20, 21, 203, 206, 207; in Java, 22, 200; retreat from Java, 44, 195, 209, 210, 212–13
Peterson, John V., 50, 302
Petrinella Hospital, 164, 165
Pettit, Robert L., 124–25
Philippines, defended by U.S. submarines, 25. *See also* individual place names
Phillips, Tom, 6–7, 38–39
*Phoenix* (CL-46), 229, 277
"Photo Joe," 99, 102
*Pickerel* (SS-177), 301
*Piet Hein* (destroyer, Dutch), 41, 197
"Pigboats," 24
*Pigeon* (ASR-6), 25, 54, 55, 299; in Philippines, 26, 28, 85, 100, 257; rescue work, 61, 87, 258; scuttled, 29, 35–36
*Pike* (SS-173), 152, 301
*Pillsbury* (DD-227), 302; damaged in collision, 38, 85; at Cavite Navy Yard, 38, 39, 86, 257; at Balikpapan, 40; in Java, 45, 270; retreat from Java, 45, 273, 274, 279
Piru (Ceram), 177
*Pittsburgh* (CA-70), 250
Plant, William H., 67, 68
*Pope* (DD-225), 226, 302; in Manila, 38, 259; at Balikpapan, 40, 152, 155, 156, 219; repaired in Java, 219; retreat from Java, 21, 44, 219–28

*Porpoise* (SS-172), 301
Port Lamon (Mindanao, Philippines), 291–92
*Port Mar* (transport), 18
Pound, H. C., 302
Pratt, J. L., 303
*President Harrison* (passenger liner), 6
*Prince of Wales* (battleship, British), 5, 7, 8, 39
Pryce, R. F., 301
*PT-31*, 63, 64, *66*, 66–68
*PT-32*, 63, 64, 65, 70–71, 74–75
*PT-33*, 63, 64, 65
*PY-34*, 63, 66–69, 71, 74–82
*PT-35*, 63, 64, 71–78, 82
*PT-41*, 63, 69–82

*Quail* (AM-15), 60, 61, 281–83, 304
Quezon, Manuel, 33, 76–78
Quinaux, K. E., 91

Ralston, Frank M., 146, 150
*Ranger* (tug), 284, 287
Rankin, Raid Ortumas, *290*, 297
*Ran Paloma* (cutter), 182
Ray, Herbert J., 74
Renard, J. C., 303
*Repulse* (heavy cruiser, British), 5, 7, 8, 39
Reynolds, Willard J., 79, 80, 81
Richardson, Bruce Roland, *290*, 297
Richardson, Iliff D., 80, 81
Richardson, James O., 4
Robinson, Arthur G., 159, 161, 163, 299
Robinson, S. E., 262, 299
*Rochester* (CA-124), 250
Rockingham (Australia), 182
Rockwell, Francis W., 10, 27, 64, 65, 72, 74
Rooks, Albert H., 18, 19, 299; in Batavia, 21–22, 196; in Flores Sea, 198; in Java Sea, 204, 208, 210, 211; in Bantam Bay, 21, 22, 215–16
Roosevelt, Franklin Delano, 3, 5, 59, 72, 210
Ross, Albert P., 80
Ross (Chief Machinist's Mate), 118
Roth, E. A., 304
Rottnest Island Light, 279
Royal Navy. *See* Navy, Royal
Royal Netherlands Army. *See* Army, Dutch
Royal Netherlands Navy. *See* Navy, Dutch
Ruzak, J. J., 184–86, 191
Ryan, T. C., 161

*S-36*, **35**, 112, 300

*S-37*, 300
*S-38*, 112, 113–19, *116*, 300
*S-39*, 300
*S-40*, 112, 300
*S-41*, 300
Sackett, Earl L., 35, 97, 100, 101, 102, 107, 299
*Sailfish* (SS-192), 300
Saint Nicholas Point Light, 211
Sajafi (East Indies), 292
*Sakura Maru* (passenger-cargo ship, Japanese), 23
*Salmon* (SS-182), *34*, 112, 301
Sanana (Sulu Islands), 149
Sangley Point, 5
*Santa Rita* (yard tug), 256, 258
Saporua (Ceram), 177
*Sargo* (SS-188), 32, 301
Saumlakki Bay, 172, 183
*Saury* (SS-189), 112, 301
Sayre, Francis B., 33
Schilling (Royal Netherlands Indies Army general), 22
Schmidt (Dutch liaison officer), 167
Schumacher, Vincent E., 70, 74, 76, 82
Scribner, James M., 126
*Sculpin* (SS-191), 300
*Seadragon* (SS-194), 300; at Cavite Navy Yard, 25, 35, 85, 87, 257, 258; ordered to Australia, 32
*Seal* (SS-183), *34*, 301
*Sealion* (SS-195), 300; sunk at Cavite Navy Yard, 8–9, 25, 35, 85, 87, 257, 258
*Searaven* (SS-196), 300
*Sea Witch* (C-3–type merchantman), 229–31, 231n, 275, 276–77
*Seawolf* (SS-197), 29, 300
Shane, Louis, Jr., 35, 301
Shanghai, 4
*Shark* (SS-174), 10, 27, 28, 35, 301
Sharp (Aviation Machinist's Mate Third Class), 174
Sharp, William F., 82
Sheil, Ted, 23
*Shikinami* (destroyer, Japanese), 23
*Shirakumo* (destroyer, Japanese), 23
Shuler, J. C., 185–89 *passim*
Siasi Island, 125, 127
Sikorsky VS-42, 141
*Silent Victory* (book), 33n
Singapore, 5, 7, 8, 9; fall of, 11, 165, 269
Sitankai (Philippines), 133, 134–36
Sixteenth Naval District, 283
*Skipjack* (SS-184), 301
Smith, Charles D., 215
Smith, **Chester** C., 33, **300**

Smith, Columbus D., 53
Smith, D. E., 303
Smith, H. P., 302
*Snapper* (SS-185), 300
*Somanoura Maru* (transport, Japanese), 155
Soriano, Andres, 77
South China Patrol. *See* China Patrol, South
South West Pacific Command (U.S.), 11. *See also* Glassford, William A., Jr.
*Spearfish* (SS-190), 32, 275, 276, 282, 301
Stark, Harold R., 6, 252
State Department, 6
Steel, James Howard, 290, 297
*Stewart* (DD-224), 302; ordered to Tarakan, 38; in Flores Sea, 40, 197; at Bandung Strait, 41, 270; end in Surabaja, 44–45
*Stingray* (SS-186), 32, *34*, 112, 300
Stone, H. L., 300
Straits of Marianna, 181
Stratton (former soldier), 134–36
Stringer, John Samuel, 290, 297
*Sturgeon* (SS-187), 32, *34*, 300
S-type submarines, 24–25, 96. *See also* individual submarines
Suarez, Alejandro, 133, 134
Submarine Division 21, 32, *34*, 301
Submarine Division 22, 33, *34*, 300
Submarine Division 201, 25, 35, 300
Submarine Division 202, 25, 29, 300
Submarine Division 203, 27, 35, 301
Submarine Squadron 20, 25–36, 299–301
Sumatra, fall of, 178
Sumbawa Island, 151
Sunda Strait, Battle of, 20, 22–23, 195, 196, 210, 213, 220, 272
Surabaja (Java): Dutch naval base, 8; U.S. Navy headquarters, 10, 30, 165, 187; bombed, 199, 263, 265, 266, 268–69; submarine action, 243
Surigao Strait, 291
Sutherland, Richard K., 74, 82
*Swan* (corvette, Australian), 18
Swisher, Glen Arthur, 290, 297
*Swordfish* (SS-193), 29, 33, 76, 300

Taam Island (East Indies), 294
Tabango (Leyte, Philippines), 289
Tacloban (Leyte, Philippines), 289
Talbot, Paul H., 152–56, *154*, 302
*Tanager* (AM-5), 60, 61, 304
Tandjungpriok (Sumatra), 263, 269
Tarakan (Borneo), 139, 151
*Tarpon* (SS-175), 301
Task Force 1, 9

Task Force 5, 6, 9, 10, 299
Task Force 42, 182
*Tatsukami Maru* (transport, Japanese), 155
Tawao (Borneo), 138–39
Taylor, Donald C., 284, 290, 296
ter Poorten, Hein, 10
Thomson, H. P., 304
Thomson, R. C., 185–87, 191
Thursday Island (Australia), 182
Tientsin, 4
Tills, Robert G., 49
Timor (Philippines), 18, 184
Tioor Island (East Indies), 293
Tijilatjap (Java), 16, 31, 163, *164*, 165, 199, 270; aircraft delivered to, 230–31, 237; evacuation of, 11, 43, 167–69, 273–74
*Tokushima Maru* (passenger-cargo ship, Japanese), 23
Tokyo Rose, 262
Tolley, Kemp, 58, 303
Townsville (Australia), 182
*Trinity* (AO-13), 10, 15, 151, 261, 303
Tripartite Pact, 3
*Tromp* (destroyer, Dutch), 16, 41, 159, 197, 265
*Tsuruga Maru* (transport, Japanese), 156
*Tsurumi* (tanker, Japanese), 23
Tual (Kai Islands), 179, 180
*Tulagi* (transport), 18
*Tulsa* (PG-22), 43, 52, 55, 61, 237, 303
*Tutuila* (PR-4), 6, 53

"Uncle Sam's Mickey Mouse Battle Fleet," 105–7
U.S. Asiatic Fleet. *See* Asiatic Fleet

Valdes, Basilio, 77
*Van Cloon* (steamer, Dutch), 267–68
*Van Ghent* (destroyer, Dutch), 197
*Van Outhoorn* (merchantman, Dutch), 269
Van Staelen (captain of *Java*), 204
Vanzant, R. B., 300
Verde Island (Philippines), 287, 288
Voge, Richard G., 35, 300

Wagner, Frank D., 47, 49, 50, 302
Wainwright, Jonathan M., 77, 108, 283–84, 288
*Wake* (PR-3), 6, 53
Wallace, L., 301
Waller, Hector M. L., 21, 22, 196, 204, 210
War Department, 6, 29
Warder, F. B., 300
Warfield, T. G., 304

*Warrnambool* (subchaser, Australian), 193–94
Wassel, Croyden M., 164–71
Waterman, Andrew K., 124, 130
Watkins, Earl Belvin, 290, 297
Wavell, Archibald Percival, 10, 11
Weinmann, Charles Ernest, 290, 297
*Whipple* (DD-217), 38, 39, 302; rescues *Langley* survivors, 61, 231, 232, 235, 237; rescues *Pecos* survivors, 238, 239–40, 273
*Whippoorwill* (AM-35), 55, 60, 304; at Cavite Navy Yard, 39, 60, 85, 86–87, 257; in Java, 60–61, 237; retreat from Java, 43, 273
Whitford, "N" "T," 127, 133, 136
Wildebush, F. F., 161
Wiley, Herbert V., 37, 301
Wilkes, John, 11, 28, 29, 30, 32, 98, 299
*William B. Preston* (AVD-7), 30, 47–51 *passim*, 94, 303

*William Van der Zaan* (minelayer, Dutch), 231
Wilson, William R. "Bill," 228
Winslow, Walter G. (as narrator), 195–218
*Witte De With* (destroyer, Dutch), 20, 205, 206
Wong (Chinese colonel), 72
*Worrengo* (corvette, Australian), 18
Woslegel, Edward Stanley, 290, 297
Wright, W. L., 300
Wurtsmith (Lieutenant Colonel), 296

Yangtze Patrol, 6, 52–53, 58, 250
*Yarra* (gunboat, Australian), 43

*Zealandia* (ammunition ship, British), 94
Zeros, 173, 174, 185–86, 265